ADVANCES IN
LIBRARY ADMINISTRATION
AND ORGANIZATION

Volume 11 • 1993

ADVANCES IN LIBRARY ADMINISTRATION AND ORGANIZATION

Editors: GERARD B. McCABE
Director of Libraries
Clarion University of Pennsylvania

BERNARD KREISSMAN
University Librarian, Emeritus
University of California, Davis

VOLUME 11 • 1993

 JAI PRESS INC.

Greenwich, Connecticut   *London, England*

CONTENTS

INTRODUCTION
Bernard Kreissman   vii

COST ANALYSIS OF LIBRARY REFERENCE
SERVICES
Marjorie E. Murfin   1

LIBRARIES, TECHNOLOGY AND QUALITY
Miriam A. Drake   37

TRANSFORMATIONAL LEADERSHIP FOR
LIBRARY MANAGERS
J. Fred Olive III   49

LIBRARY TECHNOLOGY TRANSFER: BEYOND
THE CULTURAL BOUNDARIES
Kenneth J. Oberembt   75

VOLUNTEERS IN LIBRARIES: AN UPDATE
Rashelle S. Karp   97

LIBRARIES: IMPROVING SERVICES TO
NON-TRADITIONAL STUDENTS
Ray Hall   115

NATIONAL TECHNICAL INFORMATION:
THE RED OCTOBER PROBLEM
Steven M. Hutton   131

EXAMINING INNOVATIVE APPLICATIONS
OF TECHNOLOGY IN LIBRARIES
Virginia Tiefel   143

AUTOMATED COLLECTION ANALYSIS AND
DEVELOPMENT: BUSINESS COLLECTION
Jane A. Dodd and Suzanne D. Gyeszly   201

THE TWO-YEAR M.L.S.: ANSWER OR
ANATHEMA
Ahmad Fouad M. Gamaluddin and
Jane Rogers Butterworth   217

SPECULATIONS ON SOCIAL EPISTEMOLOGY:
SPECIALIZATION IN SOCIETY, REFLECTIONS
ON EMILE DURKHEIM AND ADAM SMITH
Steven M. Hutton   245

A BIBLIOGRAPHY OF LIBRARY MANAGEMENT
IN SUB-SAHARAN AFRICA
Glenn L. Sitzman   267

BIBLIOGRAPHY OF SUB-SAHARA AFRICAN
LIBRARIANSHIP, 1990
Compiled by Glenn L. Sitzman   295

BIOGRAPHICAL SKETCHES OF THE
CONTRIBUTORS   319

INDEX   321

INTRODUCTION

In the first ten years of publication, *Advances in Library Administration and Organization* established a strong reputation as a library research publication, and as one of the very few journals in the field sympathetic to the long, sometimes very long, paper. While it is recognized universally that major research project analysis and description frequently requires lengthy documentation, few journals can afford the page requirements necessary for such extensive documentation. Thus, if it were not for *ALAO* and a miniscule number of sister publications, most of these research projects or similar analyses would go unknown to all but the authors and their circle of close associates. Consequently, the editors' original interest in publishing the longer paper has been strengthened by the experience of the last ten years.

The editors felt also that entry into the second decade should be made with a particularly strong showing. It was our desire to demonstrate that time had not dulled the zeal and vigor with which we had approached Volume 1 of *ALAO*. With Volume 11, we believe that we have achieved that goal. Volume 11, we believe, ranks with the strongest issues we have produced, and it demonstrates clearly the values of the long research paper.

Marjorie Murfin's tripartite article on library costs, particularly reference transactions, brings new insights into these often explored areas. Miriam Drake addresses a delicate subject, "Quality", in this printed version of her "Alice G. Smith Lecture."

Leadership style and perceptions are reported by J. Fred Olive. From Cairo comes Kenneth Oberembt's analysis of Egyptian cultural constraints inhibiting the introduction of technology to Egyptian libraries. Rashelle Karp takes a strong positive position on library volunteerism and recommends acceptance and recognition of volunteers. "Improving Services to Non-Traditional Students," by Ron Hall, is an analysis and recommendation of library service to that growing phenomenon—older aged college students.

The first of two papers by Steven Hutton, "National Technical Information: The Red October Problem," raises questions regarding the conflicting needs for information flow and national security in an increasingly technological information environment. Virginia Tiefel's work on the introduction of technology in public services was supported by the Council on Library Resources and Ohio State University. A second project funded by the Council on Library Resources, Dodd and Gyeszly's work, attempted to established guidelines, procedures, and methodology for an automated shelflist count and automated collection analysis.

Gamaluddin and Butterworth survey the literature and leadership opinion regarding the two-year Master of Library Science (M.L.S.) degree.

Hutton's second paper is a philosophical inquiry into social epistemology: the development of knowledge and the technologies related to discovering, storing, and transmitting knowledge.

As is proper, the volume concludes with not one, but two bibliographies from Glenn L. Sitzman on Sub-Sahara Africa.

If you think Volume 11 is a blockbuster, the editors agree with you.

Bernard Kreissman
Series Editor

COST ANALYSIS OF LIBRARY REFERENCE SERVICES

Marjorie E. Murfin

COSTING THE REFERENCE TRANSACTION: INTRODUCTION

One of the most difficult tasks facing a public services administrator today is to maintain the important balance between cost and quality. In reference service, this is particularly important since reference is a relatively expensive service and concerns about quality are increasing. Up to this point, some cost/effectiveness and cost benefit studies have been done, but as Mick notes, "we need cost studies that are conducted across a number of similar institutions ... using a common methodology" (Mick, 1979).

In order to assist reference departments to provide the best quality reference service at the least cost, it is important that a fair, reasonable, and practical method of assessing cost effectiveness be developed, particularly one which takes quality of service into account.

On the positive side, a measure of cost combined with a good measure of effectiveness might encourage quality service when that quality can be shown to be worth something, that is, to be related to values and benefits. Such a

Advances in Library Administration and Organization,
Volume 11, pages 1-36.
Copyright © 1993 by JAI Press Inc.
All rights of reproduction in any form reserved.
ISBN: 1-55938-596-0

method might also prevent the pressure for adopting inadequate measures which are poorly conceived and lower the quality of service. Under the pressures of cost containment, inadequate measures which do not take quality into account may be developed, advocated and even generally accepted and widely adopted, to the detriment of reference service.

For example, we are all aware of DRGs (diagnostically related groups) in the medical field where a cost formula has been developed without an adequate component for quality of care, because quality of medical care can't easily be measured.

Attempts are now being made to build quality into medical cost containment models. One expert says, "As other factors such as complications and readmissions are added, the ability to evaluate care will vastly improve" (McClure, 1987). This has clear implications for other professions, particularly reference service. A method of evaluation which doe not consider quality might lead to a continuing downward slide of quality by substituting less well trained and less expensive personnel at desk and emphasizing numbers as patrons are rushed through the system, regardless of outcome. Some indications in this direction can already be seen (Bunge, 1987).

It is important that reference service be in the forefront in regard to incorporating quality into a cost effectiveness model for the profession, rather than having an inappropriate and harmful one thrust upon it.

LITERATURE REVIEW

A number of studies have been done exploring methods of cost analysis for reference service. Some studies have originated within the libraries themselves, while others have been carried out by outside consultants and have sometimes involved groups of libraries. Some of these studies have utilized cost/effectiveness and cost/benefit methodology, but the majority, particularly those carried out in-house, have involved only simple costing of reference operations.

Development of Costing Methods

The earliest attempts at cost analysis were focused on simple costing of reference operations. There were, however, two difficult problems to be solved before any substantial progress could be made.

The first problem concerned the time unit to be used for representing the reference transaction. Should it be minutes, hours, months or years? The second major problem concerned *what* costs were to be included in the base figure for estimating the cost of the reference transaction. Some felt it was sufficient to include only direct (and/or indirect) personnel costs while others felt that all reference expenditures should be used as the base. Still others felt that general overhead costs should also be part of the base figure.

In early costing efforts, thinking was fixed in terms of hours. This may be because reference scheduling was done in this way, because reference volume data were usually collected in this way, and because an hourly rate of pay was fairly easily obtained. Salaries of reference librarians were divided by the total number of hours of service provided to arrive at an average hourly cost of providing reference assistance. The number of reference questions per hour was then used as a base for determining dollar cost per question (Weech, 1974). The assumptions behind this may never have been clearly thought out but use of this method implied that reference assistance to patrons was the only "output" of the reference department and *all* reference costs should be assigned to this activity. It also assumed that every minute at the reference desk was spent answering reference questions, or if not, that the "idle time" spent waiting for questions could not be otherwise utilized.

Use of the methodology of hourly or yearly "block of time" costing could give alarmingly high cost-per-transaction figures for academic libraries. Examples of this are the figure by Murphy in 1969 of $3.41 for search questions, Raffel and Shishko's figure of $2.20, also in 1969, that of Palmour and Gray in 1972 of $7.58 for a complex fact question in one library, and finally the figure of Kantor, in 1978/79 dollars, of $10.80 per reference transaction in a group of libraries (Murphy, 1978; Raffel and Shishko, 1969; Palmour and Gray, 1972; Kantor, 1981a).

Undoubtedly, a sense of unease was felt by reference department heads and personnel. This sense of unease is documented by McClure who reports reference personnel in 1985 as believing that actual costs of quality reference service are so high that, if known, they might cause serious questions to be raised, which, in turn, could result in curtailment of service (McClure, 1986). On the one hand, reference staff had serious doubts about the block-of-time methodology itself, yet they could not produce a better methodology or even clearly pinpoint the flaws of this methodology. The ominous repetition of the words, "Reference is an expensive service," echoed in many libraries. The focus on reference departments in particular was explained by Lopez when he noted, "Of all library operations the reference department is the most assailable and exposed... the staff, largely professional, is expensive, the reference collection is costly to maintain and the value of the department's contribution is difficult to delineate, much less quantify (Lopez, 1973). This targeting of reference departments was also described by Murphy in regard to the experiences of one library, "The public services department, in particular was often targeted as a splendid potential area for manpower reduction for at least 2 reasons: first because the concentration of professional personnel was usually considerably higher than in technical services and represents a more expensive mix...Second, the functions and products of public service units were less visible, less well understood and therefore less justifiable... (Murphy, 1978, pp. 98-99). The unspoken fear in the minds of reference librarians was the question of whether reference really was too expensive a service to continue to exist in its present form.

The climate of these times was best expressed by Lopez who pressed reference departments even further by insisting that the high cost figures as were then being provided were inadequate and should be raised even higher by inclusion of reference collection costs and general overhead costs. He quotes McDiarmid's ominous warning that reference service must "admit a burden of proof that it pays its way ...and display quantitized proofs (Lopez, 1973, p. 1).

This situation was further exacerbated by the "idle time" concept which grew out of the use of the hourly methodology. As reference came under sharp scrutiny in regard to its cost, questions began to be raised about "idle time" or time spent waiting for questions. At the same time, emphasis was increasingly being put on "approachability," which frowned on any other work being done at the desk because it might discourage patrons from asking questions. Articles such as that of Ellison and Molenda (1976) stressed this concept and a study by McMurdo (1982) found that 70 percent of patrons would be less likely to approach when the librarian appeared busy.

This controversy and the stress put on approachability perhaps kept reference personnel from questioning or challenging the hourly methodology. On one hand, it was stressed that, in order to be doing one's duty properly and be approachable, reference personnel must not appear busy. On the other hand they were also told that "idle time" was costly to the library. Should they challenge the concept of "idle time" they would be admitting to violation of firmly held policies of "no work at the desk," in order to insure approachability.

The hourly methodology posed serious problems for the smaller lower-volume library. To illustrate this problem, one small academic library evaluating its service through the Wisconsin-Ohio Reference Evaluation Program was found to be providing high quality reference service. In a 2-day period with single staffing the library handled 32 reference questions for a rate of less than one reference question (plus directional questions) per hour. Because of this low rate of reference questions, using the hourly methodology, the cost to the library just in staff time (adding vacations and holidays and assuming a wage of $.24 per minute, a figure taken from reference salary data from an ARL test library for this paper) would have been $10.80 per question. When overhead and other costs were added to this, reference service would, indeed, have appeared to be prohibitively expensive in this library. In actual fact, this library took only about 134 minutes or about two and one-half hours to handle these transactions with outstanding success. Thus the actual personnel time spent amounted to a cost of $1 per reference transaction to provide high quality service. The remaining desk time could undoubtedly have been spent in collection development, preparation of bibliographies and other tasks.

Not all reference personnel accepted this double bind situation. Judith King proposed the sensible alternative that was already in use in many reference departments, of making use of nonbusy desk time for professional reading, reference book selection, general collection department, preparation of bibliographies, preparation for instructional sessions, correspondence and other similar tasks. In response to a workshop stressing approachability, she argued that "idleness does not inspire confidence ... alertness and immediate response are possible without remaining idle" (King, 1977). Murphy also supports this when she notes that "theoretically and actually, a librarian could review selection media, read or answer correspondence ... all during that stint at the reference desk." She notes that this is a methodological flaw (in hourly costing) that needs to be overcome (Murphy, 1978, p. 128). William Miller also pointed out the conflict between the approachability concept and the reality of academic reference service, particularly from the viewpoint of larger academic libraries, when he noted that our most pressing problem is not to stimulate new business but to find out how to take care of the business we already have (Miller, 1984).

In addition to methods of costing by hour and by minute, another method was developed, that is, costing per unit in terms of one year. This method did not base cost on time actually taken by the activity, but on a block of time, and in that sense was similar in theory to the hourly methodology, except that the unit of time was the year. In a 1969 cost analysis of the M.I.T. Library, a reference question was found to cost $2.20 as compared to $1.10 for a circulation transaction and $7.35 for an interlibrary loan transaction (Raffel and Shishko, 1969, p. 81). This figure is termed "information and bibliographic" transactions and may also represent directional transactions. If so, costs per reference question should probably be increased to $3.67 in 1969 or close to $7.27 in 1979 or $11.85 in 1988.

A similar method was used by Paul Kantor, using data from 1977-1979, where the number of reference transactions in one year, rather than one hour, was used as a base figure. This figure was then divided by a portion of the operating budget and a similar figure of $10.80 was obtained (Kantor, 1981, p. 25). Again, all reference personnel time was allotted to desk reference service. This method was also used by the Los Angeles Public Library and the Beverly Hills Public Library, resulting, however, in much smaller cost figures (Weech, 1974, p. 325).

During this same period of time, while "block of time" costing was being used, there were others who led the way toward more precise methods of costing. This movement came from contacts with those outside the profession where costing by the minute had been used frequently in task analysis.

In 1969 Wessel did a study (to be discussed in more detail later) using minutes per transaction as the unit of time. Reference work in a special library was observed by an investigator who timed each part of the procedure (Wessel and Moore, 1969).

Palmour and Gray (1972, p. 27) used minutes per transaction as did Murphy (1978, p. 107). However, in all cases but that of Wessel, an accurate count was not obtained because the information was collected after the fact and accurate time estimations are difficult to make at a later date. Although Palmour and Gray had *intended* to cost the reference transaction by minutes taken, the log method used was inadequate and relied on memory of reference librarians to estimate, at a later time, the amount of time consumed by the question. They note that their data is more likely to represent "hours on desk" than actual minutes per transaction (Palmour and Gray, 1972, pp. 24-25).

Murphy's study remains the best example of a thorough costing study and was done in the Air Force University Library as a part of her dissertation (Murphy, 1978, p. 107). This project was done in preparation for anticipated budget cuts with possible job losses. More than 100 reference tasks, including desk reference services, were costed in terms of staff time. After a task list of 105 items was drawn up, reference staff kept dairies for a period of 10 days on the number of minutes allotted to each activity, including desk reference service. In order to make sure diaries were as accurate as possible, each staff member was also interviewed and the same data was reviewed a second time.

The most useful part of this study is the costing methodology which used wages per minute as the unit of cost, according to a formula for all Air Force academic personnel. This formula was set to allow for vacation, sick leave, etc. and provides a figure of 149 hours per month worked by civilian Air Force employees (Murphy, 1978, p. 112). Most previous thinking on costing the reference transaction had been focused on hourly wages as the unit of cost.

In spite of those few who began costing the reference transaction by minutes taken, use of the hourly methodology continued. Spencer, a reference head, in 1980 used the hourly wage costs to determine cost per question, and with a rate of 3.96 questions per hour and a wage rate of $10 per hour, arrives at a cost figure of $2.53 per question (Spencer, 1980).

One disadvantage of the use of the hourly methodology is that it rewards the library with a large volume and severely penalizes the library with a lower volume. This could create an undue pressure for big numbers at the cost of quality in libraries of all sizes. The hourly or yearly methodology continued to be used due to the greater ease of measurement and the wide availability of needed data. It was vaguely recognized that not all desk time was used in direct reference service, but no further attempts were made to adjust cost figures to take account of this, due to the perceived difficulty of obtaining such estimates.

In summarizing the work on costing of the reference transaction, the movement toward costing by minutes spent, fueled by investigators outside the reference profession, grew stronger and was demonstrated by Murphy to be an effective way of determining personnel costs for each reference activity (Murphy, 1978, p. 112). Spencer's method of using Random Alarm Mechanisms also demonstrated another viable method of determining how personnel time was being allocated and thus providing a method for proportional costing (Spencer, 1980, p. 56). So, in essence, the unit of measure and the methodology of measurement had been established for the reference transaction.

In spite of the fact that these needed elements for accurate costing had all been developed, they were not brought together in one formula for use. At this point, to arrive at an accurate and reflective cost figure, it was necessary to (1) decide exactly what areas of cost should be charged to reference, and (2) determine the different reference outputs and determine what costs should be allocated to each output, (3) determine a methodology for measuring these costs along with their corresponding outputs.

Cost Allocation

A second stream of investigation in regard to cost analysis concerned the problem of deciding what costs should be charged to desk reference service. In order to determine this, it was first necessary to (1) decide what costs, in addition to reference desk direct personnel costs, should be charged to the reference transaction output, (2) determine the number and nature of reference outputs and (3) determine the proportion of personnel time and resource costs that should be allocated to each output.

In the largest group of reference cost analysis studies, only reference personnel time was included, sometimes with overhead. In another group of studies, the entire reference budget was used as a base.

In 1969, program budgeting began to be seriously considered in libraries and was used in a cost analysis study of the M.I.T. Library. In this program budget, the costs of acquiring and maintaining all library collections, including the reference collection, was charged to a single separate fund (Raffel and Shishko, 1969, p. 81). This suggested a new way of looking at unit costs. However, it remained for Rothstein to break this impasse with a new direction. He stressed the point that "a count of reference questions dealt with represents only a rather small part of what reference librarians actually do and contribute." He speaks of a "reference activity" measure—that is, use of materials, staff, quarters, and equipment ... My experience suggests that the total reference uses of a library are probably many times as great as the number of reference questions answered ... Reference librarians reporting only on questions answered have been guilty of selling their contributions short ... Data should represent the *full* array of reference activities (Rothstein, 1984).

This clearly represented a new direction for cost analysis since it suggested that some of the expenses of the reference department should be allocated to other outputs. In the modern academic library reference department, a substantial portion of personnel time is devoted to outputs *not* usually reflected by reference question totals. Many of these outputs are patron related reference activities such as computerized searches, user education lectures, special CD-ROM assistance, preparation of bibliographies and guides to the collection and maintenance of the reference collection for users of that collection. Others of these outputs are library related and are also *not* reflected in reference statistics, such as library committee work and collection development and liaison with academic departments.

Thus, reference questions appear more costly than they should because it is assumed that all effort went into this particular output, whereas in actual fact a good part of the personnel time was devoted to other outputs. It is similar to the case of a company producing radios and refrigerators where all labor costs were attributed to the production of radios alone, making them appear to be very expensive per unit. Murphy, Spencer, and Mech, who authored a time study of how reference librarians spent their time in 4 college libraries, all found considerable amounts of personnel time to be devoted to activities other than desk reference service (Murphy, 1978, p. 121; Spencer, 1980, p. 55; Mech, 1987).

Fortunately, problems of how to allocate personnel costs were now able to be resolved since the above research has demonstrated (1) that many reference personnel activities should *not* be charged to direct reference service, and (2) that the diary or Random Alarm Mechanism plus other data should yield the necessary data on time allocations of reference personnel in a particular library.

The greatest area of concern, however, centered around the reference collection and whether or not the material and personnel costs related to the acquisition and maintenance of the reference collection should all be charged to desk reference service. The reference collection budget appears according to Cline (1987) to be the second most expensive item in the reference budget after salaries. According to Murphy, when all the collection related tasks are added up, it is also the second highest in use of personnel time, after reference desk service (Murphy, 1978, pp. 116-120). Thus, a solution to this problem was essential.

The prevailing argument over the years held that reference service could not take place without the reference collection. Therefore, the entire cost of the collection including materials and personnel time should be charged to desk reference service (Lopez, 1973, p. 239).

As mentioned before, program budgeting provided a possible solution to this problem. The work of Raffel and Shishko at M.I.T. pointed the way toward a program budget where costs of acquiring and maintaining collections was considered as one program, covering all library collections, and including reference (Raffel and Shishko, 1969, p. 81). This is in line with Rothstein's recommendations that the acquiring and maintaining of the reference collection should not be charged entirely to the reference department (1984, pp. 48-49). Raffel and Shisko did, however, include personnel administration overhead in the salaries cost figures (1969, p. 3). Unfortunately, their data failed to capture the actual time spent in reference transactions and thus allocated *all* personnel time to the one output of the reference transaction, as did Kantor (1981, p. 6, 25).

It might be said that the recommendations of Rothstein and Raffel et al. agree that the services of providing a reference collection for users should not be charged to the reference department. Provision of this collection should be included in the budget for acquiring, processing and housing collections, as for any other library collection.

On the practical level, however, reference administrators were being asked to supply line item budgets covering all costs for their own departments (Cline, 1987, p. 56). It was inevitable that these budgetary figures, including the yearly costs of the reference collection, would be used to determine the unit cost for a reference transaction. Thus, the issue of the reference collection costs could not be sidestepped by the use of a program budget for the entire library.

The only answer to a more accurate formulation for unit costs appeared to lie with a program budget *within* the reference department budget, where the correct proportion of time and materials was allocated to the appropriate output (Cline, 1987, p. 56).

Along this line, perhaps one of the more useful analyses of the cost of a reference transaction was done by Charles Anderson for a small public library in which he separated the budget into salary costs, materials costs and operating costs (Anderson, 1987).

Unit Costs

Gloria Cline, who writes on reference budgeting, notes that the original type of program budgeting begun in the 1960s was generally considered a failure, but that at present an adapted version of it could be useful (Cline, 1987, pp. 58-59, 63).

In order to obtain unit costs, it is necessary first to obtain information on costs of operation. According to Rothstein's ideas for budgeting within the reference department, when figuring unit costs, appropriate costs should be charged to appropriate outputs as is done in a program budget. This poses a great many difficulties since in order to do this accurately one must have information which is not generally available in reference departments. It is necessary to know first how reference personnel spend their time in order to allocate personnel costs to the appropriate output. For example, in academic libraries, Mech quotes studies indicating that 16 percent-21 percent of reference/public service time is spent in library related committee meetings. Mech in his study of four college libraries found rates varying from 4 percent to 17 percent of total time spent in meetings. This time clearly should not be charged to reference desk service (Mech, 1987, p. 301). Secondly, it is necessary to know the usage of the reference collection in terms of patron hours or in terms of individual patron uses versus librarian uses, so that *only* the reference librarian portion of use is charged to reference desk service, as is strongly recommended by Rothstein. Clearly both these items of data are difficult to obtain for an individual reference department. However, to obtain true unit costs for the reference question, they are essential. In addition, it is necessary also to charge a portion of operating costs to reference desk service, but this can generally be fairly easy to obtain.

While Rothstein led the way in pointing out how reference costs should be allocated by program or output, Kantor and Arrigona and Mathews led the way in developing methodology to put Rothstein's ideas into practice. Kantor developed and tested a unit of measurement and a methodology for obtaining a unit cost for patron use of library materials. Basically, this unit is based on how many persons are in a particular area at one time. "Sweeps" are made periodically in an area and the number of people are tallied. These numbers are then translated into person hours of in-house use of library materials per year (Kantor, 1981, pp. 10-13). Another unit of measurement developed by Arrigona and Mathews yields information on patron use as compared to librarian use of the reference collection, but requires an in-depth study. This methodology involves reference staff keeping a record (by broad LC class number) of sources used and shelvers keeping a record of sources shelved. The portion of use by reference librarians can then be subtracted from the portion of patron use (Arrigona and Mathews, 1988). This is, of course, extremely valuable information in line with Rothstein's ideas. The information obtained by either of these methods can be used to charge only the appropriate portion of collection costs to reference librarian use, rather than charging the entire costs of the reference collection and its maintenance to reference desk service. Arrigona and Mathews' results indicate that patron use of the reference collection may be two and one-half times that of reference librarian use (1988, pp. 78-79).

Thus, these efforts have brought us to the point where an approximation of the true cost of the reference question is within our grasp. The data required are daunting but no longer impossible to obtain. The groundwork in theory and methodology has essentially been completed.

METHODOLOGY

Based on the previous work described, it appeared to be possible to arrive at a reasonable approximation of a formula to determine the actual cost of the reference transaction in a particular library. An anonymous ARL test library which had participated in the Wisconsin-Ohio Reference Evaluation Program could be used, since a great deal of the needed cost data was available from this library. However, other data would have to be interpolated from the studies mentioned in the previous section. The final figure arrived at will, of course, not be an exact one for the test library because interpolated data have been used. It will, however, be an illustrative figure, and will probably represent what the cost in general, of a reference transaction in a large academic library might have been during the years 1982-1983.

Below are listed the data needed to determine the actual cost of the reference transaction in a particular library using this method. An asterisk before a number indicates that the data in this area were interpolated for the test library.

Cost Figures Needed

   1. Annual salaries for all reference department personnel who work at the reference desk
* 2. A personnel overhead cost figure in terms of a percentage, including vacations, sick leave, etc.
   3. Annual reference materials budget
* 4. Annual contractual costs—vendors, OCLC, Dialogue, etc.
* 5. Annual costs for supplies
* 6. Annual estimate for collection maintenance
* 7. Annual estimate for overhead for quarters and facilities

Output Figures Needed

   1. Reference transactions per year
* 2. Percent of use of the reference collection by librarians and percent by patrons

Personnel Time Allocations per Year (estimate)

* 1. Reference questions and off the desk (percent of time spent)
* 2. Reference collection development and maintenance (percent of time spent)

Following is an outline showing how cost figures were arrived at for the test library.

COSTS CHARGED TO THE REFERENCE TRANSACTION
IN THE TEST LIBRARY

	Per Year (dollars)	Per Reference Transaction (dollars)
Annual volume of reference questions	56,000	
Annual reference collection budget	$133,000	
Reference Staff Salaries	$302.118	

Costs	Per Year (dollars)	Per Reference Transaction (dollars)
All reference staff time (8 professionals & 1 clerical)	302,118	
32 percent of total time spent on reference desk (estimate)	96,687	
75 percent of desk time spent on ref. questions (includes professional reading, & up-grading of skills while waiting for questions (estimate)	75,508	1.34
Personnel Overhead for above (includes fringe benefits, pers. adm., vacation, sick leave, etc. Figured at 28 percent of salaries)	21,142	.38
Off-desk time—follow-up for reference desk questions (2 percent of time)	6,042	.11
Personnel overhead for above	1,692	.03
Personnel Skills Maintenance & Updating (estimated at 3 percent of time)	8,411 (609 hrs.)	.15
Personnel overhead for above	2,355	.04
Materials (25 percent of use of reference collection by reference librarians)	133,000	
25 percent	33,253	.59
Reference Collection Development (estimated at 3 percent of time)	9,063	
(25 percent of use of reference collection by reference libns.)	2,266	.04
Personnel overhead	634	.01
Book storage & maintenance (25 percent of use by reference libns.)	3,894	.07
Contract costs (dialog, etc.) (20 percent of use for desk reference)	3,400	.06
Reference quarters & overhead (32 percent allocated to reference desk service)	6,560 2,099	.04
Supplies (32 percent allocated to reference desk service)	700 224	.004
		2.86
GENERAL OVERHEAD		
Library overhead (estimated at 33 percent)		3.80
University overhead (estimated at 14 percent)		4.33

Now that we have arrived at a reasonable figure of what the full cost of a reference question might be in our test library, we can see how this compares with the figures arrived at by using the yearly or hourly methodology and by using the entire reference budget as a base.

Cost Without General Overhead

The actual cost of staff time in this library spent working on reference questions (plus personnel overhead) was $2.10 per transaction. At this rate, 56,000 questions per year would cost $117,600. This is only 39 percent of total reference desk personnel cost. The full cost of a reference question (all costs added *except* general overhead) in this library ($2.86) is one-and-one-half times greater than the cost of the desk time alone. If we assumed that *all* reference personnel time was spent in desk reference service (plus appropriate personnel overhead), then the cost of the reference question would be $6.90 for staffing alone.

If we go even farther and charge the entire reference budget (estimated for this library at $534,265), we arrive at a figure of $9.54 per question. This illustrates the inflation that occurs when reference time and collection costs are not prorated to other outputs and when collection costs are not prorated to patron use.

Cost With General Overhead

If, as Cochran and Warmann (1989) did, we continue even further and add 33 percent or $3.15 for library overhead ($12.69) and 14 percent or $1.78 for university overhead, we arrive at a figure of $14.477. Thus, the full cost of the reference question *with general overhead* is about 7 times the cost of the staff time (plus personnel overhead) alone. If we prorate staff time and collection costs appropriately to other outputs, as described above, *even when general overhead is added,* the full cost of the reference question is $4.33, only twice as great as the cost of the staff time alone. This illustrates the inflation that occurs when reference time and other expenses are not prorated to other outputs and general overhead is added to an already inflated figure.

CONCLUSIONS

The most accurate, fair and sensible method of arriving at unit costs for the reference question, appears to be that where the following are considered:

1. Only staff time actually spent in handling reference questions (on- and off-desk, and ready reference).

2. That portion of staff development time spent in training and upgrading skills for question answering.
3. Only an appropriate portion of collection and other operating costs.

Finally, unit costing for the reference transaction should not be done in a vacuum, but should be done for all other library services as well. Cochrane and Warmann's work illustrates the importance of placing reference desk service in perspective with other services. They report that the full cost of a reference transaction, with overhead, was $9.22, an interlibrary loan filled at $9.23, and online search at $150.83 and a user education lecture at $15 per individual patron and $359 per group. According to their figures, it cost $106.22 to purchase, catalog and shelve a monograph volume and $180.86 to purchase, catalog and shelve a serial volume (Cochran and Warmann (1989). Such studies are essential for a full understanding of service costs, and can serve as a foundation for subsequent cost benefit exploration.

COST EFFECTIVENESS ANALYSIS
IN ACADEMIC LIBRARIES

Cost benefit measures help us to determine how worthwhile an activity is, while cost effectiveness measures tell us how well we do in performing that activity. Thus, cost effectiveness measures are, in a sense, performance/cost measures and, as such, can be useful in a number of ways.

Cost effectiveness measures can be used as an exploratory tool to help in gaining a better understanding of the relationship between outcomes and costs in reference service. They can also be used to help in deciding between alternative courses of action for attaining the same goal. Cost effectiveness checks can also be made periodically as a means of improving performance over time. Finally, they can serve as an accountability measure to demonstrate that funds are well spent in an operation that is successfully meeting its goals. That is, in terms of success, the operation delivers full value for its cost.

Effectiveness Measures

In order to perform cost effectiveness studies, a good measure of effectiveness is needed. Some issues related to this are discussed below.

Input, Process and Outcome Measures

Clearly, the very nature of cost effectiveness measures requires an assessment of outcome, since a unit of cost is compared to the success of a task or event. The necessity for use of *outcome* rather than input measures is illustrated by problems encountered by efforts at medical cost containment. Quality of hospital care has been measured in the past by the Joint Commission on Accreditation of Hospitals by determining whether the institution meets input standards and by inspecting written records of procedure compliance. This failure to measure actual outcome rather than input and process factors has resulted in unacceptable conditions in some hospitals and the rejection of JCAH as a means of judging quality in both New York and California (Bogdanich, 1988).

Available Outcome Measures

What outcome measures are available for reference service? At the present time, the following have been used for academic libraries: (1) librarian self-report, (2) (researcher judgment)—presenting prepared test questions unobtrusively in the actual reference situation, (3) (researcher judgment)—testing with permission outside the actual reference situation, using prepared test questions, (4) patron report of success on actual questions.

An in-depth discussion of these methods and related issues will not be attempted here and only a brief overview of these methods will be given. Evidence is accumulating that librarian self-report is not a sufficiently reliable measure, perhaps due to the lack of feedback received by reference librarians. This lack of feedback was first noted by Carlson (1964) and has since been substantiated by Whitlatch (1990). Another reason may be that librarian ability to accurately assess the outcome of a reference transaction according to patron viewpoint, varies greatly among reference librarians and reference departments, with scores varying from 41% to 85% for individual reference departments (Murfin and Bunge, 1988b). Unobtrusive observation and testing by permission are both promising research methods and as such, are now yielding helpful information. However, for use in cost effectiveness performance measures, a rigorous measure based on patron report of success in the actual situation appears to be the truest representation of what we want to measure. This is the measure of outcome used by the Wisconsin-Ohio Reference Evaluation Program. This program measures the outcome of each reference transaction by a standard for success where the patron must (1) report that exactly what was wanted was found, (2) report that he/she was fully satisfied, (3) mark none of the 9 listed reasons for dissatisfaction. The cost effectiveness measures presented in this section are based on data for 3,588 reference transactions in 44 libraries around the country, all of whom had been participants in the Wisconsin-Ohio program.

Cautions in the Use of Cost Effectiveness Measures

A considerable danger in any attempt to explore cost effectiveness is that the *worth* and *potential benefits* of operations and activities will be judged by their cost. It must always be remembered that goals and benefits should be considered of prime importance. An activity may not be cost effective, but the benefits it brings may give it overriding importance. For example, in a hospital it is more cost/effective to treat those with minor illnesses than those with serious illnesses, yet the latter clearly have paramount importance. The values and benefits of an activity must be kept in mind at all times when interpreting cost/effectiveness data.

Cost Per Successful Question

The measure of cost per successful question has previously been suggested by McClure (1984) as a useful one, and the formula for this measure is simple. After a library has completed a sample of transactions and a percentage of success has been obtained, the following steps are taken:

1. Add minutes taken for each transaction to obtain *total minutes* for the sample period. For example, 1,150 minutes were taken.
2. Divide *total minutes* by number of *successful* transactions. Answer represents minutes taken per successful transaction.
3. Multiply *minutes taken* times cost of staff time (a figure 23¢ per minute obtained from a test library has been used with the Wisconsin-Ohio data).

Since cost is equated with staff time spent and cost differentials tend to be small, tables and discussion will focus on time spent. When used to determine the overall cost effectiveness of 44 Wisconsin-Ohio libraries, it was found that the *most* cost effective libraries took 3.5 minutes per successful question and the *least* took 17.29 minutes. This formula appeared to have power of discrimination and to be a useful one for purposes of exploratory research.

Exploration of Cost Effectiveness Relationships in the Reference Process

Clearly, it might be expected that the cost effectiveness of an operation would be affected by input factors. In this study of Wisconsin-Ohio data, input factors of patron status and major, and type, subject and complexity of question were examined in terms of their relationship to cost effectiveness. The formula of cost per successful question was used.

It was found that patron major had little effect on cost effectiveness, with it being only slightly less cost effective to help a science/technology major than a humanities major. Patron status had more effect, with it taking one-and-one-half times as long, per successful question, to help a continuing education/ nondegree student as a faculty member. Complexity of question had somewhat more effect, with a complex question taking 9.92 minutes per successful complex question as opposed to 5.92 minutes per successful simple question.

The greatest differences in cost effectiveness, however, were centered around type and subject of question. The request for compilation of a list of references on a subject took 4.7 times as long per successful question as the short-answer fact question. The greatest effect, however, seemed to be in the subject matter of the question with a question on transportation taking 11 times longer per successful question than one on etiquette.

This seems to indicate that patron input is a potent factor in cost effectiveness. The secret to more cost effective operation appears to lie in learning to deal more effectively and efficiently with our particular input, however difficult it may be. Results in regard to input factors are presented in more detail below.

Patron Major

Patron major showed a small relationship to the cost effectiveness with which the question was handled, with education, and the arts and humanities majors taking 6.87 and 7.85 minutes per successful question and medical/health and math/physical science majors taking 8.91 and 9.15 minutes per successful question.

Patron Status

Greater differences were apparent when patron status was considered, as show in Table 1.

Interpreting the above picture, it becomes apparent that generally the greater knowledge we might assume the patron to have, the more quickly and successfully he or she can be helped. Those often having the *least* knowledge

Table 1. Patron Status and Cost Effectiveness

Patron Status	Minutes per Successful Transaction	Cost per Successful Transaction
Faculty	6.23	$1.43
Library staff	6.42	1.48
Alumni	6.64	1.53
Graduate	7.63	1.75
Junior	7.90	1.82
Sophomore	8.02	1.84
Freshman	8.29	1.91
Senior	8.87	2.04
Not affiliated	8.87	2.04
Continuing education/Nondegree	9.32	2.14

Table 2.   Type of Question Asked and Cost Effectiveness

Type of Question Asked	Min. per Successful Transaction	Cost per Successful Transaction
Short answer facts	3.97	$ .91
Explanation of source or library	4.49	1.03
Smaller item in larger publication (*particular* article, speech, quote, poem, etc.)	7.03	1.62
Something by *particular* author	7.21	1.66
Type of source wanted—atlas, dict., ref. source, picture, etc.	8.74	2.01
Criticism	9.15	2.10
Facts and statistics in general—or source containing it (names, addresses, definitions, statistics, etc.)	9.56	2.20
Focus on aspect, biog., hist., other	10.7	2.46
Something, everything, everything	11.37	2.61
Analysis, trends, pro/con, cause/effect, how-to-do-it, how-it-works, other	12.41	2.85
Requests that you compile a list of references on a subject	18.81	4.33
Aspects of Questions		
Restrictions—must be certain time period, currentness, place, country, language, etc.	11.71	2.69
Multiple subject	12.55	2.89

of the library and the institution appear to be the most difficult to help successfully and efficiently. The seniors appear to be the exception to this rule. One explanation might be that seniors as a group are, perhaps, on one hand more experienced and determined and under maximum pressure, but on the other hand without the knowledge resources of the graduate. The selection procedure for graduates may generally be more rigorous, resulting in a higher level of student, and the graduate is more likely to be studying in the field of his or her choice and greatest expertise. The senior, on the other hand, may be completing disliked and difficult required courses only peripherally related to his or her major area of interest. At any rate, whatever the reason, seniors appear to be the student group presenting the greatest problem in regard to cost effective service.

Type of Question

It can be seen in Table 2 that, overall, questions with more *specific* subjects require *less* time and questions with more general subjects require *more* time to conclude successfully. For example, subjects of higher specificity such as wanting a particular small text, particular facts, particular works, criticism of particular authors, and particular types of materials tend to take less time per successful question, perhaps because it is easier and quicker to determine precisely what is wanted and to know whether or not it has been found. Those questions *not* particularized to a certain person, place, or thing perhaps tend to require more communication to assure that the question is understood and that what is found actually answers the question. Greater amounts of time also appear to be necessary to complete questions successfully, when other restrictions are added, such as currentness, or multiple subject requirements.

The low cost of effectiveness of the "request for compilation of reference on a subject" might be explained by a number of factors. Most of these questions were handled by computerized ready reference searches and probably computer situations do not allow for maximum efficiency. For example, not all libraries have facilities for ready reference searching at the reference desk, nor are sufficiently skilled personnel always available. Also, many computerized ready reference searches are done only as a last resort after other resources have been exhausted, so may have a lowered probability of success.

Subject of Question

The subject of the patron's question, as seen in Table 3, appears to be a primary factor, of those studied here, in regard to cost effectiveness. Time taken per successful question ranged from 3.75 minutes per successful question in the area of etiquette to 37.5 minutes per successful question in the area of transportation. Those subjects handled with the *most* and *least* cost effectiveness are shown in Tables 2 and 3.

It can be seen that the *most* cost effective subjects did not fall into a clear pattern, but those that were *least* cost effective appeared to fall primarily into scientific and technical areas and also into social areas, particularly around ethnic studies and ethnic relations. Comparing areas of humanities, social sciences and science and technology in regard to cost effectiveness, the following can be seen in Table 4.

With science and technology questions having a lower level of cost effectiveness in the general reference department, the question arises as to whether such questions are handled with greater cost effectiveness in special libraries devoted to these subjects. Results for two academic science and technology libraries in the Wisconsin-Ohio database were compared to these overall results and it was found that on science and technology questions, special libraries were more cost effective, with one library taking 6.45 minutes per successful question and the other 8.8 minutes per successful question, as compared to 12.04 minutes per successful question for all libraries. A social science division took 7.28 minutes per successful transaction as compared to 11.4 minutes per successful question for all libraries.

Table 3.   Most and Least Cost Effective Subjects

Most Cost Effective Subjects	*Min. per Successful Transaction*	*Cost per Successful Transaction*
Etiquette	3.75	.86
Writing	4.05	.93
Astronomy	4.50	1.03
Math	4.83	1.11
Books & Periodicals	4.92	1.13
Home Economics	5.00	1.15
Humanities in general	5.18	1.19
Films	5.76	1.32
Journalism	6.00	1.38
Physics	6.40	1.40
Communication	6.57	1.51
Costume & dress	6.71	1.54
Current events	6.97	1.60
Least Cost Effective Subjects		
Area Studies (countries)	11.03	2.54
Technology	11.13	2.56
Drug & alcohol abuse	11.31	2.60
Statistics (discipline of)	11.86	2.73
Biology	11.87	2.73
Engineering	11.93	2.74
Environment	13.67	3.14
Blacks	13.7	3.15
Military & war	14.78	3.40
Poverty	15	3.45
Energy	16.25	3.74
Architecture	16.7	3.84
Ethnic studies	18	4.14
Botany	19	4.37
Law Enforcement	19.4	4.46
Automotive	20.33	4.67
Mental health & illness	25.5	5.86
Race relations	28	6.44
Housing	29	6.67
Pollution	32	7.36
Transportation	37.5	8.62

Cost Effectiveness as an Aid in Deciding Between Alternatives

In this method, two or more alternatives for accomplishing the same goal, are examined for their cost effectiveness. In simple versions of this method, cost and effectiveness figures are compared for both alternatives. Ideally, one alternative may be found to be both more effective and less costly. If both

Table 4. Cost Effectiveness by Broad Subject Category

Broad Subject Category	Min. per Successful Transaction –average–	Cost per Successful Transaction	Min. per Successful Transaction –range for all subjects in group
All subjects in humanities	8.68	$2.00	4.05 - 16.7 (15 subj.)
All subjects in social sciences	11.4	2.62	6 - 29 (38 subj.)
All subjects in science & tech.	12.04	2.77	4.5 - 37.5 (28 subj.)

are of equal effectiveness, then the one with the lower cost would be chosen. A good example of this method is a study by Lawson where the cost effectiveness of tours versus computer-assisted instruction is compared in regard to library orientation. The effectiveness of each method was determined by testing students for retention of knowledge (Lawson, 1990). Another application of this method has been made by Havener, who compared the cost effectiveness of answering two types of questions using online and print sources (Havener, 1988). This type of application speaks directly to the question raised in our cost effectiveness exploration, of how we can deal more effectively and efficiently with our input.

Cost Effectiveness of Professional and Paraprofessional Staff in Reference Service

As an application of this method, the question of the relative cost effectiveness of professional and paraprofessional staff in providing reference service, was explored. However, when the method of cost per successful question was considered for purposes of decision-making rather than simple exploration, it was determined that the cost and quality balance needed to be adjusted.

One difficulty in making cost effectiveness comparisons using a ratio method, is that quality must be given sufficient weight so that it is not overbalanced by cost. This difficulty can be seen in that the cost scale rises in even increments, while the quality or effectiveness scale does not. Quality of reference service in academic libraries, according to Wisconsin-Ohio results, seldom falls under 40 percent success. It may be that all of the self-help mechanisms of the library provide a "floor" under the score.

At the upper end of the scale, with each patron's question being different and with no limitation on the potential difficulty of questions that might be

Table 5.   Staffing Costs per Successful Transaction with and without Penalty
for Failed Transactions

	Professional Librarians		Paraprofessional Staff	
	Complex RQ	Simple RQ	Complex RQ	Simple RQ
Total RQ	1,152	1,322	260	209
Successful	662	785	123	124
Unsuccessful	490	537	137	85
Minutes spent	6,408	4,632	1,381	749
Minutes spent per trans.	5.56	3.5	5.31	3.58
Minutes spent per successful trans.	9.86	5.9	11.22	6.04
Amount spent per minute	$.24	$.24	$.18	$.18
Amount spent per successful trans.	$2.32	$1.41	$2.02	$1.09
$2 penalty for each failed trans.	$980		$274	
Total cost per successful trans. with penalty added	$2,518		$522.58	
Total cost per successful trans. with penalty for failure	$3.80		$4.24	

asked, and 55 or more factors that might go wrong in a single reference transaction, there appears to be a ceiling of about 70 percent, beyond which it is very difficult to rise. Thus, the quality range is considerably narrower than the cost range, and a drop in cost consistently outweighs a drop in quality. For this reason, a disbenefit, frustration or hassle penalty is applied for failed questions, thus placing quality and cost in proper perspective. In the analysis below, a penalty of $2.00 has been added for each less-than-successful question.

It can be seen in this sample of libraries that overall, paraprofessionals cost somewhat less than professionals per successful complex transaction, if only cost is considered, and no penalty is given for less-than-successful transactions. This is because the 29 percent greater success of professionals is not enough to match their 33 percent greater cost (using the salary figures from our test library). However, if we consider the extra benefits gained by the higher professional success rate and the frustration and higher rate of failure on the part of paraprofessional staff important, then we might assign a penalty of $2 per transaction for frustration and wasted time for patrons. Such a penalty has been used or suggested by other investigations. Braunstein notes that in 1977 Baumol and Ordover (1976) valued waiting time at $5 per hour in the standard queuing model. Stuart (1977) refers to delay time in terms of a disbenefit. Griffiths (1982) refers to "hassle" time which includes lag time, difficulty of use and difficulty of access.

In addition to wasted time or delay time, the frustration of no answer or a poor answer should also be considered. Cronin (1977) supports the idea when he says that another possible cost to the user is the frustration encountered when the system fails to satisfy the user's particular needs.

Van House emphasizes the need to include user costs when figuring total costs. She notes that "the user trades off time and money ... library use is time intensive ... one must use the full cost, not just the monetary cost of the services (Van House, 1983). In line with this, if we assign a penalty for time wasted and frustration on less-than-successful transactions, we find that professional librarians are more cost effective on complex questions (complexity of question is measured by a special formula derived from the librarian's report of type of question asked).

This is only an overall figure and varies greatly from library to library. For example, in one ARL library we find that cost per successful complex question (without a penalty for failure) for professional librarians is $2.31 and for paraprofessional staff, $2.59. In this library paraprofessional staff took 14.42 minutes per successful complex question. In another smaller library paraprofessional staff spent 32.5 minutes per successful complex question. However, as we have noted in a previous article there were a number of libraries using paraprofessional staff effectively (Murfin and Bunge, 1988a).

The bottom line appears to be that professional and paraprofessional staff have equal effectiveness on simple questions as far as helping the patron find what is wanted. On the complex question, professional staff are more cost effective, if the increased failure and wasted time is considered important enough that a penalty be levied. If the 29 percent increase in frustration and wasted time is not considered important, then the lower rate of nonprofessional staff makes them somewhat more cost effective.

From the above analysis, we also find that complex questions are more costly than simple questions for both groups of staff. Thus, a library with questions of high complexity should recognize that highly trained staff may be needed for maximum cost effectiveness. For example, in one library, staff took 41 minutes per successful complex question, at a cost of $7.47 per question.

Cost Effectiveness as a Method of Self Improvement Over Time

Another purpose of cost effectiveness is to use it as a tool for self improvement. A measure of cost effectiveness is taken, sometimes at each stage of the reference process. Changes are made and cost effectiveness is checked again to see if improvements have resulted. This procedure is repeated until the desired level of cost effectiveness has been obtained. This method was used successfully in a special library where the reference progress was separated into steps and the step at which failure occurred in a transaction was identified. Stages where failure most often occurred were studied, new procedures were adopted and after a period of time, cost effectiveness was checked again. In this library the stages of the process were divided into (1) communication of the need, (2) search, (3) some documents identified, (4) users agree that some documents are relevant, (5) some documents arrive in time, (6) some documents received have relevance. The new procedures resulted in an increase in quality which was proportionately greater than the increase in cost (Wessel and Moore, 1969).

The difficulty of this particular method, as applied by Wessel, is that its success depends on being able to separate a task into stages and to be able to judge success or failure at each stage. An attempt was made by Kantor (1981b) to extend this research to academic and special scientific and technical libraries, but the method was not clearly demonstrated to be a viable one.

The primary problem for reference service in settings other than special libraries, may be that some parts of the process are performed by librarians and some by patrons, varying from transaction to transaction. Also, stages of the process may overlap and do not always take place in a set sequence. Finally, librarians may not receive sufficient feedback to judge success at each stage. This method, however, has potential and awaits a researcher who might possibly develop and refine it into a useful tool.

A more viable method, at this time, might be to study and improve cost effectiveness of different aspects of the reference process such as handling of types and subjects of questions, types of methods and procedures used, and type of staff utilized.

A methodology for self improvement in regard to cost effectiveness which is often overlooked, is self-testing. Such a study can be performed outside the actual setting, studying cost effectiveness in finding test questions typical of those generally asked. Much could be learned in this way of the adequacy of staff knowledge, collections and reference environment. Such a study would not take into account factors such as type of patrons, communication and pressure of business, for example, but could still provide useful information about certain very important *components* of the reference process.

Cost Effectiveness for Purposes of Accountability

One difficulty of an overall cost effectiveness measure for a service is that in order to be meaningful, it needs to be put in perspective with cost effectiveness figures from other libraries. For a number of reasons, it is difficult to make such comparisons.

Effectiveness Comparisons

If effectiveness comparisons are made on the basis of test by permission or unobtrusive observation, then we know that all libraries had the same questions and that we are comparing the same question input. However, in actual reference work, as is studied in the Wisconsin-Ohio program, question difficulty may vary greatly from one library to another. A library with easy questions might be found to be considerably more cost effective than a library with harder questions. In order to equalize this factor using Wisconsin-Ohio data, it was decided to use only effectiveness (success) on complex questions, thus assuring that the comparison would be roughly similar in regard to question input.

Cost Comparisons

Up to this point, the method selected by the Wisconsin-Ohio program has been "time taken per successful complex question." Adding cost to this ratio for purposes of comparisons between libraries across the country, poses some difficulty. First of all, methodologies for unit cost comparisons are now being developed, but have not been tested or universally accepted (See Part I of this series). Even if a methodology were finalized and accepted, the unit cost figures would need to be adjusted for a great many variables. For example, since pay levels differ in different parts of the country, one reference department might perform as well as another but would be found to be less cost effective because salaries were higher than in other parts of the country. Thus, greater effectiveness would be required of a library in a higher cost area to maintain the same level of cost effectiveness as in libraries in less expensive parts of the country.

Because of these problems in relation to cost, the best choice for purposes of comparisons across libraries appeared to be to remain with the formula of time taken per successful complex question, with a penalty of 4.4 minutes (in terms of added cost) per failed complex question. Overall figures (without penalty) for all academic libraries were 9.92 minutes per successful complex question.

The translation of time into cost could then be done at the individual library level. At such time as the problems of unit cost comparisons across libraries have been solved, cost could be added to the above comparison measure, after taking into account, variables such as library type, size and region of the country.

Conclusions

Cost effectiveness measures might also be referred to as effectiveness-efficiency measures, balanced with cost. The measure used in this study with data from the Wisconsin-Ohio Reference Evaluation Program, appeared to have sharper powers of discrimination than did the measure of effectiveness alone. As such, it should have powerful potential for future research. This measure should also prove very useful for exploring aspects of reference service, deciding between alternative courses of action, improving reference operations, and for accountability purposes.

COST BENEFIT ANALYSIS OF REFERENCE SERVICE IN ACADEMIC LIBRARIES

As in cost effectiveness analysis, cost benefit analysis may be used to explore the benefits and costs associated with an activity such as reference/information service, and to determine how to maximize benefits at least cost. It may also be used to compare two alternatives in terms of their benefits and costs, and to demonstrate the worth or value of an activity in relation to its costs. In this type of research it is usual to make an assessment of benefits and then translate these benefits into dollars and compare them to costs.

In cost effectiveness studies, the measure of value is the overall success of the outcome of a group of reference transactions, as judged by whatever method is deemed appropriate. In cost benefit studies, the outcome of a group of reference transactions is again judged, but in terms of benefits derived by users as result of reference service, such as benefits of having the information, changes made in their lives, and societal benefits in general.

Benefit Measures

Benefits may be defined as experiences which promote internal and external well being. They help individuals to attain life goals which both they and society consider desirable.

Sound, carefully developed benefit measures are essential to cost benefit analysis. Such measures have been slow in coming, particularly in academic libraries. In regard to benefit research in general, special libraries have led the way, with medical libraries in the forefront in recent years. A variety of benefits have been studied over the years, including emotional and cognitive outcomes, behavioral outcomes, and external benefits and gains.

Disbenefits

The reverse of benefits are disbenefits, where experiences exhaust individuals' personal resources of time, money, and patience, remove them further from their goals, and add to their life problems. Such experiences result in a state of distress, rather than one of well being. The negative experience of failing to find information, in particular, can, in some cases, have serious impacts on persons' lives, such as failure to graduate, loss of a prospective job, etc. Avoiding such experiences does, in a sense, improve the individual's ability to function and cope, to solve problems, and to advance toward goals. In this sense, avoidance of negative experiences can and should be considered a benefit. Benefit research done by Dervin (1985) and Wilson et al. (1989), clearly counts avoidance of negative experiences as a benefit.

Stuart (1977) has considered the effects of delay time and Flood (1973) has suggested an "Aggravation Quotient" which she maintains has a negative impact in that it affects user behavior. Users will avoid sources with high Aggravation Quotients and gravitate toward those which are less frustrating. Griffiths (1982, p. 277) speaks of a "hassle" index consisting of lag time, difficulty of access and difficulty of use.

Expected Positive Outcomes: Inferred Benefits

A number of measures are used as evidence that users *expect* that an activity has the potential to bring some benefit. Among these are frequency of use, ratings of need and importance, and willingness to pay. However, these measures do not speak to *actual* benefits obtained or to the types of benefits expected but only to the user's belief in the *potential* for benefits of that service.

Willingness to Pay

Willingness to pay may be measured by surveying users and asking them how much they *would* be willing to pay for a particular service, or by taking actual amounts paid as a measure of "willingness."

Griffiths (1982, p. 281) notes that asking users how much they were willing to pay for information should be used cautiously for judging the value of information products or services. Some users might indicate a low willingness to pay, not because the information was not valuable to them, but because of opposition to fees for library services or due to standard personal finances and competing demands for available funds. Others might give a high value to the information but in actual fact might not be willing to pay that amount. In the long run, willingness to pay is probably determined more strongly by the user's financial situation than by the nature of the information and lacks an element of validity for library purposes because it does not tell us in an unbiased way the personal value the information has for the user.

As an example of this type of research, a cost benefit study was done of online searching in an academic library. User willingness to pay was defined as the amount users were *presently* paying for searches. A negative cost benefit ratio per search was found, with costs of $16 per search and benefits of $7.50 (Standera, 1973). This supports Mason's comment that the highest price a user is willing to pay is less than the cost of the information itself (Mason and Sassone, 1978).

Overall Value Judgments

Users may be asked to rate information received for its overall value, worth, usefulness or helpfulness. Unless the question is further specified, answers do not add greatly to our knowledge and leave us with many questions as to the exact nature of the benefits and the circumstances associated with those benefits. However, if *carefully specified and well worded,* such judgments can be very helpful in identifying conditions under which benefits in general are obtained or not obtained, or in determining which alternatives bring the greatest perceived benefits for the least cost. A good example is found in a study by Saracevic and Kantor (1988) which asked users to evaluate the results of an online search performed for them in terms of its usefulness, "What contribution has this information made toward the resolution of your research problem?"

Exploration of a Wide Variety of Benefits

Exploratory research can consider a wide variety of benefits in one study, while focused research concentrates on a particular type of benefit. An example of exploratory research is that of a public library survey where users responded to an open-minded question to describe any benefits obtained from visiting the library. Responses were then categorized into types of benefits (Fairfax County Public Library User Study, 1987). A comprehensive study by Dervin classified benefits of all types into categories and a sample of California citizens was surveyed by telephone and asked if they had experienced any of these benefits in their most recent library visit to any type of library. A surprising number of persons reported benefits, indicating that this approach has much potential. This comprehensive classification of benefits represents a substantial step ahead in benefit research (Dervin, 1985, pp. 2-4).

Focused Benefit Research

Information Found or Not Found: First Level of Benefits

The question arises as to whether the finding of wanted information is a benefit in and of itself. When an individual evaluates the information found and reports it to be exactly what was wanted, then the purpose of *finding* information for decision making has been satisfied and a small advance toward a larger goal has been made. The information found has been evaluated, however, briefly, and the user's positive report indicates that the information has been processed and filtered, at least to some extent. Thus, the finding of the wanted information, itself, could be termed a benefit since it has advanced the user toward a goal, and the process of assimilation has begun. Getz, in a study of the benefits of the online catalog, counts books *found* as a benefit, even though the books were not evaluated, perhaps on the grounds that finding them advanced users a step ahead toward their ultimate goal (Getz, 1987). If we consider the reverse, we see that not finding wanted information can have negative impacts. In their critical incident reports, Wilson et al. (1989, pp. 81-83) note that failure to find wanted information can lead to unanswered questions, uncertainty, poor decision making and failure of ultimate goals.

Emotional and Cognitive Outcomes: Second Level of Benefits

It might be said that information needs to be put to use or acted upon before it can be considered that benefits have been derived. However, experiences which add to emotional well being and/or knowledge and understanding, are certainly of value. Considering the definition of impact, positive experiences which are stored internally *do* have a present impact in that they may change patterns of thinking, contribute to states of well being, result in improved decision making and generally improved functioning of the individual. Furthermore, stored information or cognitive enrichment may have strong impacts at some future time.

Desirable Emotional Outcomes. Dervin's research explores a variety of such benefits in regard to library service, including "found support/emotional control, felt connected/not alone, got rest/relaxation, happiness/pleasure, calmed down or eased worries, took mind off things, felt reassured or hopeful, and felt good about self (Dervin, 1985, pp. 11-12). Such benefits could apply equally well to the outcomes of reference service, in promoting well being and the quality of life.

Desirable Cognitive Outcomes. Although studies have not focused specifically on learning as a benefit of the reference transaction, indications are that a great deal of learning routinely takes place, with resulting increases in skill, knowledge and understanding. Unpublished Wisconsin-Ohio data indicate that 49 percent of patrons learned a new source and an additional 37 percent learned two or more new sources as the result of the reference transaction, and 77 percent reported learning something about the library. When those who reported "partly" are added, then only 7 percent of patrons reported learning *nothing* about the library as a result of reference assistance (Murfin and Bunges, 1989). This is supported by a study where 87 percent of 700 college students surveyed perceived interaction with librarians as a learning experience "sometimes" to "frequently" (Hernon and Pastine, 1977). Some research has been done dealing with behavioral change as the result of cognitive enrichment and will be discussed later.

Experiences Which Lead to Action: Third Level of Benefits

Although emotional and cognitive benefits are of high value, their present and future impact is extremely difficult to measure. Perhaps, in order to justify costs, it is felt important to demonstrate benefits beyond personal well being and increase in knowledge. Researchers continue to seek more concrete evidence that demonstrates the benefits of information to the user in external action with society and the world.

If the information is acted on, that is, used in some way to help solve problems or attain goals, then the differences made by the information can be more easily described and/or quantified and used to demonstrate impact.

Active use of information to attain goals and solve problems might be said to advance users more quickly toward goals than simple assimilation of knowledge. In this sense, as well as cognitive benefits, there are benefits in that the information is able to be applied immediately. In regard to research in this area, Goldhor (1979) found that 91 percent of public library patrons used the information obtained as the result of asking reference questions. Another study found that 46 percent of medical clinicians made decisions based on the information obtained from a MEDLINE search (Haynes, 1990). Saracevic found that 454 percent of those who received a free online search reported that it had contributed substantially to the resolution of their research problem (which indicates that it was probably utilized in some way) (Saracevic and Kantor, 1988, p. 190).

Experiences Where Use of Information Led to Successful/Desirable Outcomes: Fourth Level of Benefits

This is the highest level of impact, where positive changes can be shown to have resulted from the use of information. It goes beyond whether benefits were expected, whether information was found or not found, whether it was perceived as useful, whether it was acted upon or not acted upon. It goes, instead, to whether the outcome of the action was successful in effecting positive changes toward reaching goals and solving problems.

Desirable Behavioral Outcomes and Changes: Innovation, Creativity, Scholarship and Research Productivity

These behaviors have been explored in a number of studies, primarily in special and academic libraries. Pitlack (1980) studied creativity and innovation before and after exposing participants to online searching, and found that more new ideas were generated after such exposure. Langrish et al. (1972) also studied innovations of award-winning firms and found that 9 percent came from published literature. Garvey et al. (1972) studied research productivity in psychology and found that 14 percent of ideas originated from library channels. In these studies volume and quality of innovations and ideas were taken as measures of value or benefit, and activities such as literature/library use were examined to see if and how they contributed to those benefits.

External Benefits

Problems Solved and Individual and Societal Goals Achieved. Here again, the two exploratory studies referred to previously, uncovered many impacts in terms of goals achieved and problems solved. Dervin, for example, reports such benefits as "got ideas and understandings," "planned, decided what, when, where," "got skills to do something," "accomplished or finished something," "kept going when it seemed hard," "got started or motivated," "got confirmation that I was doing the right thing," "got out of or avoided a bad situation," "found directions," "reached goal" (Dervin, 1985, pp. 2-4). A particularly good example of this type of research is that of Haynes, where, of those clinicians who used the information from a MEDLINE search, 91% reported that patient care was improved as a result (Haynes et al., 1990, p. 81). Another study by Wilson et al. (1989, pp. H1-H2), reports that a number of lives were probably saved by use of the information obtained from a MEDLINE search.

Resources Gained or Saved. This area appears to be the most active one for cost benefit research in all types of libraries, perhaps because benefits can be more easily quantified and translated into dollars. Benefits in dollars earned as a result of information, were studied in one special library and a benefit ratio of 3 to 1 was found (Jensen, Asbury, and King, 1980).

The most usual benefit, however, is time saved. A detailed rationale for this is provided in an article by Van House (1983). A study by Getz (1987, pp. 236-239) focuses on time saved by users of the online catalog over the card catalog, with benefits being translated into dollars. Time saved by reference service has seldom been studied, but one landmark work exists, done in a special library. Users were asked how much time had been saved by literature searches and citation and reference assistance. The resulting estimate of time saved was compared to costs of staff time in answering these questions. It was estimated that for every staff hour spent on a literature search, engineering staff were saved about 9 hours of effort, thus making a benefit to cost ratio of about 1 to 9 (Kramer, 1971, p. 488).

Developing a Cost Benefit Measure for Use With Wisconsin-Ohio Reference Data

Willingness to pay was rejected as a measure for reasons previously described and valuing user time in terms of lost income was also rejected, due to the moral and ethical connotations of valuing a successful transaction for a high income patron as greater than that of a low income patron. This would be contrary to the traditions of reference service and in violation of Reference and Adult Services Division (RASD) Guidelines which state that "status of users is not to be considered" ("A Commitment to Information Services, 1979,

p. 277). Incorporating such a benefit measure could have the effect of concentrating attention on higher income level patrons to the detriment of lower income patrons because a greater benefit would be earned.

Measurement of cognitive and other later impacts which come *after* the finding of the information was not possible, because such data were not available.

It was decided that the benefit measure to be used in this study would be time and effort saved, which would then be translated into a dollar value, the same dollar value for all patrons regardless of income or willingness to pay. The reasons for selecting this measure are argued by Van House in her excellent time allocation study of public library use (Van House, 1983, pp. 382-383). She makes the point that there *is* a cost involved in going to the library, that there is considerable time, effort and related smaller costs, and that these costs to the patron *should* be considered (Van House, 1983, pp. 382-383).

Reference service, itself, is designed for the purpose of making access to information or materials quicker and easier. Thus, if we are going to assume a benefit to the patron, this is a very logical one.

A second benefit to the patron is in finding desired information or materials that he or she *might not otherwise have been able to find alone however much time had been taken.* Finding what is wanted is the first step in solving problems and achieving goals, and as such, has a positive impact. The negative outcome of not finding what is wanted is clearly a disbenefit for both the patron and the library.

A further benefit is the obvious one of knowledge gained by the patron about sources, search strategy and the library. On the basis of these benefits, it was decided that a conservative ratio of at least 3 to 1 would be clearly justified. Since the full cost, including overhead, of a reference question in a test library was $4.33, it was decided to value benefits at $13 per transaction. Since the premium was to be on quality, $12 was subtracted for each less-than-successful question on the grounds of disbenefits to the patron of the kind described before. The full amount was not subtracted because some benefits do accrue even in less-than-successful transactions. This decision means, in effect, that libraries dropping below 50 percent effectiveness may not earn benefits at all if their negative transactions outweigh their positive ones. If a negative balance remains, it will be termed as "frustration points," indicating the effect this quality of service has on patrons.

This formula was tested using all 44 academic libraries who had participated in the Wisconsin-Ohio program at that time. The statistician considered this formula to be promising, and suggested that this approach to cost benefit research should be explored. One of the most important research uses of such a formula is to determine the relative cost benefit ratios for different levels of personnel. Cost per minute for reference department personnel was estimated using the salary figures obtained from the test library. The total

Table 6.   Benefits Earned per Transaction as Compared to
Amount Spent per Transaction

	Professional Librarians		Paraprofessional Staff	
	Complex RQ	Simple RQ	Complex RQ	Simple RQ
Benefits earned	$8,606	$10,205	$1,599	f$1,612
Disbenefit cost penalty	$5,880	$6,444	$1,644	$1,020
Benefits earned per minute	$1.34	$2.21	0	$2.15
Disbenefits earned per minute	$.92	$.45	$1.19	$1.36
Benefits earned per transaction	$7.47	$7.72	0	$7.71
Disbenefits earned per transaction	$5.10	$4.87	$6.32	$4.88
Amount spent per minute	$.24	$.24	$.18	$.18
Amount spent per trans.	$1.33	$.84	$.95	$.64

amount spent for yearly reference desk personnel salaries was divided by 149 days worked per month and then by hours and minutes to arrive at a figure of $.23 per minute for professional librarians and $.18 for paraprofessional assistants. This figure was used in the cost benefit formula. Findings in regard to the 44 Wisconsin-Ohio program libraries are given in Table 6.

Conclusions

This analysis is an example of the kind of application that can be made of cost benefit data. Indications are that paraprofessionals could be used with a favorable cost benefit ratio, *if a way could be devised where they would handle only simple questions.* Unfortunately, a workable method which would achieve this is very difficult to develop.

Cost benefit research should be done on the different services offered by the reference department and the library, such as library instruction, online searching and interlibrary loan. Cost studies comparing these services have been done (Cochran and Warmann, 1989, p. 60) but need to have benefit measures incorporated.

The particular analysis just shown with Wisconsin-Ohio data represents a purely experimental approach to cost benefit analysis of reference service. It is clear that much research needs to be done on the detailed impacts of reference service, and it is hoped that such studies will soon be done. The benefits of time saved, failures avoided and life goals and satisfactions achieved as a result of reference service urgently need to be explored.

REFERENCES

Anderson, Charles. "Budgeting for Reference Services in On-Line Age." *The Reference Librarian* 19(1987):179-207.

Arrigona, Daniel and Eleanor Mathews. "A Use Study of an Academic Library Reference Collection." *RQ* 28(Fall 1988):71-81.

Baumol, William and Janusz Ordover. "Public Good Properties in Reality: The Case of Scientific Journals." In Susan K. Martin, comp., *Information Politics: Proceedings of the American Society for Information Science Annual Meeting* (Vol. 13, p. 464). Washington, DC: American Society for Information Science, 1976.

Bogdanich, Walt. "Small Comfort: Prized by Hospitals, Accreditation Hides Perils Patients Face." *Wall Street Journal,* October 12, 1988, p. 1A.

Bunge, Charles. "Stress in the Library." *Library Journal* 15(September 15, 1987):49.

Carlson, G. "Search Strategy by Reference Librarians." Part 3 of Final Report on the Organization of Large Files. Sherman Oaks, CA: Hughes Dynamics, Inc., Advances Systems Division, 1964 [PB166192].

Cline, Gloria. "Budgeting for Reference Services in the Academic Library: A Tutorial." *The Reference Librarian* 19(1987):70-71.

Cochran, Lynn and Carolyn Warmann. "Cost Analysis of Library Services at Virginia Polytechnic Institute and State University." In Janice Fennel, ed., *Building on the First Century: Proceedings of the Fifth Conference of the Association of College and Research Libraries,* Cincinnati, OH, April 5-8. Chicago: American Library Association, 1989, p. 60.

"A Commitment to Information Services: Developmental Guidelines." *RQ* 18(Spring 1979):277.

Cronin, Blaise. "Taking the Measure of Service." *Aslib Proceedings* 29(January 1977):37.

Dervin, Brenda. *How Librarians Help.* Stockton, CA: University of the Pacific, 1985.

Ellison, J.W. and Claudia Molenda. "Making Yourself Approachable." *New Library World* 77(November 1976):214-215.

Fairfax County Public Library User Study. Fairfax, VA: Fairfax County Public Library, 1987, pp. 63-71.

Flood, Barbara. "Aggravation Quotient: Search Time/User Time." In Helen Waldron and F. Raymond Long, eds., *Innovative Developments in Information Systems: Their Benefits and Costs, Proceedings of the 36th Annual Meeting of the American Society for Information Science,* Vol. 10, pp. 65-66. Westport, CT: Greenwood Press, 1973.

Garvey, William D., et al. "Research in Patterns of Scientific Communication. I. General Description of Research." *Progress in Information Storage and Retrieval* 8(June 1972): 111-122.

Getz, Malcolm. "Some Benefits of the Online Catalog." *College and Research Libraries* 48(May 1987):224-420.

Goldhor, Herbert. "The Patrons' Side of Public Library Reference Questions." *Public Library Quarterly* 1(Spring 1979):35-49.

Griffiths, Jose Marie. "The Value of Information and Related Systems, Products and Services." In Martha Williams, ed., *Annual Review of Information Science and Technology.* White Plains, NY: Knowledge Industry Publications, 1982, pp. 269-284.

Havener, Michael W. "The Use of Print Versus Online Sources to Answer Ready Reference Questions in the Social Sciences." Ph.D. dissertation, School of Library and Information Science, University of North Carolina, 1988.

Haynes, R. Brian, et al. "The Patron's Side of Public Library Reference Questions." *Public Library Quarterly* 1(Spring 1979):35-49.

Hernon, Peter and Maureen Pastine. "Student Perceptions of Academic Libraries." *College and Research Libraries* 38(March 1977):129-139.

Jensen, Rebecca, Herbert Asbury, and Radford King "Costs and Benefits to Industry of Online Literature Searches." *Special Libraries* 71(July 1980):291-297.

Kantor, Paul. "Levels of Outputs Related to Cost of Operation of Scientific and Technical Libraries." *Library Research* 3(Spring 1981a):25.

_____. "Quantitative Evaluation of the Reference Process." *RQ* 21(Fall 1981b):43-52.

Kramer, Joseph. "How to Survive in Industry: Cost Justifying Library Services." *Special Libraries* 62(November 1971):488.

King, Judith D. "On Line." *Michigan Librarian* 43(Fall 1977):25.

Langrish, J., et al. *Wealth From Knowledge*. London: Macmillan, 1972.

Lawson, Lonnie V. "A Cost Comparison Between General Library Tours and Computer-Assisted Instruction Programs." *Research Strategies* 3(Spring 1990):66-73.

Lopez, Manuel. "Academic Reference Service: Measurement, Cost and Value." *RQ* 12(Spring 1973):234, 239.

Mason, Robert M. and Peter G. Sassone. "A Lower Bound Cost Benefit Model for Information Services." *Information Processing and Management* 14(No. 2, 1978):74.

McClure, Charles. "A View from the Trenches: Costing and Performance Measures of Academic Library Public Services." *College and Research Libraries* 47(July 1986):329.

————. "Output Measures, Unobtrusive Testing, and Assessing the Quality of Reference Services." *The Reference Librarian* 11(Fall/Winter 1984):220.

McClure, Walter, President, Center for Policy Studies, *Wall Street Journal,* December 18, 1987, p. 44.

McMurdo, George. *The Effect of Busy Library Staff on Rate of Approach by Clients in an Experimental Psychology Study*. Washington, DC: Educational Resources Information Center, 1982. [ERIC Document ED221212]

Mech, Terrence. "The Realities of College Reference Service: A Case Study in Personnel Utilization." *The Reference Librarian* 19(1987):299.

Mick, C. "Cost Analysis of Information Systems and Services." In Martha Williams, ed., *Annual Review of Information Science and Technology,* Vol. 14. White Plains, NY: Knowledge Industry Publications, 1979, p. 50.

Miller, William. "What's Wrong with References: Coping with Success and Failure at the Reference Desk." *American Libraries* 15(May 1984):303.

Murfin, Marjorie and Charles Bunge. Unpublished data from the Wisconsin-Ohio Reference Evaluation Program, August, 1989.

————. "Paraprofessionals at the Reference Desk." *The Journal of Academic Librarianship* 14(March 1988a):10-14.

————. "Responsible Standards for Reference Service in Ohio Public Libraries." *Ohio Libraries* 1(March/April 1988b):1.

Murphy, Marcy. "Criteria and Methodology for Evaluating the Effectiveness of Reference and Information Functions in Academic Libraries." Unpublished Ph.D. dissertation, University of Pittsburgh, 1978, p. 117.

Palmour, Vernon and Lucy Gray. *Cost Effectiveness of Interlibrary Loan and Reference Activities of Resource Libraries in Illinois*. Springfield: Illinois State Library, 1972, p. 27.

Pitlak, Robert. *Online Data Searching as a Tool for Motivating Innovation*. Arlington, VA: Educational Resources Information Center, 1980. [ERIC Document ED190085]

Raffel, Jeffrey and Robert Shishko. *Systematic Analysis of University Libraries: An Application of Cost-Benefit Analysis to the M.I.T. Libraries*. Cambridge, MA: M.I.T. Press, 1969, p. 81.

Rothstein, Samuel. "The Hidden Agenda in the Measurement and Evaluation of Reference Service, Or, How to Make a Case for Yourself." *The Reference Librarian* 11(Fall/Winter 1984):48-49.

Saracevic, Tefko and Paul Kantor. "A Study of Information-Seeking and Retrieving: Pt. 2, Users, Questions and Effectiveness." *Journal of the American Society for Information Science* 39(May 1988):39.

Spencer, Carol. "Random Time Sampling with Self-Observation for Library Cost Studies." *Bulletin of the Medical Library Association* 68(January 1980):56.

Standera, Oldrich. "Costs and Effectiveness in the Evaluation of an Information System: A Case Study." In Helen Waldron and F. Raymond Long, eds., *Innovative Developments in Information Systems: Their Benefits and Costs. Proceedings of the 36th Annual Meeting of the American Society for Information Science,* Volume 10, pp. 65-66. Westport, CT: Greenwood Press, 1973.

Stuart, M. "Some Effects on Library Users of the Delays in Supplying Publications." *Aslib Proceedings* 29(January 1977):37.

Van House, Nancy. "A Time Allocation Theory of Public Library Use." *Library and Information Science Research* 5(Winter 1983):372, 382.

Weech, Terry. "Evaluation of Adult Reference Service." *Library Trends* 22(January 1974):324.

Wessel, C.J. and K.L. Moore. *.Criteria for Evaluating the Effectiveness of Library Operations and Services. Phase II. Recommended Criteria and Methods for Their Utilization.* ATLIS Report No. 21. Washington, DC: John I. Thompson Co., 1969, pp. 26, 31.

Whitlatch, Jo Bell. "Reference Service Effectiveness." *RQ* 30 (Winter 1990):211.

Wilson, S.R., N. Starr-Schneidkraut, and M.D. Cooper. *Use of the Critical Incident Technique to Evaluate the Impact of MEDLINE* (Final Report). Palo Alto, CA: American Institute for Research in the Behavioral Sciences, 1989. (Sponsored by the National Library of Medicine, Office of Planning and Evaluation, Bethesda, MD. NTIS order #PB90-142533/XAB.)

LIBRARIES, TECHNOLOGY AND QUALITY

Miriam A. Drake

Alice Smith has contributed much to our profession and to library/media services for children and young adults. I hope Alice's inspiration and vision will continue to motive and guide us as we deal with current difficult situations and future challenges.

While visions and dreams guide and motivate us they raise questions, challenges and, at times, frustration. How do we create a rich environment for learning? How do we change ourselves and the way we practice our profession so that we guide and direct people toward lifelong learning? How do we capture the innate curiosity of children and translate it into self motivated learning? How do we finance technology, collections and the know how needed to implement plans based on our visions and dreams?

I often am struck by the great ironies in our country. We spend more money per person on health care than any other nation in the world but we are not the healthiest people in the world. We produce more Nobel prize winners in Science than any other country, yet our children fall far below children in other industrialized countries in their knowledge of Mathematics and Science. We spend more money on education per student than any country in the world,

Advances in Library Administration and Organization,
Volume 11, pages 37-48.
Copyright © 1993 by JAI Press Inc.
All rights of reproduction in any form reserved.
ISBN: 1-55938-596-0

yet 16-20 percent of our population are functionally or totally illiterate. Many students with high school diplomas are deficient in reading, arithmetic and geography. American business and industry spend billions of dollars annually on remedial education and training.

We have developed some of the most sophisticated information technology in the world yet not all our children have access to it. $1000 buys a lot of technology today. It can buy a PC with software and a CD-ROM drive. If we purchased a personal computer for each of our 41 million children in grades K-12 we would spent 2.9 percent of the Federal Government's budget. This expenditure would be an extraordinary investment in our nation's most important asset. A PC in the hands of every child would bring significant benefits in learning and problem solving skills.

We desperately need to change our priorities, as a nation, and begin investing in people. It is clear if we do not make these investments our national well being and standard of living will decline. Reading and ability to follow written as well as oral instructions will become increasingly important for jobs at all levels.

A child born today with a life expectancy of 75 to 80 years may have two or three careers and must be a life long learner not only to adapt to change but to enjoy nature and enjoy life to the fullest. We must cultivate and nurture human abilities and the human intellect and we must begin in childhood. As Herbert Stringer has pointed out, "We do not yet comprehend that, as never before in our history as a nation, the ball game we are in will be won or lost based on how much and how wisely we invest in our human resources" (Stringer, 1987).

CHILDREN

I want to spend a few minutes on children because they are my favorite people and they are our future. Children are spontaneous, honest and hard working. The one year old works hard every day learning to walk, talk and cope with the world. Work for children is natural and effortless. Their dreams and fantasies are their visions for their futures. Dreaming and fantasizing allow children to try things out in their minds and evaluate options for themselves. In many ways, we are short changing our children by stifling their curiosity, teaching them that work and learning are difficult and stressful and turning off their imaginations. We have our exposed children to the worst aspects of television and show business. Neil Postman has observed, "Our politics, religion, news, athletics, and education and commerce have been transformed into congenial adjuncts of show business, largely without protest or even much popular notice. The result is that we as a people are on the verge of amusing ourselves to death" (Postman, 1985).

Today's children often have no way of learning through having questions answered. The days of the child being shown how to use a dictionary or encyclopedia may be over. Parents are too busy making a living. Teachers are too busy with classes, paperwork and bureaucracy. The television set gives 30-45 seconds of visual wisdom with little or no substance. We have both the challenge and responsibility to provide ways for children to learn, get answers to their questions and nurture their imaginations and natural abilities to work. We also have a responsibility to teach them to think, evaluate and question the answers they receive.

TECHNOLOGY

Technology is giving us powerful tools to bring information to people, stimulate creative thought and expand the human intellect. Computers can store and process vast amounts of data. Through graphics they can help us visualize, draw new worlds and simulate events. Computers can do mountains of drudge work and leave the thinking to us.

Telecommunications networks allow us and computers to talk to other people and other computers all over the world. The Internet provides not only access to catalogs in many libraries, but also the facility to exchange information with others in universities all over the world. The National Research and Education Network (NREN) proposed by Senator Gore will expand these facilities by providing very high speed data and information transfer.

Hypertext and multimedia technology are allowing us to combine text, graphics, still video and motion video. We can use these facilities to communicate complex concepts in a variety of ways. We can produce materials to complement and supplement classroom work and provide independent learning. These materials can be tailored to individual learning styles to enhance learning ability.

We have very powerful tools but we must keep in mind that they are only tools. Computers cannot think, invent, intuit, innovate or feel. Arno Penzias, nobel prize winner in Physics, states, "... even the best of present-day computing systems lack a key attribute of intelligence: the ability to move from one context to another ... machines only manipulate numbers; people connect them to meaning. Human intelligence almost always thrives on context while computers work on abstract numbers alone." We cannot leave the tasks of teaching and learning to computers or television. Learning depends on context and understanding. People need the time, energies and attention of other people (Penzias, 1989). Human interactions sharpen and enrich the mind.

LIBRARIES

Every day in libraries we can observe the linking of data, information, substance and context. Librarians make these linkages just as physicians and attorneys make decisions based on data within context. The physician observes, asks questions and performs tests. These data are then analyzed and synthesized to produce a diagnosis and course of action. The attorney asks questions, reviews facts, reaches conclusions and prescribes a course of action. All of this intellectual activity takes place within the unique context of an individual seeking the advice of another individual who has the professional grounding to understand, respond and recommend. Librarians perform the same sorts of functions by observing and asking, analyzing and synthesizing and prescribing a course of action appropriate to the individual's need and context.

Libraries in the future will be dependent on librarians who connect the tools of information technology and the content of information with the context of the individual. Libraries also will be more dependent on information technology. Computers and networks provide the infrastructure and information logistics needed to bring information to people. The storage, transmission, receipt, retrieval, manipulation and distribution of data constitute the logistics of information. Storage may be achieved with optical or magnetic media. Transmission may be carried out over ordinary voice phone lines or high speed optical fibers. Data may be received by a main frame or a PC on the desk top. Retrieval can involve a simple citation or billions of bytes of remote sensing data. Manipulation can be as simple as a spread sheet of the budget on a PC or as complex as thousands of equations on a super computer. The computer does not distinguish one bit of the data content from another. To the computer a byte is a byte.

Data and information are not the same. Data alone do not inform. Data are basic pieces of raw information. These pieces need to be assembled, organized and synthesized in order to be useful. Information may or may not change the state of knowledge of a person. Decisions and problem solving depend, in part, on changing the knowledge of individuals involved in decision making or solving problems. The human brain is unique in its ability to process data and information, integrate new data and synthesize with existing knowledge to form new knowledge and insight.

LIBRARY OF THE FUTURE

There will not be a generic library in the future. There will continue to be many libraries. These libraries will manage content, organize data and information, make data and information accessible and respond to the needs of individuals. Some libraries will exist in buildings. Others will exist on computers accessible through networks. Physical libraries will continue to have books, journals, maps, manuscripts, photographs, microfilm, microfiche and other objects. Books are not going to go away. They will be part of our lives for the foreseeable future. Some magazines and periodicals will continue to be printed while others will be available only electronically. Magazines and books are portable. We can take them on the airplane or to bed with us. We can browse, read and reread. Scientific and technical journals rarely are browsed and read. Usually, only a single article is needed. These journals are likely to be available electronically on an article by article basis. After reviewing a citation and/or abstract the reader will be able to order the full text of the article electronically with a variety of delivery choices.

We will be dealing with a variety of bibliographic, full text, hypertext, numeric and graphics databases. Some libraries will have databases mounted on local computers. Some libraries will use CD-ROM. All will rely on some remote online services. We will use local, regional, national and international networks to obtain information.

There will be a variety of multimedia materials available in our libraries. These materials will help children learn how airplanes fly, learn foreign languages and illustrate concepts in science and mathematics. Multimedia and interactive video will provide opportunities for faculty to create specialized learning tools.

NETWORKS

The proposed National Research and Education Network (NREN) and the existing Internet will link thousands of local, state, regional and national networks to provide high speed data transfer, high performance computing and information. The bill to establish the NREN also is known as the "High Performance Computing Act of 1991." Initial funding to establish the network is included in the President's budget for 1992. The bill's provisions include the establishment of a high capacity national network, development of an information infrastructure of databases, access facilities and acceleration of development of high performance computing systems and software.

The development and implementation of the network will be a long and complex job. There are hundreds of questions to be answered related to governance, funding, standards, use and policy. When fully implemented all colleges, universities, schools (K-12), government agencies and industry will have access to a rich store of information and computing facilities.

People will need new skills and training to navigate these new information highways and pipelines. Librarians will have new roles in teaching people how to use these networks to find the information or use other facilities they need. Now scientists and scholars use these networks to communicate with colleagues around the world. The NREN and Internet will connect many people. Classroom teachers who often are isolated from colleagues will have new capabilities for communication and sharing teaching and learning ideas and materials.

Currently, thousands of people query databases, transfer data and communicate through BITNET and NSFNET. BITNET links more than 3300 computers in 45 countries to facilitate the exchange of information related to research and education. BITNET discussion groups cover all academic disciplines.

The Internet links campus, state, and regional networks. Library catalogs, electronic journals and a variety of bulletin boards are available.

PLANNING

As we begin to plan our libraries for the future we will be faced with difficult and challenging changes and choices. While the technological issues appear overwhelming they are likely to be solved with time. The real issue is how we deliver personal services to people. We will need to look at supply versus demand. Instead of buying in anticipation of need we may choose to buy in response to need. Instead of operating in a "just in case" environment, we will operate and deliver information "just in time." Within 10 years it is likely that many scientific journals will be available online and that we will buy only those articles requested by clients. Now, many libraries are supply driven. They buy a supply of materials just in case, put them on the shelves or on CD-ROM players. People needing information or reading materials go to the library, search some sort of paper or online catalog, go to the shelves and hope the material is available. The user then brings the material to the check out counter, takes it away and hopes it will work.

The major cost of library work today is born by the user. The shift to a demand driven library will come about because people will demand more individualized service, information will be more plentiful but more difficult to fund. People will not be content to spend time searching shelves or dealing with stacks of paper, volumes of abstracting and indexing services, a print out of citations, a box of Census tapes or spending hours navigating a complex network of databases. They will find the environment of networking difficult and frustrating. Various devices and processes to help people operate effectively in a networked environment are being discussed and debated. Navigators, know-bots, information finders, information engineers and other processes based on expert systems, artificial intelligence and personal profiles may or may not succeed in finding the right information at the right time and in the right format. Changing contexts may limit the usefulness of processes based on a state of mind at one point in time. People will want librarians and information specialists to connect their unique needs to available information.

Computers offer great savings in labor and increases in productivity because they handle drudgery at low cost. Libraries will become more capital intensive and will have to invest money in computing and telecommunications equipment and facilities. The cost of providing library services will shift from the user to the institution. This shift represents an important investment in people.

In making these investments we must keep in mind that each library has a unique clientele. The needs and technological sophistication of library users should be primary criteria in selecting technologies and schedules for implementation. We must keep in mind that the keys to success lie in using appropriate and affordable technology.

OBSTACLES

Implementation of the electronic library of the future will not be without obstacles. First, standards are a major issue. We do not have standards for electronic publishing. There are several standards for optical media and no standard search engines for CD-ROM databases. Standards will emerge from the market place as they did for CD-audio, 3.5 inch disks and VHS video tape. There is no timetable for the formulation or implementation of needed standards but there are people working on them. The Coalition for Networked Information, (CNI) NISO, ALA, EDUCOM and AAP all have standards committees. Major participants and stakeholders will have to reach agreement on standards before the network and new technologies can succeed.

A second obstacle is cost. Many librarians view technology as an add-on to paper and are caught between adding to collections and buying information and the computers to access it. School and university administrators do not fully understand the potential of the library and technology to advance learning, teaching and research or the emerging benefits and costs. Publishers are reluctant to change because of their lack of experience in the electronic marketplace. Their fear of revenue losses clouds the possibilities associated with new ways of doing business. In addition, publishers are just beginning to realize that they have to change the way they deliver their products. This is a bit traumatic because they have been doing business the same way for over 400 years.

Technological development is moving more rapidly than are social and political processes. For example, our copyright laws were designed for the print era, not the electronic age. Our concepts of authorship and ownership will change as people collaborate through computers and networks. Who will own these creative works? If documents are being changed, which version becomes the document of record? Who will preserve the document? How will it be preserved? How will we preserve the achievements, history and culture of our people? How will documents published in electronic formats be preserved? Who will be responsible for preservation of electronic information?

Social change will result in new arrangements in the work place and new ways of working. Library operations will be affected by changes in the composition of the work force, an increasingly illiterate population, greater computer literacy among younger people, an aging population and the breakdown of hierarchy. We have seen significant downsizing in our corporations and the elimination of thousands of middle management positions. We are just beginning to see how information empowers the individual and nations. In universities students have access to most of the same information as faculty. Some students have more access because they use the computer to access more databases than faculty. In Eastern Europe we have seen a breakdown in tradition and hierarchy, in part, because more people have greater access to information through networks and television. During the war in the Persian Gulf, we and the enemy saw the same television news at the same time.

QUALITY

The electronic library of the future will place greater demands on librarians. Our goals will be shifting from buying and storing books to providing information to reduce user cost and contribute positively to our clients' success in problem solving, decision making and learning. There is a growing crisis in all types of services including library service. Davidow and Uttal have observed, "Crisis is a strong word but no exaggeration. Most customer service is poor, much of it is awful and service quality generally appears to be falling" (Davidow and Uttal, 1989).

Many librarians believe that they are providing services people need when they direct a user to a CD-ROM database, perform an online search resulting in a long list of citations and abstracts or show someone how to use a paper index. We often don't know and don't find out if people receiving those services are satisfied. There is the tendency to treat customer service as an add on to the collection development—something to be done if there is time.

The people we serve are the most important people in the library. They are the purpose of our work. They want more value for their tax dollars, user fees and items foregone to fund library operations. We need to learn more about their needs and expectations and provide appropriate service in a library they often do not tell the librarian. They tell their friends, colleagues and, sometimes, library funders. Ineffective library service can result in people not finding needed data or information or in people receiving inaccurate or incomplete information resulting in economic and other losses.

In short, librarians need to climb aboard the quality train before it leaves the station. In the last couple of years hundreds of articles have been written about quality assurance, quality control, quality service and total quality management. Relatively few organizations in the United States are consumer driven. Librarians, in many instances, have created libraries for the convenience of the library staff. Few libraries have been created for consumer oriented service. People are asking and increasingly will be demanding higher quality services of value from all service providers including physicians, accountants, attorneys, airlines and librarians. They will be demanding services responsive to individual need. Librarians, imbued with the value of egalitarianism will have to segment groups of customers and create services responsive to the particular needs of each group.

NATURE OF SERVICES

Service is difficult to measure because it is an intangible process. In quality service settings each person is treated as a respected individual. There is a diversity of response between the consumer and the organization. Quality service is an art, not a science. It is subjective, emotional and abstract. In quality service, process is as important as results.

A service does not exist until it is requested by a consumer. This consumer may be old, young or middle aged, a toddler or a grandparent, a student, businessperson or police officer. Service does not sit on a shelf waiting to be plucked. Service is created when the librarian and the consumer come into contact. The adult consumer will judge the quality of service in terms of expectations, satisfaction and value. The young person will judge value if a question is answered or a piece of mental puzzle is supplied. All people evaluate services on the basis of how well they were treated.

Quality service provision stems from excellent training, love of people and love of problem solving. Consumers quickly sense when the service provider is enthusiastic about the job. Quality service means keeping consumer satisfaction in mind not just for the immediate transaction but for the long haul. Quality service is not a discrete, one shot event. It is a process aimed at attracting and keeping people using and relying on library services.

The provision of quality services will require basic and substantial changes in our organizational structure, operations, education and training. Technology and electronic publishing will give us powerful tools but we must supply the motivation and creativity for change. We must set aside old assumptions about why people use libraries. We must discard the notion of the user and focus on the client for and with whom we are providing service. Users borrow material and use a facility. Customers or clients are active participants in the service transaction. Librarians often fail to listen to their consumers. The attitude appears to be, "What do they know about libraries?" Listening to customers and changing operations may be painful and traumatic because consumer oriented library service conflicts with the standards and norms of the profession. Tradition stresses a collection of printed materials, not spending time with and providing advice to clients and customers.

Service and its measurement cause difficulty for librarians who, in the past, have been urged to produce quantitative measures of their value. Service does not result in quick and easy quantitative measures. Reporting the number of customer interactions, books loaned, reference questions, online searches, citations retrieved or number enrolled in training classes tell nothing about quality or customer satisfaction. The intangible nature of information exacerbates the problems. Often the most effective indicators of service quality are anecdotes that don't translate into numbers. Unlike legal, accounting or health services, information services don't have established quantitative values. Most libraries do not have the opportunity to test pricing schemes and establish value based on willingness to pay. Tax support precludes libraries from discovering their value in the marketplace. One result is that library and librarian services are undervalued by society. When individuals, government, business or industry want and value information they usually are willing to pay more than their tax contributions.

The role of schools of library and information science also must change. They must concentrate on education and not be expected to provide a library with an employee who can work effectively the first day on the job. Libraries should welcome the opportunities to train and motivate well educated professionals.

ROLE OF MANAGEMENT

Library management will be called upon to function in new ways. Bell and Zemke, who have written extensively about service and companies providing good services, have identified four characteristics of successful service managers. They are "customer-focused," "obsessed about service," effective communicators and set examples in dealing with customers (Bell and Zemke, 1990). Their objectives are focused on satisfying the customer. Their employees are trained and flexible. "Competent, confident people have broad repertoires; properly trained and empowered, savvy employees will do the right thing at the right time" (Bell and Zemke, 1990). How many library managers believe that their staffs are competent, confident, and flexible?

Librarians often seem to seek recipes for handling all situations. Many library managers want slavish adherence to policies and rules. Breaking out of established procedures and ways of doing things is not the norm in libraries. The number of questionnaires that librarians send to other librarians suggests that librarians often are not confident about their decisions and seek confirmation through finding out what other libraries are doing. Risk taking is minimal.

Many librarians appear to be indifferent to customer satisfaction. They continue to measure their success by circulation data rather than customer satisfaction. They insist on equal treatment for all people rather than segmenting and examining what services each group of users want and need. It is rare that librarians will follow up to find out if a customer found what he/she was seeking in the library. Customer satisfaction measures and user surveys are not the same. Satisfaction is measured in a variety of ways including complaints, surveys, observation of interactions, attitudes and behaviors and informal discussion. Satisfaction is difficult to measure because it involves qualitative and subjective judgments. Information services often involve delayed satisfaction, not instant gratification. The success of a research proposal, acceptance of a publication and synthesis of new knowledge may take weeks or months. The delay in ascertaining the success of information transfer makes the measurement of customer satisfaction far more difficult than counting loans.

Communication is a critical component of effective customer service. All library personnel need to understand the service goals and objectives of the library. People dealing directly with customers must be excellent communicators. They need to know how to listen, ask, respond and observe. They cannot assume that they know what the customer wants until the customer asks or tells them.

Good service managers must set an example for all personnel in dealing with customers. Personnel can learn from direct observation of successful interactions as well as training. In many instances training has been unsuccessful because employees have been unable to translate what they have learned into action. A one or two day workshop is likely to be effective only with constant follow up training and reinforcement of desired behaviors.

Customers will be far more productive and informed when their needs are met with quality services. They will learn, make better decisions and solve problems more easily when library service is provided effectively. In many instances, the service will result in savings of time and money for people and companies. The well being of the individual customer and library employee will be improved. An emphasis on service will empower employees to make a difference for customers.

The productivity of service often extends beyond the service consumer. There are thousands of what economists call externalities created by service. These externalities may bring benefits to a classroom because a teacher learned about a new method for teaching a complex subject. Society, as a whole, may benefit by a creative person receiving the right information at the right time.

CONCLUSION

Today librarianship is the world's most exciting profession. We have a golden opportunity to change the way people learn, make decisions and solve problems, ,and we must have the persistence to make it happen. We must be guided and inspired by Alice Smith's visions, dreams and hard work. We must grow with our clients and customers and work with them to learn how technology can contribute to productivity and creativity. In the words of Lyndon Johnson, "We must open the doors of opportunity. But we must also equip our people to walk through those doors."

ACKNOWLEDGMENT

This paper is based on the Alice G. Smith Lecture presented at the University of South Florida, Tampa, February 6, 1991.

REFERENCES

Bell, Chip R. and Ron Zembe. "The Performing Art of Service Management," *Management Review,* July, 1990, pp. 44-45.

Davidow, William H. and Bro Uttal. *Total Customer Service, The Ultimate Weapon.* New York: Harper and Row, 1989, p. xix.

Penzias, Arno. *Ideas and Information.* New York: Simon and Schuster, 1989, pp. 10, 11, 49.

Postman, Neil. *Amusing Ourselves to Death: Public Disclosure* in the Age of Show Business, New York: Viking, 1985, pp. 3-4.

Stringer, Herbert, "Education: The Road to American Productivity," *Management Quarterly,* 48 (Fall, 1987), p. 43.

TRANSFORMATIONAL LEADERSHIP FOR LIBRARY MANAGERS

J. Fred Olive III

ABSTRACT

The purpose of this study was to determine whether library department heads were perceived by self and by subordinate group members as using different leadership styles when interacting with various subordinate groups.

A review of the literature indicated that there was a large body of research on leadership emphasizing the dimensions "Consideration" and "Initiation of Structure." The review also indicated that, while some research failed to find a significant relationship between these two dimensions, there was substantial research to support these relationships when situational factors were considered. The literature also confirmed that there was a body of research material on library department heads; however, literature on the subordinate groups' perceptions of the leader was sparse.

The libraries in this study were from institutions classified as private liberal arts colleges I, with participants from public service departments and technical service departments. The proportion of participating libraries (n = 55) to total population (n = 137) was 40.15 percent.

Advances in Library Administration and Organization,
Volume 11, pages 49-73.
Copyright © 1993 by JAI Press Inc.
All rights of reproduction in any form reserved.
ISBN: 1-55938-596-0

The leadership style was determined by calculating the mean score on the Ohio State University Leadership Behavior Description Questionnaire Form XII. Analysis was performed by use of the two-tailed t-test and the chi-square statistics with a level of significance less than .05 being considered significant.

The conclusions from the study are that (1) on the variable Initiation of Structure, there seems to be a difference in the technical service department heads' perceptions and the perceptions of the department's professional staff members; (2) on the variable Consideration, there seems to be differences in the department heads' perceptions and the perceptions of both the nonprofessional and nondepartment head staff members; (3) on the variable Consideration, there seems to be a significant relationship between the perceptions of (a) nondepartment head participants when the department head is female and (b) all participants when the department has held the current position for six to ten years; (4) on the variable Status, there seems to be a significant relationship between the perceptions of professional and nonprofessional staff members when assessing their respective department head; and (5) on the variable Initiation of Structure, there seems to be a significant relationship between the perceptions of participants when the department head (a) was male, (b) was female, (c) was between twenty-one to thirty-five years of age, (d) did not have any professionals reporting to the department head, and (e) had from one to two professionals reporting to the department head.

INTRODUCTION

Changes in clientele, advances in technology, and increases in the diversity of library personnel are but some of the challenges that library administrators face in their libraries. With these changes many in the library profession believe that the greatest challenge for library administrators is leading the library staff in the coming decades. Those leaders who are willing to provide support for their staff members by attempting to understand what these members need to develop professionally will be the successful leaders of the future. To become a successful leader, library administrators, department heads, and librarians need to increase their understanding of how to lead their staffs more effectively.

One way to increase leadership effectiveness is to help administrators understand how they are being perceived by their staff members. From an increased understanding of how they are being perceived, library administrators are better able to understand why they are sometimes misunderstood. They should realize that it is the diversity in one's background, experience, and role in the library that influences one's perception of the leader. Are library administrators perceived as interacting the same way with each of their subordinates, is the focus of this study.

Another way to aid library staff members in the development of their skills is to recognize the properties of transformational leadership theory. Since Burns described transformational leadership, the roles of administrators and leaders within the library setting have continued to change. Leaders recognize that subordinates are more educated and thus may suggest solutions to problems that were once nonexistent, or more likely, were left to administrators' expertise. With new demands and competing interests, the library is a perfect place for the development of a transformational leader. Such a leader makes professional development a major goal for the entire library staff.

Subordinates of these leaders are encouraged to strive to understand and to contribute to the higher group goals. Without this group effort, the changes could overwhelm the library. The department head who focuses on actions and behaviors to reduce resistance to decisions will encourage the staff to accept the vision of the leader.

"Transformational leadership is more likely to occur under conditions of rapid change, where organizational goals are complex and often unclear, and where members are highly educated and are expected to be creative" (Carver, 1989, p. 31). This statement typifies the conditions in the academic library. Likewise, "during periods of volatility, completion, and uncertainty, it is advisable to subdue the formal authority patterns and encourage a loose structure which will stimulate initiative" (p. 33). A transformational leader is needed throughout the library to "anticipate challenges, and design innovative solutions to meet the turbulent and uncertain environment of the future" (p. 33). While there is a great need for leaders to provide direction for their subordinates, and while these leaders contribute a variety of skills, one may ask if there is only one way a leader is perceived as interacting with each of his or her subordinates.

Dansereau, Graen, and Haga (1975), and Miles and Steiner (1981) discussed the relationship between the leader and the group as being less homogeneous than previously assumed, as one in which the leader interacts differently with various members of the group. This concept is called the "vertical dyad theory" (Dansereau et al., 1975). It is important for the leader and the respective subordinates to know how they are perceived by each other. The diversity in perceptions of individuals are based upon the role-episode process (Graen, 1983). This is the process by which individuals determine their roles in the group and how they are perceived by other group members.

Some of the earliest concepts of leadership were found in religious settings or in groups of primary of family relationships. In a review of the literature on leadership, Seligman (1968) discussed the different sources of a leader's authority: which is found within the group and outside the group. With the concept of "divine right of kings," the leader or king received authority from a source other than the group that was governed, while the Mayflower Compact is an example of a leader having been granted power by the members of the group. The source of authority coming from the governed gave impetus for a type of democratic leadership.

By the twentieth century, a leader's power was often vested in the office. Leadership was viewed as a role that satisfied the expectations of both leader and followers, and the success of the leader varied with the situation (Seligman, 1968).

According to Bass (1960, 1981), leadership should not be explained in terms of the leader but rather in terms of the role of the individuals in the group. These role perceptions are the critical factors for investigation. In a 1977 article, Calder indicated that trait studies have "failed to establish any strong relationship between ... [traits] and leadership" (p. 179). Miles and Steiner (1981) agreed with Calder and reasoned that the lack of correlation between behavioral style and situational model studies occurs because leadership is a first-degree scientific construct which cannot be empirically analyzed. A study of perceptions is a second-degree scientific construct which can be analyzed.

The behaviors of a leaders are perceived either by direct observation or through indirect sources. Leadership depends upon the individuals, situation, purpose of the group, background of the participants, and bias brought to the situation. Since leadership is not itself observable, only leadership action as perceived by others can be observed (Calder, 1977).

A leader may use observation in an attempt to understand how he or she is perceived by others. This understanding could assist the leader in becoming more effective. If a leader attempts to be honest and open to members of a group, they will, in turn, see the leader as more effective (Miles and Steiner, 1981). The behavior of individual members can be analyzed by how others perceive those behaviors. Also, the expected behaviors of persons as perceived by the leader can be varied. If the expectations and perceived behaviors connote to the individual that the person is a leader, then the inference is made. "Leadership exists only as a perception" (Calder, 1977, p. 202).

While few researchers have studied leadership in the library setting four researchers (Comes, 1977/78; Dragon, 1976/77; Frankie, 1980/81; Sparks, 1976) have made major contributions to the emerging literature on leadership in the academic library setting. Sparks (1976) compared staff perceptions and the administrators perceptions of themselves based on the Leadership Behavior Description Questionnaire. Findings from the Sparks study showed promise in analysis of leaders' styles.

Comes (1978/1979) described directors of medium-sized academic libraries in terms of their leadership patterns. The instrument used in his study was the Leadership Behavior Description Questionnaire Form XII (LBDQ-XII). It was found that the differences in mean scores of the director's self-perceptions and the subordinated perceptions of the director's leadership style suggested a need to improve communications and place a higher value on personal relationships rather than on task direction.

Two recommendations from the Comes study were, first, that the LBDQ-XII can be used in a larger population within the library community and, second, that four subscales appeared to be most appropriate for future studies: (a) consideration, (b) tolerance of freedom, (c) initiation of structure, and (d) production emphasis. Frankie (1980/1981) found that within the academic library profession there was a need to provide alternative organizational structures to meet the changing needs for library services. Such alternative organizational structures might replace traditional library organizational structures which are based upon distinctions between technical and public service functions. The ... head of the Catalog Department ... would very likely ... adopt a supervisory style that would be quite different from that used by the head of the Reference Department, because of the differences in staff attitudes, behavioral style and work preferences in such areas as working in groups, approval of others and preferences for directive leadership ... (Frankie, p. 172).

In the final study reviewed, Dragon (1976/1977) described the relationship between self-descriptions and subordinates' descriptions of the leadership behavior of library administrators. Dragon used the LBDQ for her study.

Focus of This Study

Is there a difference in the leadership styles exhibited by the department heads of selected liberal arts college libraries according to their self-perceptions and the perceptions of members of subordinate groups. This investigation consisted of examining the leadership styles of library department heads as perceived by their subordinates. If library department heads are perceived as using a variety of leadership styles, both they and their subordinates would be better able to understand each other and to work together more effectively. This study, centered around three questions:

1. Are department heads of liberal arts college libraries perceived by their subordinate groups as using different leadership styles when they are interacting with various subordinate groups?

2. Is there a perceived difference in leadership styles of the department head based on the role of the different subordinate groups, other background characteristics of group members (professional librarian or nonprofessional), and the particular library subgroup (public services department or technical services department)?

3. Is there a perceived difference in leadership style between the department head's self-perception and that of the subordinate groups?

Leadership Research Studies

The administration of institutions of higher education is a complex, challenging, and, in many instances, frustrating undertaking. The library administrator must be sensitive to the needs of the populations served by the library, the pressures exerted by outside groups, and the internal functioning of the library. A major component of administration is leadership. Traditionally, two styles (sometimes referred to as dimensions) of leadership theory appear in the literature: (a) the authoritarian and (b) the democratic. Authoritarian leadership is associated with a bureaucratic organizational structure; in this dimension, authority is derived from the leader. The leader initiates decisions and does not consult with subordinates.

The preferred leadership style for some administrators is democratic leadership, as seen in a participatory organizational structure. Authority in the latter type of organization stems from the group whose members participate in the decision-making process.

Stogdill (cited in Bass, 1981), in his survey of research on leadership during the past 40 years, categorized the following definitions of leadership: (a) a focus on group process, (b) a set of personality characteristics, (c) an act of inducing compliance, (d) an exercise of influencing, (e) an act or behavior, (f) a form of persuasion, (g) a power relation, (h) an instrument of goal achievement, (i) an effect of interaction, (j) a differential role, and (k) an initiation of structure.

Trait Studies

The attempt to identify traits of leaders has been an outgrowth of the lack of a single definition of leadership. Early studies described the characteristics of an effective leader but not the actions of the effective leader. Barrow (1977) identified personality characteristics, social traits, and physical characteristics of leaders; some examples of Barrow's personality characteristics are (a) originality, (b) initiative, (c) persistence, (d) knowledge, and (e) enthusiasm. His list of social traits includes (a) tact, (b) patience, (c) prestige, and (d) sympathy. Physical characteristics, according to Barrow, are (a) height, (b) weight, and (c) physical attractiveness. He recommended that these traits and characteristics be used as guidelines to determine important attributes of effective leaders.

Tannenbaum and Schmidt (1958) proposed one of the first classifications of leadership for defining an effective leader in terms of style. Tannenbaum's leadership behavior continuum provides an illustration of degrees of authority and group freedom. The unique feature of the continuum is that it provides flexibility for the leader to change style, according to the situation, based on experience and training.

Gibb (1969) stated that in the study of relationships between personality traits and leadership, two factors seem to be well established: one, that numerous studies of the personalities of leaders have failed to find a consistent pattern of traits that characterize leaders, and two, that there is abundant evidence that member personalities affect group performance.

There is reason to believe that personality traits and leadership affect that aspect of the group's behavior to which the leadership concept applies (Mann, 1959; Stogdill, 1948). However, the lack of evidence to demonstrate a definitive relationship between personality and leadership may be due to the inadequacy of personality description and measurement. This lack of evidence also may be due to the situation which overrides personality factors (Cunningham and Gephart, 1973). The literature suggests that the type of leadership to develop is determined by the nature of the group and the problems it must solve (Borgardus, 1918). Murphy (1941) supported this conclusion by saying that leadership does not reside in a person but in the function of the occasion. Gibb (1954) suggested that leadership is interactional, beginning with group formation. Upon creation of the group, the participants are assigned a position depending upon their relationships to other group members.

Behavioral Approaches

Since trait studies (Korman, 1966; Fiedler, 1964; Hass, 1984) have not provided a clear understanding of leadership, social psychologists have begun to study group function and structure. They have examined the acts that assist the group in achieving its goals. In these studies, leadership is based on the group rather than on the individual. From this research, two basic types of group functions are identified: task functions and human functions.

Korman (1966) summarized research on "Consideration" and "Initiating Structure." He indicated that the studies he reviewed fail to find a significant relationship between these two dimensions. With the recognition that different characteristics and behaviors are important for leaders depending on the group function and the situation, several authorities proposed what are known as contingency theories of leadership (Fiedler, 1964; Hass, 1984). These theories are referred to as contingency theories because a leader's influence on subordinates is contingent on particular situational factors.

Contingency Theories

The findings of numerous studies from the Research Center for Group Dynamics have been summarized by Cartwright and Zander (1960). These studies have shown that a group leader's objective may center either on the achievement of the group goal or on the maintenance of the group. More recent studies have indicated that leadership styles vary, some emphasizing tasks and others stressing interpersonal relationships. While studies have used a variety of names for these behaviors (Stogdill, 1963), it may be said that the dimensions represent both the task or structural function of the group leader and the human relations or consideration of the group. Researchers have attempted to represent these behaviors by the X and Y axis. This approach is the basis for two popular leadership models: the Ohio State University Leadership Model (Hersey and Blanchard, 1982) and the Hersey and Blanchard (1969) model.

The Ohio State University leadership model represents leadership behavior as having two magnitudes or dimensions. One of these dimensions is "Consideration," and the other is Initiating Structure (Fleishman, 1953, 1973). Robbins (1980) described each of these dimensions: Employer/employee relationships that include mutual trust and respect for subordinates' ideas and feelings is described as "Consideration," while "Initiating Structure" refers to the leader's role in defining and structuring group tasks to achieve the group goal.

According to Halpin (1957), leaders high in "Consideration" and "Initiating Structure" tended to achieve high subordinate performance and satisfaction more often than do those who rate low either on "Consideration" or "Initiating Structure," or both. He also found that those leaders high on "Initiating Structure" have greater rates of absenteeism, turnover, and lower levels of satisfaction among subordinates, while those leaders high in "Consideration" generally have positive outcomes in these areas. Exceptions have been found to indicate that situational factors need to be integrated into theory. Campbell (cited in Stogdill, 1974) reported that there are significant differences among leaders in different situations when described on the "Consideration" and "Initiating Structure" scales of the Ohio State University Leader Behavior Description Questionnaire. This concern for the integration of situational factors has led to the development of the Hersey and Blanchard (1969) model.

The Hersey and Blanchard model is based on the situational approach. Using the terms "task behavior" and "relationships behavior," which are similar to the Ohio State dimensions, Hersey and Blanchard assigned these terms to the X and Y axis and went one step further by labeling the quadrants: high task and high relationship, high relationship and low task, low task and low relationship, and low relationship and high task. Hersey and Blanchard also included in the tri-dimensional model the dimension of effectiveness/environment.

In summary, the Ohio State studies and the research by Hersey and Blanchard represent a dual relationship. These models presume that leadership styles are predicated on the relationship of two variables or behaviors. The variables have different names (Stogdill, 1963); however, both deal with the control of the structure and the socio-emotional aspects of the leader-subordinate relationship.

An earlier review of the literature by Cunningham and Gephart (1973) noted that (1) Leaders scoring above the mean on both Initiating Structure and Consideration were perceived ... to be most effective; those scoring below the mean on both dimensions were perceived to be least effective; those scoring high on one dimension but low on the other were somewhere in between; (2) preferences and expectations for leader behavior vary widely among reference groups (p. 148); (3) the leader's perception of his own behavior differs from others' perceptions; (4) confidence in leadership, satisfaction, effectiveness, and attitudes toward the work situation are all influenced by incongruence in expectations for leader behavior; (p. 149) (5) the effectiveness of leaders may be seriously compromised in interpersonal relationships by misperceptions and the existence of value differences; (6) relational studies indicate that leader behavior is related to many organizational variables (p. 150); and (7) situational factors influence leader behavior (p. 151).

The second generalization presented in the Cunningham and Gephart study (1973) indicates that the two dimensions (i.e., Consideration and Initiation of Structure) have an influence on a leader's effectiveness. Also, their third generalization recognizes that the leader's behavior may vary depending on the role of the group with which the leader is interacting. These findings support this study's contention that the library administrator will respond differently to an individual, based upon that individual's role within the group. Therefore, it may be concluded that leaders must attempt to tailor their relationship styles according to the different roles and needs of their subordinate groups and depending on the immediate situation (James, 1985). In this study, role differentiation is categorized by the subordinate groups: public services and technical services, professional and nonprofessional.

Calder's (1977) study led to the conclusion that while leaders may use various leadership styles in different situations, they may also vary their leadership styles with individual members of the same group. Based upon this research, the leader may think he or she is behaving in a similar manner toward individuals, while the individuals may simultaneously perceive that the leader is behaving differently toward particular individuals.

This difference in perception led to the recognition of what came to be known as the "attribution theory" (Calder, 1977). The follower's perceptions of the leader's behavior is based on the follower's internal as well as external beliefs. Thus, the follower may infer that particular behaviors are caused by traits or external constraints (Miles and Steiner, 1981). According to Bass (1960, 1981), leadership is not explained in terms of the leader or the group but is explained in terms of the roles of the individuals in the group and their perceptions of the leader. These, Bass said, were critical factors that needed to be studied because each individual in a group plays a changing role and is influenced by the attributes that a person is perceived to possess.

In 1977, Calder stated that trait studies have "failed to establish any strong relationship between ... [traits] and leadership" (p. 179). The lack of positive findings with behavioral style and situational/contingency models studies has occurred because leadership is a first-degree construct that cannot be observed (Calder, 1977; Miles and Steiner, 1981). The behaviors of a leader, according to Calder, are evidenced by direct observation or indirect sources. Leadership depends upon the individuals, situation, purpose of the group, background of the participants, and biases brought to the situation.

The private/personal behaviors of individuals are also largely unobservable, for these may include beliefs rather than observed behavior. If the expectations and other observed behaviors connote to the individual that the person is a leader, that inference is made. "Leadership exist only as a perception"(Calder, 1977, p. 202).

Some factors suggested by Robbins that could prejudice individual perception are selectivity, interests, experiences, expectations, cultural background, motives, halo effect, projection, and a person's attribution of reasons for other individuals' behaviors. These factors can create a distorted view of reality. Thus, if the same leadership style were being used for all group members, then an individual member might perceive a difference in the leadership being given.

Dyadic Linkage Model

The dyadic linkage model is based on the assumption that the group is not homogeneous. The research that supports the theory that various leader-follower relationships may exist in the same group simultaneously is based upon the vertical dyad theory advocated by Graen and Cashman (1975) and Miles and Steiner (1981). The vertical dyad theory is particularly appropriate for this study, which attempts to view the leadership style of the library department head by surveying and analyzing subordinates' perceptions and the department head's self-perceptions. In this study, the various roles a subordinate group plays (divided into areas of responsibility, such as public services and technical services), as well as personal characteristics, have a major emphasis on the way the library department head is perceived to interact with the subordinate. While the role that a subordinate plays in a group can influence the library department head, others in the group may perceive the library department head as having a different leadership style depending on the individual. The actual process of determining a leader's or follower's role is called the Role Episode Process (Cashman, Dansereau, Graen, and Haga, 1976; Dansereau et al., 1975; Graen, 1983; Miles and Steiner, 1981). This is the process by which the leader and followers observe each other and perceive whether the person observed is effective or ineffective in his or her role.

Library Leadership Studies

Sparks (1976) compared staff perceptions and administrator's self-perceptions of the administrator's leadership using two dimensions (sometimes referred to as "styles"): consideration and structure. Spark's study shows promise in this use of these two dimensions as models for personnel in academic libraries. While both dimensions have been found to be essential for leadership to be effective in the area of structure, subordinates have shown a close correlation with the administrator's perceptions, while in the area of consideration the leader's self-perception has been shown to be considerably higher than that of subordinates. Sparks also found that structure is positively correlated to effectiveness, since in professional positions (i.e., librarians), the tasks are unstructured and goals are routine. Sparks stated that her model would be useful for small- and medium-sized libraries in which the Association of Research Libraries' Office of Management Studies is inappropriate.

Martin (1981) cited Gorman as arguing that technology has rendered the technical services and public services divisions of academic libraries as obsolete because technical achievements have made the past physical restrictions of the technical services division no longer necessary. He indicated that the functions of cataloging and other technical services do not require the physical location of the shelf list and authority files to be in close proximity to the individuals using them. With the computerized access of such available at remote locations, the divisions are not necessary. However, while there is justification for this viewpoint, there are also problems with it. While the training of technical service librarians is similar to that of public service librarians, the specialization of these two areas is evident by course work provided for in the Master's in Library Science program. One usually concentrates on one area of specialization or the other. For a person to become proficient in both would require more time for the Master's program, and for a librarian to meet the requirement of both jobs does not appear possible in the near future.

One of the recent studies of leadership style within the academic library was that of Comes (1978/1979). Comes described directors of medium-sized academic libraries, in regard to their leadership patterns, using the Leadership Behavior Description Questionnaire Form XII (LBDQ-XII). Implications from the Comes study suggested that since there are differences between the director's self-perceptions and the subordinate's perceptions of the director's leadership style, there may need to be an improvement in communication and a higher value placed on personal relationships than on task direction. Two recommendations from the Comes study are (a) that the LBDQ-XII be used in a larger population within the library community and (b) that four subscales appear to be most appropriate for future studies: consideration, tolerance of freedom, initiation of structure, and production emphasis.

Frankie (1980/1981) identified a subculture within the ranks of academic librarians. Her major findings were that there was a need for a reassessment of profession of university librarianship to face today's new challenges (p. 164) and that there were differences in staff attitudes, behavioral styles, and work preferences of catalog and reference librarians, thus the supervisory style that would be used by the catalog department head would be different from that used by the head of the reference department (Frankie, 1980/1981).

The two predominant groups of librarians recognized by Frankie were public services and technical services librarians. She described reference librarianship as client-oriented, requiring little supervision and considerable discretion in decision making. In contrast, she described catalog librarianship as needing closer supervision, and systematic/methodical conformity to the requirements of the work situation (p. 147).

The Frankie study found that the reference librarians' mean scores on the LBDQ-XII were significantly different (in the predicted direction) from the mean scores of the catalog librarians. The reference librarians' scores were lower than those scores of the catalog librarians in the characteristics of orderliness, systematic-methodical, and directive leadership. The reference librarians' scores were higher than those of the catalog librarians in the characteristics of take leadership, social interaction, act independently, group participation, and activity-frequent change.

The most comprehensive study of library leadership was completed by Dragon (1976/1977). Dragon's study was a replication of leadership research conducted in business and military organizations. She attempted to investigate and describe the relationship between self-descriptions and subordinate descriptions of the leadership behavior of library administrators.

After considering other instruments, Dragon used the Ohio State University (LBDQ-XII). Dragon's review of the literature on theoretical models and major methodologies also supported the use of the LBDQ-II instrument.

Institutions and Participants

The institutions for this study were selected from those United States institutions classified as private Liberal Arts I (LAI) institutions, as determined by the Carnegie classification. LAI institutions are described as highly selective undergraduate colleges that award more than half of their baccalaureate degrees in arts and science fields ("Carnegie Foundation's Classifications," 1987, p. 22).

Due to the small number of LAI institutions in this classification ($N = 140$), all private LAI institutions were surveyed. The names, titles, and addresses of the library directors were obtained from the *Higher Education Directory* (1987) and other appropriate sources. At the conclusion of the study, all evidence of identification was destroyed.

Instrument and Ancillary Materials

Instrument

The Ohio State University LBDQ-XII, which has dominated much of leadership research in the past 20 years (Stogdill, 1974) was the primary instrument of data collection for this study. Support for use of the LBDQ-XII was found in its successful use in the Dragon (1976/1977) and Comes

(1978/1979), and in other studies discussed in Chapter II. For a thorough review of the Ohio State University leadership studies (specifically the LBDQ), see Dipboye (1978). Since the 1957 LBDQ manual, much research has been done in the area of leadership (Bass, 1981). Both "Consideration" and "Initiation of Structure" have been found to have high coefficients of internal consistency.

While there were several factors previously mentioned that led to the acceptance of the LBDQ-XII as the appropriate instrument for this study, there were two factors not previously mentioned that support the use of this instrument: validity and reliability. While Dragon (1976/1977) noted the LBDQ-II does need further refinement, it is superior to hastily developed alternatives.

Demographic Data

Personal demographics were requested by the LBDQ-XII using a demographic data section (divided into sections to be completed by all participants and a section to be completed by the department head only). No names were requested, to insure confidentiality. The identifying information requested from the subordinates was (a) status (professional or nonprofessional), (b) gender, (c) library subgroup (public service or technical service) and (d) department head/subordinate status. This information was sought for all participants. The information requested from each department head was (a) number of subordinates (professional and nonprofessional) reporting to the department head, (b) number of years the department head had been in the current position, (c) academic degrees earned by the department head, (d) age range of the department head, and (e) title of the last position held by the department head on the current campus.

Methods of Data Collection

Each director was sent a packet of materials that included (a) a letter stating the study's purpose and instructions for distribution of the instruments, (b) a letter from the director of a state university library soliciting the director's cooperation, and (c) surveys and return-addressed stamped envelopes for return of the survey. The director was requested to distribute the surveys to the library staff, giving one to the public services department head and one to the technical services department head. The remainder of the surveys were to be divided between each department (public services department and technical services department) and each library subgroup (e.g., professional and nonprofessional staff members). The survey form was designed to contain the letter to the participant, the demographic data requested and the LBDQ-XII instrument.

Treatment of Data

The *Statistical Package for the Social Sciences PC+ Version 3* (SPSS, 1988) was used to perform the analysis of the data. Following the receipt of the completed questionnaires, data were analyzed to determine the acceptability of the hypotheses. Analysis was performed by use of a *t* test and the chi square statistics.

A comparison of "Consideration" and "Initiation of Structure" was completed to determine the differences in mean scores for each of the following groups: (a) public service departments, (b) technical service departments, (c) professionals, (d) nonprofessionals, (e) department heads, and (f) nondepartment heads. These scores were produced by totaling the responses for each statement for each group. The comparison was made by use of the mean score of each group. The mean is a descriptive measure of central tendency. The mean, standard deviation, *t* test, significance level and related discussion are presented for each hypothesis. For each group of statements (i.e., 10 "Consideration" statements and 10 "Initiation of Structure" statements), the frequency and the percentage of response for each statement is included for comparison to other studies and for future research.

The inferential measure that was used in this study was the *t* test. The *t* test is a statistic was used to examine the difference between the sample means and whether or not the sample means were significantly different beyond the expectations due to sample variation. This test was used to compare the sample mean of "Consideration" to the sample mean of "Initiation of Structure" for each group. This was done to determine if there was a significant difference between the two dimensions of leadership. The sample means for the variables of "Consideration" and "Initiation of Structure" were calculated by using the raw scores from the participants' surveys. A *t*-test, score with a level of significance less than .05, was considered significant. The confidence level was 95 percent with a .05 probability of the difference occurring by chance.

Since the hypotheses were written as nondirectional, a two-tailed test of significant was appropriate. The two-tailed test was suggested for most social science research (Slavin, 1984). Slavin stated that a one-tailed test generally should not be used, since there is at least a possibility that the results will turn in the opposite direction of the hypotheses.

The LBDQ-XII includes 100 items of which 80 were scored 1=always, 2=often, 3=occasionally, 4=seldom, and 5=never. The LBDQ-XII included 20 items that were written in the negative and were scored in the reverse order. The SPSS/PC+ was used to recode the 20 negative items to reflect the scoring of the 80 positive items. The analysis was then carried out on the variables "Consideration" and "Initiation of Structure" with the recoded data. Items representing other variables were: representation, demand reconciliation, tolerance for uncertainty, persuasiveness, tolerance for freedom, role assumption, production emphasis, predictive accuracy, integration, and superior orientation. While these dimensions were included in the instrument administered, this study did not analyze the data from these dimensions.

PRESENTATION AND ANALYSIS OF THE DATA

Demographic Information

The total number of Liberal Arts I institutions in the survey population was 140, with 4 of the institutions participating in a library consortia agreement that decreased the total number of libraries in the study to 137. The proportion of participating libraries ($n = 55$) to total population ($n = 137$) was 40.15 percent. The number of libraries indicating (by way of the director communicating with the researcher) that they were not able to participate was 25 for a total of 80 (58.39 percent) libraries responding in some way to the survey. While some libraries did not participate in the survey, the library director's comments were of interest and contributed to insight into the unique leadership concerns of library administrators. The data from correspondence received from the library directors were not used in the testing of the hypotheses; however, selected comments were included to illustrate the need for additional research and consideration of the organizational structure of the libraries when conducing research on leadership within organizations.

The numbers of individuals by grouping returning the survey were as follows: 153 (45.8 percent) professional librarians, 181 (54.2 percent) nonprofessional staff, 162 (51.6 percent) public services department staff members, 152 (48.4 percent) technical services department staff members, 102 (30.4 percent) department heads, 233 (69.6 percent) nondepartment heads, 276 (85.7 percent) females, and 46 (14.3 percent) males. The data from all libraries were pooled to have a sufficient number of subjects in each group. The numbers reported for various groups did not equal the total number of participants because some individuals did not respond to some of the items requested in the survey. For example, one individual commented that the survey should not request the gender of the participants and thus declined to respond to that item.

Treatment and Analysis of the Hypotheses

An alpha level of .05 was used as the criterion for statistical significance for all hypotheses. The analysis for each hypothesis follows in both parenthetical and tabular forms.

Hypothesis 1: There are differences in the mean scores of "Consideration" and "Initiation of Structure" on the LBDQ-XII utilized by the public services department head as perceived by the public services professional librarians.

The first hypothesis was addressed by calculating descriptive statistics for public services department heads and public services professionals on the variables "Consideration" and "Initiation of Structure." The *t* test was used to test the group means for statistical significance. There were no statistically significant differences in the mean scores for public services department heads and public services professionals on the variables of "Consideration" or "Initiation of Structure."

Hypothesis 2: There are differences in the mean scores of "Consideration" and "Initiation of Structure" on the LBDQ-XII utilized by the technical services department head as perceived by the technical services professional librarians.

The second hypothesis was addressed by calculating descriptive statistics for technical services department heads and technical services professionals on the variables "Consideration" and "Initiation of Structure." The *t* test was used to test the group means for statistical significance. There were no statistically significant differences in the mean scores for technical services department heads and technical services professionals on the variable of "Consideration." However, there was a statistical difference found in the variable of "Initiation of Structure" scores for the technical services department heads and those for technical services professionals. In addition, the mean scores for the technical services professionals were larger for both variables (Consideration and Initiation of Structure) than for the technical services department heads.

Hypothesis 3: There are differences in the mean scores of "Consideration" and "Initiation of Structure" on the LBDQ-XII utilized by the public services department head as perceived by the public services nonprofessional staff.

The third hypothesis was addressed by calculating descriptive statistics for public services department heads and public services nonprofessionals on the variables of "Consideration" and "Initiation of Structure." The *t* test was used to test the group means for statistical significance. There were no statistically significant differences in the mean scores for public services department heads and public services nonprofessionals on the variables of "Consideration" or "Initiation of Structure."

Hypothesis 4: There are differences in the mean scores of "Consideration" and "Initiation of Structure" on the LBDQ-XII utilized by the technical services department head as perceived by the technical services nonprofessional staff.

The fourth hypothesis was addressed by calculating descriptive statistics for technical services department heads and technical services nonprofessionals on the variables of "Consideration" and "Initiation of Structure." The *t* test was used to test the group means for statistical significance. There were no statistically significant differences in the mean scores for technical services department heads and technical services nonprofessionals on the variables consideration or "Initiation of Structure." The mean scores on both "Consideration" and "Initiation of Structure" were larger for technical services nonprofessionals than for technical services department heads, though on "Initiation of Structure" the degree was slight.

Hypothesis 5: There are differences in the mean scores of "Consideration" and "Initiation of Structure" on the LBDQ-XII of the department head when interacting with the professional librarians.

The fifth hypothesis was addressed by calculating descriptive statistics for all department heads and all professionals on the variables of "Consideration" and "Initiation of Structure." The *t* test was used to test the group means for statistical significance. There were no statistically significant differences in the mean scores for department heads and professionals on the variables of "Consideration" or "Initiation of Structure." The mean scores on both "Consideration" and "Initiation of Structure" were larger for professionals than for department heads.

Hypothesis 6: There are differences in the mean scores of "Consideration" and "Initiation of Structure" on the LBDQ XII of the department head when interacting with the nonprofessional staff.

The sixth hypothesis was addressed by calculating descriptive statistics for all department heads and nonprofessionals on the variables of "Consideration" and "Initiation of Structure." The *t* test was used to test the group means for statistical significance. There was a statistically significance difference found on "Consideration" scores for the department heads and nonprofessionals. However, there were no statistically significant differences in the mean scores for department heads and nonprofessionals on the variable of "Initiation of Structure."

Hypothesis 7: There are differences in the mean scores of "Consideration" and "Initiation of Structure" on the LBDQ-XII of the department head as perceived by the department head and by the nondepartment heads.

The seventh hypothesis was addressed by calculating descriptive statistics for all department heads and all nondepartment heads on the variables of "Consideration" and "Initiation of Structure." The *t* test was used to test the group means for statistical significance. There was a statistically significant difference found on "Consideration" scores for all department heads and all nondepartment heads. However, there were no statistically significant differences in the mean scores for all department heads and all nondepartment heads on the variable of "Initiation of Structure." The mean scores on both "Consideration" and "Initiation of Structure" were larger for nondepartment heads than for department heads, though on "Initiation of Structure" the degree was slight.

Hypothesis 8: There are no differences in the mean scores of "Consideration" and "Initiation of Structure" on the LBDQ-XII utilized by the department head, as perceived by different subordinate groups (professional and nonprofessional staffs, public services and technical services staffs, department heads, and nondepartment heads) for the following variables: (1) number of professional librarians in the library, (b) number of professional librarians reporting to the department head, (c) number of years the department head has been in his or her current position, (d) academic degrees earned by the department head, (e) age of the department head, (f) gender of the department head, and (g) number of professional staff members reporting to the department head.

The eighth hypothesis was addressed by calculating descriptive statistics for all participants and various subordinate groups (i.e., professional staff members, nonprofessional staff members, public services staff, technical services staff, department heads, and nondepartment heads) on the variables of "Consideration" and "Initiation of Structure": (a) number of professional librarians in the library, (b) number of professional librarians reporting to the department head, (c) number of years the department head has been in his or her current position, (d) academic degrees earned by the department head, (e) age of the department head, (f) gender of the department head, and (g) number of professional staff members reporting to the department head. Further analysis was attempted by use of chi square for the all participants and various subordinate groups (i.e., professional staff members, nonprofessional staff members, public services staff, technical services staff, department heads, and nondepartment heads). There was a significant difference found between the variables of "Consideration" and status (chi square = 49.1584, $df = 34$, $p < .05$). Also, there was a statistically significant difference between the variables "Initiation of Structure" and gender (chi square = 54.77394, $df = 34$, $p < .05$). Similarly, there was a statistically significant difference between the variables "Consideration" and gender (chi square = 49.01724, $df = 34$, $p < .05$). There was a statistically significant difference between the variable of "Initiation of Structure," when controlling for status (professional/nonprofessional) and the variable of one or two professional staff members (chi square = 24, $df = 13$, $p < .05$). There was a statistically significant difference between the variable of "Consideration," when controlling for status (professional/nonprofessional), and the variable of 6-10 years in the position (chi square = 21, $df = 11$, $p < .05$). There was a statistically significant difference between the variable of "Initiation of Structure," when controlling for status (professional/nonprofessional) and the variable of age range (21 to 35 years) (chi square = 18, $df = 9$, $p < .05$). There was a statistically significant difference between the variable of "Initiation of Structure," when controlling for department head status (department head/nondepartment), and the variables of no professional staff members (chi square = 40.14026, $df = 26$, $p < .05$) and one or two professional staff members (chi square = 24, $df = 13$, $p < .05$). There was a statistically significant difference between the variable of "Initiation of Structure," when controlling for department head status (department head/nondepartment), and the variable of age range (21 to 35 years (chi square = 19, $df = 20$, $p < .05$). There was a statistically significant difference between the variable of "Consideration," when controlling for department head status (department head/nondepartment) and the variable gender (female) (chi square $= 51.27601$, $df = 33$, $p < .05$). No other differences were found to be statistically significant.

Library Directors' Correspondence

An unexpected outcome of this survey was the data collected from the correspondence received from the library directors of institutions that decided not to participate in the survey. Of the 25 directors who corresponded with the researcher, there seemed to be three main reasons for their declining to participate in the survey: (a) the size of the library staff, (b) the time required to complete the survey, and (c) the organizational structure of their library was considered incompatible with the design of the study. When categorized, the reasons mentioned by directors were of the following frequencies: size by 12 directors, time by 7 directors, and organizational structure by 8 directors. Several of the directors indicated that there might be more than one reason for their decisions to decline to participate. Only four of the directors who corresponded gave no reason for their declining to participate. The correspondence from directors produced comments centered around three concerns: size of the staff, time constraints, and organizational structure. In regards to size of the library staff one director noted that after sharing the request for participation with the library supervisory and support staff, they felt they were too small a group to do what needed to be accomplished to remain afloat. Time constraints was another concern noted by one director who was endeavoring to complete an addition to their facility. Organizational structure seemed to be of concern from some libraries since they did not have a department similar to the one described in the study. They described an organization designed apparently with more of a team or participatory management focus.

Discussion

As a result of the data analysis of this study, the following findings are presented:

1. There is no evidence to support the statement that there are differences in the mean scores for the variables of "Consideration" or "Initiation of Structure" utilized by the public services department heads as perceived by the professional librarians or nonprofessional staff.
2. There is no evidence to support the statement that there is a difference in the mean scores for the variable of "Consideration" utilized by the technical services department head as perceived by the technical services professional librarians.

3. There is evidence to support the statement that there is a difference in the mean score for the variable of "Initiation of Structure" utilized by the technical services department head as perceived by the technical services professional librarians.

4. There is no evidence to support the statement that there are differences in the mean scores for the variables of "Consideration" or "Initiation of Structure" utilized by the technical services department heads and technical services nonprofessional staff.

5. There is evidence to support the statement that there are differences in the mean scores for the variable of "Consideration" utilized by department heads when interacting with the nonprofessionals or by department heads when interacting with nondepartment heads.

6. There is no evidence to support the statement that there are differences in the mean scores for the variables of "Consideration" or "Initiation of Structure" utilized by department heads when interacting with the nonprofessionals.

7. There is no evidence to support the statement that there is a difference in the mean scores for the variable of "Initiation of Structure" utilized by department heads when interacting with the nonprofessionals.

8. There is no evidence to support the statement that there is a difference in the mean scores for the variable of "Initiation of Structure" utilized by department heads when interacting with the nondepartment heads.

9. There is evidence to support the statement that there is a statistically significant relationship between the demographic variable status and the variable of "Consideration."

10. There is evidence to support the statement that there is a statistically significant relationship between the demographic variable Gender and the variables of "Initiation of Structure" and "Consideration."

11. There is evidence to support the statement that there is a statistically significant relationship between the demographic variable of Years in the Position (6-10 years) and the variable of "Consideration."

12. There is evidence to support the statement that there is a statistically significant relationship found on the demographic variable of Age Range (21-35 years) and the variable of "Initiation of Structure" for both department heads status (department heads and nondepartment heads) and professional status (professionals and nonprofessionals).

13. There is evidence to support the statement that there is a statistically significant relationship between the demographic variable of Number of Professional Staff Members (0 and 1-2) and the variable of "Initiation of Structure."

14. There is evidence to support the statement that there is a statistically significant relationship between the demographic variable of Gender (female) and the variable of "Consideration."

The research findings of this study support the following conclusions concerning the leadership style of academic library department heads as they are perceived by the department head and the subordinates:

1. For the variable of "Initiation of Structure," there seems to be a difference in the technical services department heads' perceptions and the perceptions of the technical services department professional staff members.
2. For the variable of "Consideration," there seems to be differences in the department heads' perceptions and the perceptions of both the professional staff members and nondepartment head staff members.
3. For the variable of "Consideration," there seems to be a significant relationship between the perceptions of nondepartment head participants when the department head is female.
4. For the variables of "Consideration" and "Status," there seems to be a significant relationship between the perceptions of professional staff members and nonprofessional staff members when assessing their respective department head.
5. For the variable of "Consideration," there seems to be a significant relationship between the perceptions of all participants when the department has held the current position for six to ten years.
6. For the variables of "Initiation of Structure" and "Consideration," there seems to be a significant relationship between the perceptions of participants and the gender of the department head.
7. For the variable of "Initiation of Structure," there seems to be a significant relationship between the perceptions of all participants when the department head was between 21 to 35 years of age.
8. For the variable of "Initiation of Structure," there seems to be a significant relationship between the perceptions of all participants when the department head (a) had no professionals or (b) had from one to two professionals reporting to the department head.

Implications for the Profession

Being aware that library department heads are perceived as using a variety of leadership styles may help both the department heads and their subordinates to understand each other and work together more effectively. The application of this study's findings for the library profession may be accomplished in two phases. The first phase is training of department heads to evaluate perceptions. The recognition that other people may perceive a situation differently is the first step toward improvement in leadership. Department heads should learn to understand that each person has different perceptions of the same situations. The second phase is training of all staff members to be cognizant of differences in the perceptions of others.

In the first phase, the training provided the department heads may help them understand that there is a need for differences in the leadership based on the organizational structure of the library. This finding seems to be apparent from the correspondence from the directors of the library. This finding has implication for the department head that has a small staff and is trying to treat all the staff in the same manner.

The second phase of training in the library staff involves a need to become aware of possible perceptual differences that may be based on gender, experience level, or professional status. Since there seems to be indication that there is significance in relationships on "Consideration" and "Initiation of Structure" for both females and males, it would be wise for the library staff to discuss why, when the majority of the librarians are female, the majority of the library leadership is male.

This study's findings seem to indicate that there needs to be made to understand the perceptions of the individual rather than the group. Each staff member comes to the work place with a different background and thus a different perception about what the leader is attempting to do, or for that matter, what a leader is supposed to be. Diversity in the library setting seems to be the norm rather than the exception. The staff and users of the library will become more diverse in the future and all library staff should become more aware of and understanding of the positive nature of a diverse work setting.

The relationship between the perceptions of all staff members when the department head has held the current position for 6 to 10 years indicates that the department head with a number of years' experience may understand the dynamics of the department staff and provide more effective leadership. The amount of time in the position is probably a stabilizing factor that gives the individuals in the department time to learn about the department head. This study's findings indicate that training offered to a new department heads could provide a better understanding of how these individuals could improve their leadership as well as their sensitivity to the diverse nature of the library staff members.

The findings indicate a significant degree of difference in the perceptions of the department head and both the professionals and the nonprofessionals on the variable "Consideration." Since the backgrounds are different between the professional and nonprofessional staff members, the differences in perceptions is not surprising. When current professional staff, and more importantly the department heads and administrators, were in school, nonprofessional staff members were less well educated; however, now the level of education has increased. The professional expectations may be for a collegial relationship that supports the professional activities, and the nonprofessional may expect to be supported on a more personal basis.

Since the libraries in this study are small, it is possible that the size of the department may be a factor in the leadership style of the department head.

The department that has few professionals may require them to be responsible for all duties in the department, both professional and nonprofessional. This may impact the satisfaction level of the professional staff.

This study's findings indicate that there is need for a better understanding of the department head by the staff to improve the productivity of the nonprofessional staff in the work attempted by the staff members. The profession of librarianship needs to examine itself to provide for improvement of the all staff members and recognize the needs of all staff for structure and consideration depending on the roles and tasks to be attempted at a particular time. The empowerment of the professional and nonprofessional staffs to grow is needed to if the profession is to continue to address the changes and challenges of the future.

Recommendations for Further Study

These recommendations are based on the findings and conclusions of this study:

1. Further research should be conducted to include all types of college and university libraries to provide a broader base for future research studies.
2. Further research should be conducted to identify other methods of assessing the leadership behaviors of college and university library staff members as well as other academic departments.
3. Further research should be conducted to identify more appropriate assessments of the leadership behaviors of library personnel that are based upon different organizational structures.
4. Further research should be conducted to identify institutions that provide leadership training for library department heads.
5. Further research should be conducted using the Leadership Behavior Description Questionnaire Form XII to increase the amount of data for analysis and comparison of perceptions on leadership at various organizational levels in college and university libraries.
6. Further research should be conducted using the Leadership Behavior Description Questionnaire Form XII to include additional personnel categories to provide a broader picture of the perceptions of leaders and staff member in college and university libraries.

REFERENCES

Barrow, J. C. "The Variables of Leadership: A Review and Conceptual Framework." *Academy of Management Review, 2*(2 1977), pp. 231-251.
Bass, B. M. *Leadership Psychology and Organizational Behavior.* New York: Harper, 1960.

Bass, B. M. (Ed.) *Stogdill's Handbook of Leadership: A Survey of Theory and Research* (rev. ed.). New York: Free Press, 1981.

Borgardus, E. S. *Essentials of Social Psychology*. Los Angeles: University of Southern California Press, 1918.

Burns, J. M. *Leadership*. New York: Harper & Row, 1978.

Calder, B. J. An Attribution Theory of Leadership." In B. Staw & G. R. Salancik (Eds.), *New Directions in Organizational Behavior* (1977) pp. 179-202). Chicago: St. Clair Press.

"Carnegie Foundation's Classifications of More Than 3,000 Institiutions of Higher Education." *The Chronicle of Higher Education* (1987, July 8). pp. 22-26, 28-30.

Cartwright, D., and Zander, A. *Group Dynamics: Research and Theory*. Evanston, IL: Row, Peterson, 1960.

Carver, D. A. (1989). "Transformational Leadership: A Bibliographic Essay." *Library Administration and Management, 3*(1 1989) pp. 30-34.

Cashman, J., Dansereau, F., Jr., Graen, G., and Haga, W. J. "A Vertical Dyad Linkage Approach to Leadership within Formal Organizations: A Longitudinal Investigation of the Role-making Process." *Organizational Behavior and Human Performance, 13,* (1975) pp. 46-78.

Cashman, J., Dansereau, F., Jr., Graen, G., and Haga, W. J. "Organizational Understructure and Leadership: A Longitudinal Investigation of the Mangerial Role-making Process." *Organizational Behavior and Human Performance, 15,* (1976) pp. 278-296.

Comes, J. F. "Relationships between Leadership Behavior and Goal Attainment in Selected Academic Libraries." (Doctoral dissertation, Ball State University, 1978). *Dissertation Abstracts International, 39,* (1978/1979) pp. 5782 A.

Cunningham, L. L., and Gephart, W. J. *Leadership: The Science and the Art Today*. Itasca, IL: F. E. Peacock, 1973.

Dansereau, F., Graen, G., ,and Haga, W. J. "A Vertical Dyad Linkage Approach to Leadership in Formal Organizations: A Longitudinal Investigation of the Role Making Process." *Organizational Behavior and Human Performance, 13,* (1975) pp. 46-78.

Dipboye, R. L. (1978). "Leadership Behavior Description Questionnaire." In O. K. Buros (Ed.), *The Eighth Mental Measurements Yearbook* (Vol. 2, (1978) pp. 1742-1747). Highland Park, NJ: Gryphon Press.

Dragon, A. C. (1976/1977). "Self-descriptions and Subordinate Descriptions of the Leader Behavior of Library Administrators" (Doctoral dissertation, University of Minnesota, 1976). *Dissertation Abstracts International, 37,* (1976/1977) 7380 A.

Fiedler, F. E. (1964). "A Contingency Model of Leadership Effectiveness." In L. Berkowitz (Ed.), *Advances in Experimental Social Psychology* (Vol. 1, (1964) pp. 150-190). New York: Academic Press.

Fleishman, E. A. "The Measurement of Leadership Attitudes in Industry." *Journal of Applied Psychology, 34,* (1953) 153-158.

Fleishman, E. A. (1973). "Twenty years of Consideration and Structure." In E. A. Fleishman and J. G. Hunt (Eds.), *Current Developments in the Study of Leadership* (1973 pp. 1-40). Carbondale: Southern Illinois University Press.

Frankie, S. (1980/1981). "The Behavioral Styles, Work Preferenecs and Values of an Occupational Group: A Study of University Catalog and Reference Librarians." (Doctoral dissertation, The George Washington University, 1980). *Dissertations Abstracts International, 41* (1980/1981) 3307 A.

Gibb, C. A. (1954). "Leadership." In G. Lindzey and E. Aronson (Eds.), *Handbook of Social Psychology* (Vol. 4, (1954) pp. 205-282). Reading, MA: Addison-Wesley.

Gibb, C. A. *Leadership: Selected Readings*. Baltimore, MD: Penguin Books, 1969.

Graen, G. (1983). "Role Making Process within Complex Organizations." In M. D. Dunnette (Ed.), *Handbook of Industrial and Organizational Psychology* (1983) pp. 1201-1245.

Graen, G., and Cashman, J. (1975). "A Role Making Model of Leadership in Formal Organizations: A Developmental Approach." In J. Hunt and L. L. Larson (Eds.), *Leadership Frontiers* (1975) pp. 143-165). Kent, OH: Kent State University Press.

Halpin, A. W. *Manual for the Leader Behavior Description Questionnaire.* Columbus: Ohio State University, Bureau of Business Research, 1957.

Hass, F. W. "A Study of the Applicability of Contemporary Contingency and Situational Management Theory to Higher Education." *Dissertation Abstracts International, 45* (1984) 704A.

Hersey, P., and Blanchard, K. H. *Management of Organizational Behavior.* Englewood Cliffs, NJ: Prentice-Hall, 1969.

Hersey, P., and Blanchard, K. H. *Management of Organizational Behavior.* Englewood Cliffs, NJ: Prentice-Hall, 1982.

Higher Education Directory. Washington, DC: Higher Education Publications, 1987.

James, T. O. "Can We Choose a Management Style." In R. J. Fecher (Ed.). *Applying Corporate Management Strategies.* (1985, p. 59-74). San Francisco: Jossey Bass.

Korman, A. K. "Consideration," "Initiating Structure," and Organizational Criteria." *Personnel Psychology, 18,* 1966, pp. 349-360.

Mann, R.D. "A Review of relationships between Personalitiy and Performance in Small Groups." *Psychological Bulletin, 56,* 1959, pp. 241-270.

Martin, M. S. *Issues in Personnel Management in Academic Libraries.* Grenwich, CT: JAI Press, 1981.

Miles, A., and Steiner, P. *Winners, Losers, Hired Hands: Leadership Theories Applied for Student Affairs Officers.* Tuscaloosa, AL: Randall Publishing, 1981.

Murphy, A. K. "A Study of the Leadeship Process.' *American Sociological Review, 6,* 1941, pp. 674-687.

Robbins, S. P. *The Administrative Process.* Englewood Cliffs, NJ: Prentice-Hall, 1980.

Seligman, L. G. "Leadership: Political Aspects." In D. L. Sills (Ed.), *The International Encyclopedia of Social Sciences* (Vol. 9, 1968, p. 108). New York: Macmillan Company and the Free Press.

Slavin, R. E. *Research Methods in Education: A Practical Guide.* Englewood Cliffs, NJ: Prentice-Hall, 1984.

Sparks, R. "Library Management: Consideration and Structure." *Journal of Academic Librarianship, 2*(2) 1976 pp. 66-71.

Statistical Package for the Social Sciences PC+ Version 3. Chicago: SPSS Inc., 1988.

Stogdill, R. M. "Personal Factors Associated with Leadership: A Survey of the Literature." *Journal of Psychology, 25,* 1948, pp. 35-71.

Stogdill, R. M. *Manual for the Leader Behavior Description Questionnaire-Form XII.* Columbus: Ohio State University, Bureau of Business Research, 1963.

Stogdill, R. M. *Handbook of Leadership.* New York: Free Press, 1974.

Tannenbaum, R., and Schmidt, W. H. "How to Choose a Leadership Pattern." *Havard Business Review, 36,* 1958, pp. 95-101.

LIBRARY TECHNOLOGY TRANSFER:
BEYOND THE CULTURAL BOUNDARIES

Kenneth J. Oberembt

ABSTRACT

Computer and telecommunications technologies are being introduced into Third World library contexts where they confront some serious transfer problems. The paper discusses four cultural constraints—elitism, authoritarianism, atomism, and groupism—that impede technology transfer in an Egyptian library and offers guidance to library change agents who must reconcile transfer technology to the cultural realities of their specific library settings.

We are all aware of how much contemporary information technology is impacting the library profession. There was a time, not long ago at all, when information was simply a reference librarian's answer to a patron's question. Now the workaday lives of library staff are steadily being transformed by information retrieval, information science, and information theory—concepts that have become named realities only since 1950.[1] Savants in the library profession who dwell on future possibilities even predict the disappearance of the library altogether. Time will prove or give the lie to such a forecast, but

Advances in Library Administration and Organization,
Volume 11, pages 75-95.
Copyright © 1993 by JAI Press Inc.
All rights of reproduction in any form reserved.
ISBN: 1-55938-596-0

meanwhile telecommunications and computer technologies are radically altering what libraries do and how they do it. We do not any longer so much collect as access recorded knowledge and our work with users is increasingly information service rather than library reference.

Technological change, well advanced in libraries of the Developed World, is now invading library operations and services in the Developing World. Reflecting on four years of technological change at the library I administer in Egypt, where American and Egyptian cultures are in continuous and sometimes frictional interaction, I am well aware of just how challenging—and daunting—library technology transfer is in a Third World context. Some problems are purely technical, others systemic and environmental. Still others, which I have identified from a particular set of experiences at the American University in Cairo and which are the focus of this essay, are cultural.

None of these problems, I can report happily, is irremediable. None, on the other hand, is remedied easily. To understand them is, however, a necessary precondition for development of a truly international and intercultural information technology and for universal library and information networking. There cannot be a wholly successful implementation in libraries worldwide of interconnected information systems without it.

To this end I will examine some of the constraints to acculturation of new library technologies at my home institution, an Egyptian case study intended to elucidate a general problem of concern to all whose library vision is global. The American University in Cairo Library permits an unusually focused look at cultural constraints to transfer because other types of impediments often associated with technology transfer programs, particularly those bi-national in nature, are absent.[2] Technology transfer is a continuous rather than an intermittent activity at the American University in Cairo.

THE AMERICAN UNIVERSITY IN CAIRO CONTEXT

The American University in Cairo (hereafter AUC) is a seventy-year experiment in bi-culturalism. It operates as a private cultural organization under a 1962 Egyptian-American Cultural Cooperation Agreement and a 1971 Protocol with the Government of Egypt which recognizes AUC's degrees as equivalent to those awarded by Egyptian national universities. At the same time incorporated in the United States, AUC is licensed by the Educational Institution Licensure Commission of the District of Columbia and accredited by the Commission on Higher Education of the Middle States Association of Colleges and Schools to confer U.S.-approved university degrees.[3] Beyond the fact of its statutory existence in two different—and two culturally different—countries, AUC formally acknowledges a dual culturalism "exemplifying American educational principles and practices and recognizing the heritage and customs of Egypt and the surrounding Arab world" as infusing its teaching, research, and service functions.[4]

The outward sign of AUC bi-culturalism is the mixed national origin of the administrative, teaching, and support staff cadres. The staff composition of the AUC Library quite well mirrors that of the parent institution as a whole. AUC Library professionals, who are classed as faculty and for organizational purposes constitute an academic department, number 16 all together—10 (63 percent) Egyptian, five (31 percent American, and one (6 percent) Third Country Nationality. Although the 1971 Protocol explicitly defined by percentage the faculty to be hired as American (45 percent), Egyptian (45 percent), and Third Country Nationality (10 percent),[5] American-hire faculty overall have fallen in recent years far short of their 45 percent target figure to approximately 1/3 of the total AUC full-tome faculty, the same proportion as American-hire faculty in the AUC Library.[6] The 77 Library non-professionals (42 full-time and 35 part-time) are with one exception Egyptian Nationals. The 1971 Protocol set a 5 percent foreign-hire maximum on this large and diverse employee group and thereby guaranteed that below the administrative and faculty ranks the Egyptian presence would predominate.[7] Imbalance in the mix of nationalities on the AUC Library staff overall—5 percent American or 7 percent Foreign as against 93 percent Egyptian—is a limiting factor in the transfer of non-indigenous technologies.

Technology transfer specialist Susan Scott-Stevens, after studying several transfer projects in Indonesia, has emphasized the context dependency of technology: "Technological packages are created, shaped, and learned in specific contexts, and are transferred to other equally specific contexts, where they undergo further change."[8] Although her observation is adduced from the discipline of engineering, it has most certainly a cross-disciplinary validity. The library technology in process of transfer to AUC depends upon an overwhelming number of staff unacquainted with its contextual origins to assimilate, to modify, and to use it in its new environment. The transfer is understandably complex and problematic.

KEY CONCEPTS

At the outset, let me delimit several key interpretive concepts. The term *technology,* with or without a qualifying adjective, refers to computer-based information systems developed over the past 25 years, either already used or potentially usable in the library setting. Hardware, software, documentation, technical knowledge are all components of these systems and, therefore, aspects of both technology and its transfer. A specific discussion sometimes invites mention of a specific technology, such as electronic mail or computer cataloging, but the range of technologies presently adopted in the library setting or adaptable to it is very broad indeed and my intent is to be all-inclusive.

Since my subject is technology *transfer,* the library technology I have in mind exclusively is that which is developed in one country and imported into another. I deliberately exclude home-grown technology, the better to emphasize the phenomenon of cultural constraint.

In using the term *cultural constraint,* I do not mean to invoke any particular theoretical model of culture developed by scientists or humanists. Rather I have directed my attention to what Edward T. Hall calls the "situational frame." It is, as he has described it, "the smallest viable unit of a culture" and is

> made up of situational dialects, material appurtenances, situational personalities, and behavior patterns that occur in recognized settings and are appropriate to specific situations.[9]

The situation which I, for analytic purposes, have framed is the work environment of the AUC Library, and the cultural constraints identified derive from the value, proxemic, social, and behavioral components of this environment. In order of discussion, these are *elitism, authoritatianism, atomism,* and *groupism.*

ELITISM AS CONSTRAINT

The image problem of the library profession in Egypt is the lowly image of Egyptian libraries. Public sector libraries, which comprise the great bulk of libraries in Egypt, are overstaffed and underfunded, unmanaged or undermanaged, inaccessible and underused, storage rather than service oriented, untouched to date in any really important ways by informatics, disregarded (except for a few scientific disciplines) in the planning process for national socio-economic development, and marginal in the cultural life of the nation generally. The Dar El-Kutub, so undervalued within the General Egyptian Book Organization (GEBO) bureaucracy that it cannot gain the resources to exercise the National Library functions assigned to it, or the Cairo University Library, fractured into discipline-based libraries each wholly owned by its respective faculty or research institute and so wanting in basic bibliographic control that the collective information resources are unknowable and therefore largely unusable, can be cited as examples of an endemic problem.

Much, it is true, has happened in recent years to give the library profession and librarians a better image. Mrs. Suzanne Mubarak, wife of the President of Egypt, has focused her energies on the foundation of children's libraries, and the publicity surrounding successive inaugural ceremonies has alerted the public to the cultural and educational importance of libraries. Early exposure to libraries, it is hoped, will encourage children to become lifelong users, and their library requirements as they mature into adolescence and adulthood will then give impetus to other libraries in the public sector to upgrade operations and services. Private sector libraries, particularly those associated with embassies and consulates in the Cairo area, are distinguished by service programming and by staff orientation to user need. The libraries of the American Cultural Center and the British Council are especially noteworthy. And in the public sector the newly founded Council of Ministers' Library has a similar reputation.

Despite the present glimmer of change on the Egyptian library scene, the state of affairs in the early 1970s when the AUC Library was seeking to rebuild its professional cadre was most inauspicious for the recruitment of Egyptian nationals. Those with academic training in librarianship above the level of the baccalaureate were very few in number, and this small applicant pool was reduced still further by the AUC-required score of 80 percent (minimum) on the University of Michigan English Proficiency Examination. Since English is the language of instruction of AUC, written and spoken mastery of the tongue are indispensable for AUC Library professional-level performance, both on the job and in university governance. Therefore, the AUC Library decided to rely on its in-house support staff as the chief source of supply for Egyptians filling professional positions. The in-house recruitment procedure established in the 1970s, as it has turned out, inhibits technological development and technology transfer in the 1990s.

Underlying that procedure was an elitist concept of professionalism grounded in cultural attitudes and values. In a very real sense its inspiration was the lowly image of Egyptian librarianship and its goal to create a countervailing prestigious image. The cultural observation that "the Arab is a strict observer of rank in the social order"[10] is apposite because position consciousness came to dominate the content of library professionalism at the expense of intellectual and skills content.

The goal of dignifying the position of the library professional in the AUC social order was entirely successful. Professional appointment now confers automatic faculty status. I am not aware of any academic librarians in Egypt, except those at AUC, having such parity with teaching faculty. The benefits are enormous and, indeed, prestigious: academic year contract equity, salary equality, equal responsibility in the committee and governance structure of the university. It is no small matter that AUC Library Faculty work under contract for only nine months of the academic year, have an annual three-month paid vacation, receive a portion of salary in hard currency, are guaranteed membership in AUC standing committees (e.g., Undergraduate, Graduate, Academic Board, Publications, Faculty Senate) and can stand for election to others.

Although the library-related titles Senior Librarian (non-administrative) and Deputy Librarian (administrative) are used to classify Library Faculty in

AUC's faculty rank schema, these are equivalent to the titles Instructor and Assistant Professor reserved for the AUC teaching cadre. Such is the power and prestige of faculty status that AUC Library professionals think of themselves on and off the job primarily as faculty. Librarianship and the tasks associated with it tend to take second place.

To gain a share in faculty prestige has long been the incentive for AUC Library staff to obtain promotion to professional status. And the process for doing so, created in the 1970s, was eased considerably by omitting any requirement for Egyptians to hold a degree in Library Science or to have academic training in librarianship. The effect of this was to bifurcate professionalism because the masters degree in Library Science, or equivalent formal certification, remained a prerequisite for ex-patriate hires. Egyptian and non-Egyptian professionals in the AUC Library were, thus, not bound by the same entry requirement. Another result was to weaken the already tenuous affective link, on the Egyptian side, between Library Faculty status and the library profession. To become a library professional without formal library study was the ordinary procedure at AUC. Finally, there was a diminishment in the intellectual content of library professionalism. Knowledge of librarianship as a science became unnecessary for the exercise of professional library responsibility.

Allied to the aim of ennobling library professional status through its subsumption in faculty status was that of enhancing the status of professionalism in the AUC Library workplace by isolating it from subprofessionalism. It springs from what I call the *mudiir/a motive* (Arabic masculine/feminine forms combined), the desire to be a manager. In principle this motive outwardly resembles that of contemporary American librarians to redefine the duties of the library professional in the technological age by distinguishing as clearly as possible between professional and non-professional roles. In actual fact, however, the *mudiir/a motive* focuses on library management as a state of being rather than a state of action, on managerial perks rather than tasks.

To say that Arabs are "utterly contemptuous of all manual labor"[11] or that in "Muslim societies" the "concept of service connotes menial work and is not considered to be the province of an educated person such as the librarian"[12] is to utter at best only partial truths, but these cultural observations do capture what management means—or, rather, does not mean—to many Egyptian managers. Manual or practical skills are regarded as sub-managerial. They are relevant to the managed but irrelevant to the manager. This is a view inculcated and reinforced by the Egyptian educational system, where, it has been pointed out, there is "a marked reluctance among students to go into technical occupations" despite the demonstrable need "for skilled manpower."[13] Reluctance is strictly a matter of "social status" which "places academic above technical education." Egyptians are guided by the view that "social status is enhanced by having an academic degree" whereas "to have a technical degree" is "neither prestigious nor economically rewarding."[14]

The Egyptian managerial elite are the product of the academic educational track, not the vocational. These are rather more rigidly separated in Egypt than in, for example, the United States and mean that such technical skills as typing or keyboarding are not included in the academic curriculum. In fact, these skills can all too easily be regarded as secretarial and an active aversion to ever acquiring them develop. I emphasize keyboarding intentionally because it is indispensable for computer literacy and for mastery of new computer-based information technology. Fully one-third of the professionals in the AUC Library have never acquired this skill. Several have indicated no intention of ever doing so. Others have referred to the personal difficulty they had in overcoming a practical skills mindset while learning how to keyboard, despite a conscious decision to learn.

Built into the AUC Library's in-house method of professional appointment, additionally, was a major systemic flaw: it was left as a matter of personal choice for non-professional staff to decide to become professionals and to position themselves for eventual professional-level promotion by acquiring English language proficiency and a masters degree, discipline unspecified. Those who met these qualifications entered a special pre-professional category and were cycled in seniority order into professional rank as vacancies occurred. The process was a fairly mechanical one. No job descriptions were developed when vacancies occurred nor were professional skills nor knowledge prerequisites established. Candidates neither prepared curricula vitae nor interviewed. The process of filling each opening with the next most senior pre-professional was so automatic that even an adverse judgment about that candidate's suitability for the job available was generally insufficient reason for denial of appointment.

This procedure was systematically applied for some 10 years until a 1984 decision by the University administration, responding to amendment in Egyptian National Labor Law and mandating that all Egyptian faculty be hired only under secondment, meant the termination of Library professional appointments from on-staff.[15] During that ten-year timespan the procedure yielded a group of professionals whose knowledge of librarianship was confined mainly to what the AUC Library already knew and did. It did not involve any significant value-added learning and it had no built-in incentive to exceed the knowledge limits of actual on-the-job duties or to master new concepts of library operations and services. It was not conditioned by either an expertise in library theory, verified through formal examination, or a carefully crafted program of job cross-training comprehending the full range of library public and technical service functions. Inbreeding was its hallmark, and its emphasis, one might say, was on the manners of professionalism, not on the professional metier. Professionalism became a reward, an end in itself, the capstone to a career and not the commencement of a new one.

Given its proactive stance in adopting new technologies, the AUC Library is concerned about the steady diminishment of its Egyptian professional contingent through retirement and resignation with no yet identifiable source of resupply in prospect. Technology transfer in the terms which fulfill the AUC mission is frustrated indeed if there are no Egyptian professional recipients to whom knowledge can be transferred and who, in turn, can share their acquired expertise extramurally with co-national peers.

Of equal concern is the technological unreadiness of the present AUC Library Faculty cadre. Computer literacy and decision-making skills are the sine qua non of library professionalism in the post-industrial era. Even expatriate AUC Library Faculty must struggle to stay abreast of the times, but their prior academic training in librarianship and computer-related skills training, their continuing education activities while on home visits (once a year for most, twice annually for several), and their personal motivation to emulate their library colleagues back home in automation knowhow are advantages largely inaccessible to the Egyptian Library Faculty. For the Egyptians hired into professional positions since the mid-1970s, on the other hand, neither the Egyptian Association for Library and Information Science (EALIS) nor the departments of Library Science at the Egyptian national universities, the most readily accessible associations of library educators and practitioners, offer schematic training relevant to the needs of working professionals. Only the highly motivated among the Egyptian Library Faculty have entirely on their own tried to make up for what was lacking in their academic and work experience. Several have become computer literate and one, completing a Masters of Business Administration degree, has upgraded her management skills. The number of the highly self-motivated is still small, less than half of the total.

Because the introduction of computer-based library technology is itself so recent at AUC—1986-1987, to be precise—the AUC Library is only now realizing the need for a new type of library professional, a new standard of professionalism, new criteria for selecting the professional staff of the future, and, finally new in-service training programs for professionals presently on-staff. More will be said later about addressing these needs.

Whether all of the current AUC Library professionals can adapt to the technological revolution underway is uncertain, but adaptation and new role identity are necessary to cope with it. What the AUC Library is facing is a generic and not a unique problem. Libraries everywhere in the Third World positioning themselves for entry into the age of electronic information may well be forced to circumvent cultural barriers if they too are to create professional leadership sympathetic to technological change. None should expect to be spared this problem and the need to resolve it indefinitely.

AUTHORITARIANISM AS CONSTRAINT

In the West, and particularly in the United States, where technology diffuses through library operations and services there is widespread reflection on new organizational structures more suitable to the computerized library than current hierarchical arrangements of authority and function. Data access and distribution on a scale impossible in the pre-automation library invite, and likely even mandate, broader sharing of authority, more flexible organization, and greater individual initiative. Similarly the AUC Library, where an authoritarian supervisor-supervisee relationship impedes technology implementation and transfer, finds itself impelled to adopt the more democratic structure library technology educes. Here too culture poses constraint.

Authoritarianism is well documented as the prevailing management style in the Egyptian public sector, which is, given the dominance of that sector in the socio-economic life of the nation, in fact to say that it is normative in Egypt. The findings of an American-Egyptian research team based upon a 1983 study of the Egyptian bureaucracy by the Al Ahram Center for Political and Strategic Studies (Cairo) confirm the "popular assumption that bureaucratic authority is heavily centralized." Furthermore, its causes "are rooted both in the pragmatic realities of bureaucratic life as well as in the broader culture of Egyptian society."[16]

Some have opined that authoritarianism in the Arab World derives from the subservience towards political and religious authority inculcated by Arab Abbasid and Ottoman Empire rulership[17] or originates in bedouin patriarchal society[18] or, with reference to Egypt specifically, that it is "the main structural characteristic" of an "hydraulic society" and has pre-Islamic roots in the hierarchical organization of society and authority in the Pharaonic Era.[19] The 1983 Al Ahram study surveyed, both formally by questionnaire and informally in discussion, Egyptian bureaucrats who readily accepted historical explanations for the centralizing behavior of the Egyptian bureaucracy. Personal considerations—"concerns of *wasta* (i.e., mediation or influence) and power," "the technical inability of subordinates to execute the tasks delegated," and "the reluctance of subordinates to accept responsibility"[20]—were cited too as reasons for centralism of authority.

It should come as no surprise that a place where group work is conducted, whether that be a library or the office of a government ministry, will adopt an administrative style harmonious with the surrounding external culture. The micro-environment will invariably display the predelictions of the macro. And so it is with the AUC Library.

More than just a cultural inclination, however, centralizing behavior is a by-product of the elitist professionalism, discussed previously, which injects an authoritarian dynamic into relationships between professionals and subprofessionals, between supervisors and supervisees. It evolves quite naturally from the inequality of faculty and non-faculty status and is heightened by Library Faculty disassociation from daily library tasks that would compromise their status. Those promoted to the professional ranks from on-staff seem particularly keen to break with their past by drawing a firm line between current and previous work and between present and past roles in the workplace. They expect the same deferential treatment from subordinates that they once themselves conferred upon superiors.

The authoritarian dynamic affects people in the way they work and, therefore, it affects the character of work itself. One result noticeable in the AUC Library and elsewhere in Egypt is the elaborate system of protocols developed over time for requesting and granting approval, what I like to call the *bureaucracy of permission*. Typically requests must be documented in order to be processed. Then they have to be submitted to multiple ascending authorities, a process open to additional authorizations extending as far as the director's office in the case of timid supervisors. The chain is easily broken by the unavailability of a key person. Meanwhile action requested waits incomplete or undone, encumbered in time-consuming delay.

For library professionals who find fulfillment in the sheer effect of their word and signature to empower or disempower subordinates, authoritarian behavior is a forceful assertion of self-importance. Staff control is identified frequently by AUC Library staff as the attribute nonpareil of a library manager—from director to unit head—and it has encouraged the professional cadre to specialize in the politics of authority and in the manipulation of the levers of authority. Such specialists are interested, ultimately, in controlling people rather than in understanding technology and in guiding its implementation.

Bureaucratic rigidity has tended to freeze staff in inflexible postures, non-professionals not daring to be very innovative with the computer literacy skills they employ daily in their work and professionals not caring too much to develop hands-on knowledge of technology. The slow pace of IBM Dobis/Libis Library System implementation in the AUC Library, less than half as far along as it should be at this point, is due in large measure to an authoritarian organizational structure and group dynamic that reduce personal commitment to technology and its transfer, that lessen the sense of staff ownership of the transferred technology. Tactics to address this problem will be dealt with later on.

Not only in Egypt and the Third World but also in portions of the Developed World command style management is a forceful presence. Supplanting it with the more democratic style within which technology can thrive is, as world events in these early 1990s remind us, not a problem unique to the AUC Library or to librarianship.

ATOMISM AS CONSTRAINT

Something of the Egyptian fixation on status and fervor for status mobility is rather nicely encapsulated in the novelette *Respected Sir* by 1988 Nobel Prize winner Naguib Mahfouz, where Othman Bayyumi, newly appointed petty clerk in the Archives Section, contemplates the formidable series of promotional steps separating him from the Director-General and vows to devote his life and energies to covering that long distance:

'I am on fire, o God.'

Flames were devouring his soul from top to bottom as it soared upwards into a world of dreams. In a single moment of revelation he perceived the world as a surge of dazzling light which he pressed to his bosom and held on to like one demented. He had always dreamed and desired and yearned, but this time he was really ablaze, and in the light of this sacred fire he glimpsed the meaning of life.[21]

Othman's perception of job advancement as spiritual quest, of course, exaggerates reality. At the same time it illuminates a respect for orderly structure and a dedication to step-by-step upward progress that imbues the Egyptian work ethic. Mahfouz's portrait of the career civil servant who becomes little more than a slave to the career ladder, achieving his goal of Director-Generalship only on his deathbed, is ironic. Spirituality sinks into mundanity and globality into minutiae, and so Othman loses his ultimate goal even while he seems to gain it.

Othman Bayyumi is, in a rather interesting way, an embodiment of the Arab temperament which has been delineated as giving "overattention ... to minute details, but without integrating them into a composite and well-organized whole" or, again, which "atomizes the world and then views each atom as a stable monad."[22] This habitude of conceptualizing reality is particulate rather than universalistic in its mode of analysis. Its tendency is myopic—a "can't see the forest for trees" narrowness of vision that is caught so well in the following summation of the prevailing view among Egyptians of the relationship between remunerative position, education, and certification:

People have become ... used to the notion of education merely as a mean (sic) for obtaining a certificate which would lead to a job, a job which is associated with a specific certificate and preceded by a specific number of years in education which would mean a specific salary and a specific place on the social ladder. If, however, the job was connected with a different certificate, preceded by a different number of years, it would mean a different salary and a different place on the social ladder.[23]

"Certificate pricing," to use the term fashionable with contemporary Egyptian economists, is the logical conclusion to a reductive process that abolishes the "link" between "pay" and "productivity."[24] Dividing and delinking are the tenor of the atomistic impulse.

Generally speaking, schemes designed to satisfy worker need for job status and mobility must extend for the entire worklife of Egyptian employees, few of whom, compared to their counterparts in the West, leave permanently for jobs elsewhere or build careers based on a need to find jobs with a succession of employers. Such schemes are also especially vulnerable to atomism, to division into uncoordinated elements. This is discernible in the AUC Library's system of employee placement and promotion which effectually disjoins job, rank/status, pay, and productivity and, as a result, constrains technology transfer which depends upon their jointure.

Under the guaranteed job security provisions of Egyptian Labor Law, the full-time Egyptian worker becomes a tenured employee automatically upon renewal of contract. For Egyptian non-professionals in the AUC Library that happens one year from the date of first employment.[25] For AUC Library Egyptian faculty, tenuring would also at the present time immediately follow renewal of the initial contract, except that AUC, starting in 1984, has required seconded employment for Egyptians. All current Egyptian Library Faculty were employed before that cut-off date and were grandfathered into tenure at that time.

Advancement incentive schemes get such extraordinary emphasis in the Egyptian workplace and at AUC just because other motivations, both positive and negative, are excluded by law and circumstance. The method of advancing personnel in the AUC Library is a rather complex one, and it is not the same for faculty and support staff. For the former, the method is mandated by University policy. For the latter, it is the creation of the AUC Library itself and modeled, mutatis mutandis, on the method of faculty advancement.

Professionals are ranked, in ascending order, Senior Librarian and Deputy Librarian, equivalent to Instructor and Assistant Professor, respectively. University Librarian (i.e., Library Director) is an administrative rather than faculty position, although it is roughly equivalent to Professor.[26] The professional nomenclature, as previously mentioned, is reserved exclusively for the teaching faculty as a matter of institutional policy. Upward movement for Library Faculty is severely restricted. University Librarian rank is limited to the Director, and Deputy Librarian to the one or two professionals who with the Director form the Administrative Council.

The recompense for lack of mobility between ranks is in-rank movement according to a system of "steps"—19 for Senior Librarians and 10 for Deputy Librarians.[27] Work performance is evaluated annually and submitted for approval to the University's Committee on Appointments, Promotion, and Tenure. A favorable committee decision means advancement of one step in the gradation and an unfavorable a step freeze without advancement for at least one year. Annual evaluations over time have become pro forma and step increases virtually automatic.

The method of advancing library non-professional staff is more complex. A combination of placement ranks and grades is used to mark each employee's stage of progress. The ranks, six all together, are arranged according to interrelated promotional tracks. The Library Assistant, Senior Library

Assistant, and Junior Librarian ranks represent one track for staff who score 60 percent, the minimum hiring level, on the University of Michigan English Proficiency Examination, but who have less than a baccalaureate degree. The second track comprises the ranks of Assistant Librarian and Librarian, the first requiring English proficiency at the 70 percent level and a baccalaureate degree and the latter 80 percent-level English proficiency masters degree.[28] Additionally, the latter has come to be regarded as quasi-professional and, until recently, constituted the Egyptian applicant pool from which professional vacancies were filled. Crossing over from the first to the second track is merely a matter of satisfying degree and enhanced language prerequisites. Finally, the rank of Administrative Assistant, a third track unto itself, is the exclusive preserve of that handful of support staff who perform office management functions for the Director. Although without a degree requirement, excellence in English and Arabic, in typewriting and keyboarding, and in handling office routines are mandatory.[29] Recruitment is usually from without rather than from within current staff.

The six placement ranks, moreover, interact with 10 placement grades to round out the promotional system. Whatever their advancement track, all support staff can attain placement grade VIII. Staff in Librarian and Administrative Assistant rank can achieve grades IX and X. The engine for both rank and grade movement is seniority. Thus, a Library Assistant after five years on the job will move automatically to the Senior Library Assistant rank and to the Junior Librarian rank after ten, and the same Library Assistant after fourteen years will move automatically to grade VIII.[30] Annual evaluations have become perfunctory and, consequently, do not effect rank or grade movement.

The petty clerk of Naguib Mahfouz's *Respected Sir* would find the AUC Library's placement and promotion scheme both intelligible and satisfying. Every stage is denoted by its appropriate rank, step or grade, and prerequisites, and the stages are sequenced in superabundant detail. The deficiency in the scheme is that staff and institutional benefits are disjunctive. Staff need for status mobility is fulfilled but Library need for job enhancement is not.

Job functions, in fact, play no role in staff advancement. They have become marginalized to the extent that AUC Library staff, professionals and non-professionals alike, have for many years not worked at all within written job descriptions. Titles such as Senior Librarian at the faculty level and Junior Librarian at the non-professional in no way indicate the job duties of the bearer. Personnel with responsibilities varying widely in skill and authority can share in same rank/grade, or those in high skill and authority jobs can even be outranked/graded by those in low skill. Supervisors can easily hold lesser rank/grade than those they supervise. That salary and other kinds of compensation are driven by rank and its associated steps and grades only increases the disparity between status on the promotional level and job functions on the operational. One very obvious consequence is that the status structure is taken much more seriously than job structure. A job represents the daily grind but status confers both prestige and monetary reward.

In a work environment where the job itself is undervalued and relationships between job, status/rank, and pay are indeterminate, productivity and accountability inevitably suffer. Employees tend to seek the least onerous work, to care less about improving their work, and to resist new work challenges when actual job tasks and the quality of their performance do not affect promotion. A library undergoing simultaneous technological change and job evolution in response to changing technology is obviously constrained if the reward system for staff, who must bear the brunt of the change pain, is unsupportive and is disproportionate to institutional need.

This is the situation in which the AUC Library finds itself. It is a situation, perhaps, shared by many libraries. From the perspective of the Third World it is well worth asking whether something of the Western competitive environment within which library technology developed will have to be adopted wherever that technology is implemented. Competition in the form of a hierarchy of jobs based on a gradation of automation and management skills, progressively more demanding, and a staff concentrating on skills upgrade to ascend the job ladder could create conditions amenable to technology transfer. Recommendations to follow later will pick up on these themes.

Competition would go against the grain of Egyptian cultural attitudes that sanctify seniority. Contesting peers for advancement within a job hierarchy, with all the risks to personal pride and to fellowship in the workplace this poses, would be very difficult for Egyptian staff to accept. So too the reality of increasingly limited opportunities for upward progress as the job scale narrows and of increasingly expanded opportunities for personal frustration as career blockage looms. It simply must be admitted that library technology makes demands of its own, and, if unmet, the technology will not transfer.

GROUPISM AS CONSTRAINT

Sociability is a trait that travellers and visitors have consistently attributed to Egyptians. Edward Lane, among the most famous of these for the enduring quality of his early nineteenth-century description of Egyptian mores, identifies "(a)ffability" as "a general characteristic of Egyptians of all classes."[31] And observations similar to Lane's reappear in the popular Cairene press of today, where, for example, an Egyptian critic will remark in passing that "the Egyptian temperament" is "intrinsically gregarious, and tends to regard even the most private of experiences as communal property."[32] Sociability is cultural, emanating from the group consciousness that defines Arab society, which, according to an acute observer, "starts with the family" and "is patterned on it" and "extends outward from it." This family "comprises more than just the members of the nuclear unit of procreation and orientation" but is, in fact, "an extended group, covering non-blood relationships and friends to whom kinship terms are given as an index of nearness, love or respect."[33]

Familism is the term often used to describe the Arab social pattern that places family and familial solidarity in the ascendance.[34] Because of that term's association with blood ties and because blood-link is no longer the essential ingredient of group formation in modern Arab society, groupism is, perhaps, preferable as the more generic. No less than familism, however, it recognizes the family overtones and behaviors associated with group bonding in the Arab World, such that Arab social organization is of an "emphatically personal and intense character."[35]

Groupism extends quite naturally to the workplace, where form group friendships which adopt the familiar family patterns and behaviors. These friendships develop organically from tasksharing and physical proximity, and their most visible expression is in group sociability, which both bonds each group internally and strengthens it in its relationship with other groups in the work environment.

Of more than passing interest at this moment in Egypt, as the nation is moving from a command to a market economy, are the interrelated issues of worker attitude and work productivity. The assumption has long been that a socializing rather than productive ethic governs the Egyptian workplace, an assumption that the 1983 Al Ahram study of the Egyptian public sector bureaucracy tends to confirm: "group dynamics ... depress rather than stimulate professional (i.e., 'flexible,' 'innovative,' 'productive') behavior."[36] A group dynamic directed more towards socialization than production is also the pattern in the AUC Library where it tends to bar a fully effective technology implementation and transfer. There is, in brief, dissonance between the people orientation of the staff and the machine orientation of the technology that is being introduced.

A strong sense of community exists within the workforce of the AUC Library. It is valorized even by the frequent use of such words as family, father, mother, brother, sister to exemplify this community and its internal relationships. Staff develop a network of friends on the job and carry their friendships over from work into their private lives. In the work setting they are very solicitous toward each other. Those present assume temporarily the duties of others who are absent, the more skilled assist the lesser with difficult tasks, and the experienced form patron-client relationships with the inexperienced. In their dealings with each other they emphasize person-to-person contact. The average workday is punctuated with conversation, telephone calls, tea and coffee breaks, meetings with supervisors on all manner of job-related and personal matters, and visits to colleagues in remote units. Even in carrying out their individual job tasks they prefer spacial proximity.

Provision of services to library clientele is equally personalized. The clear preference is for conducting business face-to-face or voice-to-voice, if by telephone, rather than through more impersonal written communication. These patterns of staff and patron-staff interaction can easily be generalized to work settings throughout Egypt.

Computer-based information technology introduced into the AUC Library has interrupted the customary patterns of social interaction and has, as a consequence, met staff resistance. The depersonalizing effect of technology is a case in point. A recent pilot test of the electronic mail component of IBM's Professional Office System (PROFS) was, for example, only a qualified success. To be sure, a variety of factors figured in this result. Some staff did not have a readily accessible terminal to send and to receive mail. For this inconvenience they did not experiment with electronic mail beyond the training period. Other staff did not gain much familiarity with computerized messaging because people with whom they normally conduct business were not among the test users. The innovation for them had no convincing purpose and their interest subsided after the training period as well.

The pilot test, however, provoked still another reaction which bears upon the issue of technology's depersonalizing potential. Some staff expressed the opinion that computer mail was too impersonal for their use. They would rather the give-and-take of conversation to handle business with colleagues inside and outside of the Library. Except for such rote matters as scheduling meetings and posting notices, they want to be able to pick up on the subtleties of tone and nuance in the respondent's words and they judge terminal talk a wholly inadequate substitute for live discourse. There is something to this, for Egyptians do have a habit of speaking by indirection, especially on sensitive subjects. To do this is only to be polite, to avoid giving offense. They are also rather reluctant to commit thought and opinion to writing because documentation is evidentiary.

Beyond the impersonality of technology is apprehension about technology's potential for devaluing the human connections of traditional library service. The paradigm par excellence is the person-to-person link between librarian and user. Possible technology disruption of this bond surfaced in the process of planning for the incorporation of non-print media and computer-assisted instruction (CAI) into the Bibliographic Instruction Program of the AUC Library. There was a measured enthusiasm for these innovations by some staff because earlier experimentation, prompted by an emergency situation, demonstrated that students and their teachers responded quite well to the technology and that the Bibliographic Instruction team itself gained from it efficiences in workload. For others, the reduced time spent face-to-face with students, eliciting questions and answers, as well as a lower profile in the classroom—as adjunct, actually, to educational technology—and apparent diminishment of their expertise were all viewed as definite new technology liabilities.

Perhaps of greatest concern to the staff is any rupture in the social fabric of their work environment, a threat they suspect library technology may well pose. This view gained currency and credibility during preliminary discussions about merging AUC Library's Acquisitions and Cataloging Departments, the logical response to the way the IBM Dobis/Libis applications software operates. Staff most immediately affected have offered at best tepid endorsement of the idea. Anxieties about changed job duties, workflow, and lines of report are the frequently cited reasons for their hesitation. Expressed too is fear about interrupting long-standing work partnerships—and friendships—if the two separate departments are united and reorganized. Preservation of community, of group integrity, of the family interaction that pervades staff relationships is an issue that is increasingly capturing the attention of staff with the advancement of computer-based technology in library operations. It cannot be ignored.

The emerging library technologies are, as indeed is so often said, a significant change force in the library environment. And because they can so radically alter the nature of library work and, therefore, the interrelationships of staff who perform it, acceptance by staff is crucial to successful technology transfer. The key to acceptance is correspondence between technology's technical demands and a library staff's need for personal and social fulfillment in the workplace.

Job satisfaction in the AUC Library rests so very much on interpersonal relations with colleagues, more so than on job duties and indeed for many on status and salary as well. No one wants robot-like staff as soulless as computing machines. At the same time individual and group routines must yield in a reasonable measure to machine routines, and staff must change, and unavoidably, feel the pain of change. As even libraries in the Developed World know, technological implementation inflicts trauma. This cannot be helped.

BEYOND THE CULTURAL BOUNDARIES

Changing technology is a fact of life for libraries in this last decade of the twentieth century. Scarcely a library anywhere in the world should expect to remain untouched much longer by the computer and telecommunications revolution or by the eventuality of universal information networking. That said, libraries should then dare to take a proactive stance on technology, to plan for it and to further its progress. This is far easier to say, of course, than to do. The technical, cognitive, managerial, and fiscal hurdles can be quite daunting. And so too the cultural, judging from the experience of the AUC Library.

The host culture that invigorates the American University in Cairo is the context within which the AUC Library carries out its mission. That host culture is both supportive and, as I have argued, constraining. Although I have discussed only the latter, I must emphasize here that AUC is completely in tune with its counterparts in the United States on the need to accommodate informatics in academe. It is, moreover, a pacesetter among institutions of higher learning in Egypt for its readiness to adopt high tech and to incorporate it into academic programs and support services. Egypt itself has for almost 200 years been the leader of the Arab World in hosting Western science and technology and, capital-poor though it may be, it is still "(a)mong the Arab states ... considered to be the most scientifically and technologically advanced."[37]

Nonetheless, my intent has been to demonstrate the presence of certain cultural phenomena inhibiting the transfer of information technologies to the AUC Library and to indicate that these must be circumvented if transfer is to succeed. These, described in the preceding pages, are an elitist concept of professionalism counterproductive to acquisition of technological knowledge and skills, an authoritarian behavior discouraging staff ownership of technology, an atomistic system of personnel placement and promotion disjoining reward from job skills enhancement, and a group consciousness polarizing sociability and machine methodism. My intent is also to suggest that variations of these are present in other library settings as well.

Culture manifests itself through people, and cultural impedance to technology and its transfer through human resistance. Cultural resistance to technological innovation is not amenable to simple remedy but, on the other hand, is not impervious to remediation. Shrewdly applied, prescription can ameliorate cultural constraints and generate behavior conducive to technology transfer. Cultural boundaries are not fixed, never to be redrawn or exceeded. They can be made pliable and even transcended.

In this spirit I offer a series of recommendations based upon the exigencies of technology transfer experienced by the AUC Library. Addressed most immediately to the Third World realities of the technologizing library, they are not, however, necessarily limited to Third World libraries. Admittedly idealistic, they nonetheless offer guidance to library change agents who must reconcile transfer technology to the cultural realities of their specific library settings.

1.0   Leadership Development:
    1.1   Computer literacy should become a requirement for all professionals on staff and a prerequisite for professional appointment. The computer literate professional will know what constitutes correct machine interaction, how to follow software applications, and how to evaluate new programs for functional effectiveness and task suitability.

1.2 Advancement to professional leadership responsibility should be preceded by a formal and directed library training program. Assuming the inaccessibility of an external center for training in librarianship, on-staff professionals will mentor preprofessionals and direct their program of study. Learning experiences will be both theoretical and practical and the modes of instruction both instructor-led and self-guided, but the focus will be on the science of librarianship. The program will incorporate benchmark testing and evaluation.

2.0 Management Development:

2.1 Appropriate authority should be allocated to each organizational level (e.g., unit, department, division, executive council, directorship) of the library. Authority assignments will be documented, included in all job and position descriptions, and published librarywide.

2.2 In-service managerial training should be instituted. The emphasis will be on the behaviors (flexibility, innovativeness, decisiveness, productivity) and skills (analytical, generalizing, decision-making) that constitute good management. Those with managerial responsibility, including subprofessionals, at all organizational levels will participate.

3.0 Organization Development:

3.1 All jobs should be individually described, grouped into positions sharing common knowledge/skills characteristics and authority levels, and arranged in a hierarchy of positions. Jobs and positions (i.e., job groupings) will have definite titles. Position titles will reflect their hierarchical order.

3.2 Grade promotion should be integrated into the total job/position structure of the library. It will be designed to reward the good performance of employees working continuously in the same job or at the same position level.

3.3 Appointment and promotion should be based strictly on merit. Evaluation of knowledge, behavior, skill will determine both initial job/position/grade assignment and subsequent mobility. Neither seniority nor personal influence will affect appointment and promotion.

4.0 Staff Development:

4.1 A merit system of annual bonus awards, monetary and symbolic, for computer skills enhancement should be established. High achievers in computer performance will serve as models for other staff. Rewarding them will help strengthen their resolve to withstand negative work group pressures.

4.2   In-service training in computer skills and operations should be provided. Ongoing computer training will increase familiarity with machine methods and promote the people-machine interface.

Librarians in the Developing World would provide a most useful service to colleagues everywhere if they would report with clarity and candor their experiences with the way imported technologies adapt culturally in specific local settings. Were these technologies modified or customized to accommodate certain cultural needs? What culturally-based phenomena, organizational or attitudinal, were themselves corrected to smooth the way for technology adoption? The collective answers would help advance a truly international and intercultural library technology.

NOTES

1.   *Webster's Ninth New Collegiate Dictionary,* Springfield, MA: Merriam-Webster, Inc., c1988, s.v. "information retrieval," "information science," "information theory."

2.   Constraints of time, language, consultant/recipient relationship, for example, are identified in two engineering technology transfer projects in Indonesia analyzed by Susan Scott-Stevens, *Foreign Consultants and Counterparts: Problems in Technology Transfer* (Boulder, CO: Westview Press, c1987), p. 106-120.

3.   *American University in Cairo 1992-1993 Catalog,* p. 16.

4.   *Ibid.,* p. 13.

5.   "Protocol Between the Government of the Arab Republic of Egypt (Ministry of Higher Education) and the American University in Cairo (Board of Trustees of the American University in Cairo, incorporated in Washington, D.C. in the United States of America) concerning the Status and Organization of the American University in Cairo," Articles 4 and 5. Original document in the AUC Archives of the AUC Library.

6.   "Minutes of the Faculty Meeting of December 19, 1990." Original in the AUC Archives of the AUC Library.

7.   "Protocol Between the Government of the Arab Republic...," (*op. cit.*), Article 5.

8.   Scott-Stevens, *op. cit.,* p. 154.

9.   Edward T. Hall, *Beyond Culture* (Garden City, NY: Anchor Press/Doubleday, 1976), p. 113.

10.   Sania Hamady, *Temperament and Character of the Arabs,* (New York, NY: Twayne Publishers, c1960), p. 71.

11.   *Ibid.,* p. 147. So too Raphael Patai, *The Arab Mind* (New York, NY: Charles Scribner's Sons, c1973), p. 114-115: "In the Middle Eastern ethic, from pre-biblical times down to the present, the ideal has always been to escape the curse of work.... This ethic considers all work a curse, but expecially work that makes you sweat."

12.   Ziauddin Sardar, *Information and the Muslim World, A Strategy for the Twenty-First Century* (London, U.K.: Mansell Publishing Limited, 1988), p. 91.

13.   Derek Hopwood, *Egypt: Politics and Society 1945-1984,* 2nd ed. (Boston, MA: Allen & Unwin, 1985), p. 139.

14.   Judith Cochran, *Education in Egypt* London, U.K.: Croom Helm, c1986), p. 64-65.

15.   As stated in the AUC handbook *Personnel Policies and Procedures for Teaching, Research and Library Faculty and Related Staff,* Section II. "Appointment of New Faculty," p. 3: "New

Egyptian faculty members are normally appointed only on secondment from national universities or other institutions, initially for one or two years." What is involved is temporary detail to AUC from regular duties at another institution.

16. Monte Palmer, Ali Leila, El Sayed Yassin, *The Egyptian Bureaucracy* (Syracuse, NY: Syracuse University Press, 1988), pp. 78, 81. Similarly, although in the manner of a cri de coeur, has the celebrated contemporary Egyptian playwright, Alfred Farag, complained in his essay "Put the boot on another foot," *Al-Ahram Weekly* (Cairo: Egypt, Thursday, October 1991), p. 5: "If ever asked to explain the causes for the crises we face in our economy, public-sector industries, education, culture and sports, I would have to answer that the source of all problems lies in the authoritarian nature of the relationship between the boss and his subordinates, the manager and employees, and so on down the ladder and that whoever is caught red-handed contradicting his boss is given the boot in no time flat."

17. For example, Hamady, *op. cit.,* pp. 103-127.

18. Patai, *op. cit.,* pp. 77-78. In *Neopatriarchy, A Theory of Distorted Change in Arab Society* (New York, NY: Oxford University Press, 1988) Hisham Sharabi expatiates on the 200-year modernization process at work in the Arab World which has produced not modern society but rather modernized patriarchal or "neopatriarchal" society. At its center is the "Arab neopatriarchal family" and "this family continues to nurture the values and attitudes of heteronomy" (p. 45).

19. Nazih N.M. Ayubi, *Bureaucracy & Politics in Contemporary Egypt* (London: Ithaca Press, 1980), p. 126.

20. Palmer, *op. cit.,* pp. 80-81.

21. Naguib Mahfouz, *Respected Sir,* trans. by Dr. Rasheed El-Eneny (Cairo: Egypt: AUC Press, 1988), p. 4.

22. Hamady, *op. cit.,* p. 209.

23. Abdel Aziz El-Koussy, "The Need for Change," *The Specialised National Councils Magazine* (Cairo, Egypt: Presidency of the Republic A. R. Egypt, 1977), p. 43. This attitude prevails no less in 1991 than in 1977.

24. Khalid Sherif, "Reforming Law 48: Another Step Toward State Enterprise Reform," *Middle East Times/Egypt,* Vol. IX, No. 18 (30 April - 6 May 1991), p. 6. El-Khoussy, *op. cit.,* p. 51, likewise refers to "certificates which are evaluated on almost a commercial price base...."

25. AUC's *Employee Handbook,* Section 3: Performance Appraisal, p. 8.

26. *Personnel Policies and Procedures...* (*op. cit.*), Subsection A. "Guiding Criteria" of Section II. "Appointment of New Faculty," p. 5-6.

27. *Ibid.,* Supplement on Compensation and Allowance Scales.

28. "New Position Titles & Structure for Library Personnel." Memorandum from the Director of the AUC Personnel and Legal Affairs Office, dated June 20, 1984. Original document in the AUC Archives of the AUC Library.

29. *Ibid.*

30. *Ibid.*

31. Edward Lane, *Manners and Customs of the Modern Egyptians* (retitled from the original *An Account of the Manners and Customs of the Modern Egyptians*) (London: J.M. Dent, 1954), p. 211.

32. Nehad Selaiha, "All the World's a Stage!" *Al-Ahram Weekly* (Cairo, Egypt: Thursday, 8 August 1991), p. 8.

33. Hamady, *op. cit.,* p. 88-89.

34. See, for example, Patai, *op. cit.,* pp. 280-283.

35. *Ibid.,* p. 284.

36. Palmer, *op. cit.,* p. 140.

37. Ziauddin Sardar, *Science and Technology in the Middle East, A Guide to Issues, Organizations and Institutions* (London, U.K.: Longman, 1982), p. 129.

VOLUNTEERS IN LIBRARIES:
AN UPDATE

Rashelle S. Karp

INTRODUCTION

Over 38 million people in the United States do some type of volunteer work on a regular basis ("38 Million ..." 1990). If one includes children and people doing nontraditional volunter work (e.g., helping neighbors or relatives, volunteering in a family business), this number jumps to a staggering 92 million ("1983 Gallup ...", 1984), or about half of the total U.S. population (Nightingale, 1989), representing a total value in terms of staff time of over $65.5 billion ("Dollar Value ...", 1982). In just one small public library (Lewin, 1987), the value of volunteer service (using a minimum wage figure of $3.55/ hour) was computed to be in excess of $54,457 for one year (169 volunteers who worked 16,226 hours). Other literature cites the savings realizing by institutions that employ volunteers (Luloff, 1984). In 1986 the library literature on volunteerism, 1909-1985, was reviewed for this series (Karp, 1986). Nearly seven years later, the amount of library literature produced annually that deals with volunteerism has not increased, but, to the extent that the professional literature reflects practice, librarians' acceptance of volunteers has. Volunteers,

Advances in Library Administration and Organization,
Volume 11, pages 97-114.
Copyright © 1993 by JAI Press Inc.
All rights of reproduction in any form reserved.
ISBN: 1-55938-596-0

or individuals who freely contribute their services, without financial compensation, to public or voluntary organizations (National Association of Social Workers, 1977, p. 1582; Barker, 1987, p. 173), seem to have become the norm rather than the exception in libraries. And, perhaps more importantly, objections previously raised seem to have metamorphosed into realized opportunities, creative solutions, and a growing consensus regarding the appropriateness and appropriate use of volunteers.

THE LITERATURE OF CONFLICTS

In 1986 this writer identified 10 major conflicts around which debates about the use of volunteers in libraries revolved. They are summarized following.

Conflict 1: Value of Services. The old adage that people only value what they pay for (Levine, 1980) is at the root of debates in this area. It is claimed that the use of unpaid staff in libraries results in lowered esteem (Corbett, 1941; Farrington, 1943; Tabor, 1940; Schumacher, 1943) and public perceptions that librarianship is not a profession (Anderson, 1983).

Conflict 2: Public Support. It has been indicated in the literature that the use of volunteers may result in decreased human resource support and a lowering of the library's financial base (Flanagan, 1976; Dolnick, 1987).

Conflict 3: Obligations. There is a perception among some professionals that the use of volunteers represents an administrator's abrogation of his/her obligation not to overcommit library professionals. The use of volunteers is sometimes viewed as overcommitment because training and supervision are very time consuming (Cribben, 1974; Kies, 1976; Savage, 1976; Cooper, 1983), and because when volunteers leave, the work they had been doing is overwhelming to a professional with an already filled schedule (Levine, 1980).

Conflict 4: Cost Effectiveness. It is persuasively argued by some that the training and supervision of volunteers far outweighs the good that they do. Although this has been refuted, both on an intuitive level ("Volunteers... 1942; Greer, 1974) and via statistics (Lewin, 1988; Longeway, 1979), many still see this as an issue.

Conflict 5: Staff Morale. The cost of training and supervising a volunteer can lead to a situation most practically described as "protecting one's investment" (Trainer, 1976), or giving volunteers choice assignments which will keep them interested enough to stay, while relegating paid staff to more tedious and mundane jobs. Obviously, staff morale suffers when this happens.

Conflict 6: Exploitiveness.   Although men and women volunteer in about the same proportions (19 percent and 22 percent respectively), a greater proportion of women with part time jobs volunteers (29.9 percent of the women vs. 18 percent of the men) and a greater proportion of college educated women volunteers (41.4 percent of the women vs. 36 percent of the men). This, along with statistics indicating that men volunteer largely for civic or political organizations (perceived by the public as activism) while women volunteer in schools or other educational institutions which are perceived by many as social service but not activism (Kaminer, 1984; "38 Million...", 1990), leads some to charge that volunteerism exploits women (Nyren, 1981; Bolger, 1975).

Conflict 7: Obedience to the Unenforceable.   Since the nature of volunteerism precludes monetary incentive, and thus any "real" control over volunteer workers, it is sometimes claimed that they are likely to be unreliable, unmanageable, and more likely to quit if not totally satisfied with their assignments (Tucker, 1973; Pearce, 1983; "Volunteer Use...", 1982; Park, 1989).

Conflict 8: Professionalism.   The argument that volunteers "deprofession-alize" the field is convincingly made in the literature (Anderson et al., 1983; Farrington, 1943; "Volunteers...", 1942; Carvalho, 1984), and the need to limit volunteer responsibilities to nonprofessional tasks is broadly propounded (Carvalho, 1984; Gale, 1976; Schumacher, 1943). A question echoed by many is: Do volunteers know what they are doing and should they be doing it (Flanagan, 1976). Also within this category are concerns from professionals about the ethics of using volunteers (Netting, 1987) and particularly for libraries, whether confidentiality (Masek, 1984; Byrne and Caskey, 1985) is compromised when volunteers are privy to the internal records of an institution.

Conflict 9: Job Security.   Fears that volunteers will replace or supplant paid professionals (Dolnick, 1987; Gale, 1976; Stephan, 1976; Trainer, 1976), along with uneasiness about volunteers' effects on the salary levels of paid professionals (Library Association, 1982) are often at the root of objections to their use in libraries.

Conflict 10: Essential vs. Nonessential Tasks.   In an attempt to solve questions about professionalism and salaries, some propound the division of library tasks into essential jobs that should only be filled by paid professionals and nonessential jobs that can be filled by volunteers. This type of logic is seen by others as dangerous to library survival since nonessential services are likely to be cut entirely from already over-taxed institutions (Karp, 1986).

THE LITERATURE OF USE

The literature of conflicts is compelling and must be reckoned with. It is, however, interesting to note that for the most part, literature dealing with volunteerism in libraries since the middle 1980s focuses not on conflicts but on creative solutions. The incidence and varied use of volunteers reflected in the library literature since the middle 1980s seems to indicate that, at least in practice, librarians *have* resolved many of the conflicts. A tremendously varied picture of what volunteers do in libraries emerges from the literature; a partial list of their activities includes:

1. Document preparation, including sorting, shelving, mending, and filing (Strickland, 1989; Behrman, 1987);
2. Fixing library equipment (Dalrymple, 1990);
3. Recording books for the blind ("Ceremony...", 1990; Keltner, 1989; Pfeifer, 1968);
4. Architectural design and facilities preparation (Brown, 1985; Seguin and Jarlsberg, 1976);
5. English as a Second Language (ESL) training (Hill, 1988);
6. Summer reading program help (Eisenhut, 1988);
7. Outreach services (LeClair-Marzolf, 1981) including reading to nursing home residents ("Need for Volunteers...", 1974; Watson, 1987);
8. Information and Referral Services (Levinson, 1988);
9. Grant writing ("Clayton...", 1988);
10. Fundraising (Haeuser, 1986) through activities such as auctions (Bryant, 1989), friends of the library activities and membership drives (Kochoff, 1989; Clark, 1990), booksales (Brawner, 1985; Rutledge, 1985), and mystery parties (Cooper, 1989);
11. Storytelling (Holden, 1987; Petgen, 1966; Inglewood California Public Library, 1975; Blair, 1982);
12. Writing overdue notices ("Computer...", 1986);
13. Adult literacy programming ("Volunteers...", 1976; "Forming...", 1985; "Illinois...", 1987);
14. Booktalking (Overmyer, 1987);
15. Children's programming (Genson, 1975; Schuckett, 1985);
16. Public relations (Logan, 1947; "Volunteers...", 1977; "Hayden...", 1982; "Such..." 1980);
17. Preservation of library materials after a flood or fire (Gaughan, 1989);
18. Genealogy ("Genealogical...", 1978; "LSCA...", 1982);
19. Oral history (Taylor, 1975);
20. Circulation control ("Proposition 13...", 1979; "Libraries of...", 1975);
21. Library orientation tours ("Docents at...", 1983)
22. Special collections development (Parsons, 1943);

23. Tutoring ("METRO...", 1976);
24. Running the entire library (Sannwald and Hofmann, 1980); Detweiler, 1982; Burson, 1986);
25. Reading aloud (Munson-Benson, 1988; Smith, 1990); and
26. Staffing the reference desk (Souza, 1989).

The benefits derived from such varied and increasing uses of volunteers in libraries include (1) volunteers' many ties to the community which result in greater public relations and greater financial commitment from the community (Deckoff, 1983; Gray, 1982; Trainer, 1976; Tucker, 1973; Wells and Ihrig, 1988); (2) volunteers' ability to lobby for libraries (Levine, 1980; "Edmonton...", 1983); (3) the exposure that the library receives because of the many services it can provide when volunteers help out; (4) the personal benefits to volunteers that library work provides (O'Neill, 1983; Howarth, 1965; Jenner, 1982; "Volunteers in Libraries...", 1982; Lucas, 1980); (5) the fact that the introduction of a new service via volunteer staffing often turns into a permanent paid staff position (Gale, 1976; Stephan, 1976; Detweiler, 1982; Warner, 1977); (6) the additional hours that volunteers allow libraries to remain open (Casey, 1984), and in some cases stay open at all (Chugh, 1980; and (7) potential recruitment into the profession. It is especially interesting to note that the library literature since the middle 1980s neither extols nor derides the virtues of volunteers, but for the most part, focuses on methods for managing volunteers.

THE LITERATURE OF SOLUTIONS

The key to effective use of volunteers is effective management. The "Guidelines for Using Volunteers in Libraries" adopted by the American Library Association (ALA) in 1981 lists 17 broad principles upon which the use of volunteers should be based. In summarized form they include: preplanning; application of sound administration; clarification of volunteers' status in terms of library liability for injuries and for work-related expenses; consideration of volunteers as temporary measures pending employment of staff; formal recognition mechanisms; appropriate placement of volunteers in specific jobs and according to specific schedules; codified job descriptions for each volunteer position; programs of training and evaluation for volunteers; hiring of a volunteer coordinator; and establishment of a backup system in the absence of regularly scheduled volunteers (ALA, 1971).

The ALA "Guidelines" provide broad statements, most of which, with the exception of the prohibition against using volunteers as a permanent measure, are still followed today. The literature provides more specific suggestions. They are described below.

Preplanning

Before any volunteer program can be initiated, the concept and practice must be approved by the library staff, in writing ("Volunteer Projects...", 1979) by the library's administrative and funding bodies (Gray, 1982), and by any collective bargaining agencies that operate for library employees (Skory, 1989). It is especially important that collective bargaining agencies be involved from the very beginning of discussions about volunteers since they are legally and ethically bound to protect the jobs and welfare of paid employees. For example, the Domestic Volunteer Service Act of 1973 (PL 93-113) has been interpreted, at least for ACTION volunteers, to mandate that "volunteers may not perform any services or engage in any duties which would otherwise be performed by an employed worker as part of his assigned duties, [or which would result in] the displacement of employed workers" (45 CFR Sec 1216.1-1). No volunteer program can succeed unless all groups associated with library operations are committed to it.

The process of preplanning (Bennett, 1984) also involves prioritizing the needs of the library and then determining if volunteers can be helpful within the institution's formal structure and overall planning (Tedrick, 1984). It may be that volunteers are only feasible in certain areas of a library's planned efforts to achieve its mission and objectives; it may be that volunteers are appropriate in all areas. The important issue is to reach consensus and overall commitment to a volunteer program (Snider, 1985); top down mandates to use volunteers will not work and grass roots decisions without the commitment of management and labor unions will be equally unsuccessful.

Planning

Background Knowledge. After a consensus has been reached and a clear commitment from library staff, library administrators, and labor unions has been received, the planning of specific services can begin. Information necessary for adequate planning starts with a general knowledge of why people volunteer. This is because the longevity of a volunteer depends, in part, on how well the original motivations for volunteering are satisfied (Morrow-Howell, 1989), and on how well a program of recruitment matches a volunteer's motivations to the job to be done (Sergent and Sedlacek, 1989; Murk and Stephan, 1990). Additionally, a person's motivations for volunteering relate directly to the impact on the organization (Jenner, 1981). The literature of social work (Stanton, 1970; Morrow-Howell, 1989), education (Reichlin, 1982) and psychology (Pearce, 1983) identifies various types of volunteers who are characterized by their motivations for volunteering. A typology (Dodson, 1980) might include:

1. Altruistic or Others-Oriented Volunteers. These volunteers are primarily devoted to doing things for others (Henderson, 1981; Kratcoski, 1989).
2. Issue- or Cause-Oriented Volunteers (Murk and Stephan, 1990). People in this category are concerned with specific public issues and with effecting change (Luloff, 1983; Whaley, 1984; Luloff, 1984).
3. Self-Expressive Volunteers. Here, the volunteer is primarily interested in enjoyment of activities for his or her own self-expression and realization (Rubin and Thorelli, 1984; Williams, 1986), for the feelings of affiliation that volunteering affords (Balenger, et al., 1989), and for the social interactions within a work environment (Ozawa and Morrow-Howell, 1986).
4. Self-Interest or Occupational/Economics Volunteers. Sometimes referred to as career volunteers, these individuals are primarily interested in furthering their occupational or economic goals through experience gained and contacts made while they volunteer (Parker, 1988; Reichlin, 1982; Jenner, 1982; Green, 1984; Altman and Sedlacek, 1990).
5. Philanthropic Volunteers. This type of volunteer is primarily concerned with raising funds (Weinberg, 1990).
6. Pattern Volunteers. Although not often discussed in the literature, some people volunteer merely because volunteering has been a part of their lives since infancy as they have watched role models who volunteered (Fitch, 1987).

Budgeting. All costs (both direct and indirect) must be considered before instituting a volunteer program. Although volunteers are unpaid, they not a free source of help. There will be substantial costs involved in the recruitment, training, supervision and recognition of volunteers. Also, if the volunteer program is to be a sizeable one, it may be necessary to hire a paid volunteer coordinator.

Knowing the Law. Before instituting a volunteer program, librarians must become aware of their legal responsibilities toward volunteers ("Legal Status...", 1979) and their liability for volunteers. Liability basically comprises three areas: injury caused by a volunteer, injury to a volunteer, and a volunteer's right to maintain her/his job (Tedrick, 1989). Although a small percentage of volunteers have actually filed lawsuits against a parent institution, librarians must take the measures necessary to deal with a lawsuit situation, or better, to prevent such situations. One example of legislation in which the institution is clearly responsible for injury can be found in the laws of some states, which have interpreted their Workers Compensation Acts so as to allow certain volunteer worker compensation benefits. The Pennsylvania Workers Compensation Act (PWCA), for example, defines "employee" as "All natural persons who perform services for another for a valuable consideration" Penn. Stat. Ann. Tit. 77, Sec. 22 (Purdon Supp., 1982). Section 1031 of the Act, as interpreted by the Pennsylvania courts, recognizes that "certain classes of volunteers who [perform] public services merit compensation under the PWCA for injuries received while carrying out their Good Samaritan activities." *Guffey v. Logan,* 563 F. Supp. 951, 957 (D. Penn., 1983). Locating and understanding the impact of certain legislation upon a volunteer program may require the services of an attorney.

Recruiting

Job Descriptions. After identifying areas in which volunteers will be most valuable, job descriptions must be written (Taylor, 1986) for each volunteer position or, if desirable, for each job that a volunteer will be doing. Especially in libraries which use high-risk volunteers—for example, people who have been sent by the court to do community service as part of their sentence (Childress, 1989)—or other "special" (Behrman, 1987) volunteers (e.g., developmentally or physically disabled individuals), job-specific descriptions might be preferable. Job descriptions for volunteers should be prepared with at least the same amount of care used to prepare descriptions for the recruitment of paid staff. Librarians must be cognizant that the pool of applicants for volunteer jobs will be local. This necessitates more detailed lists of objective criteria for screening to eliminate personal biases and hopefully reduce the number of local people whose "feathers are ruffled" at not being selected for a particular job. Potentially good public relations that can be generated by volunteers can quickly turn into monstrously bad publicity by unjustifiably rejected volunteer applicants.

Advertising. A carefully developed advertising plan which properly reflects the library's professional image should be implemented. Advertisements should include job specifications and minimum qualifications. Again, the same care that would be taken to advertise paid positions should be taken to advertise volunteer positions.

Interviewing. It is critical that volunteers be interviewed and thoroughly screened before being hired. Librarians should not accept everyone who applies (Whipple, 1982). Only one out of many applicants is hired for a paid position; the same should hold true for volunteer positions. The interview process is two-way; potential volunteers should be encouraged to ask questions which will help clarify whether or not they really want the job, and interviewers should ask enough well designed questions to ascertain which position or tasks are most suitable for each volunteer ("Recognize Volunteers", 1987). It has also been suggested that potential volunteers whose motivations are primarily egoistic should be weeded out during the interview process (Rubin and Thorelli, 1984).

Orienting

The interview has already begun the process of orientation, because it included a thorough description of the job. A formal process of orientation which is separate from volunteers' formal training, is necessary to make new volunteers fell welcome ("Volunteerism", 1980) and to facilitate the process of social interaction, often cited as a major motivation and reward for volunteers (McClam, 1985). An appropriate orientation will include introductions to all of the staff, a thorough tour of the facilities, an overview of the library's operations, and, most importantly, a clear explanation of the volunteer's valuable role within the library. It cannot be emphasized enough that all volunteers must have a clear understanding of why their jobs are important, how their work feeds into other's work, and how what they do contributes to the overall operations of the library. A sincere attempt to orient volunteers helps immeasurably to integrate them with staff ("Success...", 1985).

Training and Supervising

The literature of training is linked to supervision since adequate training involves a constant contact person to answer volunteer's questions as they come up (Hoagland, 1984) and involving volunteers in their supervisors' decision-making (Adams, 1988). Some practitioners advocate a manual for volunteers (Gallo, 1985) and others believe that extended training programs are necessary (Weinschenk, 1986). The types of training run the gamut from correspondence courses (Hannaford, 1984) that teach volunteers how to run a library to minute controls over volunteers that include daily and weekly assignment slips (Burson, 1986). Regardless of the methods used, the literature agrees that (1) a volunteer must know his/her supervisor and must have already access to that person; (2) duties must be patiently and clearly demonstrated (Hoagland, 1981); (3) volunteers' roles must be well delineated (Zischka and Jones, 1987); (4) volunteers should be included in some staff meetings so that they are up to date on institutional changes (Vafa, 1980); and (5) volunteers should be encouraged to participate socially and professionally within the library's working group.

Evaluating

Volunteers must be evaluated on a set schedule and using a preapproved rating scale. It is also important that volunteers be involved in planning how they will be evaluated (Obrokta, 1989). Evaluations should be kept in a personnel folder so that they can later be used to provide job references (*Documenting Volunteer Experience,* 1986), as reminders to recognize special achievements, and (if necessary) as documentation for dismissal. Librarians must be prepared to dismiss volunteers if they do not perform up to preset standards. The point to be remembered is that if they are hired, they can be fired. However, the purpose of evaluation is not to provide grounds for dismissal, it is to provide volunteers with a sense of value and a sense that their jobs are critical to the library.

Recognizing

The volunteer's "paycheck" is recognition. Formal appreciation of a volunteer's work is essential to their retention (Kendall and Kenkel, 1989) and may be accomplished in many ways, limited only by the creativity of the supervisor. However, it is equally important to "keep the contributions of both volunteers and paid staff in perspective. [Agencies] make great efforts to recognize and honor volunteers who are performing essentially the same service as paid employees who receive little or no special recognition. Such contradictory reward systems can sabotage effective volunteer service if a antagonism develops between paid staff members and volunteers" (Lucas, 1980). Some librarians balance recognition of volunteers by setting a minimum number of hours of service that must be met before any formal recognition is received ("Volunteers...," 1986); others advertize volunteer successes in newspaper articles (Brownlee and Ney, 1988). Additional ways in which volunteers can be recognized include granting of privileges (i.e., use of the library photocopy machine at a reduced rate, extended loan periods for books, use of the library lounge), annual recognition dinners, and, most importantly, positive feedback on jobs well done.

CONCLUSIONS

In 1986, the writer indicated that there was a need for the profession to produce a definitive manual on the use of volunteers. Also indicated was a need for national and state leaders to upgrade standards for providing library service to include a recognized role for volunteers (Jenkins, 1982). Finally it was indicated that library schools should conduct workshops and include coursework in their curricula on the use of volunteers in libraries. Although the literature indicates greater acceptance of volunteers from a practitioner's standpoint, formal acknowledgement of their role in libraries has not yet been achieved. A thorough search of the literature on volunteers reveals manuals only in areas where a program primarily comprises volunteers—for example, the Peace Corps, (Vittitow and Elster, 1985), the Volunteer Support

Management Program (*Volunteer Support Management Program,* 1984), Job Training Partnership Act activities (Nightingale, 1989), or social service agencies—literature which identifies the need for such training tools (Wilson, 1984), and models for certain aspects of volunteer programs (Boyles, 1987; Gerhard, 1988) or for specific volunteer programs—most notably in the field of adult education (Borden, 1984; Freireich, 1984; Miller, 1983) and school libraries (*Adult Volunteers,* 1982; Gray, 1984). The only manual found for library volunteer programs was the excellent *Volunteers in Network Libraries* (1986), which describes the management and procedures of the exemplary volunteer programs in the National Library Service for the Blind Network libraries. The 1971 ALA guidelines on the use of volunteers have not been updated. A course by course examination of catalogs from all of the accredited library schools in the United States reveals that no formal coursework devoted to the use of volunteers exists. And, there is still a "nationwide need to increase the status...of voluntarism..." (Ray, 1982). Given the current widespread use of volunteers in libraries, the lack of formal acknowledgment in the literature and coursework designed to help librarians recognize and appropriately utilize them is unfortunate.

As before, it is strongly recommended that librarians publicly accept and recognize the value of volunteerism at all times, and not just during times of budget crisis (Fredenburg, 1989). Such public acclamation can only help as it codifies the process and places volunteers in an appropriate and well deserved position of high regard.

REFERENCES

Adams, C. H., et al. "Communication and Motivation within the Superior-subordinate Dyad: Testing the Conventional Wisdom of Volunteer Management." *Journal of Applied Communication Research, 16* (Fall, 1988), pp. 69-81.

Adult Volunteers. A Handbook for Teacher-Librarians in the Vancouver School Board to Provide Assistance to Teacher-Librarians Who Are Establishing Adult Volunteer Programs, [and] *to Suggest Ideas for Teacher-Librarians Who Wish to Enlarge or Enhance Their Volunteer Programs.* British Columbia: Vancouver School Board, 1982.

Altman, J. H., & Sedlacek, W. E. *Differences in Volunteer Interest by Level of Career Orientation. Research Report N5-90.* College Park, MD: Counseling Center, University of Maryland, 1990.

American Library Association, Library Administration Division. "Guidelines for Using Volunteers in the Future of Libraries." *American Libraries, 2,* (April, 1971), pp. 407-408.

Anderson, A. J. (1983, May 1). "Why Not Volunteers?" [Solving the Problem of Staff Reduction.] *Library Journal, 108,* (May 1, 1983), p. 883.

Balenger, V. J., et al. *Volunteer Activities and Their Relationship to Motivational Needs: A Study of the Stamp Union Program Research Report 18-89.* College Park, MD: Counseling Center, University of Maryland, 1989.

Barker, R. L. *The Social Work Dictionary.* Silver Spring, MD: National Association of Social Workers, 1987.

Bennett, L. L. *Volunteers in the School Media Center.* Libraries Unlimited, 1984.

Behrman, S. "Autistic Teen Takes to Library Work: NYPL Center Teaches Marketable Skill in School-Sponsored Project." *American Libraries, 18,* (May, 1987), p. 375.

Blair, I. L. "Medford Storytelling Guild: Or Volunteers, Unlimited.' *Emergency Librarian, 10,* (Nov./Dec. 1982) pp. 19-20.

Bolger, E. "Volunteerism, Take It Out of My Salary." *MS.,* (Feb. 1985), pp. 71-74.

Borden, J. *Volunteerism in Adult Education. A Guide Book for Increasing the Scope and Quality of Volunteer Programs in Adult Education.* Phoenix, AZ: Phoenix Union High School District, 1984.

Boyles, A. *DYS Volunteer Services Manual.* Raleigh, NC: North Carolina State Department of Human Resources, Division of Youth Services, 1987.

Brawner, L.B. and Clark, E. "Anatomy of a Library's Experience with Four Book Sales.' *Public Library Quarterly, 6,* (Fall, 1985), 9-24.

Brown, C. "Developing Houston's Alief Branch, with a Little Help from Our Friends." *Texas Libraries, 46,* (Fall, 1985), pp. 66-68.

Brownlee, E. U., & Ney, N. J. "Alice B. Toklas and the Liberries: Building a successful Friends group." *Library Journal, 113,* (Feb. 1, 1988), pp. 41-43.

Bryant, D.C. "Fun Auction." *Unabashed Librarian,* no. 73, 3, 1989.

Burson, L. E. *Recruiting and Training Volunteers for Church and Synagogue Libraries. CSLA Guide no. 14.* Bryn Mawr, PA: Church & Synagogue Library Association.

Byrne, R. and Caskey, R. "For Love or Money? What Motivates Volunteers?" *Journal of Extension, 23,* (Fall, 1985), pp. 4-7.

Carvalho, J. "To Complement or Compete? The Role of Volunteers in Public Libraries." *Public Library Quarterly, 5,* (Spring, 1984) pp. 35-39.

Casey, D.W. "Volunteers—How They Serve in Public Libraries." *CLIC Quarterly, 3,* (Dec. 1984), pp. 26-27.

"Ceremony Inaugurates New DBPH Recording Booth." *Texas Libraries, 51,* (Spring, 1990), p. 10.

Childress, C. P. "The Community Service Volunteer: Boon or Bane?" *Library Journal, 114,* (Feb. 15, 1989), pp. 137-138.

Chugh, R. L. *Voluntary Contribution of Service: A Priceless Resource for the Potsdam Community.* Potsdam, NY: State University of New York, 1980.

Clark, C. K. "Getting Started with Annual Funds in Academic Libraries." *Journal of Library Administration, 12,* (1990) pp. 73-87.

"Clayton Library Friends Group Receives Grant." *Texas Libraries, 49,* (Summer, 1988), p. 53.

"Computer Replaces Volunteers." *Library Journal, 111,* (Oct. 15, 1986), p. 22.

Cooper, G. "Mystery Party Raises $1000." *Unabashed Librarian,* no. 72, (1989), p. 5.

Cooper, G. "Plan for Reductions." *Library Journal, 108,* (May, 1983) 884.

Corbett, E. V. "The Layman Looks at Librarianship." *Library World, 44,* (Oct. 1941) pp. 43-45.

Cribben, Sister M. M. "Browsing: Library Volunteers' Projects." *Catholic Library World, 46* (Nov. 1974), p. 181.

Dalrymple, H. "NLS Thanks Telephone Pioneers for 30 Years' Service." *Library of Congress Information Bulletin, 49,* (Dec. 17, 1990) p. 435.

Deckoff, M. J. (1983, October). "The Volunteer: Key to Successful Fund Raising." *Independent School, 43, ,* (Oct. 1983) pp. 34-38.

Detweiler, M. J. "Volunteers in Public Libraries: The Costs and Benefits." *Public Libraries, 21,* (Fall, 1982) p. 5.

Detweiler, M. J. "Volunteers Are One Option." *Library Journal, 108,* (May 1, 1983) pp. 883-884.

"Docents at Los Angeles Public: An Elite Volunteer Corps." *Library Journal, 108,* (Oct. 15, 1983) p. 1917.

Documenting Volunteer Experience. Volunteer for Minnesota: A Project for Developing Public Private Partnerships in Communities. St. Paul, MN: Minnesota Office on Volunteer Services, Department of Administration, 1986.

Dodson, K. (1980, July). "Help! The Answer Can Be Volunteers." *Idaho Librarian, 32,* (July, 1980) pp. 112-115.

Dolnick, S., (Ed.). (1987, March). "Friends of Libraries." *Library Association Board, 89,* (March, 1987) p. 139.

Dolnick, S., (Ed.). *Friends of Libraries Sourcebook,* 2nd ed. Chicago: American Library Association, 1990.

"Edmonton Lauds Its Volunteers at Tenth Year Birthday Party." *Library Journal, 108,* (Oct. 1, 1983) p. 1834.

Eisenhut, L. "Teen Volunteers." *Voice of Youth Advocate, 11,* (June, 1988) pp. 65-67.

Farrington, A. "Hospital Library Volunteers," no. *ALA Bulletin, 37,* (Sept., 1943) pp. 261-263.

Fitch, R. T. "Characteristics and Motivations of College Students Volunteering for Community Service." *Journal of College Student Personnel, 28,* (Sept., 1987) pp. 424-431.

Flanagan, A. "Some Thoughts on Survival in the Seventies: or Two Views of the Volunteer Dilemma." *Catholic Library World, 48,* (Oct. 1976) pp. 112-115.

"Forming a Volunteer Literacy Program." *Illinois Libraries, 67,* (Sept. 1985) pp. 584-586.

Fredenburg, A. M. *Keeping the Special Library-Volunteer Initiative Going.* Paper presented at the Annual Conference of the Special Libraries Association (80th, New York, NY June 10-15, 1989).

Freireich, S. *Handbook for Volunteer Coordinators/Trainers.* Boston, MA: International Institute of Boston, 1984.

Gale, S. R. "Volunteers and Patient's Libraries." *Catholic Library World, 48,* (Oct. 1976) pp. 116-118.

Gallo, P. "A Manual for Pages—One Library's Experience." *Ohio Library Association Bulletin, 55,* (Oct. 1985) pp. 19-21.

Gaughan, T. M. "CBS Evening News Lauds LAPL Volunteers." *American Libraries, 20,* (April, 1989) pp. 282-283.

Genson, T.J. "Use of Volunteers in Michigan Public Libraries." *Michigan Librarian, 41,* (Summer, 1975) p. 18.

Gerhard, G. W. *MVP: A Volunteer Development & Recognition Model.* Paper presented at the Annual Meeting of the American Association for Adult and Continuing Education (Tulsa, OK, November 1988).

Gray, S. T. "Working with Volunteers." *Voc Ed, 57,* (June, 1982) pp. 49-51.

Gray, S.T. *Managing School Volunteers-Eight Keys to Success.* Paper presented at the International Conference for Parent/Citizen Involvement in Schools (Salt Lake City, UT, July 1982).

Gray, S. T. "Increase Productivity with Volunteers." *School Business Affairs, 50,* (Feb. 1984) p. 36.

Green, S.K. *Volunteer Motivation and Its Relationship to Satisfaction and Future Volunteering.* Toronto: American Psychological Association, 1984.

Greer, E. "Volunteers in the Chapel Hill Public Library." *North Carolina Libraries, 32,* (Spring, 1974) pp. 25-27.

Haeuser, M. (1986, May). "What Friends Are for: Gaining Financial Independence." *Wilson Library Bulletin, 60,* (May, 1986) pp. 25-27.

Hannaford, C. "The Church Librarian: An Essential Volunteer." *Catholic Library World, 56,* (Dec., 1984) pp. 217-222.

"Hayden, Colorado Survey Finds People Love Their Library." *Library Journal, 107,* (Nov. 15, 1982) pp. 430-431.

Henderson, J. A. "Motivations and Perceptions of Volunteerism as a Leisure Activity." *Journal of Leisure Research, 13,* (1981) pp. 208-218.

Henderson, K. A. "Women as Volunteers." *The Humanist, 44,* (July/Aug., 1984) pp. 26-27+.

Hill, J. "Salute to a Public Library Volunteer." *Public Libraries, 27* (Winter, 1988) 0. 176.

Hoagland, Sister M.A. "Library Skills—Caught or Taught!" [Instruction to Volunteers]. *Catholic Library World, 53,* (Nov. 1981) pp. 173-175.

Hoagland, Sister M. A. (1984, December). "Training and Gaining School Library Volunteers." *Catholic Library World, 56, 1* (Dec. 1984) pp. 213-216.

Holden, S. and Albano, C. "Do You Have a Knack for Storytelling?" *School Library Journal, 34,* (1987) p. 50.

Howarth, E. "Personality Characteristics of Volunteers." *Psychological Reports, 38,* (1976) pp. 855-858.

"The Illinois Adult Literacy/Volunteer Initiative 1984-1986: Chronology of Events." *Illinois Libraries, 69,* (June, 1987) pp. 395-399.

Jenkins, H. "Volunteers in the Future of Libraries." *Library Journal, 97,* (April 15, 1972) pp. 1399-1403.

Jenner, J. R. "Participation, Leadership, and the Role of Volunteerism among Selected Women Volunteers." *Journal of Voluntary Action Research, 11,* (Oct.-Dec. 1982) pp. 27-38.

Jenner, J. R. "Volunteerism as an Aspect of Women's Work Lives." *Journal of Vocational Behavior, 19,* (Dec. 1981) 00. 302-314.

Kaminer, W. *Women Volunteering: The Pleasure, Pain, and Politics of Unpaid Work from 1830 to the Present.* Garden City, NY: Anchor Press, 1984.

Karp, R. S. "Volunteers in Libraries." In Gerard B. McCabe and Bernard Kreissman (Eds.) *Advances in Library Administration and Organization,* vol. 5, (1986) pp. 15-32. Greenwich, CT: JAI Press, Inc.

Kendall, K.S., & M.B. Kenkel. "Social Exchange in the Natural Helping Interaction." *Journal of Rural Community Psychology, 10,* (Winter, 1989) pp. 25-45.

Keltner, C. "Bringing Books to Life." *Texas Libraries, 50* (Fall, 1989) pp. 77-79.

Kies, C. "And Whom Have I Done What For?" *Catholic Library World, 48,* (Oct. 1976) pp. 102-103.

Kochoff, S.T. "Alternative Funding Sources: Friends as Fund Raisers." *Bottom Line, 3,* (1989) pp. 35-36.

Kratcoski, P.C., & S. Crittenden. "Criminal Justice Volunteerism: A Comparison of Adult and Juvenile Agency Volunteers." *Journal of Offender Counseling, Services and Rehabilitation, 7,* (Winter, 1989) pp. 5-14.

Kuras, C. *Volunteer Assistance in the Library.* Ingelwood, CA: Inglewood Public Library, 1975.

Lafata, L. *The Effective Coordination of Volunteers. Domestic Monograph Series No. 1.* Rockville, MD: National Clearinghouse on Domestic Violence, 1980.

LeClair-Marzolf, M. "Fairly Boring Jobs for Young People" [Reprinted from Main Entry, February 1981]. *Unabashed Librarian, 38,* (1981) pp. 2-5.

"Legal Status of Volunteers Clarified in Florida." *Library Journal, 104,* (Nov. 1, 1979) pp. 2274.

Levine, E. "Volunteerism in Libraries." *Bay State Librarian, 69,* (Summer, 1980) pp. 11-14.

Levinson, R. W. "New I and R Teams in Library-Based Services: Librarians, Social Workers, and Older Volunteers." *The Reference Librarian,* no. 21, (1988) pp. 121-134.

Lewin, M. "Library Volunteers, a Growing Phenomenon." *Bookmark, 46,* (Summer, 1988) pp. 249-51.

"Libraries of All Types Depending on Volunteers." *Library Journal, 100,* (Feb. 1, 1975) 0. 254.

Library Association. "Library Association Policy on Unpaid Volunteers." *Library Association Record, 84,* (Feb. 1982) p. 72.

Logan, G. K. "Volunteers for Publicity." *Louisiana Library Association Bulletin, 10,* (March, 1947) 00. 72-74.

Longeway, B. (1979, January). "Examining Volunteer Expenses." *American Libraries, 10,* (Jan., 1979) p. 10.

"LSCA Funded Volunteer Program Catches on in Carroll County." *Library Journal, 107,* (March 1, 1982) p. 500+.

Lucas, L. "Volunteers: Altruists or Primadonnas?" *Public Libraries, 19,* (Fall, 1980) pp. 87-89.

Luloff, A. E., et al. *Characteristics, Motivations and Costs to the Community of Town Government Volunteers. Research Report 101.* Durham, NH: New Hampshire Agricultural Experiment Station, University of New Hampshire, 1983.

Luloff, A. E., et al. "Local Voluntarism in New Hampshire: Who, Why, and at What Benefit." *Journal of the Community Development Society, 15,* (1984) pp. 17-30.

"Many Outreach Services Depend on Volunteers." *Library Journal, 99,* (Nov. 1, 1974) p. 2795.

Masek, D. B. "Parents as Partners in the School Library Media Center.' *Catholic Library World, 56,* (Oct. 1984) pp. 132-134.

McClam, T. *Volunteer Motivations and Rewards: Shaping Future Programs.* Paper presented at the Annual Conference of the American Association for Counseling and Development (New York, NY, April 2-5, 1985).

McKinley, C. "Volunteer Efforts Recognized at Laramie County." *Wyoming Library Roundup, 37,* (Summer, 1982) pp. 50-51.

"Metro Studies Volunteer Use; Tucson Urges Program." *Library Journal, 101,* (July, 1976) pp. 1480-1481.

Middleton, S., and S. Fernando. "Volunteers in Two Hospital Library Settings." In *Health Information: New Directions* (pp. 359-369). New Zealand Library Association, Health Library Section, Conference Commission, 1990.

Miller, J. M. *ABE/ESL Volunteer Program Organizational handbook.* Seattle, WA: Washington Literacy, 1983.

Morrow-Howell, N., and A. Mui. "Elderly Volunteers: Reasons for Initiating and Terminating Service." *Journal of Gerontological Social Work, 13,* (1989) pp. 21-34.

Moussa, L. "Volunteers Offer Library Services to Shut-ins." *Catholic Library World, 48,* (Oct. 1976) pp. 119-121.

Munson-Bensen, T. "Books in the Classroom." *Horn Book, 64,* (March/April, 1988) 00. 251-253.

Murk, P. J., and J. F. Stephan. *Volunteers Enhance the Quality of Life in a Community... or How To Get Them, Train Them, and Keep Them.* Paper presented at the Annual Meeting of the American Association for Adult Continuing Education (Salt Lake City, UT, October 28-November 3, 1990).

National Association of Social Workers. "Volunteers." In *Encyclopedia of Social Work,* vol. 2, 7th ed. (1977) pp. 1582-1590. Washington, DC: National Association of Social Workers.

"Need for Volunteers Cited: New Projects Reported." *Library Journal, 99,* (Sept. 1, 1974) p. 2026.

Netting, F. E. "Ethical Issues in Volunteer Management and Accountability." *Social Work, 32,* (May/June, 1987) pp. 250-52.

Nichols, B. M. "Enrich Your Library with Volunteer Programs." *Show-Me Libraries, 31,* (Aug. 1980) pp. 24-26.

Nightingale, D. S., et al. *The Potential Role of Voluntarism in JTPA. Urban Institute Policy Memorandum.* Washington, DC: Urban Institute, 1989.

Nyren, K. "News in Review, 1981." *Library Journal, 107,* (Jan. 15, 1982) pp. 139-150.

Obrokta, C. (1989, May/June). "Media in Catechesis: Volunteer Management." *Catholic Library World, 60,* (May/June, 1989) pp. 247-248+.

"One Volunteer Experiment." *American Libraries, 5,* (May, 1974) pp. 231-232.

O'Neill, P. C. "New Volunteer Venture is a Two-Sided Service." *Phi Delta Kappan, 65,* (Oct. 1983) pp. 145-146.

Overmyer, E. "Bookleggin: Community Wide Booktalking Through Library-Trained Volunteers." *Journal of Youth Services in Libraries, 1,* (Fall, 1987) pp. 82-86.

Ozawa, M. N., and N. Morrow-Howell. *Elderly Volunteers and the Time They Contribute: An Empirical Study.* Paper presented at the Annual Scientific Meeting of the Gerontological Society (39th, Chicago, IL, November 19-23, 1986).

Parikh, N,. and M. Schneider. "Book Buddies: Bringing Stories to Hospitalized Children." *School Library Journal, 35,* (Dec. 1988) pp. 35-39.

Park, C. S. (1989, Winter). "Public Library Volunteers." *Texas Library Journal, 65,* (Winter, 1989) 126-128.

Parker, M. A. "Student Volunteers: An Endangered Species?" *Campus Activities Programming, 20,* (March, 1988) 49-51.

Parsons, M. P. "One Library's Volunteers." *Wilson Library Bulletin, 18,* (Sept., 1943) pp. 34-35+.

Pearce, J. L. "Job Attitude and Motivation Differences Between Volunteers and Employees from Comparable Organizations." *Journal of Applied Psychology, 68,* (Nov. 1983) pp. 646-652.

Petgen, E. A. "Inside to Outside and Back Again." *Southeastern Librarian, 16,* (Summer, 1966) 107-112.

Pfeifer, D. B. "Meeting the Needs of the Physically Handicapped," *Library Occurrent, 22,* (Aug. 1968) pp. 289-290.

"Proposition 13 Spurs Use of Volunteers in Ventura." *Library Journal, 104,* (May 1, 1979) p. 996.

Ray, G. W. "Meeting Volunteers on Their Own Ground." *New Directions for Experiential Learning,* no. 18, (Dec. 1982) pp. 5-15.

"Recognize Volunteers." *Unabashed Librarian,* no. 64 (1987) 27.

Reichlin, S. (1982, December). "Volunteering and Adult Education: A Historical View." *New Directions for Experiential Learning,* no. 18 (Dec. 1982) pp. 25-33.

Rubin, A., and I. M. Thorelli. "Egoistic Motives and Longevity of Participation by Social Service Volunteers." *Journal of Applied Behavioral Science, 20,* (1984) pp. 223-235.

Rutledge, J. "Used Book Sales: Some Practical Advice." *Show-Me Libraries, 36,* (March, 1985) pp. 22-25.

Sannwald, W. W., and C. M. Hofmann. "Practicing Librarians: Volunteerism in Ventura County." *Library Journal, 107* (ie 105), (March 15, 1980) pp. 681-682.

Savage, N. "Volunteers in Libraries." *Library Journal, 101,* (Dec. 1, 1976) pp. 2431-2433.

Schneider, M. "Book Buddies: Volunteers Bringing Library Services to Hospitalized Children." *Unabashed Librarian,* no. 64, (1987) pp. 21-22.

Schuckett, S. (1985, January). "You too Can Start a Local FOCAL!" *Illinois Libraries, 67,* (Jan. 1985) pp. 41-44.

Schumacher, M. Hospital Library Volunteers, Yes. *ALA Bulletin, 37,* 258-260.

Seguin, M. M., and J. Jarlsberg. "Vintage Volunteers in the Library." *Catholic Library World, 48,* (Oct. 1976) pp. 109-111.

Sergent, M. T., and W. E. Sedlacek. "Volunteer Motivations Across Student Organizations: A Test of Person-Environment Fit Theory." *Journal of College Student Development, 31,* (May, 1990) pp. 255-261.

Skory, V. "Friends of the Library." *Canadian Library Journal, 46,* (Oct., 1989) pp. 317-321.

Smith, A. L. "A Lifeline to Beginning Readers." *School Library Journal, 36,* (April, 1990) 48.

Snider, A. "The Dynamic Tension: Professionals and Volunteers." *Journal of Extension, 23,* (Fall, 1985) 7-10.

Souza, M. B. *Library Information Desk. An Organizational and Operating Guide.* Alexandria, VA: ERIC Document Reproduction Service, operated by Computer Microfilm Corp., (ERIC reports; ED 315 089), 1989.

Stanton, E. *Clients Come Last.* Beverly Hills, CA: Sage Publications, 1970.

Stanton, V. C. "Volunteers, Another View: How Do the Volunteers Feel about Their Work?" *Wisconsin Library Bulletin, 74,* (Sept., 1978) pp. 235-236.

Stephan, S. "Assignment: Administrative Volunteer." *Catholic Library World, 48,* (Oct., 1976) pp. 104-107.

Strickland, C. "Young Users: Library Volunteers and You." *Wilson Library Bulletin, 64,* (Nov. 1989) pp. 72-73.

"Success with Volunteers at Community College Library." *Library Journal, 110,* (Feb. 1, 1985) pp. 29-30.

"Such Good Friends." *American Libraries, 21,* 2 (Dec. 1990) p. 1021.

Tabor, F. T. "What Price Volunteers?" *Wilson Library Bulletin, 15,* (Nov. 1940) p. 269.

Taylor, B. "Volunteers Aid Oral History Project." *Focus on Indiana Libraries, 29,* (Spring, 1975) p. 23.

Taylor, K. "Peaceful Coexistence." *Currents, 12,* (April, 1986) pp. 14-18.

Tedrick, T., et al. "Effective Management of a Volunteer Corps." *Parks and Recreation, 19,* (Feb. 1984) p. 55-59, 70.

Tedrick, T., and K. Henderson. *Volunteers in Leisure. A Management Perspective.* Reston, VA: American Alliance for Health, Physical Education, Recreation and Dance. American Association for Leisure and Recreation, 1989.

Trainer, L. (1976, December). "METRO Workshop on Volunteers in Libraries Sparks Controversy, Offers Practical Advice." *American Libraries, 7,* (Dec. 1976) pp. 66-67.

Tucker, M. P. (1973, Winter). "Volunteers for the Library." *California School Libraries, 44,* (Winter, 1973) pp. 21-22.

Vafa, A. "Volunteer Literacy Tutors Must Have Training and Support." *Canadian Library Journal, 37,* (Aug. 1980) pp. 267-269.

Vittitow, D., and J. Elster. Working as Counterparts. A Peace Corps In-Service Training Manual. Training for Development. Peace Corps Information Collection and Exchange Training Manual No. T-6. Washington, DC: Peace Corps, Information Collection and Exchange Division, 1985.

"Volunteer Management Support Program Handbook." Washington, DC: ACTION, Department of Commerce, Minority Business Development Agency, 1984.

"Volunteer Projects: Reports from the Field." *Library Journal, 104,* (Feb. 1, 1979) 341.

"Volunteer Use Up in Phoenix." *Library Journal, 107, 1* (Oct. 1, 1982) p. 1804.

"Volunteerism." In E. Silverman, *101 Media Center Ideas* (1980) pp. 157-177. Metuchen, NJ: Scarecrow.

"Volunteers." In J. B. Turner (Ed.), *Encyclopedia of Social Work* (Vol. 2, 7th ed. (1977) p. 1582-1590). Washington, DC: National Association of Social Workers.

"Volunteers in Libraries: Comments to Marjery Quigley." *Library Journal, 67,* (May 1, 1942) p. 401.

"Volunteers in Libraries: Guards, Public Relations, Outreach." *Library Journal, 102,* (Oct. 1, 1977) p. 1996.

"Volunteers in Libraries: Reports from All Over." *Library Journal, 107,* (Jan. 1, 1982) p. 20.

Volunteers in Network Libraries: A Manual of Procedures. Washington, DC: Library of Congress, National Library Service for the Blind and Physically Handicapped, 1986.

"Volunteers Rally in the Iowa City." *Library Journal, 111,* (June, 1986) p. 44.

Warner, A. S. *Volunteers in Libraries: LJ Special Report N2.* New York: Bowker, 1977.

Warner, A. S. *Volunteers in Libraries II.* New York: Library Journal, 1983.

Warnsholz, F. *Making the Most of Volunteers and Friends in Libraries.* Lincoln, NE: Nebraska Library Commission, 1978.

Watson, T. "Reading Aloud in Seattle: A Good Idea Getting Better." *Wilson Library Bulletin, 61,* (Feb. 1987) pp. 20-22.

Weinberg, B. M. *Scholarship Fund Development: The Art of Successful Begging.* Arnold, MD: Anne Arundel Community College, 1990.

Weinschenk, D. "I&R Service from Volunteer Senior Citizens." *Library Journal, 111,* (Oct. 15, 1986) p. 50.

Wells, L. B., and Ihrig, A. B. "Volunteers in the Library: The Role of Trustees." In *The Library Trustee,* 4th ed. (1988) pp. 144-151. Chicago, IL: American Library Association.

Whaley, C. and Wolfe, D. "Creating Incentives for Cooperating Teachers." *Journal of Teacher Education, 35,* (July/Aug. 1984) pp. 46-48.

Whipple, M. "Creative Use of Volunteers [at Acton Public Library]." *Connecticut Libraries, 24,* (Spring, 1982) pp. 15-16.

Williams, R. F. "The Values of Volunteer Benefactors." *Mental Retardation, 24,* (June, 1986) pp. 163-168.

Wilson, M. "The new Frontier: Volunteer Management Training." *Training and Development Journal, 38,* (July, 1984) pp. 50-52.

Zischka, P. C., and I. Jones. Special Skills and Challenges in Supervising Volunteers. *Clinical Supervisor, 5,* (Winter, 1987) 19-30.

LIBRARIES:
IMPROVING SERVICES TO
NON-TRADITIONAL STUDENTS

Ray Hall

Through the doors of each of your libraries is coming in ever increasing numbers a new population of students. This student population will shortly, if it has not already, surpass the traditional student population on your campus. It is the adult student—the non-traditional student. One may define the adult/ non-traditional student as "one whose learning activities are secondary to other social or economic roles." (Loewenthal, Blackwelder, and Broomall, 1980, p. 34) another definition of adult/non-tradtional students qualifies them as anyone over 25 years of age; but whatever the definition, they are a growing force in higher education.

Much has been written in recent years about the increasing number of non-traditional students. They are receiving a higher profile in today's educational environment which features declining numbers of traditional students. In 1983 a *New York Times Educational Supplement* noted that between 1973 and 1983 the percentage of students in the over-25 group grew from 29 to 35 percent. (Rubin, 1985, pp. 33-34) The trend continued through the 1980s and in 1988

Advances in Library Administration and Organization,
Volume 11, pages 115-130.
Copyright © 1993 by JAI Press Inc.
All rights of reproduction in any form reserved.
ISBN: 1-55938-596-0

a survey conducted by the College Board and reported in the *Chronicle of Higher Education* found that six million adult students were enrolled for college credit each year, comprising 45 percent of the undergraduate and graduate student body. The study concludes with a prediction that by the end of the century at least 50 percent of the students enrolled in colleges and universities would be non-traditional students. (Hirschorn, 1988, p. A35) That prediction has already been met or exceeded in some states. In Arizona, if community college enrollment is included, 80 percent of higher education head count is non-traditional students (Nordstrom, 1989, p. 11).

The implications of these demographic statistics for higher education should be obvious—no longer can teaching strategies and motivational techniques used for traditional students apply. Change is necessary. The same must be said for libraries and librarians.

In order to examine the implications for library service to non-traditional students, we need to consider the reasons that non-traditional students return to academia and the characteristics of these non-traditional students. Silling (1984) has noted four (4) categories of reasons why non-traditional students are returning to school, and while some students return for one specific reason, most return because of a combination of these factors:

Identity Crisis.   Many adults are drawn to college in an attempt to develop a more far-reaching identity. During the middle-age years, individuals often question their own abilities and limitations, values and attitudes. In a collegiate environment, they seek a means to attain a better sense of themselves and expand their concept of how they fit into society.

Preparation for a Career.   Most adults cite preparation for a career as one of the most important reasons for continuing their education. Sometimes their goals are to learn new skills or earn degrees required for raises in salary or for promotions. Other times, returning to school is a defense against loneliness (for housewives in particular), and fulfills needs to prove their worth in roles besides those of housewife or mother.

Greater Realization of Potential.   Many adults go to college because of an interest in developing a lifestyle that gives life more meaning and makes life more enjoyable. Many women begin college immediately after high school, but leave prior to earning a degree in order to get married and have children. Returning to school fulfills a need to complete this unfinished part of their lives and provides an opportunity to develop a new set of relationships. Because our society places value on a college degree, increasing numbers of adults are seeking the status of being a college graduate.

Life Transition. A majority of adult students are returning to higher education due to a major life transition. Many adults who are divorced or widowed seek new friendships, additional income-producing skills, and insurance for a more stable future. Others seek less tangible rewards such as skills in decision-making and assertiveness, or a renewed belief in themselves as whole and adequate persons (p. 11).

What are the characteristics of non-traditional students? Some demographic information about non-traditional students will provide insights about this increasingly significant group of students.

1. Eight percent of all non-traditional students are attending college because they are in life role or life circumstance transitions. (See Beder, 1985) Most of these transitions are triggered by some life crisis, such as divorce, retirement, empty nest syndrome, etc. (Queeny, 1984, pp. 2-6)

2. Over fifty percent are seeking to make career moves: "A May, 1984, government survey of 40,752,000 courses taken by adults during the previous 12-month period revealed that most adults took courses for job related reasons. Of that group, 14.6% reported wanting to change occupations, 3.6% reported wanting new jobs within their current occupations, and 75.3% reported that they were simply seeking advancement in their current jobs." (Nordstrom, 1989, p. 4) Other changes relate to the student's family life, health, and leisure time. (See Aslanian and Brickell, 1980, for an in-depth discussion) While these situations may be critical and often are traumatic, they provide the motivation for the adult student to initiate change. This change is often through the avenue of higher education; thus, the non-traditional students comes to higher education highly motivated and focused on definite goals. "In contrast to adolescents who tend to take college for granted, adults place more value on going to college because they have waited longer to attend—and usually attend at greater personal and economic sacrifice. Because of the higher value placed on college education, the adult learner is more likely also than his younger counterpart to find his college experience deeply satisfying" (Nordstrom, 1989, p. 11).

3. More than 50 percent are adult women who tend to be older than adult male students and move at a slower pace academically. (Iovacchini, Hall, and Hengstler, 1985, p. 43)

4. Thirty-three percent have high school diplomas, 20 percent have some college, 13 percent have a degree, and 17 percent have a graduate degree. Most are returning to school after a hiatus of some years. (Sheridan, 1986, p. 157)

5. Most are first generation college students coming from working class backgrounds. (Iovacchini, Hall, and Hengstler, 1985, p. 44)

6. Adult students indicate that the desire to live at home, the educational programs offered at the institution, the low tuition and the availability of financial aid are very important in their selection of college. (Iovacchini, Hall, and Hengstler, 1985, p. 44)

7.   To finance their education, non-traditional students are more likely to work full time, utilize GI benefits, or rely on their spouse's income. (Iovacchini, Hall, and Hengstler, 1985, p. 44)

Collette Wagner and Augusta Kappner, (1987) in their work "The Academic Library and the Non-Traditional Student", make the following observations about non-traditional students:

- *academically,* they are at high risk in the traditional college classroom due to insufficient preparation at lower levels of the educational system;
- *economically,* they are struggling for survival and require financial assistance in order to undertake college study;
- *socially,* they are predominantly members of minority groups or first generation college students. In urban centers, they are also likely to be first generation Americans as well. As first time college students, they share the expectation that the college experience will provide them with a means to occupational success;
- *experientially,* they are likely to be older and more accustomed to bearing the wage-earning, child-rearing, and other responsibilities of a mature adult, and,
- *attitudinally,* they are less likely to take college for granted, skeptical of authority, interested in exerting some "ownership" rights over their own education, and highly motivated (pp. 4-5).

Furthermore, the non-traditional student is often under a great deal of stress. Demand and conflicts between the parent/spouse/worker role and their new student role often result in feelings of stress and confusion. This is often coupled with resistance from family and/or peers as the non-traditional student attempts to further their education. (Sheridan, 1986, p. 157) There may also be concern or doubt about their ability to compete with other younger, more assertive students.

In addition, non-traditional students are faced with new and bewildering issues or questions: getting academic and/or experiential credits, learning registration procedures, understanding classroom protocol, developing study skills, and selecting a degree (Sheridan, 1986, p. 158).

Finally, non-traditional students are apprehensive—not comfortable with their new and often bewildering educational experience. They can be easily frightened away if they do not feel welcome when they first experience the new educational environment of the academic library. It has been observed that "the typical non-traditional students seems to approach the academic library as if it were a dangerous pit of intellectual quicksand" (Wagner and Kappner, 1987, p. 5).

There are several reasons non-traditional students are apprehensive when they first approach the library. The first relates to their own past—concepts about libraries and librarians developed during their childhood or young adulthood. They may not have been library oriented or they may have had unpleasant library experiences (Hine, Meek, and Miller, 1989, p. 20). They may also perceive barriers to their use of academic libraries—such as "inadequate information and other academic skills, limited time with many competing demands on it, lack of confidence in their ability to do research, and the many recent changes in libraries brought about by information technology " (Steffen, 1989, p. 97).

A second source of apprehension relates to what Connie Mellon (1988) calls "library anxiety": the student's fear of the library. The following three student quotes are from her article "Library Anxiety and the Non-Traditional Student":

> Using the library is a scary prospect, especially when I think about in-depth research. I know that research cannot be done without frequent visits to the library and I know that nothing in here will hurt me, but it all seems so vast and overpowering.

> When I first entered the library, I was terrified. I didn't know where anything was located or even who to ask to get some help. It was like being in a foreign country and unable to speak the language.

> I was scared to ask questions. I didn't want to bother anyone. I also didn't want them to think I was stupid (pp. 78-79).

Perhaps as you are questioning exactly what the non-traditional students could be anxious about? There are several possible factors. Some additional student comments from Mellon's article illustrate them.

> I am not accustomed to such a high library. I came to the library not too long ago to gather information for a paper I had to write. I had no idea where to begin.

> I think it's great that the students have access to such a vast store of information, but I certainly do not know how to find anything in there, except for a table, maybe. There have been several occasions where I needed to use materials in the library, but I am accustomed to the good old Dewey Decimal System and it was pretty disheartening to look in the catalog and find tons of books on Eli Whitney, but then realize that there is no way I can locate them. And who am I supposed to ask for help? No one looks too interested in what I'm doing. And the one little chart I saw on a shelf was quite a disappointment. It just confused me even more. It is not a good feeling to be lost in a library. Especially when I am supposed to be somewhat intelligent. After all, I am attending an institution of higher learning, am I not? Talk about a hard blow to the ego!

> Presently I don't have any feelings about using [the] Library because I haven't had the opportunity of doing a research paper. I hope to god that somebody will help me! It seems kinda scary going in there with everybody expecting me to know how to get information— seems like nobody cares and no one wants to help you. I know how to use the card catalog, so maybe that'll help me out a little bit. I certainly do hope so. The library is so big and uncaring looking with all those rows and rows and shelves and shelves full of nothing but books, magazines, journals, encyclopedias—seems endless! (p. 79).

In concluding our examination of the characteristics of the non-traditional student it might prove beneficial to make a brief comparison of traditional and non-traditional students. An interesting comparison is given by D.R. Hameister (1977) in his article "Traditional and adult students: A dichotomy." Hameister characterizes traditional students, in part, as students who are continuing their schooling, who are strongly influenced by formal education, who are familiar with educational routine, who are full time students, who have adequate communication and study skills, who have minimal work experience, who frequently have no clear vocational goals, who put a strong emphasis on grades, who have goals of receiving a degree, and who possess an idea of how he/she compares with fellow students.

Non-traditional students, on the other hand, are students who are returning to school, who are strongly influenced by informal education, who are unfamiliar with educational routine, who are part time students, who have communication and study skill deficiencies, who have extensive work experience and clear vocational goals, who put less emphasis on grades, who may or may not have goals of receiving a degree, and who have no clear basis of how he/she compares to fellow students (pp. 6-8).

A part of the task facing the academic library is to support the non-traditional student and successfully ease them into the intricacies of library research. One method is to build on those particular strengths which the non-traditional student possesses. While a few non-traditional students enthusiastically "dig in" to the modern academic library for their information needs, the majority are much more reticent. Support from library faculty can help these less assertive adults overcome any doubts about their ability to master the techniques of research in the library. Andrea Wyman (1988) has several observations about methods to serve non-traditional students. Becoming involved with networks for non-traditionals opens doors of opportunity for reaching this student group. Since not all orientation sessions and other meetings are publicized, this provides an avenue to contacts with the non-traditionals. Designating specific librarians to work with non-traditional students can promote a valuable rapport between student and librarian. Always advertise programs for non-traditional students well in advance of the event because scheduling is sometimes difficult for them. Recognize that experientially there is a vast difference between traditional and non-traditional students. A concrete approach to learning is more applicable than an abstract approach for non-traditionals. They often ask more questions and want more detailed answers than traditional students. Quiet study areas are highly desirable and attempts should be made to provide them. Non-traditional males may be reluctant to ask for assistance and the librarians should be sensitive to this situation (pp. 32-33).

Librarians can be quite beneficial in assisting non-traditional students to achieve a positive educational experience. Keenan (1989) suggests four types of services librarians can provide non-traditional students to enhance their learning. These services (improving the self-concept, drawing on self-experience, recognizing self-readiness, and utilizing self-motivation) will assist in providing a relevant knowledge base. By empowering the non-traditional student to master research techniques, the need for being master of his/her own destiny is met for the non-traditional student. This mastery will improve the students self-concept. For the librarian serving non-traditional students, an emphasis on individualization is necessary. Activities or processes that draw on the experience of the non-traditional student will reinforce the relevancy of the learning experience. The librarian should be attuned to the non-traditional student, seeking to recognize that the student has mastered one stage and is ready to progress to the next; non-traditional students are strongly motivated to learn when they perceive the new knowledge or skill as helpful. The librarian can use this as a tool to motivate non-traditional students to master new information or abilities (pp. 153-155).

It may seem unreasonable to expect librarians who are already very busy and overextended to develop this kind of relationships with all students, not just non-traditionals, that will permit the librarian to recognize when these individual goals have been mastered. It is necessary, however, to become more involved in the needs of all students, dealing creatively and enthusiastically with them.

Let us examine five areas of library service, emphasizing meeting the needs of non-traditional students.

1. Cooperation with other libraries. Cooperation with different types of libraries (i.e., public, school, special) is an effective method of utilizing a broad gamut of library resources to meet the educational needs of the non-traditional student. The objective is to assist the non-traditional student to make the most efficient use of available library resources.

The traditional answer to the needs of the part-time student is to push for an extension of library hours. In the best of all possible worlds, all the libraries would be open all the time, and have all of the material that all of the students need for all of their assignments. Terrific!

Closer to reality, however, is the fact that all the libraries are open some of the time, and have some of the materials that some of the students need for some of their assignments.

Clearly, we can never provide all of the *all's* in the first statement; but we can and should make an effort to define the *some's* of the second statement. Students who will have difficulty getting all of their library work done in the home library should be made aware of the resources of other libraries in the area.

It takes awareness, a conscious decision, and perhaps a *soupçon* of humility on the part of any academic library administrator to acknowledge that some students are best served by using a combination of libraries, and to incorporate a thorough awareness of the resources of neighboring institutions into the public service policy (Lutzker, 1982, pp. 249-250).

2. Reference. Let us examine Reference next. Carefully listen to the non-traditional student. Ask appropriate questions to determine the information needs. (Does this sound like a lecture on the "Reference Interview"?) Wagner and Kappner (1987) point out the importance of the reference interview when working with non-traditional students:

> While the depth and breadth of the library's collection and the expertise of the reference librarian are important elements of the reference scenario, it is the student who initiates the action and dominates the drama. Thus, to a great degree, the success of the reference interview is dependent upon the skills and attitudes of the student—i.e., the student who is articulate, at ease in the library environment, and self-confident enough to approach a librarian to ask questions, reveal needs, listen and follow directions is more likely to benefit from the reference encounter. The non-traditional student—the hit and run library user—typically possess very few of these prerequisites for success in the library research game as played by the traditional rules of reference. By reinventing the research game, defining the librarian as enemy rather than ally, and waging a campaign of blitzkreig attacks on the academic library, the non-traditional student has tossed the gauntlet of challenge onto the reference desk. In response to such desperate action, academic libraries have hastened to undertake special instructional initiatives while reach beyond the physical limits of the reference desk and, indeed, beyond the walls of the library itself (pp. 9-10).

After the reference interview, concisely target the reference requirements, and then lead the student to the most relevant source(s) while giving brief explanatory comments. Don't overwhelm the student! Tuckett and Stoffle (1984) have argued against problem specific instruction, maintaining that students cannot synthesize random bits of information into a cohesive approach to information retrieval (p. 60). However, this is not necessarily so for non-traditional students who are more adept than traditional students at synthesizing seemingly unconnected facts into a cohesive entity.

Tomaiuolo (1990), however, agrees with Tuckett and Stoffle, noting that:

> Some library school reference course instructors have said, "Err on the side of providing less information. The patron can always come back and ask for more." Having once considered this axiom antithetical to good library service, I now realize that to provide more information than is necessary, particularly with respect to reentry students, is gratuitous pedantics (p. 53).

A key factor to remember is the importance of developing an active communication with the non-traditional student; once that is in place, they will feel comfortable to return to ask additional questions. Additional sources can then be introduced, and ultimately, self-reliance will come.

Other methods utilized by reference departments to meet non-traditional students' needs include arranging for the library to accept collect calls from off-campus students or providing toll-free numbers for requests for reference assistance; offering computer searches; doing photocopying; and, processing interlibrary loan requests. On-line database searches can be performed by the on-campus librarian and sent to the students. Although many librarians feel it is necessary to have the student present during the search, this is not feasible for off-campus students. A telephone interview between the librarian and student combined with bibliographic instruction in on-line searches should be sufficient (Courtney and Tiller, 1989, p. 123).

One final observation about reference service for non-traditional students relates to their time management priorities. A humorous, but hauntingly accurate, view is given by Wagner and Kappner:

> In their lives, time is one of their most precious commodities, and they are impatient and frustrated to learn that the library reference desk is not a McDonald's service counter where quick stops yield fast information in neat, take-out containers. Unwilling to waste time learning how to find required information because every second must be spent mastering the subject at hand, non-traditional college students will frequently reject what appears to be time-consuming and arcane research methodology in favor of clutching a few comfortable sources which can be located by fast-paced browsing. It seems that they will settle for anything as long as they escape without being ensnared by learning a complicated new research process which will interfere with their primary studies (p. 6).

3. Reserve and Circulation. In the areas of Reserve and Circulation, it might be best to remember the advise of R. Dean Galloway and Zoia Horn: (1985) "The emphasis should be upon serving the need and making it easy for the user. As long as no one else is hurt by granting the request, it should be done" (p. 125).

The non-traditional student has very little spare time to spend reading in the library, reserving library time for research that can only be done there. How then can reserve items be effectively administered. If there are limited copies of an item and a large class needs to read significant amounts, then limited reserve is the answer. If, however, the choice is one or two items from a list of 10-20, then circulation for 1-2 weeks certainly seems in order.

Another possible alternative when reserve is unavoidable is to cooperate with other libraries. Public libraries may own items on your reserve list and might place their items on reserve (See Cowser, 1978). If there are other academic libraries in your area, perhaps a cooperative agreement could be forged with reciprocal borrowing, especially when there are variations in the weekend hours (Lutzker, 1982, p. 250).

Utilizing the faculty member is also an alternative. Here the teacher would check out the materials and circulate them him/herself. This would give the instructor a handle on who was attempting to do the reading. There are several obvious disadvantages to this approach such as the limited amount of information which can be conveyed, the burden put on the instructor, and the clerical hassles of checking books in and out.

Circulation has two areas where a deviation from tradition might be possible: circulation of microformat materials and seldom-used reference materials. (Lutzker, 1982, p. 251) With the proliferation of portable microform readers that are relatively inexpensive, there is more access to machines outside the library. Perhaps purchasing a microform reader to "circulate" is an alternative. It would certainly help the student, traditional or non-traditional, with little spare time to spend in the library.

Limited-use reference materials (or items in Reference Storage—if you have such an area) are also candidates for circulation. By usage they are "seldom used" so why not allow circulation if it will make life a little bit easier for the occasional student requesting the material.

Many libraries do not circulate periodicals and therefore limit their use by off-campus students. Another means of access must be provided so that off-campus students can make use of periodical articles. A photocopying service is one answer. Students can submit written requests for articles by mail to the on-campus library or send them via the instructor. Requests might also be made by telephone. The library should also handle interlibrary loan requests from off-campus students. Again, requests can be made by mail or telephone, and materials delivered by the method chosen for book delivery from the on-campus library (Courtney and Tiller, 1989, p. 123).

These particular ideas may not work, but taking a fresh look at policies and procedures might provoke some new untried ideas that just might be the answer to meet the needs of the non-traditional students.

4. Bibliographic Instruction. Probably the instruction librarians are the ones in the best position to help the non-traditional student. As discussed earlier, the library is usually one of the places on campus where the non-traditional students feels most apprehensive. An effective bibliographic instruction program can go far to alleviate the fears of students confronted with the need for library research. There are several key elements to remember:

1. Bibliographic instruction methods used successfully with traditional undergraduate students are usually not adequate for non-traditional students unless modified.
2. Bibliographic instruction programs must be rooted in a framework that embodies flexibility, adaptability, and the notion of "learning how to learn." Considering the diverse backgrounds, experience, and knowledge that [non-traditional] students bring to the classroom, the content of the instruction must be both meaningful and placed within a broad context (Brown, 1986, p. 180).

3. Librarians must exhibit an unusual degree of compassion and understanding as they offer assistance and guidance in teaching these students how to negotiate the library (Ford and Bennett, 1987, p. 32).

4. Since non-traditional students are often short of time means they may want to progress from little or no knowledge to conducting a meaningful information search in one visit (Howard, 1983, p. 153).

5. Large doses of formal bibliographic instruction (i.e., classroom presentations) may not be the most effective method of instruction. There personal contact, which non-traditional students need and from which they learn best, is precluded. Individual accommodation is best because non-traditional students have individual questions, insights, and experiences.

6. Respect between the library faculty and the non-traditional student is paramount; the librarian must take the first step to ensure that the non-traditional student never construes asking for assistance as dependency. This is accomplished during the fist exchange by verbally demonstrating a willingness to work with the non-traditional student. Tone of voice and phrasing of comments are crucial (Knowles, 1968, p. 351).

7. Instruction librarians must shift from a passive to an active role concerning outreach to faculty members who are teaching courses that have been identified as quite frustrating to non-traditional students. Another possible result is better relations between the teaching faculty and the librarians. Better relations can lead to improved service to the teaching faculty (Sheridan, 1985, p. 185).

Adults have accumulated experience and attained maturity. They chose to reenter higher education for diverse, practical reasons. Libraries would be wise to recognize this experience and maturity, and capitalize on it. Librarians must also recognize and analyze the contrasts between younger and older students; the instructional approaches that are particularly successful with the latter group must be noted. Research and empiricism shows that an informal, practical approach is indicated. Relevancy works. Utilizing this orientation, the librarians make the reentrants' time spent retrieving information less laborious, but also immensely productive. As adult enrollment continues to increase, this issue becomes salient. Librarians can effectively serve adult students by recognizing their needs and addressing those needs with the most practical instructional tools and methods available. These methods will satisfy the reentry students' need for respect, autonomy, and relevancy (Tomaiuolo, 1990, p. 53).

5. Off-Site Libraries. Recognizing the importance of meeting the educational needs of non-traditional students (especially in light of the current decrease of traditional students), colleges and universities are increasingly developing programs such as evening and weekend courses, compressed time

courses, telecourses, and offering classes at a variety of locations removed from the campus. These accommodations for the needs of the non-traditional student are creating new relationships between students and faculty and the academic library. Librarians have been challenged to creatively develop programs to meet the needs of students and faculty in these innovative programs, each of which presents its own unique set of challenges.

Off-site courses particularly offer a number of challenges to effective library services! The following are some aspects from a number of successful programs:

1.   Promote library "visibility" on the main campus. If there is an absence of library representation in planning off-site programs, it comes from a lack of visibility. Librarians should be an integral part of the planning process and programs should not be allowed to become operational without provision of adequate library support. Collaboration between the Continuing Education Office (or comparable academic office) and the library are essential to the successful implementation of an instructional program at a distance. Libraries need to establish a viable presence for off-campus programs and to inform their community of users of the services available. This can best be accomplished through ongoing library involvement in the off-campus planning process (Kascus, and Aguilar, 1987, pp. 87-88).

2.   Aggressively market library services. Virginia Witucke (1990) of Central Michigan University has developed an extensive list of suggestions, which include publicizing the library to individuals, especially new students and faculty, through letters or packets (piggybacking on someone else's mailing or program might make this more feasible); using existing campus publications to publicize the library by actively seeking opportunities to submit library-related copy; personalizing service through more liberal use of names of both librarians and patrons through use of photographs of librarians in publications or display areas; promoting telephone reference service, since it appears to be more comfortable to some people; initiating class visits by choosing courses to be visited in a systematic way; and, participating actively in institution-wide functions, whatever their significance or direct library relevance (p. 254).

3.   One traditional limitation to learners in off-campus setting has been the inability to browse the collection. If your library has an online catalog with browse capability, every effort should be made to have at least one available to students in all off-campus locations (Keenan, 1989, p. 157).

4.   Providing access to bibliographic tools, collections, and trained staff is a major consideration. Some of the solutions that other libraries have utilized have been

a.   to establish branch libraries at the site;
b.   to use the on-campus library to serve all users;

    c. to use the trunk delivery system to transport material to remote sites; or,

    d. to use some combination of these options (Lessin, 1985, p. 5).

Courses may be taught in a variety of locations. "Unless permanent college or university learning centers with libraries are located in each community, the local public, school, hospital, community college, or even college or university library may be looked to for library services for off-campus students. Contact should be made with appropriate libraries, and in some cases legal and monetary agreements may be needed between the two institutions if effective support is expected" (Johnson, 1988, p. 250).

5.   Programs offered at a distance require complex delivery systems. Book and document delivery, both outgoing and incoming, poses problems. Trunk delivery physically limits the number of items that can be delivered at one time. Use of the U.S. Postal Service can result in delays in receiving material, a high cost per transaction, and practical problems in returning borrowed books. Technology, such as telefacsimile, can help to shorten the distance between the library and the user, but ultimately cost becomes the critical factor in determining the choice of the delivery system (Kascus and Aguilar, 1988, p. 34).

6.   Speed is of the essence in serving non-traditional students who are often short of time; at a distance, the time factor becomes even more critical. Most library users want an immediate response to a request for information or resources, whether on-campus or off-campus. Timeliness in responding to a information request would be an important measure of library performance in the user's evaluation of library services (Kascus and Aguilar, 1988, p. 34).

7.   In offering academic programs at remote sites, faculty may be reluctant to make library assignments to off-campus students. Yet, the faculty should be responsible for preparing library assignments that will give off-campus students an equivalent educational experience and satisfy the same standards of rigor applied to on-campus programs. The library's responsibility is to work to establish its presence and insure that off-campus faculty are fully aware of the library support available for the instructional program. In order to do this, the library should develop a good marketing strategy that alerts off-campus faculty to the full range of library resources and services that are available and how these can be packaged and delivered to serve off-campus needs (Kascus and Aguilar, 1988, p. 34).

8.   Successful utilization of the library's resources to satisfy information needs is dependent on the student's research skills. While on-campus students have access to the advice and expertise of instructors and reference librarians, off-campus students may be limited in the amount and quality of assistance they receive. Therefore it is essential that a sound bibliographic instruction component be built into any library's off-campus services. The most effective

method would be an on-site visit by the bibliographic instruction librarian from the home campus. A successful on-site visit requires cooperation with the instructor as well as other librarians from institutions that off-campus students might use (Courtney and Tiller, 1989, p. 124).

9. Flexibility is the key word in managing an off-campus branch library so completely removed from the rest of the University. The librarian must respond to the needs of two separate groups—the university library and the off-campus library. Loyalties can become split, and it is frequently advisable for this library to function independently of the main library. Because the librarian is isolated from professional colleagues, library staff participation in the development of policies and procedures is encouraged at all levels. Often this input is more practical than that of librarians 45 miles away. Ultimately it is those on the scene who must live with the policies and procedures—it is usually best if they feel some responsibility for their development and implementation.

Not only must the librarian at the off-campus library practice flexibility, but supervisors on campus must use forbearance when dealing with exceptions to established practices. Often, goals for the off-campus library are set at the administrative level without considering how they can be met. An inflexible administrator who "goes by the book" can severely limit the innovative approaches necessary for a successful off-campus branch library. The off-campus library should try to work within the general framework of policies established on campus; if it is not practical to follow them exactly, their spirit should generally be maintained (Burich, 1980, 649-650).

Supporting the non-traditional student in the library is an ever-changing aspect of academic librarianship. The energy and motivation that this very special group of students brings to the library is real and contagious; it is exciting to work with non-traditionals. It is also extremely rewarding to work with them. Students have been known to introduce their families at graduation or describe the librarians as "life savers." Boxes of cookies or candy have periodically appeared and sharing a cup of coffee occasionally happens.

Taking extra effort to provide services for non-traditional students in the academic library may help students become reacquainted with library research skills, will introduce them to the new technologies of online catalogs and databases, and become more than a pleasurable part of the academic librarian's job—it will also prepare librarians for the large numbers of future non-traditional students that are predicted to turn up on college campuses and in academic libraries (Wyman, 1988, p. 33).

REFERENCES

Aslanian, Carole B and Henry Brickell. *Americans in Transition: Life Changes as Reasons for Adult Learning.* New York: College Entrance Examination Board, 1980.

Beder, Hal. "The Relationship of Knowledge Sought to Appropriate Teacher Behavior in Adult Education." *Lifelong Learning, 9,* (1985) pp. 14-15, 27-28.

Brown, Karen. "A Bibliographic Instruction Model for Reaching Adult Part-Time Students." *Off Campus Library Services Conference,* Knoxville, TN, 18-19 April 1985. Mount Pleasant, MI: Central Michigan Univ. Pres, 1986.

Burich, Nancy. "Coping with Changing Tradition: The University of Kansas Regents Center Library." *Wilson Library Bulletin, 54,* (1980) pp. 654-650.

Courtney, Nancy and Kathleen Tiller. "Off-Campus Library Services." In G. B. McCabe (Ed.), *Operations Handbook for the Small Academic Library* (1989) (pp. 121-126). New York: Greenwood Press.

Cowser, R. L., Jr. "Cooperative Activity Links College and Public Library." *Texas Libraries 40* (1978) pp. 179-181.

Ford, Robert B., Jr. and Yvonne S. Bennett, (1987). "Bibliographic Instruction for the Nontraditional College Student: The Medgar Evers Experience." *The Bookmark 46* (1987) pp. 31-35.

Galloway, R. Dean and Zoia Horn. "Alternative Ways to Meet User Needs." In E.J. Josey (Ed.) *New Dimensions for Academic Library Service.* (1975) p. 121-131. Metuchen, N.J.: Scarecrow Press.

Hameister, D.R. "Traditional and Adult Students: A Dichotomy." *Lifelong Learning: The Adult Years 1,* (1977) pp. 6-8.

Hine, Betsy N., Janet Meek, and Ruth H. Miller. (1989). "Bibliographic Instruction for the Adult Student in an Academic Library." *Journal of Continuing Higher Education 37* (1989) pp. 20-24.

Hirschorn, Micahel W. "Students over 25 Found to Make Up 45 Pct. of Campus Enrollments." *Chronicle of Higher Education 34* (1988) p. A35.

Howard, Sheila. "Library Use Education for Adult University Students." *Canadian Library Journal 40* (1983) pp. 149-155.

Iovacchini, Eric V., Linda M. Hall, and Dennis D. Hengstler. "Going Back to College: Some Differences Between Adults and Traditional Students." *College and University 61* (1985) pp. 43-54.

Johnson, Jean S. "Off-Campus Library Services and the Smaller Academic Library." In G. B. McCabe (Ed.) *The Smaller Academic Library.* (1988) pp. 249-256. New York: Greenwood Press.

Kascus, Marie and William Aguilar. *Problems and Issues in Providing Library Support to Off-Campus Academic Programs: A Pilot Study.* Washington, DC: Alliance, an Association for Alternative Degree Programs, American Council on Education. (ERIC Document Reproduction Service No. ED 321 625), 1987.

Kascus, Marie and William Aguilar. "Providing Library Support to Off-Campus Programs." *College and Research Libraries 49* (1988) pp. 29-37.

Keenan, Lori M. "Andragogy Off-Campus: The Library's Role." *Reference Librarian 24* (1989) pp. 147-158.

Knowles, Malcolm S. "Andragogy not Pedagogy." *Adult Leadership 16* (1968) pp. 350-352, 386.

Lessin, Barton M. "Keynote Address." *Off-Campus Library Services Conference,* Knoxville, TN, 18-19 April 1985 Mount Pleasant, MI: Central Michigan Univ. Press, (1986) p. 5.

Lowenthal. N., J. Blackwelder, and J.K. Broomall. "Correspondence, Instruction, and the Adult Student." In A.B. Knox (Ed.) *Teaching Adults Effectively* (1980). San Francisco, CA: Jossey-Bass.

Lutzker, Marilyn. "Full-Time Thinking About Part-Time Students." In M.D. Kathman and V.S. Massman (Eds.) *Options for the 80s: Proceedings of the Second National Conference of the Association of College and Research Libraries.* (1982) pp. 247-254. Greenwich, CT: JAI Press Inc.

Mellon, Constance A. "Library Anxiety and the Non-Traditional Student." In T. Menching (Ed.) *Reaching and teaching Diverse User Groups* (1989) pp. 77-81. Ann Arbor, MI: Pierian Press.

Nordstrom, Brian H. *Non-Traditional Students: Adults in Transition.* (ERIC Docment Reproduction Service No. ED 310 686), 1989.

Queeny, D. S. "Adult Learners: A Focus on Who They Are, What They Need, and the Problems They Face." *Journal of Continuing Higher Education 32* (1984) pp. 2-6.

Rubin, Nancy. "Meeting Adult Needs: Colleges Providing New Services for Mature Students." *The New York Time Education Fall Survey* (Nov. 10, 1985) pp. 33-34.

Sheridan, Jean. "Andragogy: A New Concept for Academic Librarians." *Research Strategies 4* (1986) pp. 156-167.

Sheridan, Jean. "Teaching Part-Time MBAs to Use a Library." *Research Strategies 3* (1985) pp. 184-190.

Silling, M. A. "Student Services for Adult Learners." Dayton, OH: Annual Conference of the Williams Midwest Region Academic Affairs Administrators. (ERIC Document Reproduction Service No. ED 253 809), 1984.

Steffen, Susan S. "Removing Barriers: Bibliographic Instruction for Adults." In T. Menching (Ed.) *Reaching and Teaching Diverse User Groups* (1989) pp. 97-87. Ann Arbor, MI: Pierian Press.

Tomaiuolo, Nicholas G. "Reconsidering Bibliographic Instruction for Adult Reentry Students: Emphasizing the Practical." RSR 18 (1990) pp. 49-54.

Tuckett, Harold W. and Carla J. Stoffle. "Learning Theory and the Self-Reliant Library User." RQ *24* (1984) pp. 58-67.

Wagner, Colette A. and Augusta S. Kappner. *The Academic Library and the Non-Traditional Student,* New York: Proceedings of the Arden House Symposium. (ERIC Document Reproduction Service No. ED 284 589), 1987.

Witucke, Virginia. "Off-Campus Library Services: Leading the Way." *College and Research Libraries News 3* (1990) pp. 252-256.

Wyman, Andrea. "On My Mind: Working with Nontraditional Students in the Academic Library." *Journal of Academic Librarianship 24* (1988) pp. 32-33.

NATIONAL TECHNICAL INFORMATION:

THE RED OCTOBER PROBLEM

Steven M. Hutton

In democracies there is a natural conflict between national secrets and the public's right to know. Rarely has this conflict intruded on libraries. Throughout the period of the Reagan Administration, however, the concerted efforts of Executive Branch departments to tighten security impinged on the nation's libraries and information services. The impact was on several fronts, including the confidentiality of patron access to materials, restriction of scholarly communication, and limiting access to national technical information.

While the public record is not entirely clear, it is likely that two particular events precipitated this conflict. The first of these was the publication of the novel, *The Hunt for Red October* (Clancy, 1984). The novel presents a realistic account of submarine warfare in the North Atlantic. At a White House dinner party John Lehman, Secretary of the Navy, jokingly told the author, Tom Clancy, that he would have been charged with treason had he been in the military (Pear, 1987a).

Advances in Library Administration and Organization,
Volume 11, pages 131-142.
Copyright © 1993 by JAI Press Inc.
All rights of reproduction in any form reserved.
ISBN: 1-55938-596-0

The second event occurred shortly after the 1984 election. On 17 December a spokesman for the Department of Defense announced restrictions on the press coverage of the Discovery shuttle mission to take place on 23 January 1984 ("Secrecy Planned," 1984). This was the first of what was to be several shuttle missions of a completely military nature. Information which would not be made available included the lift-off time, flight path, and cargo.

Prior to this announcement Secretary of Defense Caspar Weinberger had contacted the editors of *Aviation Week and Space Technology* and the *Associated Press,* as well as the heads of the news divisions of CBS and NBC (Hiatt, 1984). He requested that certain information about the shuttle mission, information already in the hands of journalists, not be published. This was the first instance during his tenure that Weinberger had ever made such a request. Responses varied from assurances of no publication, to no commitment of any kind. Nevertheless, none of the agencies contacted by Weinberger released any information about the nature of the shuttle mission.

On 19 December *The Washington Post* did publish a story revealing that the shuttle mission would launch a signal intelligence satellite into geosynchronous orbit over the western territory of the Soviet Union (Pincus and Thornton, 1984). In responding to Weinberger's furious reaction to the publication of this story, Bill Bradlee, editor of the *Post,* stated that he had not been contacted by Weinberger and that all the information in the story had been previously published elsewhere (Hiatt, 1984).

In both cases information considered vital to the security of the United States had been pieced together from unclassified technical and other publicly available information.

The impact of these two events must be viewed within the context of the Reagan information policy that was being formulated from the very beginning of the Reagan first term. According to one journalist (Armstrong, 1986),

> There was an attempt to orchestrate with precision and with symphonic results the national
> security information that comes from the highest level leaker. Of course, this was not new
> to the Reagan administration ... this use of the strategic leak was perfected by the Reagan
> administration...[and] has become the principal tool for manipulating the public record,
> even for announcing policy (p. 27).

Under the Reagan Administration there was also a reversal in the policies for classifying information (Mitchel, 1987, p. 446). The Nixon and Carter administration has made efforts to better organize the classification system, to classify fewer documents, to put time limits on the classifications, and to declassify more documents. In 1974 the Freedom of Information Act was extended to provide better and faster access to documents by requestors. But as early as July 1981 the Reagan Administration supported efforts in the Congress to weaken the Freedom of Information Act (Lardner, 1981), and in June 1982 Presidential Executive Order 12356 modified the criteria for classifying documents. The prior criteria had been not to classify a document if there were any doubts about whether the document should be classified. This was reversed to "if in doubt, classify" (Mitchel, 1987, p. 449).

To better organize the classification system and to make it appear that fewer documents were being classified, the Department of Defense began to use "derived classifications" more frequently (Pear, 1987b). Under this system, when a Defense Department project is contracted, a list is created detailing the types of information that should be classified for that project The list is classified, and any subsequent classified documents for the project are considered derived classifications. It appears statistically that less information is being classified, when in fact more information is being classified.

Another method of securing information is to compartmentalize it into smaller sets, with fewer and fewer people having access to large sets of data. This strategy was also adopted; now there are as many as 10,000 compartmentalized programs in the U.S. government. Theoretically only the President has access to all of them (Armstrong, 1986, p. 28).

While compartmentalization was increasing, an additional strategy of extending pre-publication review was implemented (Shattuck, 1986, p. A4). Generally, pre-publication review had applied only to employees of the Central Intelligence Agency, its purpose being to ensure that classified information did not inadvertently appear in print. On 11 March 1983 the White House issued National Security Decision Directive 84. This extended pre-publication review to 120,000 government employees. It also authorized government agencies to order polygraph examinations on employees during investigations of unauthorized leaks.

With an apparently successful strategy in place, government agencies began to extend the concept of pre-publication review to scholars working under government contract. Testifying before a Congressional Sub-committee, Thomas Ehrlich, Provost of the University of Pennsylvania, stated that NSDD-84 would result in academics not wishing to serve in government, since they would be unable to publish the results of their work. He further stated that those who had already served in government would no longer be able to discuss their work on returning to academia. Thus, the "traditional role of academia in providing a forum for criticism and debate," would be reduced (Shattuck, 1986, p. A8).

NSDD-84 not only effected the hard sciences, but also the social sciences. Some agencies extended pre-publication review apparently to ensure that the research being done "was consistent with their view of the mission." Other contract clauses known as "technical direction" and "changes" clauses could potentially be used to alter the outcome of the research itself (Shattuck, 1986, pp. A10-A11).

NSDD-84 also provided for the classification of information already made public, so long as the information could be realistically retrieved, and provided for the classification of research projects in progress. (Shattuck, 1986, p. A17). This would inevitably influence the decisions of scholars in their choices of research direction. Two particular areas researchers might avoid would be laser and super-conductivity research, since potentially the results could be classified at any time.

Another government strategy has been to monitor technical and scientific conferences and to force the withdrawal of unclassified papers prior to their presentation. On one occasion in August 1982, about 100 papers to be presented for the Society of Photo-Optical Instrument Engineers were censored by the Defense Department. Many of these papers were not the result of any government funded research (American Library Association [ALA], 1986a, p. 61).

Still another strategy for limiting the distribution of technical information was to extend the lists of technologies prohibited from export. These lists include the Commodity Control List, the U.S. Munitions List, and the Military Critical Technologies List. The last is perhaps the most controversial, since it is over 700 pages long and is itself classified (Shattuck, 1986, pp. A17, A25). At the present time it purportedly "covers all newly created technical documents by DoD-funded research, development, test, and evaluation programs" (Kaplan, 1984).

In July 1987 the Reagan Administration held a national conference on super-conductivity research which excluded foreigners (McDonald, 1987). At this conference President Reagan proposed to exempt research results in this area from the Freedom of Information Act.

Responses by scientists were mixed. Some favored the Reagan proposal as a means of maintaining reciprocity, in that several nations have erected information barriers after the fashion of trade barriers. Many other scientists objected. In particular, James A. Krumhansl, professor of Physics at Cornell University, stated that he doubted the Japanese would continue to invite American scientists to conferences, if Americans excluded them. Another problem for the scientific community is that many research teams in government funded technical research are comprised of foreign nationals. Philip Anderson, professor of physics at Princeton and a 1977 Nobel Price winner, stated that his own "theoretical group consists of an Indian scientist, three scientists from Communist China, two from Canada, one from Ireland, and two Americans" (McDonald, 1987).

From these events it is clear that national technical capability has become a major area of contention among nations. The question is not just which has the most weapons, or the best defense, but which nation has the lead in technology—not only for the sake of military superiority, but also for national economic superiority.

The Reagan Administration also extended the legal framework under which a person can be prosecuted for violating security laws (Armstrong, 1986, p. 32). In the case of *United States v. Morison* (1985), the defendant, a government employee, transmitted three satellite reconnaissance photographs to Jane's Defence Weekly. Morison was himself an editor for *Jane's Fighting Ships,* and this was known to the Government. While the defense showed that there was no real damage to U.S. security and no intent to damage that security, Morison was convicted of espionage on the theory that he broke the circle of control around the photographs. The decision represents a major extension of the parameters under which charges of espionage can be brought.

Finally, the Government has made cutbacks in the gathering of statistical information. These cuts have been a means to reduce staff and paperwork, but also demonstrate a philosophical bias—if the information is not useful to the Government itself, then there is no reason to collect it. Significant information reductions have occurred in the ares of health, education, and energy statistics (ALA, 1986a, pp. 56-58).

Of these strategies—controlled leaks, compartmentalization, pre-publication review, polygraphs, weakening the Freedom of Information Act, extending the export control list, censoring conference papers, restricting foreign nationals from conferences, extending the legal parameters for espionage, and eliminating some statistical information—only the elimination of some statistical information had to that point in time any direct impact on the nation's libraries. Then came the publication of *The Hunt for Red October* and *The Washington Post* story on the Discovery shuttle mission. These two stories evidently represented significant blows to the perception of the state of national security by several Executive Branch agencies.

A major component of overall espionage activity is the collection of bits and pieces of information regarding the enemy's strategic and tactical capability. From the pieces an overall picture is assembled. Obviously then, much of the national security effort is directed toward limiting the distribution of information so that the enemy cannot collect the bits and pieces. With these two stories it became clear to the military that while they had been protecting a large number of fairly large bits of information, they had failed to protect an even larger number of small bits of information from public distribution. Given enough of the small bits and enough time, a studious novelist could derive a useful, overall picture of U.S. military capability. What the novelist could do, the enemy could do also.

For those charged with maintaining national security several questions arose. How much technical information had been distributed? Where was it located? Where did it originate? What could be done to protect this information in the future? And finally, what could be done to limit the damage?

Because the situation was extraordinary, the security measures taken in response to these questions were, for a democracy, extraordinary. Again it is not clear from the public record when the first response came. According to a Department of Defense announcement on 17 March, 1986 the CIA and the DOD initiated a disinformation strategy about this time. "Incorrect performance figures for aircraft and weapon systems, and other altered technical information," were included in press releases (North, 1986). Other channels for technical disinformation were also used, so that it even became feasible for the disinformation to reach the Congress through public hearings. The DOD justified this by stating that the Congress had direct channels to the DOD to verify its information. The disinformation program was not centralized within any government agency and was also compartmentalized. This organization arrangement raises the uneasy specter of the U.S. Government disinforming itself more than it was disinforming the Soviets. The question must also be asked as to whether a democracy is capable of effectively using disinformation in times of peace.

Besides this particular damage control effort, on 6 November 1986 Admiral John Poindexter, head of the National Security Council, created a new classification for information described as sensitive (Schrage, 1986). (This was just prior to the beginning of the Iran-Contra Scandal.) The authorization for this classification came from National Security Decision Directive 145, signed by President Reagan in September 1984. The sensitive information class was directly aimed at unclassified information which in combination with other information could produce an aggregate picture of U.S. military capability. This class could encompass, "government or government derived economic, human, financial, industrial, agricultural, technological and law enforcement information." Also under review at this same time were two proposals. The first would require licenses for foreign nationals to search databases which are part of the National Technical Information Service (NTIS) database, Dialog, or other privately owned databases. The second suggested that software be installed on the database search systems to monitor anyone accessing national security related topics.

This problem of sensitive or gray information had been discussed several years earlier in the Corson Report (National Academy of Sciences, 1982, p. 49). Commissioned by the National Academy of Sciences and other agencies, the report was intended to answer questions regarding technology transfer to the Soviet Union and other foreign governments. Following more than a year of debate within the Defense Department, the Government announced on 24 May 1984 that there would be no category of classification for the sensitive or gray information (Walsh, 1984). Between this announcement and the Government's reversal of that policy in November 1984 (Kaplan, 1984) was the publication in October of Clancy's novel.

As the Iran-Contra Affair progressed, pressure from Congress forced the White House on 18 March 1987 to withdraw plans for the sensitive class of information (Engleberg, 1987). About this same time, however, the Office of

Management and Budget (OMB) renewed its efforts to privatize NTIS (Farnsworth, 1987). The privatization issue first arouse in early 1985 when Malcolm Baldridge, Secretary of Commerce, became alarmed about the transfer of technical information to foreign governments through NTIS (Norman, 1985). Subsequently in April 1986, the Department of Commerce published a request for public comment (Department of Commerce, 1986). Several possible privatization alternatives were discussed and numerous issues were raised. Would government agencies continue to place documents in a privatized NTIS? Should there be legislation requiring the placement? Would government-to-government document exchange programs continue? Would documents continue to be permanently available as they are now? Should the government impose price controls on a private company to prevent the information from becoming overly expensive? Should the government copyright information prior to distributing it through a private company? What rights do citizens have to the results of federally funded research?

From the viewpoint of public administrators (Moe, 1987), questions of this type are often of lesser importance than "the key question... which sector [public or private] performs the function more efficiently and economically?" (p. 453). Primarily, the privatization movement has aimed at reducing the role of government to allow market forces to determine the growth and/or decline of products and services. Within the United States the movement became intertwined with Reaganomics and the Reagan philosophy of reducing the size and scope of the federal government. However, correctly viewed, the privatization movement is international in scope. But "...compared to most other nations, developed and less developed, relatively few candidates are available for full divestiture by the United States government" (p. 456).

According to one researcher (Moe, 1987), economic theory alone cannot justify privatization. There are organizational and legal problems in determining the assignment of functions between the public and private sectors. These problems include the loss of decision-making authority to the private sector, loss of personnel and continuity in administration of services, loss of accountability of officials to the public, the possibility of corruption, conflict of interest, and protection of citizens' privacy. Additional jurisdictional and legal questions relate to public budget review, taxation of the privatized service, bankruptcy, and liability. At the present time, "...the political actors, both executive and legislative, are assigning functions with a public character largely without criteria and with consequences that are expensive to both the public and private sectors" (p. 456).

While there are sufficient philosophical grounds upon which to attack the privatization movement, the library community has generally confined the arguments against the privatization of NTIS to the practical matters of what information will be available and how much it will cost. Historically librarians have favored privatization when the issues of availability and cost of information have not been significant. In 1982 the National Commission on Libraries and Information Science (NCLIS, 1982) issued a report which delineated the issues related to public and private sector information functions. The report showed that the greatest conflict between the sectors arises over government information that is of high economic value to the private sector. However, the task force specifically excluded technology issues (in this case, computer searching, etc.) and international data flow from their discussion (NCLIS, 1982, p. 4).

In 1986 the American Library Association's Committee on Freedom and Equality of Access to Information described many of the Reagan Administration's efforts to limit access to information. But in this report, also, there was a tendency to view favorably the privatization of the delivery systems of government derived information (ALA, 1986a, p. 77).

Librarians have rarely seen the privatization of NTIS as the Government's means to diminish or even eliminate it as a source of national technical information. More typically they are inclined to answer the threat that privatization poses with questions on the order of, "How is this going to work?" (Moody, 1986). Only slight attention is given to the issue of what information will be permanently lost. Yet, according to Kurt N. Molhom, Administrator of the Defense Logistics Agency at the Defense Technical Information Center (DTIC), it is doubtful that the DTIC would continue to provide information to a private contractor that it currently provides to NTIS (Moody, 1986, p. 160).

Perhaps the strongest response to the issue came on 28 May 1987 in the Special Library Association's testimony to the NCLIS. In this testimony SLA linked the NTIS matter with other government tactics to restrict access to information (Morton, 1988, p. 192).

It is clear that the Government's motivations go beyond any economic savings or increase in inefficiency. NTIS is a profit-making agency and has on four separate occasions in the last decade failed to pass reviews for privatization (DeCandido, 1988). The Information Industry Association, one of whose members would be a likely purchaser of NTIS, has stated in a letter to the chairman of the House Sub-committee on Science, Research, and Technology, that the privatization proposal is "fatally flawed in conception." And finally, both houses of Congress have passed legislation prohibiting any further contracting-out of NTIS services ("NTIS Privatization," 1988).

While there are ample philosophical grounds for opposing the privatization of NTIS as an ill-conceived target of the privatization movement, it seems obvious that, for the Government at least, privatization is not the true issue. The library community should not be deceived by the rhetoric, or swayed into modifying a reasonable history of opinion about privatization, when the true issue is censorship.

In the field of public administration there is growing evidence that privatization is being used as a tool for infringing upon the rights of private citizens. According to Sullivan (1987), "Although the United States Constitution provides many protections for citizens against arbitrary government action and infringement of individual liberties, it provides no protection from abuses by the private sector" (p. 461).

After reviewing pertinent legal cases from the last several years, Sullivan concludes:

> To political leaders or public administrators who review constitutional due process requirements as onerous limits on the efficiency of government agencies, the possibility of escaping such restraints can only add luster to the possibilities of privatization. To those who share the concerns ...for maximum protection of citizens from arbitrary decision matters, however, the current drive for privatization poses a major threat (p. 466).

Another episode in the Government's damage control efforts has been the FBI's "Library Awareness Program." According to the FBI, the program was designed to inform librarians that foreign agents are using the nation's libraries to gather technical information (McFadden, 1987). the FBI also requested information on materials used and database searches performed by specific persons. An additional justification for this program has been the "mosaic theory." In 1986 a number of private vendors of technical information were visited by the FBI, Department of Defense, CIA, and the Air Force. According to Jerry Yung, Mead Data's vice-president for government relations, "Their position was that, though available publicly, once aggregated with powerful computer software, [technical information] could be used against national interests" (Hagedorn, 1988). Both Mead Data and the library community have rejected the mosaic theory (Foerstel, 1991, p. 72). In addition, at nearly every juncture the library community has opposed the FBI's program. The National Security Archive and the Intellectual Freedom Committee of the ALA continue their efforts, with litigation and Freedom of Information Act requests, to uncover the full extent of the FBI's program (Foerstel, 1991, pp. 158-160).

It appears doubtful that the OMB or any other government agency will pursue the privatization of NTIS in the foreseeable future. In January 1988 President Reagan signed legislation instructing the National Bureau of Standards to devise guidelines for the classification of, and access procedures to, national technical information in the Government's electronic databases. If any standards have been devised, these have not been made publicly available. The problems of sensitive and aggregate information are likely intractable. According to Robert L. Park, professor of physics at the University of Maryland:

> What these cases tell us is that information cannot be only a little bit secret ... We are
> eventually led to treat "sensitive information" like any other classified material—that is,
> to keep it secure and release it only to persons with proper clearance and a need to know
> (Park, 1988, p. 66).

Both the ALA ("Resolution", 1986) and the Association of Research Libraries (1985) have passed resolutions in response to the Government's increasing restrictions on access to information. Still the library community tends to argue the privatization of NTIS as an issue of economy and efficiency, rather than one of censorship. To paraphrase Chief Justice John Marshall, the power to privatize is the power to destroy. While the issue of the FBI's Library Awareness Program is one of confidentiality, it is also an issue of failure. From the perspective of the Government, there was a failure to protect national security by allowing technical information to be publicly distributed. It is doubtful that the FBI program has deterred any Soviet agents. That technical information currently resides in the nation's libraries does not make the librarian the villain.

The Reagan Presidency significantly restructured foreign policy away from the support of military dictators favorable to the U.S. and toward the support of freely elected democracies. There has also been considerable rhetoric and some progress toward lowering national economic trade barriers. It is odd that simultaneously there has been an agenda to limit access to information within the republic itself. The military's censorship of the media during the conflict in the Persian Gulf has resulted in the further extension of government control over information ("No News," 1991). Additionally, the war with Iraq has once again raised questions about the export of technology and technical information (Smolowe, 1991).

It is not apparent that this agenda is solely the product of a philosophical or political bias. Military and economic competition among nations will become increasingly a competition for the technological edge. The relative importance of national technical information will increase correspondingly.

The problem of aggregate information is one of mesh. How finely must the Government sieve information to protect national security? It is also a problem of time. Today's insignificant bit of information may be tomorrow's key to an information mosaic. It is also a problem of personal freedoms. How many government employees, scholars, and researchers must sign away their First Amendment rights? It is also a problem of confidence and trust. Can the U.S. promote democracy in the world by censoring its own citizenry?

The publication of *The Hunt for Red October* was a decisive turning point, from which undoubtedly there is no turning back. Researchers and librarians must be prepared to address the problems posed by the increasing importance of national technical information.

REFERENCES

American Library Association. *Freedom of Equality of Access to Information: A Report to the American Library Association.* Chicago: American Library Association, 1986a.

American Library Association. "Resolution Concerning the Collection and Dissemination of Governmental Scientific Information." *Newsletter on Intellectual Freedom, 35,* (1986b), p. 238.

Armstrong, Scott. "The Restrictive Effects of Government Information on Scholarship and Research: Two Views from Users, the Journalist." *Minutes of the 107th Meeting of the Association of Research Libraries* (1986, pp. 24-31). Washington, D.C.: Association of Research Libraries.

Association of Research Libraries. "Access to Information: A Statement from the Association of Research Libraries." *Minutes of the 107th Meeting of the Association of Research Libraries* (1986, pp. E1-E2). Washington, D.C.: Association of Research Libraries.

Clancy, Tom. *The Hunt for Red October.* Annapolis, MD: Naval Institute Press, 1984.

DeCandido, Graceanne A. "Voices Raised in Subcommittee Against Privatization of NTIS." *Library Journal, 113*(6), (1988), p. 16.

Department of Commerce. "Study of Alternatives for Privatizing NTIS." *Federal Register,* (April 28, 1986) pp. 15868-15870.

Engleberg, Stephen. "U.S. Drops Efforts on Sensitive Data." *The New York Times,* (March 18, 1987) pp. A1. A21.

Farnsworth, Clyde H. "U.S. Plans to Spin off Technical Data Service." *The New York Times,* (March 18, 1987) p. D1, D21.

Foerstel, Herbert N. *Surveillance in the stacks: The FBI's Library Awareness Program.* New York: Greenwood Press, 1991.

Hagedorn, Ann. "FBI Recruits Librarians To Spy on "Commie" Readers." *Wall Street Journal,* (May 19, 1988) p. .32.

Hiatt, Fred. "Secretary Says Shuttle Report is Irresponsible." *The Washington Post,* (Dec. 20, 1984) pp. A1, A14.

Kaplan, Fred. "Pentagon Order to Curb Public Access to Military Data." *The Boston Globe,* (Nov. 4, 1984) p. 9.

Lardner, George, Jr. "FOIA Ball Bounces into Congress' Court." *The Washington, Post,* (July 16, 1981) p. A6.

McDonald, Kim. "Reagan's Plan to Limit Foreign Access to Data Opposed By Scientists." *Chronicle of Higher Education,* (Sept. 9, 1987) pp. A1, A10.

McFadden, Robert D. "F.B.I. in New York Asks Librarians' Aid in Reporting on Spies." *The New York Times,* (Sept. 18, 1987) pp. A1, B2.

Mitchel, Steven E. "Classified Information and Legal Research," *Law Library Journal, 79,* (1987) pp. 445-454.

Moe, Ronald C. "Exploring the Limits of Privatization." *Public Administration Review, 47,* (1987) pp. 453-460.

Moody, Marilyn. "The Privatization of NTIS: What Are the Implications?" *RQ, 27,* (1986) pp. 157-162.

Morton, Sandy I. "SLA Responds to U.S. Government Issues in the '80s." *Special Libraries, 79,* (1988), pp. 189-193.

National Academy of Sciences. *Scientific Communication and National Security.* Washington, D.C.: National Academy Press, 1982.

National Commission on Libraries and Information Science. *Public Sector/Private Sector Interaction in Providing Information Services.* Washington, D.C.: National Commission on Libraries and Information Science, 1982.

"No News: Bad News." *The Nation,* (Jan. 28, ,1991) pp. 75-76.

Norman, Colin. "Commerce Secretary Wants Technical Data Restricted." *Science, 227*(4691), (1985) p. 1182.

North, David M. "U.S. Using Disinformation Policy to Impede Technical Data Flow." *Aviation Week & Science Technology, 124*(11), (1986) pp. 16-17.

"NTIS Privatization Proceeds Despite Congress's Opposition." *American Libraries, 19,* (March, 198), p. 156.

Park, Robert L. "Restricting Information: A Dangerous Game." *Issues in Science and Technology, 5*(1), (1988), pp. 62-67.

Pear, Robert. "For the Patient Reader, Military Secrets are Self-revealing." *The New York Times,* (Aug. 30, 1987a) p. E5.

Pear, Robert. "Washington Feeling Insecure about Non-Secret Information." *The New York Times,* (Aug. 30, 1987b) p. E5.

Pincus, Walter and Mary Thornton. "U.S. To Orbit 'Sigint' Craft from Shuttle." *The Washington Post,* (Dec. 19, 1984) pp. A1, A8-A9.

Schrage, Michael. "U.S. Limits Access to Information Related to National Security." *The Washington Post,* (Nov. 13, 1986) pp. A1, A29.

"Secrecy Planned for Shuttle Mission: Pentagon Acts To Conceal Satellite Cargo from Soviets." *The Washington Post,* (Dec. 8, 1984) p. A8.

Shattuck, John, "Federal Restrictions on the Free Flow of Academic Information and Ideas." *Minutes of the 107th Meeting of the Association of Research Libraries* (1986) pp. A1-A31. Washington, D.C.: Association of Research Libraries.

Smolowe, Jill. "Who Armed Baghdad?" *Time, 137,* (Feb. 11, 1991) pp. 334-35.

Sullivan, Harold J. "Privatization of Public Services: A Growing Threat to Constitutional Rights." *Public Administration Review, 47,* (1987) pp. 461-467.

Walsh, John. "DOD Springs Surprise on Secrecy Rules." *Science, 224,* (1984) p. 1081.

EXAMINING INNOVATIVE APPLICATIONS OF TECHNOLOGY IN LIBRARIES

Virginia Tiefel

I am extremely grateful to the Council on Library Resources, The Ohio State University, and the University Libraries for the opportunity to do this study. The Council provided grant support for travel and the University also funded travel support. The University Libraries provided a five month leave to make the site visits and write the report. The generous support from the Council, the University, and the Libraries made this study possible.

Over a period of six months I visited and talked with personnel in 13 institutions. My purpose was to examine innovative applications of technology to public services in libraries. Working for four years on the Ohio State University library's Gateway to Information project had increased my curiosity about how projects develop. I was interested in such issues as how projects were started, and developed, whom they served, and what problems were encountered. I created 17 criteria for exmaining the projects (see back of report) and applied for grant money to support the necessary travel. I believed it was necessary to visit the sites and talk with the people involved in the project to

Advances in Library Administration and Organization,
Volume 11, pages 143-200.
Copyright © 1993 by JAI Press Inc.
All rights of reproduction in any form reserved.
ISBN: 1-55938-596-0

understand the issues. I didn't want to undertake a scientific study as such but rather to get a feeling for the projects and determine what the major elements are in implementing innovative projects, how people on the cutting edge develop their projects, and what and how they plan for the future. This is an impressionistic study and, therefore, very subjective. I have tried to capture the "flavor" of the projects and provide some insights for others who are or would like to become involved in forward-thinking, innovative library projects.

There is some repetition in the report. This was done deliberately to enable the sections of the report to stand alone and allow the reader to focus on specific issues without reading the entire report.

SOME OBSERVATIONS

There are some common issues or themes that become apparent in the site visits and while writing this report. This brief summary is not comprehensive or all-inclusive but suggestive of what was learned.

In terms of users, most librarians observed that users often don't know what they need and how the information may be packaged. They don't understand how to search and often don't know if what they found is the best, most relevant information. Brevity and speed are important to users. They usually prefer electronic to print format and don't like extra key strokes. The emphasis of most of the projects was on students—23 of the 25 programs served students (but not exclusively). Faculty have increased expectations about information and user education and these increased demands are putting pressure on libraries. Usage was growing steadily in most projects.

There is a perception that most libraries, as they function now, require users to know and understand how libraries are organized. Many librarians are tying to change this by developing systems that will meet users' needs and are easy to use. Most libraries wanted to develop improved interfaces. Their goal was to develop systems with transparent delivery using laymen's language. They want to build systems for usage, not experimental purposes. Librarians are striving to meet the total needs of the users and put them in control of their own information-seeking. They want to provide information regardless of location or format with a heavy emphasis on access, especially remote access. Circulation status is seen as important and there is increased development of local databases.

Librarians are using computers to support user education, especially, at the lower undergraduate level to reduce demands on staff and provide information at the time of need. Many believe computers are cost-effective in meeting user education needs and will enable libraries to provide better instruction for students with less staff involvement. Even though librarians want to provide more help for users, they are often reluctant to refer users to computers.

A common question was at what point the project should be made available to users. There was a lot of concern about how to limit printing. The issue of whether to acquire CDs or tapes was a prominent one with wide variation in opinion. Most librarians wanted more support but weren't sure how to get it. Many were uncertain where the project fit in the library as a whole.

In terms of technology there appears to be a move from main frame to a distributed system. The reasons given for this move were to reduce costs and have windowing capability which enables users to track their searches. Most systems were on the campus networks which was perceived as important, as is dial-up access. A common user interface to mail, bulletin boards, and library and campus-wide availability was seen as desirable. Librarians recognized the capability of computers but also noted computers are expensive and require instruction in usage. Other detriments noted were their often slow response time and the inflexibility of standardized formats.

Written goals and objectives appear to be useful in giving a project direction and keeping the project on track. There seemed to be a correlation between the size of the project, the number of people working on it, and clearly stated goals and objectives.

In general, these libraries were in a proactive mode. A common belief was that if the library didn't take a proactive role, it would be subsumed by the campus computer center. Most administrators provided strong support even with severe budget cuts and almost every library had some staff skepticism regardless of the project's apparent success. There appears to be a strong commitment to sharing resources with other libraries.

PROJECT DESCRIPTIONS

Carnegie Mellon University

Carnegie-Mellon University has three major projects in development: Project Mercury; LIS II; and INSPEC. In 1980-81 before Project Mercury was begun, the decision was made to acquire an integrated online catalog. The Library Director wanted to expand the program beyond an online catalog so a strategic plan was written (subsequently three were done). Carnegie-Mellon is an example of the convergence of campus computing services with the libraries. System development is divided into system contents, user interface, and system distribution. They want their systems to be generally and easily available without requiring computer accounts, if possible, and without complicated log-on protocols.

They view the problem with most systems (including print) as requiring users to know and understand how libraries organize information. Complicating this is the librarians' perception that users often have no clear idea what they need and how the needed information may be packaged.

LIS I attempted to respond to these problems. The user selects the database and enters key words for Boolean searching. Additional screens offer help in modifying the search, using the system, and doing more sophisticated searching. LIS I is a menu-driven system with some written, brief instructions. The popularity of LIS I has proven that users prefer to use information in electronic format over print. Operational for 5 years, (first public system in March 1986), LIS I is being phased out and being moved from a mainframe to a distributed system. Reasons for moving in this direction are to be able to use windows and reduce costs of maintaining a main-frame system.

LIS II uses OCLC EPIC tapes and, by being able to open four windows simultaneously, the user is able to track his search more easily. LIS II is based on the campus network Andrew which is a distributed file system with hundreds of file servers, thousands of workstations, and more than 50 LANs. The workstations provide windowing capability and a common user interface to network services including electronic mail, bulletin boards, printing, and access to LIS. Andrew provides access to Internet. By using the OSF's Motif Style Guide, LIS II will avoid some of the problems users encountered with LIS I. Because users commonly have difficulty keeping track of where they are in a search, windowing screens were used to help this problem. Multiple windows provide a window for each conceptual task, enabling the users to keep their context and build a better conceptual model of information searching and online retrieval. LIS II allows other institutions access to their local databases, but restricts access to commercial databases.

LIS II will provide a one-line record display, a brief record display that includes variant journal titles and library holdings, and a full record display. It will also provide an item or issue display with updates of latest issues, a table of contents display, a simple way to track journal title changes, links with other databases and journal records and a simple way to submit an ILL request and request a photocopy or FAX.

There was much discussion about when to put it out and the projected time was the fall of 1991. This was somewhat dependent on how much time would be required to change from the main frame to the distributed system. It had been observed that users don't like extra key strokes and LIS II will reflect that. With half of the searching in LIS I related to the catalog, it was decided to have the LIS II screen default to the catalog. By fall, users will be able to set their first screen to whichever database they primarily use.

Future plans for LIS II include providing access to bibliographic and full-text databases in business, the social sciences, and humanities. These will be supported by the distributed system and CD-ROM jukeboxes. The system will offer access to more than 1000 full-text journals and 2300 journals in index or abstract form. Scanned articles will be available on 240 CDs for reading at the workstations. Users will be able to e-mail requests for printouts of the articles. Because the library wants to provide campus-wide availability, there has not been a strong emphasis on acquiring CDs. The library has been adding CDs to the collection since July 1988. They want the access to the CDs to be transparent to the user.

Project Mercury has been in development for two years. It is the same as LIS II with the same interface and databases except Mercury has full text. Both systems have the same software and hardware; OCLC furnishes the search software. The full text is in the areas of computer science and artificial intelligence: these were selected because the users would be computer literate, the text doesn't have a lot of visuals, and the discipline is a prominent one on campus. Project Mercury was funded by the Digital Equipment Co. and the Pew Memorial Trust. Access is restricted because of licensing agreements, so users must have an I.D. password. They plan eventually to have automatic authentication in LIS II. Fifty percent of all searchers are in the catalog. Results have shown users only change databases once or twice, including the catalog. Faculty want to see more records at a time and select into one list. Some faculty look at as many as 500 titles. The system allows them to cut and paste and save their searches. The full text has a page-like look—can zoom in, etc. It is possible to browse indexes by a single word and there are multiple indexes to a database. More stand-alone databases on CDs and more information about the contents of recently acquired books are being added. The number of commercial and locally mounted databases is being increased. Three enhancement projects have been undertaken in the library:

1. Contents notes for plays in collections.
2. Separately authored chapters in books and art exhibition catalogs.
3. Abstracts to computer science reports (EDRC).

Two catalog enhancements from commercial vendors are being added. One is *Choice* book reviews that will be brought up with the catalog record. The other is ISI analytic and full records for books and conference proceedings in science and engineering. INSPEC covers four publications in Physics, Electronics, and Computing and became available in November 1989.

CARL Systems

The CARL System serves over 1000 terminals and houses over five million bibliographic records from the Denver site. Replications of the system serve single institutions and consortia. A total of 75 libraries are presently supported on the system from 11 interconnected CPU locations linking 3500 dedicated terminals that reach from Hawaii to Boston and Maryland. CARL also provides circulation, acquisitions, and serials control systems.

In addition, approximately 150 libraries access the CARL System databases via gateway connections and most libraries in the country can access CARL through the Internet. CARL provides gateway access to *UnCover* and a wide variety of union lists: over 150 libraries use *UnCover* through gateway agreements.

UnCover covers 10,000 unique multi-disciplinary journals. The database is updated daily and indexed overnight so it is current within 24 hours of receiving the journal: no other article citation database offers this currency. *UnCover II* will deliver the first copy of the articles within 24 hours and then delivery of that article becomes instantaneous.

UnCover provides article records taken from tables of contents of all journals received by selected CARL Systems libraries. In addition to the 10,000 multi-disciplinary journals, it can be expanded by other institutions to reflect their special collections. *UnCover* contains article citations with descriptive information or abstracts from the contents pages, therefore users can search by topic or look at the tables of contents. There are two ways to search *UnCover* . The user can:

1. Search the bibliographic record of individual libraries and then go into *UnCover,* see the table of contents of individual issues, and look at the article record.
2. Select generic *UnCover* and do a subject search in all *UnCover* journals.

UnCover II which is document delivery is to be available in mid-1991. CARL can refer the user to information beyond what is available locally. CARL provides information access and delivery for more than 50 different community and commercial information indexes, using a variety of formats including full text and optical images.

CARL Systems, Inc. (formed in 1988) has increased the number of systems from six to 11 (three more were to be added by the end of 1991) and increased the number of libraries supported from 20 to 71.

Libraries using CARL as an integrated online library system can also provide access to *UnCover* as a local menu item, although the database resides in Denver. CARL supports gateways via the Internet or through dedicated connects. In either case, customization of front screens, menu choices, and exact messaging is possible. PAC is based on simplicity and flexibility in layman's terminology, not a controlled language.

Their PAC provides word, name, and browse (call number, series, title) access including Boolean capability in single word search. A name and word search can be qualified by format, media type, and date of publication. Name and word indexing is emphasized over traditional string indexing. Sophisticated searching techniques such as automatic threading, search history, and search edit are available. They strive to put the content in simple language for the novice user. Help screens are available and they can be customized according to library, branch, and even terminal. Menu prompting can be bypassed by "Quick Search."

An expert mode which will include full Boolean, explicit truncation, and explicit subject searching, is planned for 1991. For ILL, the user has access to other catalogs including circulation status which encourages borrowing. User-initiated ILL is in the planning stages. Electronic mail is available and is used primarily for internal staff communication. It will be expanded into ILL and acquisitions and will eventually extend to users for communication with the library staff. The PAC's current issue display can provide access to a recreated table of contents or the user can search for articles in *UnCover*. On order information is available to circulation for user holds.

Visual image database storage and retrieval are available. In external databases the system provides access to 75 different information databases (not including library catalogs) from such publishers as Wilson, UMI, Groliers, and IAC. It is planned to add databases at logical sites on the network and offer them to all network participants. Thus, a database available at one site can be available to the rest of the network members.

CARL supports local files like Maggie's Place (see Pike's Peak District Library description) and provides *Choice* reviews. It can accept any machine readable data files for uploading into the system. Updating records can be added through keyboarding at the system terminal and updated through the terminal or by tape-disk loading. It can produce a wide range of reports for members. Geography has had a major impact on how CARL has been developed: users are widely scattered which mandates dial-up access.

CARL sells software and hardware, provides operating training and application, gives upgrades, and provides workshops. The Information Access Committee works with technical and public service librarians. CARL Systems, Inc. services include network design, network installation, on-site maintenance, and equipment repair.

Pike's Peak District Library

Maggie's Place at the Pike's Peak District Library has an online catalog; community events calendar; clubs; courses; local documents; local authors; senior housing options; social and economic indicators; El Paso country legislative districts; child care; Grolier's on-line encyclopedia; city hall online; *Columbia Electronic Encyclopedia;* PPLD news; CARL, MARMOT, and BOULDER catalogs; and computer assisted searches. *Facts on File* was being added in 1991. The system consists of a main library, seven branch libraries, and a country hall library.

The system's policy is to have fewer books and put more emphasis on public computer information. It was one of the first libraries to offer online service for community resource files. This service was first offered in 1978. Important factors in the success of the community resources files have been community concern for information, interest of individuals and groups, and the willingness of the library to try new approaches. The library has talked community agencies into letting them do local databases. Two people are assigned to develop a local database: a librarian works with a paraprofessional to develop the database and the paraprofessional keeps the database current.

The library worked with the local Junior League to develop an information and referral service in 1977. The library's Community Interaction Team (CIT) was effective in getting feedback from the community to help the library decide on what related materials and activities to acquire and continue. The services were advertised with a media blitz and since then, they have done flyers, brochures, radio, television, and speaking to community groups. The theme has been "The Information Place." The PPLD has more databases than any other member of CARL. PPLD has been a special district—not county or city—since 1965. It is an associate member of CARL.

It was noted that libraries have created local files for a long time, but computers offer several advantages: they can save time, arrange and sort information, allow random access, do automatic compilation of statistics, provide different formats, updating capability, consistent patterns for information format, and the capability to dial-up and use on home computers. Some disadvantages of computers are the reluctance of some patrons to use computers, (computers and the expertise to learn how to use them are expensive), slow response time, and the inflexibility of a standardized format.

The library has provided dial-in access since 1978 and currently has 12 dial-in lines. The library has four programmers (two FTE) and 30 public service librarians to serve 400,000 local users. The system can determine usage which is 60 percent local and 40 percent commercial and usage has continued to grow. This library is well known for creating local databases. One that is heavily used is the *Social Economic Indicators* database. It covers statistical information to reflect the trends in the region, tracking changes in demographics, health care statistics, vacancy rates, business starts, etc. It contains current statistical information concerning the Pike's Peak region.

Goals and objectives are clearly stated. Goals are to provide social/economic indicators of the region online and in a timely manner. Targeted users are business people, developers, sales representatives, etc. It's a large database. The software developed for this has been used in developing other databases, especially Quikref. The project has been evaluated by the staff.

The Arts database is the current project. Proposed by Sydney Caler in January 1991, it is planned for availability in late December of 1991. It covers information on cultural, visual and performing artists, rehearsal and performance spaces, practice rooms, costume and equipment sources, etc. Users will be individuals, schools, businesses, program planning staff, etc. The goal is to provide online access to the most current information available on the visual and performing arts and artists of the Colorado Springs area. Benefits will be ease of access, availability to remote users, more current information than is available now, and hard to find information. The skeleton of the system is similar to the local authors database.

University of Southern California

The University of Southern California has two major projects: Project Jefferson and USC Info. USC Info contains Homer (USC's online catalog), periodical databases, and campus information. Homer provides information on materials added since 1978 and covers only some of the materials added before then. The user is advised to look first in Homer, which is the only source for availability, and if not found there, the use is directed to the card catalog.

USC Info has 14 different databases grouped into six broad categories: arts and humanities; general interest; biomedical sciences; science and technology; business and industry; social sciences. Subject selection brings up descriptions of the databases. The contents include five IAC databases: *Magazine Index; Trade and Industry Index; Management Contents; Computer Database; National Newspaper Index* and provides access to over 1000 periodicals. They plan to load six Wilson databases: *Art Index; Humanities Index; Social Sciences Index; Applied Science and Technology Index; General Science Index; Library Literature* and eventually *Psychology Index* and *Medline.* Search Constructor is available in all of the USC Info services:

1. Elect search type (for Homer title, subject, etc.)
2. Type search words.
3. Select preference ("find all of the words above," "find at least one," "find words as a single phrase").
4. Click on boxes to set language, date, material, library.

All four of the above qualifications are placed on a single screen. Users can view records individually or browse a list of 10 records at a time.

The individual record display has four sections: author; title; partial record; full record. The user can opt also for abstracts and holdings. Use of tracings is encouraged. Users are reminded the library holdings are available only in Homer. The record display for database shows author, title, source (bibliographic citation), and how to find out if the library has it—all on one screen.

The user can print or download records which are stored on the mainframe and transferred to Macintosh workstations when printed or downloaded. Printing is limited to 50 records and downloading is limited to 200 records: the same number can be saved. Several Macs share the same printer. Computers have an on-screen suggestion box. The system provides access from home and office. HyperCard access was developed to help students log-on and assist them in searching for and downloading citations.

Using the BRS Information Technologies search system, they can use free text searching, type in the desired subject terms, and use Boolean operators. The system also allows truncation and adjacency operators. The user can return to a previous search by clicking a button, combine and modify previous searches, and scroll citations which include descriptors. Users can pull up abstracts and save them. USC Info is used heavily by undergraduates for term papers. For dial-up access, someone checks for a valid library card. A VT100 emulation is available for non-Mac users. USC has approached service to the user from the aspect of access.

Background: Ten years ago the university president decided to move USC forward academically and in research. The library was historically underfunded so the advancement couldn't be in collections because that takes too long. They decided to build a great library through technology.

Discussion about the Teaching Library began in 1982 and was crystallized in USC's 1986 Re-accreditation Self-Study entitled "Designs for Leadership." The Library Committee headed by Library Director Ritcheson recommended three goals:

1. To support USC's continuing emergence as a research university of great eminence.
2. To provide a state-of-the-art center of learning for students at both the undergraduate and graduate levels.
3. To reject the role of passive service, in favor of interactive electronic learning.

A grant from the Omnunson Foundation was a beginning step. They mounted five additional databases on the BRS mainframe in 1986. They began work on the GEAC circulation system in 1984. USC Info came up in the spring with five terminals in the library and others in the computer labs (Macs were not involved). When they realized that these computers are were dominated by word processing activity, they pulled out the databases and the encyclopedia. By fall of 1988, 100 GEAC catalog terminals came up and crashed.

The failed catalog presented a real problem. There was a BRS mainframe available which performed better than the GEAC system. They decided to move the catalog to the BRS mainframe and put internal functions like acquisitions and circulation on the GEAC system. The library had to get the approval of the vice provost who thought it was a great idea, as did the budget officer. The Center for Scholarly Technology was then brought in. They liked Apple products and thought HyperCard would be a good option to pull the two systems together. A whole new fiber system was being created to deliver this technology across the campus.

There have been two cycles in USC Info: initially databases were set up and the catalog was added in 1987 when they went to Macs. The initial effort came out of the information desk and when the GEAC system failed, additional impetus was added to the project. The library was pushed to produce something quickly because of the catalog failure and Apple's donation of SE/30 terminals.

The team consisted of three staff members: one handled the mainframe, another was responsible for the network, and the third handled the front-end. Librarians selected the databases. Pressure forced them to be practical: deadlines were very important. Bringing in the campus network (on TCPIP) was a major decision and perceived as a very important one. They got the University to finalize the contract with AT&T in 1988 (2 years late). Some said it wouldn't work: there are still some doubts about its future because it is cumbersome to run two systems. An example of the cumbersome nature of the system is the need to acquire catalog records from OCLC, put them on the GEAC system, and then run the tapes to the BRS mainframe. They are now working on software to combine database index and catalog searching.

Using Pro-Cite they plan to create databases to update and produce library publications like pathfinders and bibliographies. They predict that some journals will be published online only. In the library of the future, high speed printers and hand-held machines will be needed. It will be necessary to anticipate what a computer will look like in 20 years to be able to plan the library of tomorrow. A number of small rooms will be needed for collaborative work. Audiovisuals will be computers. New workspaces need to be designed by furniture companies. The profession will need to create a new breed of librarian with computing knowledge. They believe we are in a revolution as important as printing.

A Project Jefferson shell is being developed to enable non-programming faculty and librarians to create and incorporate material for their own assignments and databases. This will be available through Kinko's Software Catalog and will run on a Mac SE with a 20 MB hard disk.

Project Jefferson is a library program in collaboration with the English Department. The director of the writing center is concerned with critical thinking. The project was given impetus when Apple donated 30 Mac SEs for the project for use in the Freshman Writing Lab and College Library. Library Macs were put to additional uses such as database management and the development of front-end searching capabilities for USC Info.

Project Jefferson is a cooperative effort between the library, the Freshman Writing Program, and the School of Industrial and System Engineering. Its goal is to encourage the development of research and critical thinking skills among freshmen. It provides students with interactive access to information, supporting specially formulated writing assignments which ask students to use background information and citations to support a position in one of several constitutional issues like racial discrimination.

Students supply disks for their notebooks and access the assignments on computers. Students have an outline, organization paper, and saved information tabs to view and rearrange background information and citations. A preference tab allows them to choose MLA and APA format. The staff has created an encyclopedia and citation database for the assignment. Encyclopedia articles are linked to broader, narrower, and related topics so students pursue different paths. They presently have 196 citations relating to three different topics in a specially created database. Saved information goes into a notebook which also has a notepad for jotting ideas.

The University of Cincinnati

The University of Cincinnati has two major projects: Medical Information Quick (MIQ) and the Integrated Academic Information Management System (IAIMS). MIQ covers approximately 25 percent of MEDLINE which includes 325 journals. Faculty were involved in selecting the titles from MEDLINE. The journals were grouped by broad subject and covered the current year plus the two previous years. The journals are in the clinical and basic life sciences, and are English language only. Only the journals in the library collection are included. With limited space in the database, the faculty opted for no abstracts in favor of more titles.

Fifteen to 1800 searches are done monthly. The system can accommodate six simultaneous users. There are two workstations in the library and the system provides dial-up access. It's on the campus network. Their license with NLM requires the system be restricted to primary users. It is available 24 hours daily, seven days a week. After several years of examination, installation, and testing it became available in February, 1986. It has two dial-in access phone lines. The intention was to give no formal instruction, but they have done some instructional materials which are online help screens and a quick reference card. MIQ has created a need for one-to-one tutorials which required more back-up at the reference desk. About one-third of the questions on MIQ are technical. With the introduction of CDs, there has been a drop in the usage of MIQ. The Ohio Board of Regents funded the network with the general library. Licensing can be expensive: it's possibly $20,000 with the NLM.

They don't know whether to maintain both systems. They believe there is a need to teach the intellectual process. They perceive a need to teach people how to use MEDLINE. Grateful Med is the instructional software for MEDLINE, but it runs on Procom which isn't compatible with the University's system. They have set up a program for small communities to teach the use of Grateful Med. Pharmacy has a course requiring the use of information, so the library teaches students in this program. They taught 24 students with an emphasis on MEDLINE, its headings and strategies. They get articles by FAX from NLM (Loansome Doc is NLM's ILL).

NLM has funded IAIMS in 14 institutions for years. IAIMS helps academic health centers transform their various information databases into integrated systems. The IAIMS project at the University of Cincinnati is going into phase three (Georgetown University and Columbia University are already in phase three). Georgetown has pulled together the information systems.

The medical school at Cincinnati is strong on clinical medicine and the system is especially appropriate to the needs of the medical faculty and staff. The IAIMS project is designed to develop systems linking research and educational information with clinical data. The IAIMS staff goes on rounds and charts reviews, recording problem-oriented patient data and medication profiles: this information goes into the Patient-Centered Database (PCD). The PCD generates daily census sheets (CS), residents' sign-out cards (SC) with current patient data and discharge summaries. Patient data include demographics, active problem lists, current medications, and ultimate disposition. Residents receive daily printouts analyzing possible drug interactions (DI) and journal articles pertinent to patient management/ diagnostic issues. The project provides data that 83 percent of the team members would not otherwise have seen and the PCD-generated information and forms save time. The project is on Internet and therefore it reaches beyond the library. All workstations are outside the library.

San Diego State University

At the San Diego State University Library, Robert Carande is one of five librarians in the science division: he reports to the head of the science division. The entire library has 26 librarians and four temporary positions (A California State University campus can have only one library.) The systems office in the library has five computer people and reports to the Assistant University Librarian for Technical Services.

Inopac "The Pac" is their online catalog. They work with Innovative Interfaces, Inc. The library is putting coin-operated printers on their OPAC. PIN is a CD—ROM network made up of periodicals arranged by subject. It was planned by a committee and begun three years ago when lottery funds became available. The main frame and CD-ROMs are in the library.

Robert is developing Reference Advisory Systems (RAS). He has one running now: other librarians are working individually on their own RAS projects. There is one workstation with eight modules and a hard disk. It runs on a color PC. Robert's project is Materials Librarian (material sci/ engineering): other projects are Public Health Librarian; Nursing Librarian; and Computer Science Librarian. Robert's system emphasizes brevity: he tries to keep the narrative to two screens. It is menu-driven with the first screen containing the main menu: type of literature (journal, report, standards, etc.). The second screen is a materials menu (type of material (plastics, metals, etc). Reference tools are recommended on the third screen. Robert doesn't alphabetize because he believes that encourages skimming. In developing a

RAS, Robert identifies three factors that need to be determined: subject;, type of information (statistical/factual, general overview, and recent research), and level of user expertise (specialist or generalist).

Each RAS is linked to a knowledge base which has two parts:

1. Bibliographic—subject and format fields—includes title, location, online status, and brief annotations.
2. Directional—suggests subject terms for searching OPAC.

The second screen on all RAS workstations requires natural language input from the user. Then the user is given the subject menu automatically (this step isn't related to the second screen choice). This is done so librarians can:

1. Determine if the user's second step would have produced what he needed.
2. Identify gaps in the subjects offered.
3. See if the user and the programmer have the same understanding of the subject menu.
4. Use in the future development of a natural language interface.

A larger system is Science Library Board which contains a front end that is programmed in HyperPAD's PAD talk. It is object-oriented with a cluster of RAS modules. It's a natural language interface in Dialog NLI (Natural Language Interface). The databases are related to RAS or the interface.

The University of Houston

The University of Houston has two projects: Intelligent Reference Information System (IRIS) and Reference Expert which is the expert system portion of IRIS. Charles Bailey, the Assistant Director of Systems, is the project Manager and Tom Wilson, Director of Systems, also works on the projects.

A third project, The Information Machine, is a stand-alone terminal used to orient users to library procedures, floorplans, and how to use the library, i.e., basic library information. It provides downloading capabilities and printing. Available for use since 1987, it is text-based with a few simple graphics and 350 screens. A committee was appointed to develop it. Questionnaires were done in 1987 resulting in eight responses. According to the results, the least successful module was the one on finding articles on a topic.

The Index Report is the public prototype system designed to suggest relevant reference materials based on a hierarchy of subjects and questions answered by users to go from a broad field of "Humanities" into a specific film review source. Reference Expert is a new version of Index Expert. IRIS combines Reference Expert and CD-ROMs.

The Electronic Publication Center Projects created a CD-ROM network and mounted 19 CD-ROMs. The Reference Expert expands the prototype Index Expert to allow searching on the network of CDs. The Intelligent Reference Information System (IRIS) is the name for the overall project (mounting a CD-ROM network, creating an expert system for finding materials, and linking them together). It combines a new version of the Index Expert (The Reference Expert) with the Electronic Publication Center Project to allow identification of significant materials and, if searchable via the network, permit searching the CD-ROMs. Because the knowledge base is separate from the expert system, it can be easily maintained by librarians.

Arizona State University

The Arizona State University Library is a member of the CARL System. Its online catalog provides access to the *Academic American Encyclopedia* online and the *Song Index,* which covers popular songs in the collection of the ASU music library. The Career Development Center has information on careers and lists books on career-related topics that are in the Center. The *Company Index* provides names and addresses of companies referred to by the career database. A campus calendar lists scheduled orientations, workshops, special events, advisement, and interview dates. A *Map Index* lists maps in the library collection and historical maps in the Arizona Collection and the Arizona Historical Foundation.

Arizona State subscribes to the CARL *UnCover Index* which is an up-to-date database indexing articles in 10,000 journals. A number of Wilson indexes are on the system including *Applied Science and Technology; Business Periodicals Index; Education Index; General Science Index, Humanities Index,* and *Social Sciences Indexes.* Advanced Communication Support System (ACSS) is a broadband network providing on-and-off campus access to the online catalog. It requires no special passwords, has no use charges, and is available 24 hours a day. Virtually any microcomputer or terminal with a modem and appropriate communications software can access it. A brochure describes the procedures.

They are working on frequently-asked questions which were collected from service points in the Hayden Library for three weeks and updated regularly. These had been put on a rolodex for service points and used for staff training. The previous library director wanted their catalog to be one of the top five in the country, so they put their money in Tandem hardware for an online catalog.

Machine Assisted Reference Services (MARS) and CD-ROMs are in one place where assistance is available. Help is provided by librarians and available during reference hours (until 10:00 P.M.). The MARS room is under the reference department. The coordinator of computer services is in the reference department and he is responsible for maintenance. The selection of databases is done by librarians. MARS is in the science library also: it is installed where online searching used to be located until CDs became so popular. MARS is in the government documents department and the head of that department is responsible for the CDs. They use CARL to provide access to government documents. They are working with SDTAT Master developing a database for County and City Data. None of the MARS sites is connected to a LAN or in the online catalog. MARS librarians are responsible for instructing the other librarians. [They have done a video, "A day at the ASU Libraries" on HyperCard to distribute to high schools.]

Texas A&M University

Texas A&M has developed a front end to NOTIS using HyperCard. MacNOTIS is designed to help users search the online computer system. Available from the MacNOTIS workstations are Wilson CD-ROM indexes on a mainframe with a HyperCard front end, the Medical Sciences Library catalog, and the Prairie View College online catalog. Wilson is available on 80 NOTIS workstations and dial-up access to over 199 terminals is available. Instruction on how to use Wilson indexes is in a printed guide. Only one in 20 catalog users also uses a Wilson index. Evaluations have been done by observation and transaction logs.

Inmagic is an expert system for an upper level undergraduate technical writing course in the colleges of business, agriculture, and engineering. The assignment requires students to locate reference materials for a paper. Librarians created the special database to support the course. Written evaluations showed that one third of the students didn't find what they are looking for and one half needed to consult a librarian for help. Students had problems with the help screens and complained that the printers were slow, difficult to read, and required multiple screens of instruction every time they used them. The subject headings used in the database presented some problems and were found to be limited in scope. The software provided inadequate help screens and the system was vulnerable to tampering. Plans are to expand the databases to other disciplines and improve the subject headings. Software more appropriate to their needs will be sought. The library plans to publicize to all sections of the course to reach more classes.

University of California, San Diego

RoboRef and Remote Access Interface Design [RAID] are two projects under development at the University of California, San Diego. RoboRef involves four libraries. Instructions are individual library specific. The libraries are Biomedical, Central University, Science and Engineering, and Undergraduate. RoboRef is planned in three phases:

1. A guide to the library provides general information but is not interactive. This has been completed and is being evaluated using unobtrusive methods of questionnaires and logs.
2. A Computer Assisted Instruction (CAI) program covers how to use such major tools in the science library as *Chemical Abstracts* and *Beilstein*. It provides instruction on single sources at both the beginning and advanced levels, offers help on what type of information is needed, and refers users to other libraries too. Funding is needed to continue development of this expert-like system.
3. This program will cover how to use other types of tools.

Some librarians want to add pathfinders, but the lack of a keyboard presents a problem. RoboRef isn't on the campus network yet. They have found that many students are "hackers."

Remote Access Interface Design (RAID) provides dial access to Roger (the local catalog) and Melvyl (the California state catalog). Some information from RoboRef is on RAID. The library wants to add access to databases with a common interface. This project has been funded by the library. The systems office reports to the Assistant University Librarian for Technical Services (14 staff support the catalog and library network). The reference department in the main library isn't comfortable referring users to computers unless the reference desk is closed.

Pennsylvania State University

Pennsylvania State University Library is working on three projects: the course-related program in the English 15 (freshman), English 202, and Business 202 courses; the Ask Fred project; and changes in the catalog. The change in the course-related instruction in the English and Business courses involves an attempt to move the program from a very staff intensive one to a Computer Associated Instruction (CAI)/computer program. In the English 15 course, the English department wanted students to use the library so a workbook program was developed: it contains three modules (periodicals, catalog, and reference sources). There is no prescribed library assignment in the course but there is a test. The workbook is required and the library is responsible for grading the workbook which is done by library science students. The library wants to put the test on computer and ultimately the whole program to save staff time. The computer center would then be responsible for grading the test. The program reaches about 40 percent of the classes and includes freshman and transfer students. Limited evaluation has been done. There are 100 sections of 25 students each in the English 202 program every semester.

The library recently studied the course syllabi in the Business 202 program and found they weren't teaching what students needed. The librarians decided what students needed was not an instruction class but the required information when they were ready to do the assignment, which might be any time of the day or night even at 2:00 A.M. (This principle of help at time of need has long been espoused by user education librarians but often difficult, if not impossible to apply). They decided that since technology could provide information at almost any time and is cost-effective, it might provide the solution to their problems. They also wanted to teach students how to ask intelligent questions.

Computer Assisted Instruction (CAI) is used for the business program. Students can dial in. Students need information on professional careers, industries, and companies. For the professional segment, students need information on how to write a cover letter and resume, and find information about the profession, professional issues (ethical, legal, etc.), and additional statistical information. In the section on industries, students can find information on the industry (projections, work place, etc.), trends, issues, companies, forecasts, financial, statistical, history, biography, company rankings and industrial ratios. The company segment provides information about companies (public/private, etc.), addresses, financial information, company image, corporate climate, issues, statistical data, history, biography, rankings, and parent/subsidiaries. All three categories list the SIC numbers. The program is designed to provide answers to the following questions: What is it? How do I find it? (strategies) Where do I find it? Why do I use it? How do I use it?

The library administration is committed to instruction and they believe that technology holds the only answer. The administration said there are too many classes in the English 202 program for the library to continue to provide instruction. Teaching this program's 60 classes a year and other writing courses impedes the library's ability to develop other courses.

Another factor is the Writing Across the Curriculum program which is being developed and will generate a whole new demand for library instruction. The administration wants to reduce staff time now involved with the English 15 and 202 programs so they can meet the anticipated increased demand made by the Writing across the Curriculum program. They are moving in that direction with the English 202D project which is a CAI program with two databases. One is a teaching database that is organized into four sections: career, industry, corporate, and the fourth section which provides information about specific reference sources and functions as an enhanced English 202D bibliography. The first three sections correspond in content to the English 202D library instruction lecture. The second database is a database shell that surrounds the teaching database. This might be mounted on Macs in public labs where they could be downloaded and would be widely accessible.

They are pilot-testing the teaching of information seeking skills and decision making on a CAI program mounted on three computers. They want to teach why and when you should use periodical indexes, reference sources, and the online catalog. Penn Pages is in the agriculture department: it provides an online catalog and document delivery for extension agents. CARL's *UnCover* is available on the Internet.

The second project, Ask Fred, is available on one terminal. The first screen categories are: locations, services, materials, subjects, and instant access. The third project involves moving the catalog from Honeywell to Digital equipment. The project director wants to change the LIAS interface: she believes librarians need to develop "engaging systems." The catalog provides supplementary information like subject bibliographies and new book lists. The library administration has found that younger faculty have higher expectations about library user education. They have no undergraduate library: the freshman and 202 programs are in general reference. The administration plans to rearrange the large library into five or so smaller libraries and set up a "general" library.

Northwestern University

At Northwestern University Brian Nielsen is providing the leadership for developing the NuInfo project in the main library. In addition, three projects are under development in the Science and Engineering Library at Northwestern University. NuInfo was conceived and developed by Brian Nielsen in early 1990, working with the Vice President for Information Services and the Associate Provost. NuInfo was created in response to recommendations by the Task Force on Undergraduate Student Life. Structurally it's an ad hoc project with the description and vision provided by Brian. Its acceptance is demonstrated by the fact that the Vice President has included it in the University's computing strategy plan.

The University's Computing Center has provided technical support in the loaning of a low level programmer. NuInfo runs on software from Princeton and an IBM 4391 main frame and is accessible on the campus network, Nunet. The planning process was begun by a library technical task force in January 1989 and continued into summer 1990. It was perceived that the library needed to be visible on the University network and to provide access to library services beyond NOTIS. The main library is well situated politically on campus.

In early 1990, the Vice President for Information Services had identified an immediate need for information for students and sent memos to the two computing units and Brian. The Vice President had thought of putting the student information system on NOTIS But Brian said that was not possible. The Vice President asked for proposals to establish an information system for students. Academic Computing's proposal required a considerable investment of money, but the University Administration didn't want to spend any money and wanted it by fall 1990. Brian talked with Academic Computing and identified Princeton's software as workable and they acquired it. The system has eight dedicated terminals: two in the student union; three in the dormitories; and three in the library. Being main frame-based, adding terminals wasn't prohibitive in cost. It operates on the Esprit VT100 with a very simple interface of 80 characters. Dial-up access is available and almost any PC can dial in, so students can use their own computers. The University gave 35,000 dollars to do this not including staff and other costs.

NuInfo has the campus phone book, the undergraduate catalog, campus events, program requirements, class schedules, student handbook, current news, etc. The current news section was generated during the Gulf crisis when the University took a proactive policy about informing students about the war. The newswire was taken from another computer and was loaded on NuInfo. It was felt that Lexis-Nexis could have been used too. The library has had good experience with that database. The computer center will give students a floppy disk for NuInfo. The library is responsible for keeping NuInfo current and makes the decisions as to what goes on NuInfo. An advisory board will monitor the growth and development of NuInfo. It is planned to connect the library network to the campus network. A Macintosh connection of NuInfo is also being planned.

A number of campus-wide information systems (CWIS) are being tried at universities around the country. There is a special interest in the communication of text and menu from one computer to another. The University of Pennsylvania, Cornell, MIT, and Princeton all have campus information systems like NuInfo. Some see systems like NuInfo as more important for intra campus than inter campus communication and information. The library believes a human structure is needed within the University for an effective computer campus and the library can be more effective than the computer center in accomplishing that.

The Curriculum Innovation Project will integrate computing technologies into faculty research and ultimately into the University curriculum. The project will promote the use and dissemination of new information technologies in the library, teaching, and research community. The library will pursue the faculty outreach component of the Library's user education efforts and foster faculty interest in and use of the Library of Congress American Memory Project.

In the Science and Engineering Library at Northwestern, Lloyd Davidson is developing a menu-driven system on an IBM computer. It can search a number of variables and produce a list. One project is Biography Index which differentiates by country, time, how well known, biography and directory and covers 60 sources. It prints a brief descriptive list. Knowledge Pro combines expert system and hypertext and is used to train staff on how to use NOTIS. Index Selector is for use after reference hours: it doesn't give specific information. It does scan tables of contents and subject lists.

At the Chicago campus of Northwestern University the emphasis is on night school with three major extension programs: management; University College (general, undergraduate); and journalism. The campus has a CD-ROM local area network with nine databases on 12 workstations. This was funded by a 250,000 dollar grant from the Kellogg Foundation.

GOALS—SECTION ONE

Of 12 institutions, nine had written goals and objectives covering in some cases two or more projects within the institution. One library had written the goals as an afterthought, but the other eight institutions had clearly defined goals before the projects were underway. The size of the project appeared to be a factor in having stated goals and objectives. Generally speaking, the projects involving three or more people had written goals; conversely, the three projects with no stated goals were created by one or two persons who had the goals in their heads.

Many of the project goals described or implied a strong proactive role for the library. Some librarians even said they believed if the library didn't assume a leadership role in providing electronic information, the computer center would assume that role and the library would end up reporting to the computer center.

Goals and objectives were written by librarians, computer staff, library staff, faculty, and library users. The Pike's Peak District Library has sought involvement from members of the community for more than 15 years in setting its goals. Its programs are really models of community participation, reflecting the library's attention to user needs.

Among stated goals, a sharing of resources between institutions was stated and the desire to provide the needed information regardless of location or format. Libraries want to become a facilitator of information and strive to meet the total needs of its clients. They want to provide access outside the library and increase the use of library collections and provide efficient delivery of materials. To increase usage, they were trying to reduce the cost of finding and using information. They wanted to put the user in control of his/her own information seeking. Libraries want to anticipate user needs to select databases, formulate a search strategy, and interpret results. User needs were categorized into three tasks: mastering the mechanics of the system; understanding the process of searching; and knowledge of a given file's content.

To accomplish these goals, one library envisioned the necessary objectives. They proposed to expand the electronic bibliographic table of contents of books. They needed to improve retrieval and interfaces keeping screens brief because they found that users won't read a lot of narrative. They wanted to eliminate the need for printed instruction or help sources and make the system available campus-wide to all kinds of computers and workstations. They planned to reduce the costs of a large scale system by using advanced workstations. They wanted to demonstrate the feasibility of the proposed technology, not build an experimental system but one that demonstrated the affordability and usability of the system for any size campus. They wanted to produce an affordable library information system for networked campuses and they planned to document and disseminate the results.

One campus wanted to provide a convenient alternative to asking in-person and dial-in questions and the reference department was eager to make the system more widely available than originally planned. In a project where the goals were set by the project director, they wanted to measure the difference in usage of CDs with a front-end with that of usage without the interface. One institution's faculty had set the objectives to achieve the goal of teaching students information skills to meet academic needs. In another institution, librarians had set detailed goals and learning and enabling objectives for specific course information needs. Their goals included the desire to move that course instruction entirely to computers to free their time for instruction in other courses.

Another library system had involved staff, community groups, and individual library users in writing lengthy goals and objectives. This system had used goals written 15 years ago to establish far-sighted programs that included a referral service to all community human service organizations and to provide greater citizen participation in culture and planning and more effective coordination of delivery of human services. They wanted to develop an information and referral service for citizens needing information, referral, or help with a problem. They wanted to make the library the primary community materials and information center. Community resources files were seen as central to the accomplishment of this goal and the development of such files remains a primary goal of this system. Their goals originally included a pledge to follow through on an individual basis with all who sought help to assure they received the needed assistance, but as outside support for this task dwindled, this goal was eliminated.

Doing a self-study of the library led to long range goals for another institution. Written by a library committee led by the library director, the three goals were; to support the institution in becoming an eminent research university; to provide a state of the art learning center for students; to assume a proactive role in development of interactive electronic learning; and create a large, online information system that provides access to a wide selection of information resources and services.

One of the goals for Project Jefferson is to encourage the development of research and critical thinking skills among freshmen. They planned to accomplish this by providing students with interactive access to information, supporting specially formulated writing assignments which ask students to use background information and citations to support a position on one of several constitutional issues like racial discrimination. One library wanted to create a prototype intelligent expert system that combines an expert system with a CD-ROM network. The system would identify and describe appropriate networked CD-ROM databases.

AUDIENCE/INTENDED USERS—SECTION TWO

Of approximately 25 different programs ranging from single purpose, limited audience [Project Jefferson] to a consortium's entire public service program [CARL], six (CARL, PPDL, Info Machine, MacNOTIS, RoboRef, and Ask Fred) served all potential library users. Three (Project Mercury, Inspec, and IAIMS) were programs for faculty but were also used by students. Seven (Project Jefferson, MIQ, San Diego State's RAS program, Inmagic, RoboRef [phase I], the English and Business programs at Penn State, and Davidson's reference systems at Northwestern) concentrated on students. Emphasizing service to students but also helpful to faculty were seven programs (LIS II, USC Info, Reference Expert and IRIS, Arizona State's programs, RAID, and NuInfo). One program (Penn Pages) was created for extension agents and one (Knowledge Pro) was done for library staff.

TYPES OF INFORMATION—SECTION THREE

Carnegie Mellon University's first online catalog was available in 1984. In March 1986, LIS became available. LIS contained the catalog, on-order file, and several local test files. In November 1986, *Magazine Index* and Grolier's *Academic Encyclopedia* were added. In 1987 more IAC databases, a dictionary, and local databases were added. LIS II enables the library to provide access to other institutions to their local databases but cut out their access to commercial databases. LIS II will provide a one line record display, a brief record display that includes variant journal titles and the library's holdings, and a full record display. It also provides an item or issue display that includes updates of latest issues, a table of contents display, and a simple way to track journal title changes and browse variations of journal titles. LIS II provides links between records in other databases and journal records and a simple way to request a photocopy or FAX or to submit an ILL request.

INSPEC covers four publication full text in Physics, Electronics, and Computing and was available in November 1989. Three enhancement projects are being developed: contents notes for plays in collections; separately authored chapters in books and art exhibition catalogs; abstracts to computer science reports (EDRC).

Two catalog enhancements from commercial vendors are being added. *Choice* book reviews will be brought up with catalog records. I.S.I. analytic and full records for books and conference proceedings in science and engineering are being added. The library plans to use CD-ROMs to rectify historical inadequacies in the collection and to improve the delivery of materials not held in their library. CDs can add needed balance to the collection. They have been purchasing them since 1987. In 1990 they had ERIC (OCLC's CD-350), *Dissertation Abstracts, Psych LIT* (Silverplatter), *ABI/INFORM* (University Microfilms). *Math Sci,* and five databases from IAC (Magazine Index, National Newspaper Index, Management Contents, Trade and Industry Index, and *Computer Index*).

The CARL System provides the *UnCover* index which accesses over 10,000 journals and their tables of contents. Arizona State University furnishes six Wilson files, Northeastern University provides UMI, and CARL in Denver furnishes ACCESS Company, *ERIC,* and book reviews from *Choice.* Any database can be accessed using CARL software as long as licensing agreements exist between the database supplier and the library. The type of information is consistent with the program's goals and objectives. It was selected by participating libraries with user input.

The University of Southern California's project, USC Info, has 5 IAC databases (the same databases as Carnegie Mellon), providing access to over 1,000 periodicals. They plan to load 6 Wilson databases (*Art Index, Humanities Index, Social Sciences Index, Applied Science and Technology Index* and *Library Literature.* They plan eventually to add *Psych Lit* and the last 10 years of *Medline.*

Project Jefferson contains USC Info, Homer (their online catalog), periodical databases, and campus information. There are 14 different databases grouped into six subjects. Project Jefferson contains 196 citations relating to three different topics in specially created databases. Saved information can be put into a notebook which also has a notepad for jotting ideas. Pro-Cite is being used to create a project to develop subject discographies.

Texas A&M's project provides access to the NOTIS online catalog, The Medical Sciences Library catalog, the Prairie View Catalog, and certain Wilson databases. The University of California San Diego project, RoboRef, contains campus maps and general campus information. RAID (Remote Access Interface Design) provides dial-up access to Roger (local catalog) and Melvyl (state catalog). Some of the information on RoboRef is on RAID.

Pennsylvania State University's English 202D project is a CAI program with two databases. One is a teaching database that is organized into four sections with the fourth section providing information about specific references sources and functions. The second database is a shell that surrounds the teaching database. The second project is Ask Fred which provides such information as library locations, services, materials, and subjects. There is also considerable work being done on their catalog with preparation to move the catalog to a new main frame.

Arizona State University is a member of the CARL System which provides access to *Grolier's Encyclopedia* and the *UnCover Index.* They subscribe to several Wilson databases including *Applied Science and Technology Index, Business Periodicals Index, General Science Index, Humanities Index,* and *Social Sciences Index.* The library has compiled several local databases and is working on creating more. They have compiled the *Song Index* which provides access to popular songs in the Music Library's collection. The *Company Index* provides names and addresses of companies about which the Career Development Center has information. The calendar lists scheduled orientations, workshops, special events, advizement, and interview dates. There is a database of career-related topics owned by the Career Development Center. The *Map Index* lists maps in the library collection and historical maps in the Arizona Collection and the Arizona Historical foundation. *STAT Master* provides county and city data. They are working on a frequently-asked-questions database which will be a compilation from questions asked at public service stations over a three week period in fall 1989. It will be updated quarterly from questions asked at the Help Desk in the main library.

The MIQ project at the University of Cincinnati Medical Library covers 325 journals from *MEDLINE,* which is approximately 25 percent of the titles in the database. The titles selected had to be in the library's collection. MIQ covers the current year and the two previous years. They are clinical and basic life science journals in English language only.

The IAIMS project contains a created database titled *Patient-Centered Database* (PCD). This is made up of information gathered by the IAIMS staff in going on rounds and chart review, recording problem-oriented patient data and medication profiles. The PCD generated daily census sheets (CS) and residents' sign-out cards (SC) with current patient data and discharge summaries. Patient data includes demographics, active problem lists, current medications, and ultimate disposition. Residents receive daily printouts analyzing possible drug interactions (DI) and journal articles pertinent to patient management/diagnostic issues. The project provides data that 83 percent of the team members would not otherwise have seen and the PCD-generated forms and information saved time.

The San Diego State University project being developed by Robert Carande focuses on materials engineering information. This content was determined by the curriculum and developed with Robert's subject expertise.

Maggie's Place at the Pike's Peak District Library contains the local online catalog, community events calendar, clubs, courses, local documents, local authors, senior housing options, social and economic indicators, El Paso county legislative districts, child care, *Grolier's Encyclopedia,* city hall on-line,

Columbia Electronic Encyclopedia, PPLD news, CARL, MARMOT and Boulder catalogs, computer assisted searches. *Facts on File* was being added. The University of Houston provides guidance in using relevant sources and 19 CD-ROMs which were evaluated and selected by the library faculty. A diversity of information beyond text-based was sought and that included citations, graphics, full text, and numeric representations.

Northwestern University's NuInfo has the campus phone book, undergraduate catalog, current news from a newswire service, weather, student handbook, information on University College and the Chicago campus, athletic schedule, placement office bulletin, film and video collection, class schedule, daily event calendar, entertainment and restaurant information for Chicago and Evanston, etc. Northwestern's Science and Engineering Library project Biography Index covers 60 sources. Knowledge Pro contains information for staff training on NOTIS and Index Selector provides basic information for use when the reference desk is closed.

THE TECHNOLOGY—SECTIONS 4-7

Texas A&M

The Texas A&M MacNOTIS system runs on HyperCard 2.0 software. Operable first in October 1988, this was the first time HyperCard was used as a library catalog front end, allowing users easy access with a mouse to a DOS-based system. It runs on Mac SE/30 terminals and can also work on Mac Classics. It was developed originally with HyperCard 1.0 and then moved to 2.0. Mitem View 2.0 B71 was used. Inmagic software was used to develop a database of questions and answers, reference aids, and library policies and procedures. The software was selected because it best fit the goals of the project. Another Mitem-like software was considered but discarded as not functional. HyperCard was used because Apple wanted to demonstrate its versatility.

CARL Systems

CARL Systems' CARL PAC is in layman's terms; it is not a controlled language and is based on flexibility and simplicity, The PAC demands little information from a request and usually responds with something. It also illustrates how a request can be revised to insure the maximum results. The system is menu driven with help screens. The menu can be bypassed by going directly to Quick Search.

In October 1983, the first prototype was out: there was one at each library. It was immediately popular. They wanted to expand and refine it so by the spring of 1984, there were 24 terminals at the University of Denver. It was designed first as a user tool, then they began developing a circulation component. The system has continued to grow. CARL is on the campus workstations in most CARL libraries.

CARL Systems Inc. is the single source for all hardware, system software, and applications software. Services include network design and installation, on-site maintenance, and equipment repair. The system, which runs on Tandem computers, provides an efficient method for storing and linking bibliographic records throughout the network while maintaining each library's capability to retain local variations. *Uncover 2* uses scanning equipment and optical disk storage. Delivery is tele-facsimile. *Uncover 2* can be accessed from any CARL system hardware site. The software makes it possible to load and support a wide variety of databases and separate hardware sites can share a single database.

All commercial databases are accessed using standard CARL searching software so any CARL site can access any database on the system, thus reducing storage requirements. The modular design of Tandem allows for expansion of databases. They are developing a system to optically scan images and link them to the catalog. The Tandem system is a network of computers within a single system.

Dynabus interprocessor bus connects two or more CPUs. The GUARDIAN operating system allows the CPUs to monitor each other and to redistribute resources of the system file. Tandem's EXPAND makes it possible to house a database at one site and make it available to other sites and still provide local menu options. Tandem's EXPAND networking software handles network connections and expansion by extending GUARDIAN. GUARDIAN monitors each CPU; EXPAND monitors the nodes and communication lines in the network and if a node or line fails, EXPAND finds an alternate communication line and then returns it to the failed line when repaired.

The CARL bibliographic file structure provides minimal redundant data storage; individual institutional differences in data; easy construction of special indexes; and rapid access to individual records. The system uses MARC records and puts in individual institutional differences (on average less than 3). It doesn't deal with merging records or variant data. The CARL/term emulation software enables PC compatible PAC terminals to display the full ALA character set. The image storage capability in the CARL terminal/PC and CARL terminal/image products enables libraries to store scanned digital copies and display them on standard PCs equipped with VGA graphic displays. Videodisc or larger graphic displays were ruled out because of cost. Search software for database access is identical across the network and all databases.

The system accepts any machine readable data files: data can be processed into MARC-like records and accessed, edited, and updated like the bibliographic databases. The system provides security with password access. Each computer system can operate independently. DYNABUS connects systems, but allows independent operating.

Disk drives are dual-ported to ensure data integrity and availability. Software provides continuous backup to data while the online system is live and available. The system can and has been expanded. There were 77 terminals in Denver in 1981 and 1000 terminals in 1990. Tandem's System Software supports such interconnecting protocols as X25, SNA, and TCP/IP allowing integration with the Online Public Access System for external gateway access as required. The CARL disk is committed to Open System Interconnection as a means of extending networks of systems. EXPAND processes through file names so programming for a network is similar to programming for a single system. CARL supports gateways via the Internet or through dedicated connects and both permit customization of front screens, menu choices, and exact messaging. Any machine readable datafile can be uploaded into the system. Updating records can be added through keyboarding at the system terminal or updated through terminal or tape/disk loading.

Carnegie Mellon University

Carnegie Mellon's LIS interface is based on these general guidelines:

1. One interface should work for all files with little or no change between files.
2. Screens should be as similar as possible across files.
3. Systems should be as self-documenting as possible; information on a given screen should cover basic options.
4. Online help should be provided to minimize the necessity for special search training.
5. The system should be designed to ensure that a user gets some useful results from each command or a helpful error message.
6. The number of choices a user has to make should be kept to a minimum without trivializing the system.
7. More sophisticated search capabilities should be available for those who want them.

Most people won't read so the screens are kept as brief as possible and consistent in design. Their search interface and retrieval system is based on IBM's STAIRS. The software was custom designed by library staff. LIS access is not password-controlled so anyone with access to campus asynchronous and TCP networks can use the system. Andrew is the campus network with powerful, UNIX-based personal workstations. LIS began when space was available on the IBM 3093 mainframe which could serve as a stand-alone database storage and retrieval machine and potential file server for Andrew. They are not going to a distributed system because of cost, flexibility, and greater capacity. They started with LS 2000-IBM 3083 in 1984.

LIS II runs on a VAX station 3100 and is mouse driven. The distributed system of LIS II was implemented in 1990-91. A special computer will be used to build databases and special machines will be used as database or retrieval servers. All computers will be used to build databases and special machines will be used as databases or retrieval servers. All computers on the campus network will have access to LIS II. Workstations with X windows are in the libraries and the workstations in offices and public computing clusters on campus will run the graphical interface being built. Users of other personal computers like IBM PC and MAC will run an interface like the LIS I.

The Open Software Foundation (OSF), a non-profit research and development company sponsored by major computer firms incorporated the Andrew File System into its Distributed Computing Environment (DCE) which indicated the acceptance of AFS as a distributed file system standard. OSF distributes a software toolkit and interface style guide that, packaged with the mwm (X.11) window manager, comprise the graphical user interface standard called "Motif" which has been adopted by the library. They have created a reasonable model for libraries to share resources under a common interface and demonstrated that the OSIZ3950 protocol can work across separate servers.

During 1991, they were to implement LIS II on a new generation of small RISC servers supported by major vendors. LIS is a menu-driven system with a Boolean capability. It provides some brief written instruction. LIS has been operational for 5 years and is being phased out. The new system will be a distributed one, not main frame. One reason for this is the new system will have a windowing capability. The library has not focused on CDs because they want to concentrate on campus-wide availability. LIS II is based on Andrew which is a campus network of more than 50 LANs, a distributed file system with the hundreds of file servers and thousands of workstations which provide windows. It provides a common user interface to network services including electronic mail, bulletin boards, and access to LIS. Andrew provides access to Internet. Project Mercury, which is the same as LIS except it provides full text, has the same software and hardware. OCLC provides full text, has the same software and hardware. OCLC provides the search software. The CDs in the Hunt library have an IBM PC/XT with a Hitachi CD drive on one setup and the other is a NCRUB< clone with a Phillips CD drive. The printers are dot matrix.

University of California, San Diego

The University of California, San Diego, uses standard HyperCard. They believe their interface is clearer than most. They believe HyperCard 2.0 isn't reliable: it crashed about every 20 minutes for them. The system runs on the Mac SE.

San Diego State University

San Diego State's interface is menu-driven like Pinter and Answerman. The subject matter is its main difference with other systems. Robert Carande doesn't consider the way the menus are structured to be novel. The software is HyperPad in Turbo Prolog; others in the library are using Spinnaker. The reference librarians are using Supercard or HyperCard 2.0. Robert looked at Exis shell, but the visual presentation was too restrictive. He chose this software because it's a logic language (if, then). He moves from the vague to the specific. Using these tools, he has more control than with a shell and it leads to knowledge that can be applied elsewhere. It can be downloaded. It is not finished. The board runs on an IBM AT and a 386 PC. A larger system in the science library is programmed in HyperPad's PAD talk which is object oriented. It's a cluster of RAS modules with a natural language interface, Dialog NLI Natural Language Interface.

Arizona State University

Arizona State University library is a member of the CARL System. They provide dial-up access to their catalog 24 hours a day. They plan to provide 75 help screens. How explicitly do screens define what they represent? The first screen doesn't do it well but the second screen does. Their maintenance is done by CARL with some corrections done locally. For the questions database they're developing, they're using Word Perfect 5.1. They plan to convert it Framework III which will work with the CARL software of the online catalog.

Their hardware is Tandem for which they pay an annual fee. They like Tandem because of its ease of use; flexibility (they can add databases); simplicity of screens; and it doesn't crash. The computer hardware used with the ASU online catalog is a five processor Tandem system. The computer handles hundreds of thousands of transactions every day. The reliability of the Tandem system significantly reduces the risk of system failure and protects the ASU databases from damage caused by electronic malfunctions. A Tandem system consists of two to 16 processors, each working independently but concurrently. This makes it possible to start with a minimum size and expand incrementally as needs grow.

University of Cincinnati

The University of Cincinnati Medical Library's Medical Information Quick (MIQ) can be accessed via phone lines. However, the VAX minicomputer used for MIQ has no protocol converter so all telecommunication software must emulate a VT 100. It runs on a Digital VAX series minicomputer with a VMS operating system. MIQ has since migrated to a VAX 11/780 minicomputer with an improvement in response time, and increase in simultaneous users, and more terminal access points. It uses BRS/SEARCH software version 3.0. Dial access requires DEC VT100 or emulation which is available commercially and a freeware package, PC-VT, is available to users with an IBM-PC or IBM compatible. It's available on Ethernet.

The Integrated Academic Information Management System project runs on MAC workstations using HyperCard. It is available on the Internet. They are considering Logic Craft. The project links to the hospital system which is IBM-based. IBM is used for the linkage and Drug Master is MSDOS based. They use SilverPlatter-VT100. There are seven workstations in the hospital and none in the library. They plan to put workstations in the library in Phase 3.

Pike's Peak District Library

The Pike's Peak District Library is on the CARL System. They have grown from four terminals in 1977 to 98 in 1985. Their system is made up of two Digital Equipment Cor. minicomputers: a PDP 11-70 and a PDP 11-44. Their first minicomputer (PDP 11-70) was chosen for its ability to handle several transactions at once, its size, and its versatility. In 1985 they purchased a new computer system based on the CARL system with hardware from Tandem and software from EYRING.

University of Houston

The University of Houston's project is an IBM-based expert system. IBM was chosen because the library is an IBM-based system. They wanted to have an "expert system project," not a HyperCard system. The project requires mounting CDs which are IBM-based.

The system was conceived and developed by Charles Bailey. The software is an IBM TokenRing Local Area Network. They are considering both VP-Expert and Intelligence/Compilerm Turbo Prolog software. They're currently using the VP-Expert Software but the final choice hasn't been made. They have Novell Advanced Netware 2.15, Above LAN (to free up memory on Novel netware); and Sabreware LAN. The Software was selected to support the existing CDs on IBM and to fit in with the IBM environment in the library.

The hardware is made up of two Meridian 80386 CD-New Model 314 servers multiple disk drive towers. They have 10 workstations of 80286-based IBM clone machines (eight are public, one is at the reference desk, and one is in the systems office). There are 10 Epsom printers with VendaCard units to have users pay for copies. (VendaCard units cost $1,500 per unit, with a $30 yearly maintenance fee per workstation.) Problems with the VendaCard units occurred because the system is placed inside the computer to become a part of the system, not allowing the computer to send the "Print" message to the printer if the user has not used a VendaCard credit card to pay for printing. As new workstations replaced older ones, the VendaCard unit has to be modified also to fit in with the new hardware stations, a real problem in maintenance. The library is committed to using the VendaCard units, but tests by the Head of Systems have shown that they could print more than twice the copies and still not spend more annually than the VendaCard unit costs.

University of Southern California

The University of Southern California has developed a HyperCard access to help students log-on and assist them in searching for and downloading citations. They use the BRS search system. Their catalog is a GEAC which makes tapes available to USC Info. Catalog records come from OCLC and they are sent to GEAC, and then run to the BRS mainframe. It's a cumbersome system; they plan eventually to make a complete conversion. A Z39.50 provides access to various databases in standard format from the main frame.

USC Info is provided through a workstation to a host-based connection via standard TCP/IP protocols on a high speed FDDI campus network. This allows them to develop access to multiple information servers via the network through a common client interface. Access is provided by MAC SE30 workstations using the power and graphics capabilities of a HyperCard front end interface to access the catalog and 14 databases and a campus information resource file. They found that when the CPU on a MAC is doing something, the HyperCard stacks can be damaged. The system is loaded on the library's IBM 3081 main frame. It requires the data storage capacity of a mainframe computer linked via a communications network to MACs. The system may not be duplicatable in other libraries.

Northwestern University

Northwestern University's NuInfo is based on Esprit VT100 which is a very simple interface system (80 characters) that can provide a dial-up access for almost any personal computer. The system was developed after looking at many other institutions; it contains a lot of text. The computer center has created an IBM interface that uses color and a mouse and will convert to a mouse. It serves as a front end for the system.

The expert system is menu driven and provides basic information. Brian Nielsen recommended buying the Princeton software because it is adaptable, ready to use, and time-saving. It's an IBM campus and the system (which is IBM-based) is available on the University network, Nunet. The IBM base makes adding terminals comparatively inexpensive. Dial-up access is available. The main problem is making the project compatible with Apple. They believe that this was the best selection for them. The projects being developed in

Northwestern University's Science and Engineering Library by Lloyd Davidson are menu-driven VP Expert on IBM. The IBM Knowledge Pro which trains staff on NOTIS combines expert systems and Hypertext. This software was chosen because it can search a number of variables and produce a list. Lloyd believes the IBM system is the best one for them.

ECONOMICS AND SUPPORT SECTIONS 8 AND 11

Funding and other forms of support come from different sources. The major sources of funding were: the library, the institutions, other departments and colleges, grants, companies, organizations, community agencies and subscribers, and the state governments. After examining the various types of funding and support, some of the consequences are enumerated and projections made for the future.

Most projects received strong support from the library's administration despite the skepticism of some staff members in almost every library. Many staff members who were doubtful at the beginning became real converts as the project developed. Many library administrators are committed to delivering the needed information in whatever form is fastest and most appropriate. Library directors have been very supportive even when faced with severe budget cuts over the last few years. Support from the library has come in the form of money, staff time, equipment, subscriptions, and development tools. Some librarians have been given a certain percentage of release time to work on projects and others have been committed full time. One library donated 80 hours of student programming to remove redundancies in the system and make it more efficient.

Many library directors have been able to get institutional support either from the administration or other departments and colleges. The medical library received a grant from the College of Medicine to help teach MEDLINE. One project director believed it helped the library in general that the administration knew about their projects. Support comes from faculty in the form of whole classes working on some phase (often evaluation) of the project. Computing centers are often contributors of staff time and equipment. In some libraries, the librarians have been taught how to do programming so they can create their projects. One librarian worked with the institution's associate provost and vice president to develop an information system for the campus: this project revealed no funding the first year, only some programming time. However, the second year the institution funded a full time programming position at $35,000.

The project of one of the most generously supported libraries was developed in the 1980s with a special grant [$300,000] and a lot of equipment from the university and subsequently received additional internal funds, equipment, and personnel. This library also received increased funding for materials over several years and was also successful in getting external grants including money for acquisitions. This library has nine FTE computer staff.

Another library received a grant to build a network from the Department of Education College Library Technology and Cooperation Grants Program. This covered 51 percent of the project's costs and the remaining 49 percent was covered by the library, mostly with personnel costs. A foundation grant supported the beginning of a project to mount additional databases and complete an online catalog.

Agencies, companies, and organizations have all supplied money. A public library received support from the now defunct CETA program and from its community. The same library also receives support from the United Way in keeping a local database current and from the Urban League with the library's Daycare file. One consortium was funded by the original member libraries and is now supported by subscribers. This group has been so successful that it has set up a corporation to run the system and return any profits to the consortium. One member library attributed a large savings in staff time to this consortium. A savings in users' money was also cited as a result of the reduction of online searching made possible by membership in the consortium. The now possible dial-up access also had reduced traffic in the libraries and saved library staff time.

Companies have provided support with money, personnel to help with software development, hardware (a main frame was given to one campus), furniture, and personal computers. The National Library of Medicine has funded the IAIMS project in 14 institutions for several years.

Most libraries remained optimistic about support for their projects. One had just undergone a change in administration and the new president was making changes in the upper-level personnel: the library was as yet unsure what impact, if any, this might have on the project. Project staff from other institutions were hoping for more support from within their libraries, usually in the form of personnel or programming. One library was pleased that their new project had already been included in the university's computing strategy plan. The consortium was expecting a very successful year in many ways including generating more income.

The support issues are far reaching and the consequences resulting from these issues are numerous. Only a few were expressed and while these may not even be the most important, they are, nevertheless, interesting. One librarian observed that the ad hoc nature of the project and its funding had impaired the library staff's perception of the project. Many librarians believed that full support would have made a significant difference in the progress of their projects but were uncertain how to bring that about.

A library director from one of the most advanced libraries observed the issues of cost between running a file/tape system and CD-ROMs. The system requires leasing charges, staff time to load and maintain the database and adapt the search interface, and disk space for storage. CDs are not only cheaper but they can be made available faster.

PERSONNEL—SECTION 9

At Texas A&M, Hal Carmichael conceived the idea of MacNOTIS. He is currently working with Mitem after leaving the University of Texas and Apple Corporation. Kelly Leeper, Programmer, and Hal Hall, Principal Investigator, have provided the leadership. Joe Jarvis in the library has helped with the testing. Kathy Jackson, Head of Automation, will take over the project if it does not receive new funding.

May Ellen Litzinger at Pennsylvania State University is the instructional specialist and provides the leadership for the HyperCard project. Torre Meringolo, Assistant Dean for Collections and Reference Services, provides direction and strong support for the projects. Carol Wright is Senior Assistant Librarian and is responsible for the Basic Skills Project which involves the freshman workbook program; she is working on a HyperCard program for support of the freshman program. Alan Claver is the programmer for the Ask Fred project and Sally Kalin, Acting Head, Computer Based Resources and Services, is working on revising their online catalog LIAS.

Susan Varca, Head of Instruction and Information at the Arizona State University Library, started the most frequently asked questions database. An information desk staff member is updating the database in Word Perfect 5.1. Another staff member will convert the Word Perfect list to Framework III. Providing technical advice for these projects and for the entire library is George Machovech, Head of Technology and Systems. George works on the catalog and CD-ROMs, negotiates site licenses, and advises on new projects. Two programmers work for Information Resources Management: one is a systems person and the other works on application (adapts systems). The reference department is responsible for the MARS room. The coordinator of computer services is in the reference department and he is responsible for maintenance. Librarians select the databases.

At San Diego State University Library, Robert Carande has developed the program described. Robert's is a one man operation. Robert is one of five librarians in the science division: he reports to the head of the science division. The entire library has 26 librarians and four temporaries. The systems office has five computer people and reports to the head of the science division. The entire library has 26 librarians and four temporaries. The systems office has five computer people and reports to the Assistant University Librarian for Technical Services.

The Pike's Peak District Library's projects started with help from the Junior League, other organizations, and five CETA employees. In 1979 the library merged the Information Services and Reference departments. Today four librarians and four technicians are responsible for the community files. Librarians provide guidance, develop policy and planning, and conduct community contacts. The library's Community Interaction Team (CIT) was effective in getting feedback from the community to help the library decide on related materials and activities. Technicians maintain the files. A team of one librarian and one technician works on one file. Tom Mihalic is the library's Systems Officer and Sydney Caler is assistant to the library director.

Charles Bailey has provided the leadership for the program at the University of Houston with the help and advice of four committees: The Project Management Group (Charles chairs); the Knowledge Engineering Group; The Electronic Publications Instruction Group; and The Research and Evaluation Group. Robin Downes, the Library Director, is the Project Director. Charles Bailey, who is the Assistant Director for Systems, is the Program Manager. Also involved are Cherie Colbert, Coordinator of Library Instruction; Kathleen Gunning, Assistant Director for Public Services and Collection Department; Judy Meyers, Assistant to the Director; Donna Hitchings, Head of Information Services; Thomas Wilson, Head of Systems; Jeff Fadel, Ivan Calimano, and Carolyn Meanly, Information Services librarians; and Derral Parkin, Head of Branch Libraries.

The University of Southern California Library conceived USC Info. They initiated contact with the computer center and out of this came the Center for Scholarly Technology which reports to both the library and the computer center. Maintenance is done by the library unit. Two to three staff do personal computer and catalog maintenance and installation. They had one handling main frame, one handling the network, and a third one responsible for the front end. The Center for Scholarly Technology looked favorably on Apple. Project Jefferson is a cooperative effort between the library, the Freshman Writing Program, and the School of Industrial and System Engineering.

Ward Shaw, Patricia Culkin, and the directors of the member libraries started the CARL System: it's a librarians' project. These are three units in CARL Inc.: Network Administration; Development; and Marketing and Support. Ward Shaw is responsible for overall direction, planning, and technology. Rebecca Lenzini is in charge of marketing, sales, and client relations. Patricia Culkin manages the system development and support. Gene Damon handles client support. As of May, 1991, they employed 32 professionals and 17 FTE clerical staff. Seven staff worked in software development; four in technical support; 15 in software. Plans were to add 10 more personnel within the next year. Ted Kopper and Wanda Zimmerman are senior programmer/analysts. User Services coordinators are assigned to each site to serve as project managers and service liaisons (all have both public and technical service experience). There are four in the User Services Department. Brenda Bailey does writing and workshops: she works also with the Information Access committee.

The library director and staff started the program at Carnegie Mellon and the library director, Tom Michalak, provided the leadership. Personnel was stable until 1991 when Michalak, Evans, and Kibbey left. They have a middle managers group. They moved the programmers into the library to facilitate their working together. The library has 95 total staff. The Academic Computing Media reports to the library director. This unit provides media for teaching, runs the computer store, and teaches a course in computer skills. All freshmen must take a course on the library's catalog. Denise Troll is a researcher who is working on Project Mercury. Barbara Richards is the library's Associate Director. The electronic information service is the responsibility of the Data and Information Services Manager with the advice of a library standing committee, Electronic Information Services Committee (EISC). The CD-ROM decisions are made by them.

At the University of Cincinnati Health Science Library, the Library Director, Phyllis Self, is responsible for MIQ and is also involved with the IAIMS project. Vicki Killion, Online Services Coordinator, was a moving force in the creation of MIQ. Nancy Lorenzi who is the Associate Senior Vice President for Medical Center Information and Communications directs the IAIMS project.

Sherry Willhite, Information Services Librarian, and Tammy Nickelson Dearie, Information Access Librarian, are the creators of RoboRef at the University of California, San Diego. NuInfo is the vision and creation of Brian Nielsen at Northwestern University. He makes all the decisions on the project in consultation with the Vice President for Information Services and the Associate Provost. NuInfo was created in response to recommendations by the Task Force on Undergraduate Student Life. Brian has a librarian and part-time programmer who report to him on the project. The project personnel has remained stable. Lloyd Davidson is the creator and developer of the Biography Index and Index Selector. Lloyd had a student programmer for one summer.

EVALUATION AND CONSULTANTS—SECTION TEN

The purpose of most of the evaluation done was to improve the projects and determine their effectiveness. One library was using the results to keep the program from crashing and to accept technical changes as they developed, and only peripherally for guidance in changing it. In one library, the results were being heavily relied on in developing the second version of the project. One library director stated that where there were conflicts between what the users wanted and the librarians recommended, he always went with the librarians. No libraries had made use of consultants.

Questionnaires and surveys were used by several institutions to evaluate their projects. Evaluation forms left at workstations for users to complete is a common form of evaluation. In one study done a few years ago, the results revealed that the most simple part of the instruction such as locations was the most successful segment but the more complex portion of finding articles on a topic was the least successful module. This same result was discovered by another library in working with a specific course. Students had to locate reference materials for a paper, so the librarians created a database for the assignment. Written evaluations showed that one-third of the students didn't find what they were looking for and one-half needed to consult a librarian. There were problems with the help screens and students found the printing to be slow and difficult to read, requiring multiple screens of instruction every time they used the printers. Problems with the database included the subject headings and the limited scope of content. There were inadequate help screens and the software was vulnerable to tampering.

A user survey in a medical library conducted in 1986 indicated that the currency of citations was the primary concern of users-obviously a reflection of the discipline. A survey of an expert system done two years ago which involved 51 responses over a three month period indicated that 86 percent had found an appropriate index, 98 percent felt the program was easy to understand, and 96 percent found it helpful. One project had a very thorough and somewhat unusual evaluation. A public library system established a local database of agencies that provided help to individuals in the community. Junior League members helped with setting up the project and they followed up on a daily basis with emergency callers and weekly basis with the non-emergency callers to determining whether the needy person had received help. This was subsequently discontinued.

Evaluating by classes either as a class project or by librarians who are doing course instruction was done by a number of libraries. In a medical library, surveys and pre/post tests were done with Psychiatry and Pharmacy classes and with groups using the project. In another institution, Education Technology classes evaluated the system as a class project. Two graduate students in the English Technical Writing program tested the project in another library and, in still another library, an Industrial Engineering class evaluated the project and gave the evaluation report to the institution's Associate Provost and a Vice President, as well as, the library.

Almost all institutions did some evaluation by observing the use of their projects. The librarians who didn't specifically mention that form of evaluation probably assumed that was understood. The small number who mentioned it (two) indicated that was the assumption. One library described their evaluation as restricted to experiential evidence and perception of the project's popularity and effectiveness with the user.

Using the transaction records to determine usage and, thereby, estimate other evaluations results was a method applied by three libraries. One librarian collected information on the users' questions and the material used to determine the success rate, which he hoped would be 50 percent. He also varied the phrasing of the system's questions to rest the success rate, which he hoped would reach 70 percent. One library used the transaction logs to determine problems with the existing systems. From this library's study, the librarians determined that users want to search the contents of journals, not just see if the library owns the journals. The logs indicated that the number of users had doubled over a six-month period.

Students were used to test the systems through interviews which could be either brief or lengthy and in some cases simply asked what they liked about the project. This form was used by two institutions. In one, the students were asked about the system's structure and interface, while in the other, students were asked what they didn't like. Lengthy interviews were conducted in a wide range of research areas to understand the human factors in online information retrieval.

Two institutions did evaluation through the computer, asking users specific questions and encouraging comments. One library had not done any formal post-implementation evaluations of electronic information resources because of lack of staff time to implement and design.

Many institutions had no plans for future evaluation studies. The two libraries that had planned future evaluation were doing so from different perspectives. One library had focused on what they wanted to know from the evaluations: impact of catalog enhancements on recall and precision; evaluate the transition from the original system to its revision; evaluate user behavior with the new system; study how users use full text databases. They planned to set up a more structured evaluation to decide on which materials to continue to purchase for the systems. The other library was planning how they would do their evaluation. They planned to use direct oral questions and more focused written questions than had been used in previous evaluations. The concept behind the new evaluation would be not so much if the system worked, but such criteria as how users conducted their research, how they made their decisions, and if the information found was relevant. Earlier evaluations had been more general in nature. They planned to use observation of user behavior, analysis of transaction logs, and a user survey.

PROBLEMS—SECTION TWELVE

Some of the same problems were shared by several institutions and some problems were unique to one institution. The shared problems can be placed into four categories: 1. Support and Funding; 2. Personnel: 3. Technology;

4. Users. Although many librarians seemed to feel a lack of support from their institutions and inadequate funding, they tended to identify their main problems as related to technology and users. Three listed inadequate support and funding as their biggest problems. Two of these said more money would have solved their major problems and they believed their institutions should have provided that funding. Their projects were different in that one was an introduction to the library on HyperCard operating on one workstation and the other was a campus-wide program that offered a variety of information in addition to the library information.

The fourth library that listed funding was well supported and funded by the institution but the librarians saw the cost of information as a serious constraint. They viewed pricing and protection as interrelated and the costs of tapes restricting what could be acquired. Licensing and copyright issues were popular topics of discussion. However, vendor-imposed conditions that were difficult, if not impossible to meet were viewed as a serious deterrent to development by only a few.

In the realm of personnel, few found serious problems. One librarian noted the difficulty of finding staff who were compatible with the project. A reference department wasn't comfortable in referring users to computers unless the reference desk was closed: this attitude had a negative impact on the usage of the system. One decried that he was the only one working on the project. The largest project examined was the CARL system with a staff of 50. The system that worked with librarians and not library users directly noted that in contracting with new library clients there was a difference in librarians' attitudes towards the system that was often the result of their experience with vendors. A good experience usually produced a positive attitude on the librarians' part and the reverse brought a negative attitude.

A failure to delineate areas of responsibility brought problems between professional librarians and paraprofessionals. This is a frequent happening when new projects are being developed and a number of people are involved. This was ultimately worked out as the project became stabilized.

One library noted the time and effort required from the staff to keep the project current and up-to-date. This was a concern expressed several times but emphasized as a potential problem by only one institution. It does reflect a common concern about the need for good staff who have good technical, planning, and people skills. One project director called for a new breed of librarian who is knowledgeable about computers. One library noted that the group appointed to develop the project wasn't a functioning team at first; there was a need to build a social structure. When all of the team's offices were assigned on the same floor, they developed good lines of communication and began continuous interaction.

Technology, as expected, seemed to bring the greatest problems. Some institutions (the most technically advanced) appeared comfortable with the decisions made about their technical future. Others were still in the process of deciding how and where their libraries and campuses were going. Most believed in the library's being on the campus workstation and the importance of providing dial-up access.

The attitude toward CDs varied from those who believed CDs are a valuable service that would be here for the immediate future to those who scoffed at the capabilities of CDs and deemed them already obsolete. On some campuses where the latter view prevailed, there was still pressure to provide CD access for users.

Some librarians were taught (or taught themselves) to use HyperCard before they could begin developing the projects. One librarian had difficulty learning to think in terms of a computer which she believed was necessary to develop her project successfully. Maintenance and down-time were cited as serious problems. This was solved in one institution by changing the reporting line of that section of maintenance from the computer center to the library which could then set priorities, etc. And one said the biggest problem was not technology, but a complex administrative structure. Slow retrieval time leading to user dissatisfaction was a concern in several institutions. Products and their selection consumed considerable staff time. One institution had difficulty running their project on the available workstation and, after spending some time trying to make it work, was forced to abandon the endeavor and charge back the lost time and money to experience. Vendor participation, including reasonable pricing and protection of copyrighted materials, was a major issue. Making the best selection in software was a frequently mentioned challenge. One institution which was creating an expert system experimented with three different software packages, weighing the positive and negative aspects of each. Some cited the difficulty of making simple changes in text created by the programming language. Technical difficulties impeded or prevented some from adding needed databases.

One library wanted to go to Sun equipment, but was hesitating because it was harder to develop an interface with that equipment than with HyperCard. They wanted HyperCard to become faster. One library could develop the needed technology but couldn't come to terms with the publisher of the database, so it was dropped.

Asyncronous lines presented problems and were expensive; a problem solved by going to telecommunication LAN systems. The need to charge for printing led to the installation of a Vendacard system which took time to integrate. Some felt the need to monitor the MARC standard format because they felt it lacked true standardization. A consortium had problems with mounting floppy disks which were created by individual libraries. An example was given of an update to a database which was not comparable in quality tot he original database. Vendor-supplied tapes also gave problems. One institution solved its problems with a computerized catalog that required a lot of user instruction by going to a completely different system.

How their systems were being used was a very common concern among institutions. Whereas, most of the systems were attractive to users, some had difficulties with attracting enough usage. One system was described as "seldom used" and little effort was being made to increase the usage. One system, which was developed for faculty and graduate students, was resisted by faculty and staff and was accepted only by emphasizing its educational role in teaching graduate students. One system that combined the use of paper and CD indexes found users had difficulty seeing the relationship between the two media; i.e., they didn't understand how the two different forms complemented each other.

The staff of one library was concerned with the quality of results when users did their own searching, but it was pointed out that this is true of traditional searching too. It was suggested that a study of the system for recall and relevance be done and an evaluation of databases be compared with the collection. There was an expressed need to develop improved interfaces for users and more effective online and printed help.

In one institution the faculty was very conservative and "not into computers." The librarians found that a lot of the software wasn't being used. They said students didn't know the value of information and that librarians needed to teach students how to evaluate information and apply problem-based learning. How to handle the sheer volume of questions and problems raised by users was a major concern in most institutions. Libraries have created greater demands and higher expectations from users. They want a more sophisticated interface and retrieval system and, overall, a more flexible system. But libraries must make decisions based on the greatest good for the most people.

Many libraries found that users frequently didn't understand the information they had selected and that they didn't know what the index they were searching could provide. Users often do not know the limitations of the indexes, e.g., only a certain period of time is covered. They tend to think that if it's found in an index, the library has it. If a search turns up nothing, they assume there is nothing and, conversely, if they find something, they tend to believe that is all there is. Users have difficulty defining and limiting their searches. These concerns are common to all library searching, but the sense of many librarians is that by making online searching so accessible, users may be less apt to ask for help.

An institution that had developed both an online database and catalog found that users had difficulty differentiating between them. Users also had problems with locating journals and with understanding such library terms as "current publication." Library jargon presents a lot of problems for users. (One study showed students understood only half of the library terms they encountered in their research.) Journal and conference titles often present problems as do truncations, inaccurate and unclear title changes, and holdings records. These, of course, are problems of long standing—not limited to online services, but maybe exacerbated by the increased accessibility of materials engendered by technology.

Finding the exact, current, meaning-laden terms and keeping use of these terms consistent throughout the system is a difficult task. In an online system that is designed to be interactive and brings up a new screen with each action, users tend to get lost easily. To enable users to keep their context clear, some systems are moving to the incorporation of windows so conceptual tasks are completed without leaving the preceding task.

Other problems cited are not easily categorized. One library had difficulty in getting the institution to recognize the library's role in developing information systems. They had to demonstrate the library's capability and did so by producing a successful project with little start-up money. On the other hand, some libraries had complete administrative support. In many of these institutions, the library took the lead in developing campus computing. Complex administrative structure was cited as a severe impediment in one institution. A common problem as the viewpoint of the project's staff that there was no clear picture of where the profit fit in the library as a whole. This presents many complications in its effect on staff acceptance and support as well as library support, and therefore has great influence on the effectiveness of the project and its future. As in the issue of institutional support, the converse was true. Many libraries provided support and encouragement for the projects, however modest, and there were many projects that had been developed by the library director.

The issue of student information literacy and the lack of any institutional response to that issue were cited as problems. A mandate by the institution to teach information skills would require a major change in curriculum which was seen as a long and arduous process, especially in a large university, and unlikely to happen in the immediate future. Handling the task of teaching large numbers of students information skills presents a real challenge. If a separate course were mandated, the librarians viewed CAI as a possible means of teaching it.

The solutions to many of these problems were in various stages of implementation from beginning planning to completed solutions. Common factors in the solutions were time, hard work, effective leadership, and capable staff—the same factors needed to develop successful projects.

LENGTH OF TIME—SECTION 13

In 1980-81, Carnegie Mellon decided to develop an integrated online catalog, but the library director expanded the vision beyond a catalog and developed a plan for a broader system. They have done three strategic plans in all. Development began on the Library Information System (LIS) in 1985 and the first public system was available in March 1986. They began to add CD-ROMs to the collection in July 1988.

Northwestern's NuInfo was started in January 1989 with the planning process extending into summer 1990. The Library Technical Task Force decided that the library needed to be visible on the University network and to provide access to library services beyond NOTIS. In early 1990, the Vice President for Information Services identified an immediate need to make more information available to students. The library provided the system. Using Princeton software, it was ready for public use in fall 1990.

Pike's Peak District Library was one of the first libraries to offer online service for community resource files in 1978. They began work on the files with the local Junior League in 1977. The University of Houston took two years to come up with a prototype version of their first project. This was longer than anticipated because of the research/development required and the lack of funding. They still don't have funding to meet their goals for public workstations. Currently, the original project Index Expert and the CD-ROM multiple network are operating on public workstations but are not joined in one workstation as planned. It has been available for use since 1987 and is text-based with a few simple graphics.

The University of Southern California came up with USC Info in spring 1988 with five terminals in the library and others in computer labs (MACs were not involved). The activity was dominated by word processing so the library eventually pulled out their databases and encyclopedias in the fall. The library then brought up 100 catalog terminals (GEAC) and they crashed. With the three factors of a failed catalog, an expensive system outside the library, and the pressure of time, it was decided to move the catalog to the IBM mainframe, which was better than the GEAC system, and move internal functions like acquisitions to the GEAC system.

Texas A&M invested the equivalent of one whole year in its project, which was more time than expected because of the problems encountered and lack of money. The project was begun two years before completion. The CARL System was formed as a consortium of the largest research libraries in Colorado to create a shared catalog in 1974. It was incorporated as a not-for-profit organization in 1978, CARL Systems, Inc. was created in 1989. Robert Carande at San Diego State University began work on his project in 1989. The University of California, San Diego began planning RoboRef in fall 1987 and began the project in fall 1988. They put it out at a computer fair in spring 1989 and got Phase I out on November 1989 making the project available in 12 to 18 months of development.

IMPACT—SECTION 14

Impact can be seen in five different but related categories; students/users; staff; libraries; other services; institutions. The medical library reported an increased users' confidence in their patient care decision-making. The popularity of their projects with their users convinced one project's staff that there was considerable impact on the students. One campus reported little effect on their students, attributing this to the fact that there were only a few workstations available and these were placed in an out-of-the-way location. However, this library reported considerable impact of the project outside of the institution.

Staff members were very much affected by the projects. One library reported an increased number of questions, about one-third of which related to the technical aspects of the project. Staff saw demand for help increase because of hardware problems and the need for more one-on-one tutorials and maintenance of terminals and printers.

Another institution reported its project created more work for the reference staff and a change in the types of questions asked. They found that users don't ask as many questions about online systems as printed indexes and that computers seemed to create a more self-service environment for the user. Librarians, as expected, were dealing a lot more with equipment than in the past.

The projects had considerable impact on most libraries and their services beside the direct effect on staff. One library said students used it heavily, but saw it as a toy. One library believed it had increased library usage by not only "the regulars," but had attracted new users. They also saw the online searching requests decrease while demand to increase the number of databases on their project continued to escalate. The impact of a multi-library system on one member library was also considerable.

Impact of the projects outside the institution was noted by two libraries although many of the others probably could have elaborated on this too. One library noted that the impact on the library and campus had been slight, but that a nationally known computer company had given the project a lot of publicity and that, as a result, the library said their institution had become well known for the library's projects.

WHAT WAS UNEXPECTED OR DIDN'T WORK SECTIONS 15 AND 16

The University of California, San Diego was surprised how long the project took; they thought it would take three months. The CARL staff was surprised at the rapid success of the project and that what started as a shared catalog grew into such a large system. Northwestern was impressed with the quantity of data in many campus offices like the English Department and the placement office. Brian Nielsen saw this as an opportunity for the library to educate people in computer literacy and build a computing infrastructure in the University. He believes that the library can set up a human structure within the University better than the computer center can.

What didn't work at the Northwestern science project was how little the system was being used. There seemed to be little support to encourage students to use it and more skepticism that it should be used. University of California, San Diego believed the timing was an impediment. The University of Southern California found that it took time to build a functioning team. They saw a need to build a social structure and spend more time on planning. They wanted to establish clearer lines of responsibility, make the interface more standard for transferring, and clean up the code.

FUTURE—SECTION 17

The University of Cincinnati Medical Library wants to acquire Baylor's science section and to do a program on nursing through Spectrum on IBM. Robert Carande at San Diego State University science library sees the RAS project as an intermediary step and believes that NREN is the future. His short term plans are to do a program on the environment and then on the history of science. He plans to do an extensive user study before undertaking these. Robert wants to go to object programming—C++. Object programming would enable librarians to share more. A few others are using PROLOG. Robert believes librarians should have their own programming language. Robert's long range plans are to develop a discourse with users about question negotiation. Robert was not currently interested in looking for more money for his project.

Texas A&M as interested in obtaining more money and had recently applied for a Title II-D grant. They saw MacNOTIS as a finished product and planned to change only the speed in an effort to increase it to an acceptable level. They might add a library tour to the program and maybe the capability to dial-up from home. They plan to distribute it as a prototype free for development by other institutions. They don't plan to sell it because it is reliant on two other pieces of software (HyperCard and MitemView). They don't plan to provide support beyond introductory workshops for institutions that obtain the program. Their plans very much hinge on the ability to obtain funding and support from the library.

At Northwestern University, Brian Nielsen plans to create a student interactive segment, such as recommending a book purchase. They were currently mounting Medline and it was to be available soon on all LUIS terminals. They plan to provide access to CD-ROMs. As a participant in LC's American Memory Project, they need $26,000 for equipment to put it on the campus video. The University computer center created an IBM interface that uses color and a mouse and Brian plans to move to this as a front end for the system. The Vice President for Information Services included the project in the University's computing strategy plan and the University provided $30,000 in the next year's budget for a full-time manager. Brian sees standards as very important for intra-campus usage. CWISP is in draft form; it looks at communication of text and menus from one computer to another. Involved in this are campuses with information systems like NuInfo: University of Pennsylvania, Cornell, MIT, Princeton. In his science library project, Lloyd Davidson is considering scanning in tables of contents and a subject list.

The University of California, San Diego library's RoboRef will be finished when Phase III is completed which may mean it is a forever project. Their short term plans are to move to Phase II and then expand Phase III indefinitely. The major factor affecting their plans is money. They are looking for support from library administration. If continuing support isn't forthcoming, RoboRef will be cut back. They think that linking it with RAID will help. Their hope is to keep it going until it becomes indispensable.

Pennsylvania State University library staff see writing across the curriculum coming to their campus soon and they believe this will generate a whole new demand for library instruction. They think that technology holds the only solution to this situation. At the Arizona State University library, Linda's short term plans are to get the questions database up by August of 1991. The long range plans are to build on the questions which would lead to more in-depth research, e.g., questions about journal location would lead to a search strategy, identification of relevant indexes, and location of indexes and journals. When the stand-alone terminals for access to Maricopa Community College databases are acquired, they may link the questions databases to the HyperCard library tour. The major factor affecting their plans is getting the staff up to speed. Their plans are subject to change if something new offers an unforeseen advantage. They are getting support from the library and other programs on campus to enable them to put their plans into action.

In general terms, the USC staff is hopeful that the proposed high speed of NREN will serve as a catalyst for the development and delivery of more materials serving a larger audience and an increase in commercial and public domain resources and services. They find the user community more knowledgeable about resources and service and more eager to have access to them. USC wants to use Sun computers, but these are not as easy to develop an interface as HyperCard. Their next step is to use X Windows on Sun. They might split up the mainframe to a unix-based system. Some think the library will report to the computing center within the next 5 years.

Currently under development now at USC are: the online catalog, bibliographic databases, indices, publications, and campus information files and services including class schedules and service directories. Also being added is information about and access to resources on local and national networks and commercial full text materials. Numeric and raw research data are stored and available only in electronic form. Other planned additions are full text versions of public domain documents, remote request and delivery capabilities, indices and guides to Image Databases and image delivery. They plan to put course reserve materials on line. Other planned additions are knowledge management tools, including system tutorials, expert system navigational tools, data and information manipulation tools, etc. USC has begun the foundation to achieve the above.

They will focus on user interfaces, system architecture and infrastructure, and standards. In terms of user interface, they have begun research into and development of sophisticated, yet easy-to-use navigation, search/retrieval, and display interfaces. These tools must utilize new and powerful graphics and windowing which is now available through workstation technology. A major expansion of campus information resources was planned for summer of 1991. In the area of system architecture and infrastructure they have begun to build a local network structure and develop a system architecture to support a distributed, client/server-based information system. The system currently provides access to multiple information servers via the network through a common client interface. They plan to connect and provide access to a second information server on the network, providing a full text based service by the summer of 1991. Standards will be a major focus point for future development efforts.

Using Pro-Cite they plan to create databases to update and produce library publications like pathfinders and bibliographies. They predict that some journals will be published online only. High speed printers and hand held machines will be needed. It will be necessary to anticipate what a computer will look like in 20 years to be able to plan the library of tomorrow. A number of small rooms will be needed for collaborative work. Audiovisuals will be on computers. New workspaces need to be designed by furniture companies. The profession will need to create a new breed of librarians with computing knowledge. They believe librarians are in a revolution as important as printing.

A Project Jefferson shell is being developed to enable non-programming faculty and librarians to create and incorporate material for their own assignments and databases. This will be available through Kinko's Software Catalog and will run on a Mac SE with a 20 MB hard disk.

The future of Carnegie Mellon's LIS project is governed by its philosophy which is "service to the broadest possible community." The new system will not be a mainframe one and will be better integrated with Andrew's (campus network) capabilities and its workstations. IBM machines are not a part of the University's plans. This reduces the number of supported operating systems on campus. The library must plan what information to deliver and how best to deliver it, i.e., collection development. They must insure a reasonable and equitable selection. One reason for going to a distributed system is cost: it gives more for the money than a mainframe. The want to add databases and campus information and a mainframe is more limited in capacity. A distributed system gives the library more flexibility.

They want to use emerging standards to link LIS II documents to word processors, databases, electronic mail, and similar applications. They are working with the University of California and Pennsylvania State University to test extensions of the Z39.50 protocol by sharing library catalog records in this project which is sponsored by Digital Equipment Corporation. They plan to deliver full text journals and technical reports in computer science and are working with MIT, Stanford, Illinois, and the University of California to collect machine-readable computer science technical reports to mount locally on databases. They will provide a full text databases with items held at separate locations but with a shared index.

They are aware that research indicated that new technology has changed information-seeking behavior, resulting in users essentialy using new search strategies with old information structures. They want to provide selected full-text materials for users when and where they need them. They want to rearrange the sequence of information on catalog records to put the information most often sought nearer the top of the record so the user doesn't have to go through so much irrelevant (to him) information.

LIS II will handle 25 simultaneous users, generating searches at the same rate and complexity of LIS I. They want to exceed the LIS I performance of 70 percent of real searches. They want to deliver complex documents over the network concentrating on image, full text, and personal databases. They will put the following Carnegie Mellon created databases on LIS II: software licensing and availability information; career resources information; Carnegie Mellon policies and procedures manual; the undergraduate catalog; the Macintosh and Andrew system user rules; faculty and staff publications and research profiles; indexes to student and faculty newspapers (perhaps with full text); full text of research materials such as encyclopedias, dictionaries, and phone books. They believe a library must be integrated into the larger work environment. They plan to broaden the range of bibliographic databases available in LIS II and provide full text databases. A long term goal is to enable users to find information without knowing which databases to search.

They want the library to become the electronic publisher for the University. By fall 1991 the user will be able to set his first screen in whatever database he uses most. Users want to leave the library connection active all day. They need a password and security system to control access to commercial databases and whatever is sensitive within databases. They must be able to limit the quantity of resources that can be consumed by a remote user.

LIS II will be expanded in the future so they are working with other groups to develop standards that all libraries can use. They are working with the Andrew system administrators to implement standards for Motif applications and window management on campus. They plan to test the graphical interface and build a terminal interface for personal computers like IBM PC and MAC.

Because of the popularity of MACs on campus, long term plans include building a Macintosh interface to LIS II.

They want to instrument the system to monitor user behavior and handle complex documents. They plan to implement LIS II on distributed file servers and release to the campus and provide training and documentation for library staff and patrons. They plan to broaden the range of bibliographic databases available in LIS II and provide full text databases. Their research plans are to evaluate the effects of catalog enhancements on recall and precision and evaluate and document the transition from LIS I to LIS II. They also plan to evaluate user behavior and preferences and study how users use full text databases. LIS has limited storage space for new files and an interface more appropriate for bibliographic and full text files than statistics or numeric data. This needs to be considered in choosing an information delivery method.

They acquire CD-ROMs to rectify historical inadequacies of their collection and to improve delivery of materials not held at CM. They have a formal strategic plan for electronic information service development over the next two to three years. They must consider how to continue to offer existing services whether by LIS, CD-ROMs or end-user systems. They will have more CDs in the next few years but long range focus continues to be campus-wide information delivery rather than services in libraries. Bibliographic databases may not be future acquisitions but rather full-text references works and numeric and statistical data which are in less demand and are more difficult to implement on LIS. CDs will continue to play an interim role in information delivery.

The University of Houston is looking for more funding. They plan to complete the new version expert system and link it to the CD network. They will expand its scope beyond indexes and abstracts and they might try to place a workstation in another library on campus. In terms of the technology, they are considering shifting from expert system to a Turbo C++—an object-oriented system. One reason for moving from AI tools to object-oriented tools is because the latter is easier for developing an interface. AI researchers have developed special sets of tools like Prolog which are difficult to use. Shells have been developed which are easier to use. Charles shied away from old languages like Fortran because they don't have the capability of AI. Publishers are now using a simple product C to produce expert system shells. New rules added to "if then" should be easy, as they use a modular-use inference engine to seek a goal and look for rules to confirm or deny. Houston plans to develop subject areas like business, incorporating databases, encyclopedias, handbooks, etc.

CARL Systems is viewed as a forever project; i.e., it will never be finished. Short term plans are to develop the document delivery segment of *Uncover 2* and add more databases. They plan to expand the number of library management system and add new information services. During 1990, they were developing the technical capabilities to scan optically a large historical collection and link these scanned images to catalog records. These would be retrievable in the online catalog and displayed on networked workstations.

Planned for release in 1991 is an expert mode search capability that includes full Boolean, explicit truncation, and explicit subject searching. They plan to add user-driven ILL soon. They plan to continue support and development of systems and provide new information services for users with emphasis on networking. They will develop capability for *Uncover 2* document delivery service and continue work on optical imaging by scanning art prints and map collections. They plan to expand the electronic mail component which is now primarily a staff communication mechanism to ILL and acquisitions (user-generated requests). The number of journals in *Uncover* will be increased. They will create special lists of databases which will be at network sites and available to all network participants. They are committed to OSI for extending the networking of systems. They will seek lots of user input in setting their goals. Their new clientele have been major factors in their planning for the future. They believe their clients need a versatile and flexible system and that CARL attracts that type of client.

NATIONAL AGRICULTURAL LIBRARY

The National Agriculture Library provides many innovative services, and, since it is a governmental agency and, therefore, is different from the other libraries examined, it isn't integrated into this report. The same criteria will be applied, but most of the issues are different. In the description section, the most innovative services will be briefly described and then a more detailed description of the Information Transfer program, which was more closely examined than the others, will be given.

The NAL offers a variety of traditional services, including specialized information centers, a large research collection, the AGRICOLA database online and on CD, electronic bulletin board, regional document delivery system, etc. NAL is working on combining microcomputers, scanners, and optical/digital disks for storage of full text databases, graphics, and images. This is a project on which NAL is cooperating with 44 land grant university libraries to test the use of optical scanning to transform full text and images to digital form for publication on CD.

Technology Transfer is the program focused on in this report. NAL's Technology Transfer program seeks to match research results and business needs to maximize the benefits of the 65 billion dollars the federal government spends on research and development every year. The Technology Transfer Information program is to act as a catalyst to bring industry and research technology together, provide information and seed money for reports, and facilitate marketing of products and research. The Federal Laboratory Consortium for Technology Transfer, which was established in 1974, was chartered by the Federal Technology Transfer Act of 1986. It is to facilitate the incorporation of federal research results and technologies into the U.S. economy as quickly as possible. This is to be done in a variety of ways, including cooperative research between government and industry, seminars, licensing, sponsored research, consulting, sharing of employee expertise and facilities, publication, etc.

Kate Hayes is the head of the Technology Transfer Office for NAL. Technology can be defined as knowledge in this connection. The federal government employs one-sixth of all scientists in this country. The program covers all federal departments. The NAL office works very closely with the Agricultural Research Service which is a USDA agency. Kate is developing a technology transfer collection for AGRICOLA. The two immediate projects for the office are a directory of technology transfer offices and an experiment with a user-driven process for technology transfer.

Kate does a monthly newsletter for the Technical Transfer Society. In working with the Agricultural Research Service, the office does searching for patent advisers including international clients. A concern of the office is that people don't know what is available. The role of libraries is seen as crucial. The office must avoid any action that could be construed as favoritism.

NAL has embarked on a project with two other agencies, USDA's Extension Service (ES) and the National Institute of Standards and Technology (NIST). Ted Maher of ES and Kate Hayes, who are the Systems Managers, selected the Hardwood Research Council for the project. This industry met the established criteria requiring that the selected industry not be dominated by a few small firms and that the industry is suffering from foreign competition. The raw material and process inputs of the selected industry must be scarce or expensive. Another factor in its selection was the industry had already established its needs. The office has contracted for four reports to be written by June or 1992 which will analyze the problems and recommend solutions.

In another project, NAL is working with 42 land grant institutions on a research and demonstration project that provides document delivery through digitized text. They are testing scanning hardware and indexing/search software to capture full text in a digital format to be published in media like CDs. They believe this is a system superior to FAX because it transmit graphics and formulae which are important to scientific research. Equipment incompatibility is another limiting factor in the use of FAX.

NAL is developing a multimedia CD-ROM that will contain textual material, a database, and an expert system. The subject covered is ornamental horticulture. The text will provide general advice for both the novice and experienced individual and will include regional requirements, citations, text of documents, illustrations, and related fields. It will have audio capability.

The software had not been selected; NAL has developed other systems (one on African aquaculture) using Knowledge Pro, so off-the-shelf software will be considered. NAL is doing other projects such as the storage of photographs on laser disks.

TECHNOLOGY TRANSFER PROGRAM

1. The goals and objectives of Technology Transfer are to develop and facilitate the merging of research and industry, often resulting in marketing. A more specific objective is to find solutions for industry-based problems. The relationship between the office and the other departments in NAL is evolving and may ultimately have some effect on the office's activities.

2. The audience is very broad and includes scientists, companies, agencies, and institutions.

3. The information provided is in science and technology.

4-7. Categories are not applicable to Technology Transfer.

8. The Department of Agriculture funds a 250,000 dollar budget. NAL has provided 23,000 dollars.

9. Kate Hayes started the program and has provided the leadership. Ted Maher, National Program Leader with the extension service and a member of the extension agents staff, worked with Kate in starting the project. Kate has a 60 percent FTE librarian and some student help.

10. Evaluation will be determined by the results of the products developed in the hardwood industry study.

11. Kate has not been successful in finding outside funding. Additional support was provided by the National Institute of Standards and Technology who gave 10,000 dollars for the hardwood study. The Agricultural Research Service has supported patent searching, and eventually the office wants to do searching for scientists before they begin their research.

12. The major problem is funding and the resultant lack of staff. NAL is at their "ceiling" in staffing and can't hire any more people. The major obstacles besides the lack of funding and staff is that it is a non-traditional program within the federal government.

13. The office came into being in September of 1990.

14. The impact could be far-reaching and might speed development and a technology or just confirm that research is needed.

15. What was unexpected was the funding from NAL and NIST.

16. What didn't work were efforts to get more money.

17. In the spring of 1992, the contracted four reports will be finished and a symposium may be held. Then they will focus on another industry. There will be a heavy emphasis on marketing results and the technological (information) needs of the industry under consideration. The industry must have already identified its technological needs and the focus will be on small companies. Kate would like to hire a staff person to complete the hardwood project so she can move on to another industry study.

CRITERIA FOR PROJECTS' STUDY

1. Goals and objectives of program:
   a. Are they written and by whom
   b. Are they measurable
2. Program's audience/intended users:
   a. Is this clearly stated
   b. Was this audience involved in the development, e.g., evaluation
   c. Has this changed (expanded or narrowed) during program's development
3. Types of information available to program's user:
   a. Is it consistent with the program's goals and objectives and appropriate for the program's users
   b. How was it selected
   c. How is it structured for the users
   d. Does it format structure and content follow educational principles
4. Type of interface:
   a. Description
   b. How was it developed
   c. Similarities to other interfaces
   d. Differences form other interfaces (unique characteristics)
5. Type of help/expert system:
   a. Which type is it
   b. Why was the system developed this way
   c. How was the system developed
6. Software used:
   a. It is unique, if not, what type of existing software is it
   b. Why this software
   c. It is finished
7. Hardware needed:
   a. What factors were important to the selection
   b. What problems are involved
   c. Would another selection have been better in their opinion

8. Economic issues:
   a. Where has money come from
   b. What other kinds of support has been sought or found
   c. How have these issues affected the program's development
9. Personnel involved:
   a. Who started the program
   b. Who has provided the leadership
   c. Has the personnel changed
10. Evaluation and consultants:
    a. What evaluation has been done
    b. What future evaluation is planned
    c. Have consultants been involved, if so, with what result
11. How and what kinds of support has been sought from:
    a. the library
    b. other units within the institution
    c. the instituition
    d. other
12. Major problems and obstacles:
    a. What were the major problems encountered so far
       * Were they anticipated
       * How were they solved
       * Could they have been prevented
    b. What were the major obstacles
       * Were they foreseen
       * How were they overcome
       * Could they have been prevented
13. Length of Time
    a. Approximately how much time has gone into the project so far
    b. Is this more or less than estimated-why
    c. How much time to accomplish established goals and objectives
14. Impact:
    a. Planned and unplanned
    b. On whom
    c. What effect
15. What happened that was unexpected/unforeseen
16. What didn't work
17. Future plans:
    a. When will the project be finished
    b. What are short-term plans
       * How were they established
    c. What are long-range plans
       * How were they set
    d. What are the major factors affecting their plans
    e. What provision is being made for future support

ACKNOWLEDGMENT

This study was funded in part by the Council on library Resources and The Ohio State University.

REFERENCES

National Agriculture Library

Andre, Pamela Q.J., "In the Field of Agriculture, CD-ROM Delivers!" *Agricultural Libraries Information Notes.*16.10 (1990) p. 1-11.
Beavers, Peggy J., "Library Services for the Agricultural Research Service: A Plan for the 1990's and Beyond." *Agricultural Libraries Information Notes* 16.1 (1990) pp. 1-6.
Casorso, Tracy M., "The North Carolina State University Libraries and the National Agricultural Library Joint Project on Transmission of Digitized Text: Improving Access to Agricultural Information." *Reference Services Review* 19.1. (1991) pp. 15-22.
Edwards, Shirley J., "Optical Scanning in a Production Environment: The TransImage 1000 Handscanner." *Agricultural Libraries Information Notes* 17.4 (1991) pp. 1-4.
Hayes, Kate, "Generating Solutions to the Hardwood Industry's Technology-Based Problems." *Agricultural Libraries Information Notes* 17.8 (1991) pp. 1-7.
"NAC/NC State Move Ahead in Designing Expanded Computer-Based Document Delivery System." *Information Alert from the National Agricultural Library* (June 1991) pp. 1-3.
Norris, Brian, "Laser Disc Technology Allows Quick Access to USDA Photos." *Agricultural Libraries Information Notes* 16.11/12 (1990) pp. 1-12.
Rand, Roberta Y., "NAL Introduces ISIS to the Public." *Agricultural Libraries Information Notes* 16.3 (1990) pp. 1-5.

Texas A&M

Anders, Vicki., "The Wiley Laser Disk Service At Evans Library, Texas A&M University." *Public Access CD-ROMs in Libraries: Case Studies* pp. 180-191.
Jackson, Kathy M., "Loading Wilson Indexes Locally—The Texas A&M Experience." *Online* (July 1990) pp. 42-45.
Leeper, Paul, and Sherrie Schmidt, "MacNOTIS: Taking On-line Library Catalogs a Step Further." *Administrative Applications* (1989) pp. 77-80.

University of Southern California

"USCInfo: A Development Platform for Tomorrow's Information Rich Environment." *Center for Scholarly Technology and the University Library* (November 1990).
Teitelbaum, Sheldon., "USC's New Teaching Library: The Future is Here." *USC Trojan Family* (September 1990) pp. 21-26.

San Diego State University

Carande, Robert, "Reference Advisory Systems (RAS): Some Practical Issues." *Reference Services Review* (Fall 1989) 87-90.

Carande, Robert, "INDEXES: A Micro-Based Expert System." *Expert Systems* (December 1988) pp. 26-27.
Carande, Robert, "Reference Advisory Systems Board." *Information Technology and Libraries* (June 1980) pp. 180-184.

Northwestern University

Weston, Norm, "NUINFO System Officially Inaugurated." *Northwestern University Computing and Networking* 6.1 (1991) 24-27.

University of Houston

Bailey, Charles Jr., "Building Knowledge-Based Systems for Public Use: The Intelligent Reference Systems Project." *Convergence: The Proceedings of the Second LITA National Conference* (1989).
Bailey, Charles Jr., "Public-Access Computer Systems: The Next Generation of Library Automation Systems." *Information Technologies and Libraries* (June 1989) pp. 178-85.
Bailey, Charles Jr., "Intelligent Multimedia Computer Systems: Emerging Information Resources in the Network Environment." *Library Hi Tech* 29.1 (1990) pp. 29-41.
Bailey, Charles Jr., Jeff Fadell, Judy E. Myers, Thomas C. Wilson., "The Index Expert System: A Knowledge-Based System to Assist Users in Index Selection." *Reference Services Review* 17.4 (1989) pp. 19-28.
Bailey, Charles Jr., "The Intelligent Reference Information System." *CD-ROM Librarian* (Sept. 1990) pp. 10-19.
Bailey, Charles Jr., "Intelligent Library Systems: Artificial Intelligence Technology and Library Automation Systems." *Advances in Library Automation and Networking* 4 (1990) p. 1-17.
Bailey, Charles Jr., "Integrated Public-Access Computer Systems: The Heart of the Electronic University." *Advances in Library Automation and Networking* 3 (1989) pp. 1-33.
Fadell, Jeff, Judy Myers, "The Information Machine: A Microcomputer-Based Reference Service." *Reference Librarian* 23 (1989) pp. 75-112.

Carnegie Mellon University

Evans, Nancy, Thomas Michalak, "Delivering Reference Information Through a Campus Network: Carnegie Mellon's Library Information System." *Reference Services Review* (Winter 1987) pp. 7-13.
Evans, Nancy, "Development of the Carnegie Mellon Library Information System." *Information Technology and Libraries* 8.2 (1989) pp. 110-120.
Evans, Nancy, "CD-ROM's at the Carnegie Mellon University." *Public Access CD-ROM's in Libraries: Case Studies* pp. 279-297.
Neuwirth, Christine M., David S. Kaufer, Ravinder Chandhok, James H. Morris, "Issues in the Design of Computer Support for Co-Authoring and Commenting." *CSCW Proceedings* (October 1990) pp. 183-195.
Neuwirth, Christine M., David S. Kaufer, "The Role of External Representations in the Writing Process: Implications for the Design of Hypertext-Based Writing Tools." *Hypertext '89 Proceedings* (1989) pp. 319-342.
Troll, Denise A., *LIBRARY INFORMATION SYSTEM II: Progress Report and Technical Plan* Mecury Technical Report Series, Number 3.(1990) Carnegie Mellon University Libraries.

Washington University

Crawford, Susan, Ronald G. Evens, "Medical School Libraries in the United States: Evolution to Information Management." *The Pharos* (Winter 1989) p. 39-41.

Georgetown University

Broering, Naomi, C., "The MAClinical Workstation." *Biomedical Information Resources Center and Clinical Informatics Center* (1990).

University of Cincinnati

Killion, Vicki, J., Leslie C. Schick, Stephena E. Harmony, Leilani A. St. Anna, "Training the End User in an Academic Medical Library." *Proceedings of the National Online Meeting* (May 1987) pp. 229-236.

Killion, Vicki J., Leslie C. Schick, Stephena E. Harmony, Leilani A. St. Anna, Ellen Marks, Mary Piper, "Enhancement of Public Services Through Medical Information Quick—A Unique End-User Search Service." *Medical Center Information and Communications* (January 1987).

CARL Systems

Technos: The Technical News of CARL Systems No. 6 (May 1991).
Technos: The Technical News of CARL Systems No. 5 (Nov. 1990).
On CARL: The Quarterly Newsletter for CARL System Users (Spring 1991).
On CARL: The Quarterly Newsletter for CARL System Users (Winter 1991).
On CARL: The Quarterly Newsletter for CARL System Users (Fall 1991).
Colorado Libraries 16.2 (June 1990).
Colorado Libraries 16.3 (September 1990).
CARL Systems Inc: System Description (May 1991).

Arizona State University

Riggs, Donald E., "Productivity Increases in Public Services: Are Expert Systems the Answer?" *Journal of Library Administration* 9.4 (1988) pp. 89-99.

Other Works

"Technology Transfer: A Profile of Agency Activities in USDA." *Submitted by the Technology Transfer Subcommittee of the Research and Education Committee U.S. Department of Agriculture* (March 1989).

Aluri, Rao, Donald E. Riggs, "Application of Expert Systems to Libraries." *Advances in Library Automaton and Networking* 2 (1988) pp. 1-43.

Wilson, Thomas C., "Zen and the Art of CD-ROM Network License Negotiation." *The Public-Access Computer Systems Review* 1 2 (1990) pp. 4-14.

AUTOMATED COLLECTION ANALYSIS AND DEVELOPMENT: BUSINESS COLLECTION

Jane A. Dodd and Suzanne D. Gyeszly

ABSTRACT

The purpose of the research was to establish guidelines, procedures, and methodology for an automated shelflist count and automated collection analysis and development using the business collection of the Sterling C. Evans Library at Texas A&M University. Aspects of NOTIS as an integrated library system, the OCLC/AMIGOS Collection Analysis CD and the OCLC/EPIC Service provided assistance to the project. The concept and the methodology could be adaptable for all types of libraries and collections. The project was funded by the Council on Library Resources.

INTRODUCTION

The intent of this project was to introduce an automated shelflist count as well as an automated collection analysis and development method for libraries using

Advances in Library Administration and Organization,
Volume 11, pages 201-215.
Copyright © 1993 by JAI Press Inc.
All rights of reproduction in any form reserved.
ISBN: 1-55938-596-0

the business collection of the Sterling C. Evans Library at Texas A&M University. The researchers chose this collection because of the growth of the student enrollment and curriculum of the College of Business Administration and Graduate School of Business (CBAGSB) over the past decade as well as the increased requirements of the faculty and its nationally recognized programs. In 1980, the College listed 5,263 declared majors, of which 4,898 were undergraduates and 385 were enrolled in graduate programs. After computed growth, the CBAGSB began to limit the enrollment. In 1992, the CBAGSB listed 6,312 declared majors in five disciplines: Accounting, Business Analysis, Finance, Management, and Marketing with a makeup of 5,691 undergraduates and 611 masters and doctoral candidates. This represents an increase in enrollment of nearly 20 percent. There are limited means for gauging comparable growth in the business collection. The researchers utilized the available automated technology for collection analysis and development and recommended lists of business titles for retrospective collection development purposes.

METHODOLOGY

Collection development policies for each of the five departments within the College of Business Administration and Graduate School of Business served as the foundation for compilation of the major subject areas and call number ranges to be included in the activities of this project. The existing collection development policies describe general collection guidelines as well as provide detailed information, by subject, on the programs to be supported, the required collection level, and the Library of Congress classification numbers (LCCN). A portion of the policy for the Finance Department is shown in Figure 1.

Subject	Serves	Required Collecting Level	Library of Congress Classification Numbers
Banks and Banking	U, G, R	A, B, C, D	HG 1501-3452.5
Credit, Practice	G, R	A, B	HF 5565-5585
Credit, Theory	G, R	B	HG 3201-3781
Credit Unions	G, R	B	HG 2033-2051
Savings Banks	G, R	B	HG 1881-1966
Banks and Banking, International	G, R	B	HG 4538
Business Enterprises	U, G, R	A, B, C, D	HG 4026-4028
Capital Budgets	U, G, R	B, C, D	HG 4028
Capital Markets	U, G, R	B, C, D	HG 4523-4557
Cash Flow/Cash Management	G, R	B	HG 4523-4557
Corporations-Finance	U, G, R	A, B, C, D	HG 4001-4480
Finance	U, G, R	A, B, C, D	HG 4173-4181
Finance, Personal	G, R	B	HG 179

Figure 1.   Excerpt from the Finance Department
Collection Development Policy

Subject	LCCN Ranges
Accounting	HF 5601-5661
Accounting	HF 5679
Accounting	HJ 9705-9931
Auditing	HF 5667-5668
Financial Statements	HF 5681-5686
Income Tax	HJ 4652-5905
Income Tax	HJ 2305-3234
Income Tax	KF 6271-6629
Finance	HG 1-1496
Corporations-Finance	HG 4001-4245
International Finance	HG 3611-3997
Banking	HG 1501-3550
Investments	HG 4501-6051
Real Estate Business	HD 1361-1395
Marketing	HF 5410-5415
Advertising	HF 5801-5828
Retail Trade	HF 5429-5437
Sales	HF 5438-5483
Management	HD 1-88
Business Ethics	HF 5386-5387
Corporations	HD 2308-3387
Executives	HF 5500
International Business	HD 2755.5
Personnel Management	HF 5549
Management Information Systems	T 56-58
Production Management	TS 155

Figure 2. Library of Congress Subject Headings and
Classification Numbers: Business Collection

Identification of relevant LCCN ranges was necessary for the automated shelflist count and for using the OCLC/AMIGOS Collection Analysis CD. The classification numbers were also used in searching the OCLC Online Union Catalog of OCLC's EPIC Service. Call number ranges were selected to encompass, as much as possible, the universe of titles in appropriate subject areas for the Library's business collection. For several subjects, identification of the call numbers was very straightforward. One of the CBAGSB's graduate programs receiving national attention is the Management Department's doctoral program in corporate strategy; nearly all titles on strategic planning and corporate planning are classified with HD 30.28. Likewise, nearly all titles related to banking are classified in the range of HG 1501-HG 3550. However, for a subject such as taxation, relevant titles can be found in various ranges of the HJ and KF classes as well as in HF. In order to avoid duplication and to simplify the search process, rather general subject groupings were used in lieu of precise call numbers for very specific subject areas. The subject groupings and LCCN ranges used are listed in Figure 2.

As an integrated library system, NOTIS has the capacity, through report writing, to complete statistics for shelflist holdings and to prepare an inventory of the entire library collection or portion of it. To implement this, a SAS (Statistical Analysis System) program was written to determine the current holdings for the business collection of the Library. The results were compared with the 1989 manual shelflist count.

The OCLC/AMIGOS Collection Analysis CD enabled the investigators to compare the Evans Library collection with ARL and peer institutions' collections, focusing on materials which were published during 1979-1989. The results of the analysis were used in assessing the Evans Library business collection. Titles not held by Evans Library were reviewed for retrospective collection development.

The OCLC/Online Union catalog on the EPIC Service helped to identify materials for collection development through the use of Library of Congress classification number search capabilities. Relevant business titles published between 1979 and 1989 were downloaded to disks for review and selection.

DISCUSSION

Automated Shelflist Count

A Statistical Analysis System (SAS) program was used to compile the shelflist count. Figures 3 and 4 show the flowchart of the program and its definitions. Blocks of the call number index, LAMCALX.KSDS, were expanded by CALLDEX into individual call number records with their NOTIS keys and stored in a file. The call number ranges that were selected to build the shelflist were stored in the file, LCSTEMS. Then, LCCOUNT compared the file created by CALLDEX with LCSTEMS sequentially. If the call number in the CALLDEX file was less than or equal to the range in the LCSTEMS file, then the counter for that range was incremented and the pointer in the CALLDEX file advanced. When the call number became greater than the range, the pointer in the LCSTEMS file was advanced and the results tallied for the shelflist count.

The programmer used the selected business call number ranges to determine the shelflist holdings of the Evans Library. The automated shelflist count for major areas within the business collection is shown in Table 1.

The researchers were unable to compare the same call numbers of the automated shelflist count with the manual count which was conducted in

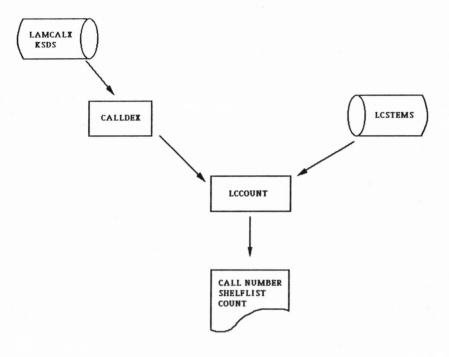

Figure 3. Flowchart for Shelflist Count

LAMCALX.KSDS	Contains call number index entries for linked and/or unlinked item records.
CALLDEX	Expands blocks of the call number index into individual call number records with associated NOTIS record numbers and places them in a file.
LCSTEMS	A list of all call number ranges to be compared with the records created by CALLDEX.
LCCOUNT	Takes the records created by CALLDEX, compares them to the call number ranges in LCSTEMS and tallies the results for the shelflist count.

Figure 4. Flowchart Definitions

Table 1. Automated Shelflist Count: Business Collection

Subject	LCCN Ranges	Shelflist Count
Accounting	HF 5601-5661	1,100
Accounting	HF 5679	66
Accounting	HJ 9705-9931	62
Auditing	HF 5667-5668	230
Financial Statements	HF 5681-5686	711
Income Tax	HJ 4652-5905	191
Income Tax	HJ 2305-3234	239
Income Tax	KF 6271-6629	769
Finance	HG 1-1496	1,459
Corporations-Finance	HG 4001-4245	738
International Finance	HG 3611-3997	847
Banking	HG 1501-3550	1,088
Investments	HG 4501-6051	1,523
Real Estate Business	HD 1361-1395	515
Marketing	HF 5410-5415	1,600
Advertising	HF 5801-5828	602
Retail Trade	HF 5429-5437	342
Sales	HF 5438-5483	585
Management	HD 1-88	5,404
Business Ethics	HF 5386-5387	194
Corporations	HD 2308-3387	467
Executives	HF 5500	316
International Business	HD 2755.5	659
Personnel Management	HF 5549	756
Management Information Systems	T 56-58	940
Production Management	TS 155	481

Table 2. Automated and Manual Shelflist Counts

LCCN Ranges	Automated	Manual
H	1,370	3,012
HA	992	1,061
HB	4,696	5,423
HC	8,005	9,483
HD 1-100	5,404	5,984
HD 101-1395	1,678	2,088
HD 1401-2210	2,210	3,325
HD 2321-4730	340	1,893
HD 4801-8942	5,982	7,500
HD 9000-9999	5,781	6,875
HE	3,722	5,246
HF 1-4050	2,270	2,740
HF 5001-6351	9,638	11,706
HG	6,054	6,732
HJ	1,635	1,870
T	3,550	4,131
TS	3,586	4,172

December, 1989. The manual shelflist count was part of the National Shelflist Count, and the call numbers covered much wider call number ranges. Table 2 lists the results of the automated and manual shelflist counts of the selected Library of Congress classification numbers.

We believe that the manual shelflist count indicated larger numbers than the automated one primarily because of the imprecise method of measurement used nationwide for preparation of the shelflist count in earlier years.

OCLC/AMIGOS COLLECTION ANALYSIS CD

OCLC/AMIGOS Collection Analysis CD (CACD) allowed the researchers to compare the Sterling C. Evans Library business collection with seventy-two participating Association of Research Libraries' (ARL) collections as well as with ten peer institutions. The ten libraries in the peer group were selected by the library and university administrators based on similar size of the library and student enrollment in addition to similar historical background. The peer institutions are listed in Figure 5.

The database of the OCLC/AMIGOS Collection Development CD is extracted from the OCLC Union Catalog for monographic titles (excluding serials, government documents, and dissertations) published between 1979 and 1989. It contains approximately 1.7 million abbreviated bibliographic records. Each record in the CACD must have a Library of Congress classification number and be held by at least one Association of Research Libraries member of some other academic library.

University of Arizona
University of Georgia
University of Illinois at Urbana-Champaign
Iowa State Univesity
University of Minnesota-Twin Cities
Ohio State University
University of Oklahoma
Pennsylvania State University
Purdue University
Texas A&M University

Figure 5. Selected Peer Institutions

GAP BETWEEN EVALUATOR AND PEER GROUP

Peer Group:	1	ARL Libraries in OCLC
LC Class Beginning:	HF 5601	
Ending:	HF 5661	This LC Class range contains 2563 records
Holdings Pct Lower:	0	
Upper:	100	Items held by 0 - 100% of the peer group
Pub. Year Beginning:	1979	
Ending:	1989	Publication years 1979 to 1989
Language:	ENG	English
Output Device:	F	Output to File
Save File Name:	EXPORT.TXT	

Figure 6. OCLC/AMIGOS Collection Analysis CD Search Format

CACD can be used for any of the following:

- Compare the user's library collection to national standards, larger institutions, and smaller libraries;
- Evaluate specific areas of the entire collection;
- Determine strengths and weaknesses of the collection;
- Choose broad or narrow subject definitions based on 32 subject definitions of the Library of Congress or the National Shelflist 500 classes;
- Generate statistical reports;
- Produce customized bibliographies for acquisitions.

The bibliographic list menu of the CACD includes overlap, gaps, unique evaluator, unique peer group evaluator, and peer group lists. The gap titles refer to titles in the database which are not held by the evaluator institution. CACD search format is illustrated in Figure 6.

All bibliographic lists can be saved in an ASCII file and manipulated as needed.

Tables 3a and 3b show the summary of collection analysis data for call number ranges associated with the business collection of the Sterling C. Evans Library. Comparison of the number of all titles in ARL libraries with TXA (Texas A&M University) gap titles indicated that Evans Library lacked an average of 51.6 percent of the available titles of ARL libraries. The largest percentage gap (81.7 percent) occurred in call number range HG 1-1496 where 2,192 titles were found in ARL libraries; Evans Library lacked 1,790 titles. In

Table 3a. Summary of Collection Analysis Data: Business Collection

Subject	LCCN Ranges	Epic	All Titles in ARL Libraries	All ARL Titles: % of Epic	TXA Gap Titles / ARL	TXA Gap Titles: % of All ARL Titles	TXA Gap Titles / Peers
Accounting	HF 5601-5661	4,075	2,563	62.9%	1,440	56.2%	692
Accounting	HF 5679	344	26	59.9%	101	49.0%	57
Accounting	HJ 9705-9931	729	248	34.0%	142	57.3%	89
Auditing	HF 5667-5668	1,034	636	61.5%	384	60.4%	193
Financial Statements	HF 5681-5686	2,365	1,589	67.2%	897	56.5%	472
Income Tax	HJ 4652-5905	1,532	667	43.5%	341	51.1%	164
Income Tax	HJ 2305-3234	1,394	676	48.5%	348	51.5%	152
Income Tax	KF 6271-6629	6,198	3,619	58.4%	2,159	59.7%	803
Finance	HG 1-1496	2,933	2,192	74.7%	1,790	81.7%	992
Corporations-Finance	HG 4001-4245	2,640	1,795	68.0%	792	44.1%	412
International Finance	HG 3611-3997	3,935	2,591	65.8%	1,109	42.8%	547
Banking	HG 1501-3550	7,176	4,304	60.0%	2,281	53.0%	952
Investments	HG 4501-6051	6,771	4,328	63.9%	2,421	55.9%	1,136
Real Estate Business	HD 1361-1395	2,033	1,264	62.2%	721	57.0%	386

Table 3a.   Summary of Collection Analysis Data: Business Collection

Subject	LCCN Ranges	Epic	All Titles in ARL Libraries	All ARL Titles: % of Epic	TXA Gap Titles/ ARL	TXA Gap Titles: % of All ARL Titles	TXA Gap Titles/ Peers
Marketing	HF 5410-5415	3,697	2,361	63.9%	1,068	45.2%	684
Advertising	HF 5801-5828	1,094	819	74.9%	406	49.6%	254
Retail Trade	HF 5429-5437	1,436	791	55.1%	385	48.7%	176
Sales	HF 5438-5483	1,892	1,266	66.9%	612	48.3%	396
Management	HD 1-88	16,414	12,757	77.7%	5,491	43.0%	2,378
Business Ethics	HF 5386-5387	714	533	74.6%	270	50.7%	187
Corporations	HD 2308-3387	5,258	3,736	71.1%	1,368	36.6%	663
Executives	HF 5500	539	307	57.0%	132	43.0%	73
International Business	HD 2755.5	436	310	71.1%	182	58.7%	101
Personnel Management	HF 5549	5,582	2,297	41.2%	1,293	56.3%	734
Management Info-Syst	T 56-58	2,239	1,468	65.6%	678	46.2%	307
Production Management	TS 155	1,129	712	63.1%	292	41.0%	168

contrast, for HD 2308-3387, ARL libraries had 5,258 titles and Evans Library had only 1,364 gaps (36.3 percent).

When evaluated with the peer institutions, the largest number of gap titles occurred in the call number range of HD 1-88; there were 2,378 gap titles of the available 12,757 ARL titles. HF 5679 had just 57 gap titles compared to peer institutions.

For collection development purposes, gap titles were downloaded to a disk and analyzed by the researchers. Numerous bibliographic data were found with only OCLC numbers and without ISBN numbers. Items without ISBN numbers were generally technical or corporate reports and papers. Titles to be considered for acquisition were checked for availability on Books in Print Plus CD. The researchers found that bibliographic records without ISBN numbers were rarely available for purchase. Therefore, many of the gap titles could not be easily used for retrospective collection development. In addition, a large percentage of titles with ISBN numbers were already out of print.

OCLC/EPIC SERVICE

Reference use of the OCLC Online Union Catalog on the EPIC Service has been discussed in the literature, but there is little mention of this database as a collection development tool. The OCLC database of more than 25 million records can be searched on the EPIC Service with many access points, including subjects, keywords, and call numbers. For reference purposes, the capability of searching for subject headings and keywords, in any order, makes this online database extremely powerful. For collection development purposes, it would be impractical, if not impossible to formulate searches using the hundreds of terms which would be required to adequately describe a collection interest such as the "business collection," whereas LCCN searching on EPIC's Database 23 (the OCLC Online Union Catalog) could be very useful.

Searches were executed on the EPIC database for all of the call number ranges associated with the business collection subject groupings. Results, in numerical totals, are included in Tables 3a and 3b along with the results obtained with the OCLC/AMIGOS CACD. The searches were restricted to English language titles, book format, published from 1979-1989. The restrictions were the same for the EPIC and CACD searches.

Figure 7 illustrates the format and provides examples of the Library of Congress classification number searches. Because the EPIC system limits the number of search elements which can be entered at one time to 300, the level at which the truncation technique can be utilized varies with the number of specific classification numbers within the range to be searched. The system also limits to 500 the number of records in a set which can be sorted. The EPIC service provides a variety of predefined formats for output as well as permits

STRUCTURE OF THE LC INDEX:

aaa	1 to 3 class letters; 1 underscore after 2 letters and 2 underscores after 1 letter
0000	First subdivision, 4 digits; leading zeros included
.000	Second subdivision; 1 to 3 place decimal number
?	Truncation sysmbol

EXAMPLE 1: SEARCH FOR HD 30.28 (STRATEGIC PLANNING)

1—>   FIND LC HD__0030.288?
S1   1324   LC HD__0030.288?   (System response)
2=>   FIND S1 AND YR 1979-1989 AND PT BKS AND LN=ENGLISH
S2   736   S1 AND YR 1979-1989 AND PT BKS AND LN=ENGLISH
3=>   FIND S2 AND YR 1985-1989   (To reduce set for sort)
S3   440   S2 AND YR 1985-1989
4=>   SORT S3 AU, TI
THE SET HAS BEEN SORTED   (System response)

EXAMPLE 2: SEARCH FOR THE RANKE HG 1-1496 (FINANCE)

1=>   FIND LC HG__000? OR LC HG__001? OR LC HG__01? OR LC HG__10?
        OR LC HG__11? OR LC HG__12? OR LC HG__13? OR LC HG__14?
S1   311   LC HG__000?
S2   98   LC HG__001?
S3   8635   LC HG__01?
S4   627   LC HG__10?
S5   354   LC HG__11?
S6   1089   LC HG__12?
S7   343   LC HG__13?
S8   108   LC HG__14?
S9   11565   LC HG__000? OR LC HG__001? OR LC HG__01? OR
                                 LC HG__10? OR LC HG__11? OR LC HG__12? OR
                                 LC HG__13? OR LC HG__14?
10=>   FIND S9 AND YR 1979-1989 AND PT BKS AND LN=ENGLISH
S10   2933   S9 AND YR 1979-1989 AND PT BKS AND LN=ENGLISH

Figure 7.   Epic Search Format for Library of Congress
Classification Numbers

user-defined formats. For the preliminary evaluation of titles for retrospective collection development, the display format, F1 (browse), was very adequate. This format includes author, titles, year, language, publications type, physical description, and series data. It is the only online format for which there is not citation charge.

There were significantly more titles retrieved with the EPIC searches than with the CACD searches. To investigate the differences, an EPIC retrieval of 736 records for HD 30.28 was compared, title by title, with the output from

Table 4. Comparison of Results EPIC and CACD Search of HD 30.28 1979-1989

	Titles on EPIC	% Total Epic Titles	Titles on CACD	% Total CACD Titles	Epic Titles Not on CACD	% Total Epic Titles Not on CACD
Titles Held by TXA	218	29.6	195	52.0	23	6.4
Duplicate Titles	77	10.5	8	2.1	69	19.1
Titles not held by TXA:						
Theses	53	7.2	3	0.8	50	13.8
Short Papers/Reports	115	15.6	27	7.2	88	24.4
Titles Inappropriate for Collection	159	21.6	67	17.9	92	25.5
Titles for Further Evaluation	114	15.5	75	20.0	39	10.8
Total	736	100.0%	375	100.0%	361	100.0%

the CACD—titles held by the Library and gap titles not held by the Library but held by one or more of the 72 ARL libraries. As shown in Table 4, 19.1 percent of the titles retrieved from the EPIC search but not the CACD were duplicate titles.

Duplication is to be expected in a database which is a union catalog. For this call number on EPIC, 22.8 percent of the titles were theses, dissertations, working papers, and other short documents. This category of material would be of interest for collection development purposes in very few circumstances; thus, the inclusion of such publications in EPIC's "book" format creates a significantly greater number of titles which are not generally useful. The remainder of the EPIC titles which were not on the CACD were reviewed for further evaluation as to suitability for the collection. Only 10.8 percent of the titles unique to the EPIC search were considered to be appropriate for additional evaluation.

SUMMARY

Discrepancies between the automated shelflist count and the manual shelflist count can be explained, at least in part, by the inaccuracies of the physical measurement for the manual count. Also, refinement could be made to the SAS program to bridge the gap between the two counts. NOTIS, Inc. has announced that it plans to develop several statistical analysis packages, including one for shelflist count.

For retrospective collection department, for the 10 year period covered, the OCLC/AMIGOS Collection Analysis CD is an excellent resource because of its comprehensive coverage. The list of individual gap titles can easily be generated for review. With each annual update of the CACD results from searching all call number ranges can be used to assess and to note changes in a library's relative quantitative strength. Use of the CACD for retrospective collection development is highly recommended for humanities and social sciences subjects. However, for science and engineering disciplines, the CACD is a less practical tool because of the need for timeliness of the materials. Timeliness is also a significant consideration for a business collection.

Because of the size of the EPIC database and because of the inability to search holdings and/or eliminate titles held, its use for retrospective collection development could be only in very limited subject areas. It would be quite impractical to review the number of titles resulting from the call number ranges searched for only the 10 year period, 1979-1989, used in this project. The OCLC/EPIC Service could be very useful for current collection development; call number searches can be stored and executed monthly at minimal charges.

The researchers suggest, for automated collection analysis and development for which classification numbers are used, that the range of numbers be as narrow and as subject-specific as possible. For collection development in subjects which are interdisciplinary or for which various classification numbers may be used, call number searches in even very limited ranges will not be useful.

ACKNOWLEDGMENTS

Research for this study was funded by grant number 879 from the Council on Library Resources. The study could not have been completed without this support. The researchers wish to thank Florencia Choto for the SAS program and Jeffrey McGuirk for his help in preparing this manuscript.

REFERENCES

Ballard, Terry. "OCLC's EPIC: Reports from the Field." *Computers in Libraries* 11, 4 (1991) pp. 47-49.

Chan, Lois Mai. "Library of Congress Classification as an Online Retrieval Tool: Potentials and Limitations." *Information Technology and Libraries* 5, 3 (1986) pp. 181-192.

Jamarillo, George R. "Computer Technlogy and Its Impact on Collection Development." *Collection Management* 10, 1/2 (1988) pp. 1-13.

Kreyche, Michael. "BCL3 and NOTIS: An Automated Collection Analysis Project." *Library Acquisitions: Practice & Theory* 13, (1989) pp. 323-328.

Lynden, Frederick Charles. "Collection Management by Automation." *Library Acquisitions: Practice and Theory* 13, (1989) pp. 177-183.

Miranda, Michael. "Developing College Business and Economics Collections." *College and Research Libraries* 49, 6 (1988) pp. 501-513.

Notress, Greg. "Searching EPIC on the Internet." *OCLC Micro* 7 (1991) pp. 23-25.

Palais, Eliot. "Use of Course Analysis in Compiling a Collection Development Policy Statement for a University Library." *Journal of Academic Librarianship* 13, 1 (1987) pp. 8-13.

Payson, Evelyn and Barbara Moore. "Statistical Collection Management Analysis of OCLC-MARC Tape Recordings." *Information Technology and Libraries* 4, 3 (1985) pp. 220-232.

Radke, Barbara A. "OCLC/AMIGOS Collection Analysis CD." *OCLC Micro* 7 (1991) pp. 28-30.

Sanders, Nancy P., Edward T. O'Neill, and Stuart L. Weibel. "Automated Collection Analysis Using the OCLC and RLG Bibliographic Databases." *College & Research Libraries* 49, 4 (1988) pp. 305-314.

Sasse, Margo and Patricia A. Smith. "Automated Acquisitions: The Future of Collection Development." *Library Acquisitions: Practice & Theory* 16, 2 (1992) pp. 135-143.

Tenopir, Carol. "Searching for Books Online." *Library Journal* 115, March 1 (1990) pp. 68-69.

Welsch, Edward K. "Back to the Future: A Personal Statement on Collection Development in an Information Culture." *Library Resources and Technical Services* 33, 1 (1989) pp. 29-36.

Whitcomb, Laurie. "OCLC's EPIC System Offers a New Way to Search the OCLC Database." *Online* 14, 1 (1990) pp. 45-50.

Zorbas, Elaine and Laurie Whitcomb. "The EPIC Experience: An Assessment of OCLC's New Online System After Its First Year." *Reference Services Review* 19, 4 (1991) pp. 45-48, 84.

THE TWO-YEAR M.L.S.:
ANSWER OR ANATHEMA

Ahmad Fouad M. Gamaluddin

and Jane Rogers Butterworth

HISTORY OF THE DEVELOPMENT OF
LIBRARY SCIENCE

Library education is in a climate of change. Several factors are responsible for this: the growth of computer technology, the changing role of libraries in society and the continuous struggle between educators and practitioners to name a few. If, as Kenneth H. Roberts states, "a principal goal for a professional school should be responsiveness to changing user needs, to changing social needs, to changing professional responsibilities, and to changing technologies," then the library school must analyze, and implement as necessary, the programs needed to keep their curricula viable and pertinent to the educational needs of the profession and career choices of their students.

The climate of change is perhaps more intense now than ever before, but has been an element of librarianship in the United States ever since the inception of libraries in colonial America. Although at least one library was evident in

Advances in Library Administration and Organization,
Volume 11, pages 217-243.
Copyright © 1993 by JAI Press Inc.
All rights of reproduction in any form reserved.
ISBN: 1-55938-596-0

Salem as early as 1629 (Smith, 1968, p. 57), the first college library at Harvard did not officially exist until 1638 (Smith, 1968, p. 58). The library at William and Mary, and the first public library (Charleston South Carolina) did not come into operation until the 1690s (Smith, 1968, p. 64). The Library of Congress was founded in 1800, but burned in 1814, only to be re-established with Thomas Jefferson's library in 1815. It was not until 1887 that attention was focused upon the education for librarianship, when the first library school opened at Columbia University under the direction of Melvil Dewey (Smith, 1968, pp. 84, 87). From 1889 to 1926, the school existed in Albany, where it is interesting to note that in 1903 the curriculum included both typing and handwriting, in case of typewriter malfunctions (Smith, 1968, p. 132). Obviously, change haunted library education at that point in history!

The development of the professional research worker, in the period from 1920 to 1960 forced changes upon the profession. Although libraries were still primarily book oriented, research workers needed access to more current data than that generally available in books (Thomson, 1982, p. 15). The research division broke off, but the inadequacy of libraries gave pause to the need for extensive change. New technology, beginning in the 1950s, echoed this message (Smith, 1968, p. 150).

According to James Thomson, who succinctly summarizes these technological changes, they can be divided into three categories (Thomson, 1982, p. 19). "First, new ways to store information compactly and cheaply... second, new mechanisms to manipulate, scan and search stored records...and third, new facilities for cheap and rapid transmission of information over long distances-telecommunications and networks" (Thomson, 1982, p. 20).

With these divisions firmly in place, Thomson goes on to assert that "The problems with libraries is that in the absolute sense they can never be convenient" (Thomson, 1982, p. 26). This does not have to be totally negative however. It is his view that libraries can definitely make use of the new technology and evolve into a survival mode. After all, even some of the "computer culprits" admit that librarians are often the most qualified to search for on line information! (Thomson, 1982, p. 39). Thomson's conclusion is simply that librarians and libraries which can not accept the inevitable change will perish, but that those able to evolve can flourish in exciting new ways (Thomson, 1982, p. 118). With this brief overview in mind, and the direction of the future of libraries and librarians, it seems only natural to examine the current directions in professional education.

One way in which to examine current opinion regarding the education of librarians is to use a survey to extract opinions from practicing librarians in the field. To that end, the following survey of 14 questions, its results and additional comments are offered. The types of libraries surveyed were evenly divided between academic and public, with school and special libraries presenting almost an equal number. Urban and Suburban libraries were the majority surveyed, although a healthy number of rural libraries responded as well. Most respondents were in a supervisory position and had a one-year Master's degree in library Science. An exact breakdown of numbers follows the survey questions.

The survey of active librarians reflected a high degree of satisfaction with the Master of Library Science program and with graduates of the one year program. Below are the questions asked and the responses.

1. Graduates of a one-year Master's program are adequately prepared for entry library positions:
   Agree: 76 percent (1472)
   Disagree: 16 percent (317)
   Neither: 5 percent (80)
   Blank: 3 percent (69)
2. A two-year library Master's program is needed to adequately prepare individuals for entry level positions:
   Agree: 16 percent (319)
   Disagree: 72 percent (1398)
   Neither: 18 percent (137)
   Blank: 4 percent (84)
3. A second Master's in a subject area other than Library Science would be more valuable than a two-year program in Library Science:
   Agree: 61 percent (1184)
   Disagree: 24 percent (458)
   Neither: 11 percent (209)
   Blank: 4 percent (87)
4. Graduates of a Master's program should be required to have knowledge of at least one foreign language:
   Agree: 55 percent (1066)
   Disagree: 31 percent (658)
   Neither: 7 percent (135)
   Blank: 4 percent (80)
5. Internships should be required as part of the Master's program:
   Agree: 80 percent (1543)
   Disagree: 13 percent (248)
   Neither: 3 percent (68)
   Blank: 4 percent (79)
6. Students should be encouraged to specialize in an area of library service, e.g., technical process, reference, academic or public libraries:
   Agree: 55 percent (1062)
   Disagree: 35 percent (686)
   Neither: 5 percent (93)
   Blank: 5 percent (97)

7. A broad liberal arts background is important for success in a library career:
   Agree: 73 percent (1415)
   Disagree: 19 percent (35)
   Neither: 4 percent (89)
   Blank: 4 percent (79)

8. Continuing education opportunities are readily available for librarians:
   Agree: 65 percent (1258)
   Disagree: 23 percent (451)
   Neither: 4 percent (76)
   Blank: 8 percent (157)

9. Potential Library Science students should be advised to enroll in a two-year Master's program:
   Agree: 20 percent (385)
   Disagree: 58 percent (1131)
   Neither: 13 percent (259)
   Blank: 8 percent (1963)

10. Potential Library Science students should be advised to enroll in a one-year Master's program:
    Agree: 58 percent (1133)
    Disagree: 18 percent (344)
    Neither: 14 percent (266)
    Blank: 10 percent (195)

11. A Master's degree should be considered the first professional degree as opposed to a Bachelor's degree:
    Agree: 56 percent (1084)
    Disagree: 12 percent (625)
    Neither: 5 percent (94)
    Blank: 7 percent (135)

12. A Bachelor's degree in Library Science is adequate for most library positions:
    Agree: 22 percent
    Disagree: 65 percent (1255)
    Neither: 6 percent (121)
    Blank: 6 percent (126)

13. Costs for a two-year program would discourage most potential students:
    Agree: 66 percent (1279)
    Disagree: 17 percent (337)
    Neither: 9 percent (178)
    Blank: 7 percent (144)

14. Libraries would be willing to pay higher level entry salaries to graduates of the two-year programs:
    Agree: 11 percent (217)
    Disagree: 74 percent (1431)
    Neither: 7 percent (1938)
    Blank: 8 percent (152)

The information below reveals the experience of the respondents.

1. The type of library:
    Academic: 592
    Public: 591
    School: 335
    Special: 420
2. Geographic location of the respondent's library:
    Urban: 764
    Suburban: 698
    Rural: 474
    Other: 2
3. Divided by supervisory position:
    Supervisor: 1404
    Non-supervisor: 527
    Not shown: 7
4. Division by educational level:
    None: 107
    Bachelor's: 175
    Master's: 1438
    Advanced: 176
    Phd: 27
    Other: 8
    Not Shown: 7
5. Division by type of MLS program:
    One-Year: 1453
    Two-Year: 133
    Neither: 332
    Other: 1
    Not Shown: 19
6. Division by years of experience:
    0-5: 417
    6-10: 497
    11-15: 402
    16-25: 408
    25+: 210

7. States participating in survey:
   Pennsylvania, Ohio, West Virginia, Delaware and New York
8. Number of surveys sent out:
   3225
9. Number of surveys answered:
   1938

SELECTED COMMENTS FROM SURVEY

1. Graduates from a one-year Master's degree are adequately prepared for entry level library positions:
   The one-year MLS program that I attended did little to prepare me for the real world. To continue another year of a similar, inept program would have been twice as worthless.
   Adequately is not a good description—not as well prepared as they might be would be a better way to put it.

2. A two-year library Master's program is needed to adequately prepare individuals for entry level positions:
   Depends on the job.
   But would be useful.

3. A second Master's in a subject area other than Library Science would be more valuable than a two-year program in Library Science:
   Librarians should be well versed in many subject areas. However, a second Master's need not be necessary, but a wide range of subjects in undergraduate programs [would be helpful].
   Probably the best or most knowledgeable librarians are those who matriculate as an undergraduate in other fields of study and then get a Master's in Library Science.

5. Internships should be required as part of the Master's program:
   I learned more in 6-8 weeks of practicum than in entire classwork for one-year.
   It is highly desirable for the grad to have worked in a real library at some point before the first professional job.
   I do think an internship would be more of value than some of the other courses that filled our schedule—especially for a librarian who finds herself in a library on her own. This is more likely to happen in a public or special or school situation than in an academic library.

6. Students should be encouraged to specialize in an area of library service, e.g., technical process, reference, academic or public libraries:

If one gets to specialize, one will never find a job in today's job market. It was also tight when I received by MLS and I began as a children's librarian. Not what I had trained for, but I did have a children's literature course as an undergraduate, and an undergraduate class in oral interpretation that helped with the story hours.

8. Continuing education opportunities are readily available for librarians:
Many in larger cities but some traveling distance.

Not truly *readily* available: too much depends on locale, travel requirements, and scheduling of courses relative to working hours.

Too costly -no commensurate salary benefit.

For music librarians, they are not readily available.

Time and money may hamper many librarians from taking advantage of such opportunities.

Courses are available, but the costs are outrageous.

We are lucky to have a library school within driving distance.

Problem with many area libraries—they do not allow people to attend them on company time.

But most tend to be rather incestuous with librarians within same field doing programs for colleagues. Need for more diversity to learn from other fields and to learn from those in library schools, etc.

State library associations, local consortia, the state library, 2nd regional meetings of the state library associations are all possible for librarians who cannot or will not attend national meetings. All these groups sponsor continuing education opportunities. Library school graduates should expect to pay a substantial amount from their own pockets to attend continuing education seminars. Many expect to attend only meetings for which they would be reimbursed. A number of libraries now reimburse only if a paper is being presented or if a session is being chaired at a regional or national meeting. Most public libraries do not reimburse except for the two top level positions. Sometimes two staff associations will contribute to attendance by one or two of the staff.

Have been to many seminars on OCLC, Dialog, various data bases.

Professional opportunities are sparse. Sabbatical leave is the answer.

10. Potential Library Science students should be advised to enroll in a one-year Master's program:
Shorter the better—get out into the field and learn from reality, not people in rich, well funded and equipped library schools.

If they have had working experience in a library system for 2+ years full time.

Inevitable if there is no practical option.

For job potential, it is not necessary, but I have had *no* problem matching my knowledge and training with *MLS* people.

There are too many accredited schools now, and all of the schools are not that good.

And take useful classes.

And encourage [them] to take a second Master's.

A well thought out program of one-year can be adequate.

Information Science should be part of the program.

This is what is acceptable in the job market around this area.

Even at my school, Catholic University of America, it was hard to fit in required and elective courses in the year and a half of study.

If School or small public library is their goal.

If the program runs more than one-year, it should be experience oriented, not book oriented—i.e. internship

Perhaps this would enable a student to better decide whether library work was for him/her.

If they survive (assuming it is a sharp school) a second Master's—special area—would then be in order.

Would prefer a 3 semester program.

11.   A Master's degree should be considered the first professional degree, as opposed to the Bachelor's degree:

Bachelor should be devoted to background in subject.

Probably, it would raise the standards of the profession. The public's perception of the librarian's worth is important.

This question makes no sense to me.

Experience is still the best teacher, and B.S. degree people could better approach a Master's after some job experience.

We need to strengthen the image of librarianship.

In a small rural library a B.S. is adequate.

For traditional library roles, yes.

Most bachelor programs are too technically oriented.

The Master's is considered the "professional" degree in most fields of work today.

I believe there is some doubt as to the validity of any MLS as a minimum job qualification. Alice N. Norton, former EEDC chair believes that the MLS would not hold up in court in a class action suit as non-discriminatory!

Students should spend their undergraduate years in liberal arts.

I do not believe a Master's degree is needed for library work.

12.   A Bachelor's degree in Library Science is adequate for most library positions:

Most of what I do now—and others here—is very basic—a lot of non professional duties.

Perhaps for technical and AV fields.

Not in academic libraries; for schools and small public libraries, it is fine as long as the basics are well learned reference skills, cataloging, etc...

No way. A potential librarian needs other education to meet and deal with user needs in many situations.

It has been for be.

B.A. in Library Science does not exist.

No, a broad liberal arts degree or anything giving a wide range of knowledge is better. In depth knowledge in one specialized field is not necessary or necessarily good for most library positions in the public realm.

A.B.S. degree is adequate to do many jobs in a library, but the profession requires the Master's degree to maintain a top level of prestige.

If it is adequate, then there are a lot of graduate programs in existence that should be phased out. With the job market oversupply, a BLS undercuts the Master's level programs.

If courses in *practical* Library Science have been adequate.

Associate degree may be adequate at times.

Some libraries are not able to afford a Master's [applicant.]

Bachelor's o.k. for paraprofessional positions, not professional.

We do not hire as professional librarians.

13. Costs for a two-year program would discourage most potential students:
Maybe that would be a help—open up the market for the rest of us.

Costs for any graduate degree are a consideration, but that doesn't alter the need for training.

With tuition increases and the costs of housing, it might be prohibitive. Taking courses while working would make the program seem interminably long.

More than likely encourage those dedicated to poverty.

When I was a library school student, the thought of two-years of that kind of "Mickey Mouse" education would have driven me to suicide.

School costs keep rising, and aids keep going down.

I think it would discourage a great many who could see no demonstrable pay off for the extra cost.

Probably yes, unless they offered at state supported colleges.

Many go on for additional education anyway.

The educational financial aid picture is not encouraging.

Unless paid traineeship offered as part of the program.

Most Master's degree programs in any field are two years. The money for costs can be obtained by students.

Salaries for library positions are commensurate with experience, not with one additional year in school. It would be a year's additional school expense which would be "reimbursed." As it is, entry level salaries are already pitifully on the low end of the scale, even lower than a number of bachelor's degrees.

Depends on goals.

14.   Librarians would be willing to pay higher entry level salaries to graduates of two-year programs:

Funds are tight and librarians as a rule earn little. With a 2-year grad, the library budget is stretched that much tighter. So, if I were a director, I wouldn't pay. I'd pay for a 1 year degree and a 1 year experience more than a 2 year degree and 0 experience.

At the present time, economic conditions being what they are, this is doubtful.

Not with a depressed economy.

From my experience, this is unimportant to libraries.

Unfortunately, they still look for that 3-5 years experience no matter how much education you have. I cannot imagine the tight-budgeted libraries willingly paying higher for a new graduate whether he be a one or two year program student.

Where are they going to get the funds? Our public library struggles with budget every year.

With our tight budget, our library could not pay more in entry level salary for a two-year program.

The job market is in the library's favor—salaries will continue to be low for many years. There are too many library schools, too many librarians, and too many graduates, and not enough job openings.

They should, but I have no idea.

We barely meet our budget needs now—money is very tight, communities give less tax support, board of trustees would probably hire a librarian for less money (with a one-year degree.)

Some libraries don't pay adequate salaries to those with vast experience. I sincerely doubt it.

Academics and Specials might—public wouldn't and I doubt that schools would unless they have salary schedules that mandate.

Never! They always pay below professional level no matter what the degree. See: *N.Y. Times* job lists.

PROFESSIONAL EDUCATION

Professional education for librarianship has been a hotly disputed topic in the scholarly journals. L.W.S. Auld is one of the many who addresses the issue of an academic or practitioner that schools with an academic emphasis stress (a) research, (b) teaching, and (c) service (albeit reluctantly.) Those programs stressing a practitioner approach place first (a) training, (b) service and (c) research. In presenting these polarized viewpoints, Auld calls for a balance between the two (Auld, 1990, p. 55).

Although this issue underscores many of the debates surrounding professional education, an even more critical issue awaits on the horizon. The growing deficit in the number of Library Science faculty could bring the profession to its knees. As many faculty members reach retirement age, there is no recruitment for their replacement. In their article, "The Faculty Vanishes" Fay Zipkowitz and Elizabeth Futas warn of the "domino effect" of this scenario (Zipkowitz and Futas, 1991, p. 152). Their research supports the gloomy outlook that as faculty disappear, more library schools will close and thus provide a future shortage of librarians. This article is relevant to the survey in that with diminishing numbers of faculty, the majority of respondents who preferred the one-year masters degree to the two-year program could find further support for their argument; A shorter program could process a greater number of librarians in a shorter period of time and require fewer faculty to teach them.

In a book entitled *Library Education* and *Employer Expectations,* editor E. Dale Cluff addresses his concerns regarding professional education when juxtaposed with employer need (Cluff, 1989, p. 246). Gathering articles on accreditation, library schools, employers and the special perspectives of recent graduates and current doctoral candidates, Cluff states in his introduction that this particular collection gives insights into the major problems facing the professional education of librarians today (Cluff, 1989, p. iv).

One such problem is accreditation, which is addressed in an article by Herman L. Totten. He provides both background information and his own appraisal of what major trends and concerns should encompass. Stating that accreditation was initially designed to improve professional education, Totter also lists other important reasons for its maintenance. Accreditation provides constructive evaluation, minimum standards, a single agency for unification and qualitative rather than quantitative appraisals (Cluff, 1989, p. v). As noted in the comments following the survey, at least one librarian feels that there are too many accredited schools already, and that they are not consistently good.

At the conclusion of his article, Totten indicates the future directions accreditation should take. He calls for enforcement of stricter admission standards, including a careful screening of personality, a longer M.S.L.S. degree and curriculum enhancement in the areas of management research, information science and automation (Cluff, 1989, p. 26). He only addresses the positive aspects of these trends, not any difficulties in attaining them. The survey responses show obvious concern for these difficulties, most especially in the context of the longer masters program.

From a student's perspective, professional education seems to provide at least adequate preparation for library employment. Lisa Spillers and Doug Bates, recent graduates perceive a difference in coming into the program with a set agenda of objectives and being willing to fall into a category once enrolled in the program. They both advise open communication with the faculty and commitment to learning as the key factors toward a successful education (Cluff, 1989, pp. 5-7).

C.F. Orgren addresses other trends in his article "Trends in Library Education." As Dean of the University of Iowa School of Library and Information Science, Orgren writes about that program (Orgren, 1990, p. 25). It is his observation that the American Library Association is successfully promoting cooperation between practitioners and educators toward the goal of increased recruitment. Beyond recruitment, Orgren sees the need for increased technological competence and skills in library management. He feels that Iowa's program is especially strong in "relevant preparation and inter-personal skill development" (Orgren, 1990, p. 25). The responses to the survey extend upon this theme and call for a broad background in liberal arts, and especially stress the importance of practical experience in the form of an internship.

In the same journal, another Library School Dean examines the role of professional education in preparing future librarians for information in a global setting. "Teaching people how to access and efficiently use information can be a cornerstone for social change," Lenox asserts (Lenox, 1990, p. 26). Far from seeing the future obsolescence of the profession, the Dean sees librarians as "gatekeepers and stewards of information" (Lenox, 1990, p. 26). Lenox echoes Orgren's call for greater management skills in professional education, and adds several other necessary skills:

- A greater recognition and acceptance of individual and ethnic differences
- A greater recognition of patrons with special needs
- The realization of greater amounts of information and a diminished library capacity
- A life-long commitment to learning
- A realization of the need for international and multi-cultural understanding

These skills would seem to be better attained in the actual classroom education and not the practical application alone, so here is support for a minimal education of one-year at the graduate level. Both educators and field practitioners must be prepared to make these skills part of the professional education.

The changing role of librarianship and the expanding career opportunities have created educational needs and educational challenges in library schools. Many schools have made an attempt to meet these needs by adding information science courses to their curricula. Various disciplines are integrated into information science: physics, biology, computer science, psychology and librarianship. Changing the name of a school, however, or adding a few new courses is not all that is necessary to meet the changing requirements of today's library education.

SUB PROFESSIONAL EDUCATION

In meeting the changing requirements of today's library education, one area which deserves important attention is that of sub-professional education. L.W.S. Auld points out that these undergraduate programs are disappearing because "LTA's [Library Technical Assistants] did not catch on due to lack of differentiation" (Auld, 1990, p. 55). Yet, it seems more important than that in the large picture.

Although the survey was not offered to an equal number of librarians with bachelor's degrees as those holding an MLS, some of the sub-professionally educated librarians felt strongly that they had adequate education to perform their jobs.

There is another possible alternative that could be considered, especially when all other alternatives do not seem convincing to students and other proponents of a solution to the anomaly supposed to be found in the present state of library education. The American Library Association has adamantly refused to consider the Bachelor's Degree in Library Science as a professional qualification. There are people who have compared the field of library science to other disciplines, and how students in those disciplines go on to complete a master's degree in those fields after a successful completion of a four year degree. The survey showed that 56 percent of those participating agreed with ALA. Further, 65 percent disagreed that a four-year degree was adequate.

Another variation of this opinion comes from those who realize that the MLS degree is not necessarily the first professional degree, especially in light of the expanding career base. As library-oriented professions open up in a business and industry, the MLS is not always a requirement for entry level positions, but a background in information processing usually is. Other examples of this nature include the librarians in small, rural libraries where funding prohibits the hiring of an MLS degree, but where microcomputers. OCLC, and networking are an important part of the library activities. Or, more specifically, the school librarian, whose undergraduate degree is certified by the state as the professional degree, and whose library might contain several microcomputers, require him or her to order the software for them, and to oversee the instruction of the machines, not to mention the utilization of available library applications. If, as these examples indicate, the impact of information technology has reached every level of the career ladder, library schools must offer the needed instruction at all levels, undergraduate through the highest degree. Obviously, not all libraries will require the range of education, but there are libraries and librarians that will prove the need for the different levels. Most of the comments following the survey, however, most strongly support the Master of Library Science degree as opposed to the bachelor degree.

TRAINING AND STAFF DEVELOPMENT

As previously mentioned, the diminishing supply of doctoral faculty may greatly lessen the ability of library schools to offer these separate levels of library science education. Two other issues affecting the training and development of staff deal with identity and accreditation. June Lester offers solutions toward addressing each of these issues. The identity problem, which concerns primarily the setting of the library school within the university can best be handled by a dialogue between practitioners and educators, with the goal of integrating the school and the field. Lester strongly advocates the continuation of the participation in the accreditation process. For the problem of faculty supply, active *planning* to increase both students and faculty should alleviate the present trend. All of these solutions rest on structured communication between the library schools and ALA to determine the "human resource needs of the profession" (Lester, 1990, p. 581).

Another champion of accreditation is J.B. Robbins, who feels that the accreditation and master's degree requirements should be defended at all costs. Claiming that the master's "may inhibit but does not prevent people from pursuing this goal" (Robbins, 1990, p. 42). Robbins supports a strong, traditional core requirement. Although supporting education for other library employees, the author vigorously contends that an undergraduate degree in Information Science does not equal the degree or expertise of the librarian (Robbins, 1990, p. 42). Most respondents to the survey certainly agree. Only 12 percent disagreed that a master's should be the primary degree for librarians.

Taking the process one step further, author Joan L. Atkinson does not feel that these two traditional strong-holds are sufficient. She advocates licensing as a "gate-keeping function" (Atkinson, 1989, p. 103) and charges that the current standards "fail as change agents." Her reason for frustration is that (1) "the process is not producing the kind of people doing the jobs we want, and (2) the process is not providing the numbers we need to fill the current positions" (Atkinson, 1989, p. 106).

Atkinson promotes four solutions to counter the lack which she feels exists:

1. National and state guidelines should be issued for youth services.
2. Competency testing at the output stage would provide a way to examine possible improvements.
3. Differentiated staffing would be more efficient.
4. A strong unified voice would provide a professional avenue for supporting necessary change.

Alan Gabehart also supports the need for accreditation, to ensure excellence, especially in academic libraries (Cluff, 1989, p. 40). Gabehart is a current Ph.D. candidate, and so provides a different perspective from educators and practitioners. His research, unfortunately, supports a "trend gone wrong." As the number of ALA accredited graduates increases, the demand for them seems to be temporarily diminishing. He voices concern, and calls on the profession to reverse this before greater damage occurs.

In the vein of offering different perspectives, Rosemary Martin looks at the training issue from the perspectives of public libraries. She feels that a continuing dialogue is needed in terms of recruitment, and to answer shortages as they occur. An Awareness of job demands, however, is of primary importance in the training and development of staff (Cluff, 1989, p. 42).

To provide a countering viewpoint, Helen Lloyd Smoke looks at training in regard to school library media centers and youth services. From her perspective, despite some concerns, this need is being satisfied in most educational programs. Her research shows that 94 percent of Library School programs provide curriculum plans for school library media specialists, but that content analysis really "provides a better gauge" (Cluff, 1989, p. 31). The faculty for this area of librarianship has decreased, but not the number of courses, a problem Smoke feels is critical. As a partial but not complete solution, she deems it necessary that these specialists be considered as part of the mainstream of the profession, and that all courses should address the needs of these groups as well as other areas of librarianship (Cluff, 1989, p. 135). The survey responses indicate that 55 percent of the participants feel that library science students should specialize, as compared to 35 percent who disagree.

Specialization can most easily be accomplished through an internship. Again, communication from practitioners to educators is seen as important. The integration of practical and academic education in the form of an internship would be invaluable, as 80 percent of the respondents indicate.

CURRICULUM DEVELOPMENT AND PREPARATION FOR THE NEXT GENERATION

The importance of an internship is just one area relevant to curriculum development. In a book comparing international curricula for library schools, Edward Reid Smith writes about the responsibility of the library schools in providing current information and training as automation continues to increase and become more complex. As further evidence of this, in the same book, Digby Hartridge bemoans the fact that public librarians lack in the development of a professional attitude. It would be easy to defend the latter complaint on the former difficulty.

Indeed, at times it is difficult to give an exact definition of library science, given the rapid and frequent changes in the field. A book which provides an interesting angle for anyone trying to pinpoint the exact position of library science in the graduate curriculum is *Information Science: The Interdisciplinary Context* by Michael Pemberton and Ann Prentice. In separate articles, Information Science is linked to the humanities, sciences, communication and seen as a multi-discipline in itself. As library science educators prepare the curriculum for the next generation, it is important to keep the unique and eclectic qualities of library science in view. It may be just these qualities which ensure its survival. It may also be reflected in the fact that 61 percent of the survey participants feel that a second masters in a field other than Library Science provides a better operating knowledge base than a two-year program could.

A diversified angle of library science education may be seen in the enhanced awareness of disabled library patrons. In her article, "Disability Awareness in the Library School Curriculum," Julie Klauber identifies a growing number of disabled clients and urges that the curriculum in Library Science program be adjusted to reflect this increase (Klauber, 1990-91, p. 154). Four major areas of disability need to be covered: those for blind, deaf, physically disabled and mentally disabled.

A recurring theme in the argument over library science course work is the issue of practice work within the curriculum. Many librarians and library science educators have indicated the need for field work as a mandatory requirement to the degree (Klauber, 1990-91, p. 157). With many of the job listings calling for experience, it seems at least prudent to offer this option as a choice, if not to mandate it. As stated earlier, the survey results support this strongly.

Paul Dumont quotes Dr. Janet Naul Naimer in his discussion of library education (Dumont, 1989, p. 70). She suggests three general requirements for curriculum development:

- computer literacy across the board
- Librarianship as a service occupation
- a greater understanding of information-seeking behavior and information itself as a commodity

Added to these requirements, Randall Simmons elaborates on the preparation which he deems most important for academic librarianship in particular: Leadership (Simmons, 1990, p. 23). "Leadership embraces the environment in which the library flourishes or flounders and the relationships which empower or impede its operation" (Simmons, 1990, p. 24). Certainly, combining leadership opportunities and skills within the context of management seems helpful, but all twenty-first-century librarians can not and will not be leaders.

Also taking a unique approach are Ian Johnson and Dorothy Williams, who pursue the context of library science curriculum in terms of the "Enterprise Culture" (Johnson and Williams, 1990, p. 31). In addition to leadership, the ability to participate well in team work and to exude "versatility and resilience" are extolled. Although this seems a bit far fetched in some respects, the library school curriculum does need to train students to expect and adapt to change.

Another area of librarianship education which is receiving some emphasis is communication. As Margaret Watson reports, "The information professional needs to be an effective communicator and therefore needs to understand the theory of communication, ranging from interpersonal communication to mass communication, before being able to interpret it into the information environment" (Watson, 1990, p. 40). On more traditional ground in terms of curriculum is Yaser Abdel-Motey, who nonetheless warns against tradition in its most severe form. "Narrowly prescriptive programmes lead to rigidity rather than flexibility in practice; emphasis in breadth at the expense of depth of knowledge and the ability to perform competently, resulting in superficiality and irrelevant to the demands of the workplace" are all dangers he foresees from this practice (Abdel-Motey, 1990, pp. 9-10).

Schools of librarianship and their faculty have the potential to broaden the scope of the education they offer and to play major role in the preparation of professionals to staff information organizations other than libraries. Faculty are important as they set examples of concern and consideration in the field. They must expand their focus to prepare students for alternate or atypical careers. In turn, this expansion will provide library school graduates, from the undergraduate level on up, with more flexibility in career development. By providing this flexibility, the library school will establish a link to a rapidly growing job market, thus promoting an expanded enrollment and corresponding growth.

What the ongoing arguments within the professional boil down to is a realization that a modification in the curriculum of library schools is necessary to compensate for the unpredictable demands of the 1990s. This modification means adding more courses, and thus increasing the length of time needed for the training of a librarian. A streamlining of the curriculum might also call for getting rid of courses which the advocates of new technology might consider not worth the investment of a student's time and intellectual energy.

It is interesting to note that all Canadian library schools with the American Library Association accredited programs are now offering two-year integrated Master in Library Science programs. On the other hand, with the exception of an insignificant number of schools, all of the ALA accredited schools in the United States are still offering the traditional one-year program. There has been a measure of pressure from concerned educators, employers, and information related associations about the possible requirement of a two-year library program to adequately prepare graduates for proficient performances on the job.

For example, the Connant Report of the University of North Carolina at Chapel Hill stated that there was a definite need for two academic years of library studies so that library schools could achieve a "thorough coverage of the common foundations, knowledge, and skills of librarianship, a substantial internship or practicum, and an opportunity for specialization" (Connant, 1978, p. 322). Little agreement, however, has been reached on the advantages of the two-year program. A number of interested observers argue that no matter how many years are devoted to study, students can never master all of the required competencies in the field. The learning process does not conclude with the granting of a diploma.

Galvin put it this way: "By definition, a professional spends his or her lifetime learning to practice his or her profession, and even at the point of retirement, has not learned it completely. This means that practitioners must assume more responsibility for the continuing education of new graduates; that employers can not expect the library schools to produce 'complete librarian'" (Galvin, 1980, p. 17). Obviously, it is a general belief that students learn more on the job than in a classroom setting removed from reality.

Yet, more than half of the U.S. Schools offer a six-year program and the number of degrees awarded is very small (Dowell, 1978, p. 332). Could these programs be made more attractive and thereby receive greater acceptance as the appropriate vehicle for dealing with increased specialization?

"If greater opportunities for internships and practice-based experiences are needed, how can these best be provided? Library education began as practice-based, in-service education. Should we now reexamine the medial education pattern which blends classroom teaching with supervised practice? Is there a possibility of developing teaching libraries with closer links to library schools just as teaching hospitals are linked to medical schools?" (Dowell, 1978, p. 332). Nevertheless, the established training processes in librarianship have been found to be beneficial proving ground for the actual work, despite the contrary views expressed in other forums.

While it has been acknowledged that a two-year program will be of immense advantage to the library schools, the benefit accrued by the students from such an extension and education will be discouraging. Students and other library education economists agree that such a two year period, which will be characterized by inflation and low salaries as a result of the current economic situation, will be highly suicidal in terms of a successful entry into the job market.

Few students would want to apply for the programs, especially if there will still be other ALA accredited schools offering the established one-year Master's degree program. As Dowell explained, "There is no indication that employers will give such students "preference in hiring" (Dowell, 1989, p. 332). The advocates of the two-year program have mentioned among other advantages the opportunity for students to take an internship. This argument does not appear convincing because there are students who enter the Master's degree program with sufficient experience in library work. For such people then, internships would be a boring and repetitive chore.

If extending the program to two-years is not the feasible thing to do, what other alternatives are left? Will a one-year program still be adequate to get the library school graduate trained to take on the challenge of a professional library career?

Getting a second Master's degree is another alternative constantly mentioned by librarians. This approach is expected to be of higher value than spending two-years in library school pursuing a single degree. Areas where such second Master's have been suggested include business, Communications, and other areas of the social sciences.

Thus those librarians who go back to college for a second Master's degree in other disciplines should display a better understanding of managerial, communication and sociological principles. All of these should be of immense help in dealings with library patrons and library related situations.

When considering the rigors of a second Master's, it seems important not to lose sight of the alternative at the undergraduate level. Perhaps the American Library Association could endorse a concentration in Library Science in conjunction with a Bachelor's degree in another major. The concentration of core library science courses at the undergraduate level should allow college students to enter library or information science entry-level positions while preparing for entry into a Master of Library Science program.

This will not imply that there are going to be more people in the profession, therefore making opportunities less available. It will put more knowledgeable individuals in library science and fill it with people capable of contributing to the well-being of the profession.

Of course, this proposal will require the restructuring of the curriculum so that students can "minor" in library science and at the same time be able to graduate as fully educated individuals. The basics of computer science, the much mentioned communication skills, the statistical knowledge students are supposed to have, will all be started in the undergraduate years and then be further developed at the Master's level. Students wishing to enter the profession from other disciplines will have to take the core courses considered to be the foundations of the profession at the undergraduate level before entering the MLS program.

Perhaps Ralph W. Connant summarizes the problems and possible solutions for all of us in his report when he says, "The library profession needs to develop a coherent basis for its claim to professionalism. There is no better way to achieve coherence than to separate professional from non-professional training in its system of education and to improve the quality and content of the master's programs" (Connant, 1978, p. 332). All of these possibilities and alternatives are easier to say than to implement into reality. Naturally, the reaction of librarians have been diverse in regard to the above series of suggestions. No two librarians can be found who share the same concerns about library education and the same required solutions to these problems. It is to be expected that any survey will produce results of varied opinions. It was against this background, and all the possible outcomes that the present survey was conducted.

THE IMPACT OF RAPID GROWTH
ON INFORMATION SERVICES

The rapid growth of information has created a major problem for libraries, and thus for library science students coming into the field. Harold Billings, in an article cleverly titled "The Bionic Library" addresses one aspect of the information explosion: scholarly journals. "The growing distance between the quantity of literature produced and the capability of academic libraries to acquire it affirms that the battle for collection comprehensiveness has already been lost. The academic research library model has been changed forever" (Billings, 1991, p. 38). Billings does not feel that all is lost for librarians, however. "It is important that librarians understand [the information] process, and help shape the flow of information (Billings, 1991, p. 40). If librarians refuse to become an integral player in this process, others will step in and take over.

A major way in which librarians can keep up and help to shape the new environment is through continuing education. Jana Varlejs feels that the current problems in continuing education must be resolved quickly, or a great opportunity will be lost. Illustrating that consumers of continuing education programs blame providers and vice versa, Varlejs places the responsibility in the lap of the American Library Association, and charges them to intensify the awareness of need in this area (Varlejs, 1989, p. 120). Part of the difficulty with the continuing education, and indeed library education in general has to do with salary levels for librarians. Some librarians contend that higher salaries would attract a better quality student, and that in turn would change the attitudes toward the necessity of librarians" (Cluff, 1989, pp. 37-45). Perhaps monetary rewards for continuing education, such as are endorsed throughout the medical profession, might make a difference as well. Paid time off and money toward the course are two such examples. Availability, at least in perception, is not the problem. Of the surveyed librarians, 65 percent felt that continuing education was readily available for librarians. The comments dealt with geography and cost as major problems, and one librarian felt that professional opportunities were non existent, with the exception of sabbatical leave.

In any case, the current information explosion clearly demands continuing education. Another perspective of viewing the information overload is to look at it within the context of post modern society. Yves Courrier does exactly that in his article. "The information needs of the emerging post-industrial society, though, are becoming clearer, and the will to take note of them in the design of teaching programmes is emerging" (Courrier, 1990, p. 223). Courrier advocates the institution of greater specialization and in-service training (Courrier, 1990, p. 233) and the mastery of information technology, but warns that, "the unity of the profession must be maintained...[it] must adapt to the relatively slow but profound evolution in social needs, and technology must be seen only as a means to an end" (Courrier, 1990, p. 234).

With the rapid increase in information comes also the rapid increase in costs. Despite decades of the "free" mentality, many libraries are charging fees for certain services. According to Steve Coffman, "even by conservative estimates, there are at least 200 to 300 libraries in the United States and Canada operating some type of fee- based information service" (Coffman and Josephine, 1991, p. 32). The authors defend the practice as a way to expand services without compromising existing practices. "Fees function as the mechanism to allow libraries to take advantage of specialized resources and expertise available at other institutions" (Coffman and Josephine, 1991, p. 36). Here again, it seems logical that librarians refusing to change will lose out to those who are willing to grow.

Daniel Barron echoes this philosophy. "If the library and information science profession is not seen in a leadership position in this important development of the information age, how can it expect to grow in influence, prestige and power?" (Barron, 1991, p. 43). In the same issue, Paul Christensen calls the reaction to the rapid growth of information "slow in coming, [but]...revolutionary" (Christensen, 1991, p. 37). If the profession can accept the change, and grow with it, the rewards will be at the very least, survival, and at the most, extraordinary.

Alan M. Rees examines this response to change from the perspective of the medical library, and the library in tandem with the medical profession. Medicine changes with the same rapidity as the current technology explosion, so this creates an interesting example. "The great popularity of the continuing education programs of the Medical Library Association reflects a concerned effort on the part of many health sciences librarians to upgrade their skills to assume such new and extended responsibilities" (Rees, 1990, p. 38). This commitment should not be espoused only by librarians in the Medical field, but must be created over into all areas of librarianship and library education if the profession is to successfully evolve amid the current growth in information services.

VARIETY OF INFORMATION REQUIREMENTS OF INFORMATION PROFESSIONALS

The survey dealt with the general needs of education for librarianship. An article which provides specific recommendations for revising the core curriculum in the library science degree was recently written by B.S. Schlessinger and collaborators. Using three criteria, (job ads for competencies sought, competencies recommended by library educators and competencies recommended by employees) they suggest 12 classes to be taken only in sequence. This provides a core of 36 hours, necessitating a two-year masters, an undergraduate major to leave room for a specialty or a sixth year option to prepare for a specialist degree. Although the core does not require internships, the authors defend the need for them. The courses are often divided into two parts and include history of librarianship, information and resource classes and also such innovative things as writing in the field (Schlessinger, 1991, pp. 16-19).

David B. Walch provides another list of functional skills, although not outlined as concretely as in the Schlessinger article. His requirements have more to do with the innate abilities of the librarian today's changing world. He lists things as basic- and often forgotten- as listening, and the moves to ideals such as a commitment for improving the "knowledge, skills and values of the profession" (Walch, 1989, pp. 87-97). Instead of examining output measures of library education, Frances Benham examines input standards into library education programs. She feels that established admission standards to library science programs and to the profession should be carefully established (Benham, 1989, pp. 73-87). Benham also espouses the need for strong information services tracks in the curriculum and plentiful on the job training, as advocated by the librarians in the survey.

Along these same lines, and in the same source, Raymond F. Vondvan expresses his opinion of curriculum changes. He contends that students must learn "Adaptability, technical comfortability, proactive professional behaviors and process skills" (Vondvan, 1989, p. 37). His opinion seem to tie in with others concerned about greater management and leadership skills. As more and more curriculum changes are occurring in library schools across the country, there is even writing being done on how to plan these changes (Poa and Warner, 1989, p. 269).

In examining how changes in information requirements affect academic libraries in post modern society, G. Van der Linde urges that knowledge should be viewed as "a network of intersecting lines which one can enter or exit at any point" (Van der Linde, 1990, p. 253). With this in mind, it is comforting to conclude with Ann Birney's feeling that "Indeed, the opportunities have never been greater and there can have been no more exciting time to be involved in library and information management education" (Birney, 1990, p. 23). In compiling all of these articles, two issues seem to stand as imperative for the continued growth of the library science profession. Again, one of these is the issue of continuing education. Library Science students must be endowed with the certain knowledge that all learned material is transient but supportive, and that the MLS is only meant to provide a base from which to continue a life long commitment to self education.

The other issue is transparently clear. If Library Education programs, practicing librarians and the American Library Association do not unify and support each other, no real progress can be made, because there will be no uniformity throughout the profession. All participants must be sympathetically aware of the others needs and difficulties, and the effort must be focused on solving these issues, not condemning other sectors for failure to produce desired results. The profession has a chance to stand up and make its presence imperative. Only in doing so can librarianship move successfully into the future.

REFERENCES

Abdel-Motey, Y. "Education for School Librarianship; the core and competency based education (comparative review of 30 education programmes and studies undertaken in the last 28 years) charts. In *International Review of Children's Literature and Librarianship* 5 no. 1: 1-11, 1990, pp. 9-10. .

Atkinson, J. L. "Credentials, Competencies and Certification." In *Managers and Missionaries*. University of Illinois at Urbana-Champaign, Graduate School of Library and Information Science. 1989, pp. 103-113.

Auld, L. W. S. "Seven Imperatives for Library Education." *Library Journal* 115:55-59, May 1, 1990.

Barron, Daniel. "The Library and Information Science Distance Education Consortium: The Profession's Virtual Classroom." *Wilson Library Bulletin* October, 1991. p. 43.

Benham, Frances. "What Do Information Services Administrators Expect of Library Education." In *Library Education and Employer Expectations*. E. Dale Cluff, guest editor. Haworth Press, 1989. Pp. 73-87.

Billings, Harold. "The Bionic Library." In *Library Journal* October 15, 1991, pp. 38-40.

Birney, A. E. "Meeting the Needs of the Library and Information Profession. Trends in Library Education." (presented at the 1989 NEMA/NLA convention) In *Nebraska Library Association Quarterley* 21: 20-23, Spring, 1990.

Christensen, Paul. "Information Power through Technology." In *Wilson Library Bulletin,* October, 1991, p. 37.

Cluff, E. Dale. (guest editor). *Library Education and Employer Expectations.* Haworth Press, 1989. Pp. iv-56.

Coffman, Steve and Helen Josephine. "Doing It for Money." In *Library Journal,* October 15, 1991, pp. 32, 36.

Connant, R. W. *The Connant Report: A Study of the Education of Librarians,* Vol. 18 No. 1978, p. 322.

Courrier, Y. "Information Services in Crisis and the Post Industrial Society." In *Education for Information* 8: 173-234, Spring, 1990.

Dowell, Arlene T. "Two Year Masters' Pre-spectives and Prospects." *Journal of Education for Librarianship.* Vol. 18 No. 1978, p. 332.

Dumont, Paul. "Library Education and Employer Expectations." *Library Education and Employer Expectations.* E. Dale Cluff, guest editor. Haworth Press, 1989, p. 70.

Galvin, Thomas J. "The Future of Education for Librarianship: The Next Fifty Years." *Oklahoma Librarian,* Vol. 31 (January, 1980) p. 17.

Gorman, G. E. (ed.) *The Education and Training of Information Professionals: Comparative and International Studies.* Pp. 47, 102.

Johnson, I. M. and D. A. Williams. "The Enterprise Culture." and Curriculum Development for Librarianship and Information Studies (at Robert Gordon's Institute of Technology). In *Personnel Training Education* 7 No. 2:31-36, 1990, p. 31.

Klauber, Julie. "Disability Awareness in the Library School Curriculum." In *Journal of Education for Library and Information Science.* 31, No. 2 1990-1991, pp. 154, 157.

Lenox, David. "Trends in Library Education." *Nebraska Quarterly.* Spring, 1990, p. 26.

Lester, June. "Education for Librarianship: A Report Card." One educator examines what course is best to solve the crisis confronting our schools. In *American Libraries* 21:580-ff, 1990, p. 581.

Orgren, C. F. "Trends in Library Education." *Nebraska Library Quarterly Spring,* 1990, p. 25.

Poa, M. L. and R. M. Warner. "Strategic Planning in the 1990's—A Challenge for Change." (Applications in schools of Library and Information Science with a case report from Michigan) *Education for Information* 7:263-271, Spring 1989, p. 269.

Rees, Alan M. "Preparing New Library Roles in the Electronic Information Environment." 9 changes due to integrated academic information, new directions. New Zealand Library Association. Health Library Section Conference. 1990, pp. 31-46.

Robbins, J. B. "Yes, Virginia, you can acquire an accredited master's degree for that job." *Library Journal* 115:40-44 Fall 1990 p. 42.

Roberts, Kenneth H. *Integration of Library and Information Science,* Bethesda: ERIC Document Reproduction, ED 208 805 p. 3.

Schlessinger, B. S. et al. "Information Science/Library Science Education Programs in the 1990s. A not-so-Modest Proposal." (how curricula compare to competencies requested in the job ads.) *Library Administration Management* 5: 16-19, Winter 1991.

Simmons, Randall C. "The College Library: Retrospective Glance from the 21st Century." In *Pacific Northwest Library Association Quarterly,* Vol. 54, Spring 1990, pp. 23-24.

Smith, Josephine Metcalfe. *A Chronology of Librarianship.* Metuchen: Scarecrow Press, 1968, pp. 57-150.

Thomson, James. *The End of Libraries.* London: Clive Bingley Limited, 1982, pp. 15-118.

Van der Linde, G. "Knowledge, Power, and the Academic Library in Post Modern Society." bibl. *South African Journal of Library and Information Science* 58: 249-254, Spring 1990, p. 253.

Varlejs, Jane. "Continuing Education: Renewal and Growth." In Management and Missionaries. University of Illinois at Urbana-Champaign. Graduate School of Information Science. 1989, p. 115-119. bibl.

Vondvan, Raymond F. "Rethinking Library Education in the Information Age." In *Library Education and Employer Expectations.* E. Dale Cluff, guest editor. Haworth Press. 1989, p. 37.

Walch, David B. "A Perspective of Academic Leadership: The Practioner's Needs and the Educator's Product." In *Library Education and Employer Expectations.* E. Dale Cluff, guest editor. Haworth Press, 1989, pp. 87-97.

Watson, M. "Communication across the Curriculum." (at Newcastle Polytechnic) in *Personnel Training for Education* 7 No. 2:37-40. 1990, p. 40.

Zipkowitz, Fay and Elizabeth Futas. "'The Faculty Vanishes' Accelerating Retirements and Difficulty in Attracting New Educators Could Spell Disaster for the Profession as a Whole." In *Library Journal* September 1, 1991, p. 152.

BIBLIOGRAPHY

Books

The Education and Training of Information Professionals; Comparative and International Studies. ed. G.E. Gorman, published in association with the Centre for Information Studies, Charles Sturt University-Riverina. Metuchen and London: Scarecrow Press, 1990. 365 pp, charts.

Information Science- The Interdisciplinary Context. ed. Michael Pemberton and Ann Prentice. Neal- Schuman, 1990 xxvi 189 pp. il. See attached review. C*Main Z668.I469.
Library Education and Employer Expectations. E. Dale Cluff, guest editor. Haworth Press, 1989. 256pp.
Thomson, James. *The End of Libraries.* London: Bingley Limited, 1982.

Articles

Abdel-Motey Y. "Education for School Librarianship; the core and competency based education [comparative review of 30 education programmes and studies undertaken in the last 28 years] charts. in *International Review of Children's Literature and Librarianship* 5 no. 1: 1-11 '90.

Alley, B. "CULA: Not just another acronym" in *Technicalities* 10:4 D '90.

Atkinson, J.L. "Credentials, Competencies and Certification." in *Managers and Missionaries* University of Illinois at Urbana-Champaign Gradaute School of Library and Information Science. 1989 pp 103-13, bibliography.

Auld, L.W.S. "Seven Imperatives for Library Education" bibl por *Library Journal* 115:55-9, My 1, '90.

Billings, Harold. "The Bionic Library" in *Library Journal* October 15, 1991. p. 38.

Birney, A. E. "Meeting the Needs of the Library and Information Profession. Trends in Library Education." [presented at the 1989 NEMA/NLA convention] in *Nebraska Library Association Quarterly* 21: 20-3, Spr. '90.

Bobinski, G.S. "How do Current Library School Curricula prepare Librarians for all types of Specialization?" in *Bookmark* 48:19-23 F'89.

Broadway, M.D. and Smith, N.M. "Basic Reference Courses in ALA accredited Library Schools." charts. in *Reference Librarian* 25-26: 431-48 '89.

Clark, A. J. "Education and Training for Librarianship and Information Work" annual Bibliography. 1989 in *Education for Information* 8: 173-221 S '90.

Connant R. W. *The Connant Report: a Study of the Education of Librarians* vol. 18, no 1978, p. 332.

Courrier, Y. "Information Services in Crisis and the Post Industrial Society" in *Education for Information* 8 173-221 S'90.

De Candido, G. A. "The Year End Review" 1990 [Closing of yet Another Graduate Library Program and Perennial Issues in Salaries and censorship] in *School Library Journal* 36:34-8 D. '90.

Dowell, Arlene T. "Two Year Master's: Perspectives and Prospects." *Journal of Education for Librarianship* vol 18 no (1978) p. 332).

Futas, Elizabeth and Zipkowitz, Kay. "The Faculty Vanishes: Accelerating retirements and difficulty in attracting new educators could spell disaster for the profession as a whole." in *Library Journal* September 1, 1991.

Galvin, Thomas J. "The Future of Education for Librarianship: The Next Fifty Years." *Oklahoma Librarian* vol 31 (January, 1980) p. 17.

Hart, T. L. "Development of Technical Standards for Library Sources" in *School Library Media Annual* v 8, 1990, in *Libraries Unlimited,* 1990, p. 191-7.

Hayes, R. M. "Education and Training of Librarians" in "Rethinking the Library in the Information Age VII" *U.S. Office of Education Res. and Improvements* Office of Library Programs, 1988, p. 43-74 bibl.

Hyman, R.J. "Library Schools in Crisis: Stemming the Tide" in Wilson Library Bulletin 65:46-9 Ja. '91.

Johnson, I.M. and Williams D.A. "The Enterprise Culture" and Curriculum Development for Librarianship and Information Studies [at Robert Gordon's Institute of Technology] in *Personnel Training Education* 7 no 2:31-6 '90.

Jul E. "Looking at Library and Information Science Education [Research of T. Hawood, reprinted from OCLC Newsletter, My/Je '89 in *Pacific Northwest Library Association Quarterly* 54:23-4 Winter, '90.

Klauber, Julie. "Disability Awareness in the Library School Curriculum" in *Journal of Education for Library and Information Science"* 31 *v*2 1990-91 pp 153-161.

Lenox, David. "Trends in Library Education." Nebraska Library Quarterly Spring, 1990, p. 26.

Lester, June. "Education for Librarianship: a report card" one educator examines what course is best to solve the crisis confronting our schools. in *American Libraries* 21:580-ff Je '90.

Lowry, C.B. "An Interview with Beverly Lunch [new dean of UCLA's Graduate School of Library and Information Science] por *Library Administration Management* 3:165-6 Fall '89.

Lynch, B.P. "Education and Training of Librarians" in "Rethinking the Library in the Information Age VII" *U.S. Office of Education Res. and Improvements* Office of Library Programs, 1988, p. 75-91. Charts.

McClure, L. W. "Influencing Our Future" [Interview with F. W. Roper, University of South Carolina Library School] por *Bulletin of the Medical Library Association* 78:413-15 O '90.

Main, L. "Research vs Practice. a 'no' contest" [the place of information technology in the curriculum] *Journal of Education for Library Information Science* 30:226-8 W'90.

Manley, W. "Professional Survival. It's Academic.' [Library Science closings] *Wilson Library Bulletin,* 65:79-81 F'91.

Orgren, C.F. "Trends in Library Education" [1989 NEMA/NLA] por *Nebraska Library Association Quarterly* 21:24-5.

Poa, M.L. and Warner, R.M. "Strategic Planning in the 1990's-A Challenge for change." [applications in schools of Library and Information Science with a case report from Michigan] *Education for Information* 7:263-71 S' 1989.

Rees, Alan M. "Preparing New Library Roles in the Electronic Information Environment" [changes due to integrated academic information, new directions. New Zealand Library Association. Health Library Section Conf. Com. 1990, p. 31-46.

Robbins, J.B. "Yes, Virginia, you can acquire an accredited master's degree for that job" por *Library Journal* 115:40-4 F 1 '90.

Roberts, Kenneth H. *Integration of Library and Information Science* Bethesda: ERIC Document Reproduction ED 208.805.

Rothstein, S. "A Forgotten Issue: Practice Work in American Library Education. An International Survey. [Reprinted from University of Illinois at Urbana-Champaign Graduate School of Library and Information Science 1968]. *Reference Librarian* no. 25-26: 199-224 '89.

Royal, S. W. "A Profile of Selected Characteristics of Faculty in non ALA Accredited Library Education Programs [In School Library Media Annual, V8 1990] *Libraries Unlimited* 1990, p. 154-71 charts.

Schlessinger, B.S. and others. "Information Science/Library Science Education Programs in the 1990's. A not-so-Modest Proposal" [how curricula compare to compentencies requested in the job ads.] charts. *Library Administration Management* 5: 16-19 W '91.

Schmidt, F. L. "Technical Reports and Non-Depository Publications" *Government Publication Review* 17:513-20 N/D '90.

Simmons, R. C. "The College Library: A Retrospective glance from the 21st century. *Pacific Northwest Library Association Quarterly* 54: 23-4 S '90.

Smith, Josephine Metcalf *A Chronology of Librarianship* Metuchen: Scarecrow Press, 1968, p. 57.

Stefani, J. "Using Vendors as Educational Resourrces" bibl. *Southeast Libraries* 40: 9-11 Spr. '90.

Van der Linde, G. "Knowledge, Power, and the Academic Library in post modern Society." bibl. *South African Journal of Library and Information Science* 58:249-54 S '90.

Varle, J.S. "Continuing Education: Providing for Change, Renewal and Growth" in *Managers and Missionaries* University of Illinois at Urbana-Champaign, Graduate School of Information Science, 1989, p. 115-19, bibl.

Watson, M. "Communication across the Curriculum" [at Newcastle Polytechnic] in *Personnel Training for Education* 7 no 2: 37-40 '90.

White, H. S. and Mort, S. L. "The Accredited Library Education Program as Preparation for Professional Library Work." [choice of school and job preparation survey of 1980 graduates of 13 accredited programs.] charts. *Library Quarterly* 60: 187-215 Jl. '90.

Wormell, I. "State of the Art in Education and Training of Library Information Professonals in Western European Countries." *Libri* 40:97-171. 1989.

SPECULATIONS ON SOCIAL EPISTEMOLOGY:
SPECIALIZATION IN SOCIETY, REFLECTIONS ON EMILE DURKHEIM AND ADAM SMITH

Steven M. Hutton

In a speech delivered in 1960 Jesse Shera called for a new discipline, social epistemology. The area of study of this new discipline would be the "intellectual differentiation and the integration of knowledge within a complex social organization." Shera noted that this new discipline would deal extensively with communication processes, but he did not envision it as a "reworking of the old field of mass communication." It would also not be much concerned with the validity or limits of knowledge as described by philosophers or with the intellectual processes of individuals as described by psychologists. While it would include the established field of the historiography of science and knowledge, it would emphasize "the ways in which knowledge is coordinated, integrated, and put to work." Social epistemology would also include the study of "the intellectual forces that shape social structures and institutions" (Shera, p. 769).

Advances in Library Administration and Organization,
Volume 11, pages 245-265.
Copyright © 1993 by JAI Press Inc.
All rights of reproduction in any form reserved.
ISBN: 1-55938-596-0

The importance Shera attached to this new discipline and its role for the future of modern society is demonstrated in the same speech:

> The recorded history of the world of thought suggests that as man's knowledge increases in volume and complexity, it becomes increasingly interdependent, and tends toward fragmentation, centrifugation, and what we today glibly call specialization. Since scholarship and action are correlative, the atomization of the one engenders conflicts in the other, and the ultimate breakdown of a society can be averted only through the exercise of some powerful cohesive force (Shera, p. 769).

It was also Shera's intention that librarians have a prominent or even dominant place in the development of social epistemology. Libraries and librarians comprise one of the communication systems that act as a cohesive force for society. Librarianship in its various classification systems has long dealt with the intellectual differentiation of knowledge.

Over a quarter of a century since Shera's speech, social epistemology has not developed as a new discipline or interdiscipline. Yet the potential for new understandings about society and the development and uses of knowledge seems vast.

There are a number of points of departure for developing social epistemology, but perhaps the most intriguing is the subject of specialization. By definition specialization includes both the differentiation of knowledge and the integration of knowledge in society. In a sense each person, no matter how menial or sophisticated his work, is a specialist. Specialists are the means through which knowledge is put to work.

Specialization is inherently a part of Nature, of life itself. Organismic analogies are often useful, and perhaps just as often misleading. Nevertheless, the differentiation of one cell from another, the functional specialization of cells, is Nature's means for evolving life.

Speciation is the specialization of life forms to fill the available ecological niches. As a general rule the more specialized organism is the more advanced organism.

Specialization operates even at a very low level among life forms. The Portuguese man-of-war is a colony of three different species of organisms, each with its own function in the overall survival of the colony. Among the social insects can be seen a similar specialization, where reproduction is concentrated in just a few individuals, and all other functions are distributed among the "workers."

Specialization is so common in society, the degree to which it operates in life is often overlooked. Early conversations with children are frequently about "What do you want to be when you grow up?" There is strong interest in the aptitudes of children. Are they artistically or mechanically inclined? Visually or musically? What school subjects are they interested in, and which do they do well in? Will their high school curriculum be college prep or vocational training? Which occupations provide the best prospects for income? From this perspective a person's life path can be viewed as a set of choices leading to a specialization. Once again, those societies with more occupational specialties are perceived as the more advanced societies.

It is arguable that cell differentiation and making an occupational choice are totally unrelated, and that the term "specialization" is merely applied to both phenomenon. Yet in both cases the process of organization, and a higher level of survival. It can be argued on the other side that specialization is *the process* by which life evolves to more advanced forms, whether those forms are species or societies.

It is perhaps because specialization is so intimately connected with our social lives and with life itself that it has not been studied extensively. Has this mechanism or process been taken for granted? Probably.

Specialization has been the subject of study by sociologists and economists. Among sociologists the views of Emile Durkheim (1893/1933) are still prominent. Among economists the views of Adam Smith (1776/1937) on specialization in his *Inquiry into the Nature and Causes of the Wealth of Nations* are generally accepted. It is possible that the wide acceptance of their views has put closure on the subject of specialization, this being another reason why specialization has not been studied more fully. It is also possible, however, that the full complexity of the specialization process has never been appreciated, that the assumptions in the theses of Durkheim and Smith have never been fully examined.

Durkheim's focus in the *Division of Labor in Society* (1893/1933) was on the question, What will hold together the fabric of society as society grows and becomes more complex? His answer: the social fabric will be retrained through the dependence of one specialty on another and through the rules of conduct the various occupations and professions generally provide for their members. According to Durkheim, specialization is solely dependent on population growth and concentration. As the population of a society becomes more numerous and more concentrated, the number of specialized occupations increases. To the criticism that some of the more populous nations, particularly in East Asia, do not show the degree of occupational specialization evidenced in the West, Durkheim responds that these are special cases in which other factors have prevented specialization.

Implicit in Durkheim's notion is the assumption that the more people there are, the more people there will be to advance knowledge. So long as population growth is exponential, the growth of knowledge must also be exponential.

Childe (1936, pp. 140-178) has also noted the role of specialization in the "urban revolutions" which occurred in ancient Egypt, Mesopotamia, and the Indus valley.

Adam Smith described three causes for the advantages that are brought about by specialization:

> first, to the increase of dexterity in every particular workman; secondly, to the saving of time which is commonly lost in passing from one species of work to another; and lastly, to the invention of a great number of machines which facilitate and abridge labour, and enable one man to do the work of many (Smith, 1776/1937, p. 4).

Industrial society has been built on the concept of the division of labor, perhaps reaching its zenith in the modern automobile assembly line. "By the time Henry Ford started manufacturing Model T's in 1908 it took not eighteen different operations to complete a unit but 7,882" (Toffler, 1980, p. 66).

According to economists, specialization, or the division of labor, is more efficient than no specialization. A much greater quantity of work can be produced with the same investment of energy or time.

Extending this concept to nations, economists have derived the theory of the international division of labor. Due to natural differences, greater outputs were attainable by manufacturing, for example, wine in Portugal and cloth in England. In 1817 the economist Ricardo stated that, "In proportion as the market is extended, the people of every country are enabled to make the best division of their labour, and most advantageous use of their exertions."

From this point economists developed the law of comparative advantage, which basically states that any economic region has a comparative advantage over other economic regions in the production of at least one or more goods or services (Machlup, 1977, p. 47). Operating for over two-hundred years this rationale produced the global marketplace. The broken spirits and cultures of many peoples were left in the wake of this rationale as they were integrated by force into the global market. Specialization is indeed a powerful concept. Its employment as a justification for colonialism is perhaps another reason why it has not been further investigated.

Correlation does not prove causation. It can be demonstrated that population growth and concentration does not necessarily cause an increase in specializations within society, as claimed by Durkheim. It can also be demonstrated that the concept of the international division of labor and the law of comparative advantage have overlooked some factors—factors which when thoroughly examined explain more fully why modern technologies have difficulty taking root in developing and Third World countries. These questions will be more fully examined.

The first division of labor discussed by Durkheim is that based on sex. According to anthropologists there was much less physical differentiation of the sexes in early man. The female probably had as much capacity to hunt or perform any other task as the male. But of course, the male did not have the biological capacity to bear children or to nurture them in their infancy. Thus, gender-based differentiation of tasks was probably the first division of labor.

The importance of this division should not be underestimated. It has been operating in societies since there were societies and continues to operate today. It is only due to the modern feminist movement that society has begun to question the utility of gender-based distinctions in work. This movement is frequently dated to the 1963 publication of Betty Friedan's book, *The Feminine Mystique*. Others find the roots of the movement in the necessary employment of women in factories during World War II. It is doubtful, however, that the feminist movement could have occurred at an earlier time and been successful. In 1800 over 85 percent of the U.S. civilian labor force was employed in the agricultural and industrial sectors. It was not until 1955 that the combined percentage of the two sectors dropped below 50 percent (Beniger, 1986, p. 23).

Probably just as important to the success of the movement has been the invention of indoor plumbing, the furnace, the refrigerator, the range, the vacuum cleaner, the washer and dryer, and certainly the TV dinner. The reduction in the amount of time and effort necessary to maintain the household provided women with the opportunity to shift their energies to other pursuits. The more political aspects of the movement, no matter how one views them, would not have been possible without the seedbed of opportunity.

The shift of women from household labor to labor outside the home also reduced the amount of time women spent in rearing children. The occasional baby-sitter down the street has rapidly become the new social institution of pre-school day-care—the recent subject of political debate as well.

From this example it can be concluded that gender-based specializations have been prominent throughout history, until recently. The transmission of information or knowledge about child-rearing and tasks related to the household was primarily among women, especially mother to daughter. The transmission of information related to agriculture and industry was primarily among men, principally father to son. The opportunity to break down the gender-based division of labor was provided by new technologies which reduced the amount of time and effort required to maintain the household. Much of the remaining gender-based function, i.e. pre-school care, is being transferred to a new specialization.

Probably the second division of labor occurred among primitive men when one individual indicated, by whatever grunts, gesticulations and physical contest, "I'm in charge here." The world's first manager was born. The responsibilities associated with leadership include the health and welfare of the group. Without making distinctions between different types of early groups, leadership would involve decision-making about where to settle, when and where to hunt or fish, when and where to plant, the settling of disputes among members, etc. Modern law with all its specialties can be traced to tribal leadership.

Within the context of leadership is the inherent premium placed on experience. The group trusts the decision-making ability of the leader, not just for survival skills associated with hunting or being a warrior, but also because of his experience. The transmission of information and knowledge from one generation to the next has been and continues to be of primary importance to the maintenance and growth of society.

However, in some fields the value of experience is currently being questioned and appears to be declining. This is a consequence of technology changing so rapidly, that being up-to-date in one's field is more important than having worked in the field for a number of years. For some occupations life-long learning is no longer a luxury, but a necessity.

The breakdown of the generational transmission of knowledge can also be seen in the school systems. In prior years parents felt confident in being able to help their children with their school work, but this confidence has been jolted in recent years. This is perhaps best exemplified by the period when "new math" was introduced. Even in the primary grades, the mathematics that was being taught was no longer the arithmetic with which parents were familiar. Whether this factor accounts for some of the decline in the test scores of American students is unknown. However, it seems possible, if not likely.

The next significant division of labor to occur in primitive man was probably the shaman or medicine man. The primary responsibility of the medicine man was for the health of the tribe. Depending on the specific tribal type, the responsibility might also include the settling of some disputes. Among primitive peoples there was often a strong connection between physical health, mental health, and justice (Capra, 1982).

The shaman was probably also the first communication occupation or information specialist. Through whatever mystical or magical powers he might employ, he had access to information unavailable to other members of the group. This would include information about diagnoses, remedies, and prophecies. From him can be traced the field of medicine with all its specialties.

The function of medicine and public health in society is of particular importance. As life expectancy is extended, so is the capacity of society to transmit information from one generation to the next. This ability can be characterized not only by the increase in duration in which the information is available, but also by the quality. Presumably as a person grows older, new experience is integrated with prior experience and new understandings are available. Hopefully, judgement increases with age.

From the shaman can also be traced a vast array of other occupations dealing with secret or mystical information—priests, prophets, astrologers, magi, magicians, alchemists, mediums, and channelers. The concept of revealed knowledge is probably as important to society as the concept of discovered knowledge. The modern Catholic Church retains the doctrine of papal infallibility, implying a direct link between the pope and God. Western society, no matter how technologically advanced, maintains the basic social structure through the promulgation of Judeo-Christian values. These values are in their essence the result of the revealed knowledge of the Judaic prophets. No matter what the religious beliefs, or lack of belief, by most parents in Western society, a major function of parenthood is the transmission of these values to their children.

Some researchers are also beginning to question whether there might be a more scientific explanation for some parapsychological phenomena. Many major universities are sponsoring research in this area.

In the biological sciences Sheldrake (1981) suggests that genetic information transmitted from one generation to another does not contain the informational capacity to account for the shapes of species or their instinctive behavior. He hypothesizes the existence of a morphogenetic field, not yet discovered by physicists, from which each organism draws information about its own species. His book contains the results of a number of experimental studies which lend support to his thesis.

Revealed knowledge could be an important area for further investigation. For the purpose of understanding how knowledge and information operate in societies, it is just as important to understand the workings of myth, superstition, and falsehoods as it is to understand the operation of truth. The goal of sociology is the rational explanation of the behavior of groups of people. In their pursuit of that goal sociologists sometimes assume that people act rationally, otherwise the rational explanation is not possible. They forget that it is not what is true that is important, but what people believe to be true. Often the only rational explanation is that people act irrationally. We do not necessarily need to know the psychological why's. It cannot be stated with certainty that what is commonly accepted among the scientific community today is absolute knowledge. In many cases it is the best guess at this time. Even in physics, generally considered the most rigorous of the sciences, there are some who believe that the pursuit of the ever smaller, more basic particle is philosophically fruitless (Bohm, 1981). It is likely that historiographers of science will look back on this century of physics as one of major progress, but also as a period in which the correct path of inquiry was missed.

As early societies flourished into the civilizations of Egypt and Mesopotamia, librarianship found its roots. "By 2700 B.C., the Sumerians had established temple, private, and government libraries in which their varied writings could be preserved and used" (Gates, 1968, p. 8). In terms of the storage and transmission of information and knowledge this was a new and significant development. To the prior forms of gender-based, generational-based, and specialization-based transmission of information was added the new method of written communication. Knowledge could survive without direct person to person transmission.

As certain skilled occupations developed and grew within the ancient societies, the practitioners formed guilds. Little is known about the ancient guilds. It is thought, however, that in classical Greece guilds were banned (Durkheim, 1893/1933). If this is true, it provides an indication of the extent of the political and social power that guilds could wield. Perhaps the Greeks banned them as a means of limiting the power of "special interest groups."

The extent of specialization was probably not much different in ancient Egypt than in pre-industrial Europe. In Etienne Boileau's "Book of Trades," which first appeared in 1260, 100 Parisian trade associations were listed. By the mid-seventeenth century, 1,551 associations were listed (Lacroix, 1874). There may have been five associations for a single trade, but each trade may have had an average of five specializations within the trade. Nevertheless, it appears that there must have been about 300 to 50 distinct trades. This is not a large number, and it is conceivable that a similar number existed in ancient Egypt. The types of occupations mentioned by Childe (1936, p. 167) are all found in the Middle Age listings of occupations by Lacroix (1874) and show similar levels of skill or expert knowledge.

It is likely that the operation of the guilds in ancient times was also not much different than during the Middle Ages. During the Middle Ages the guild was concerned first and foremost with the economic protection of the occupation. This involved price-fixing among the members and the setting of equitable prices for goods and services among the various guilds. The cost of services could also be determined by controlling the number of practitioners of the occupation. Thus evolved the system of apprentice, journeyman, and master. The masters of the guild determined the number of apprentices that would be signed on during any given period. This system could only have evolved after the occupations had developed to the extent that the knowledge and skills of the occupation required a fair amount of time to learn.

Another method of limiting the number of practitioners was to keep secret key bits of information. Even today we speak of trade secrets and the tricks of the trade. Middle Age apprenticeship was, after all, a system in which many years of labor were traded for expert knowledge.

The guilds of pre-industrial Europe operated also as beneficent societies, taking care of many of the social needs of the members and their families. While the early guilds included both the artisans and the merchants of specific products, further development split the artisan guild from the merchant guild. The merchant guilds "acquired vast privileges and judicial and legislative powers in the cities, and it was guild officers who ruled the large commercial cities such as Genoa and Venice or Bruges and Nuremberg" (Hoselitz, 1948, p. 26). While the powers of the guild system were greatly diminished by the rise of the nation-states, vestiges of the guild remain today. In the building trades the apprentice system still operates. Universities offer Master degrees. Labor unions strive for the economic protection of their members. Some professions, notably medicine and law, maintain control over the number of practitioners by controlling admissions to medical and law schools. A practical requirement of any professional association is the setting and maintenance of standards of education and practice among the members.

The guild has operated throughout much of history as one of the primary means of transmitting expert knowledge from one generation to the next.

Another institution developing during this same period was the Medieval university. During the twelfth century, "many of the earliest universities were simply federations of students who employed scholars to teach them" (Marsh, 1948, p. 416). Borrowing its organizational structure both the church and the guilds, the university by the thirteenth century had organized faculties and granted degrees. The birth of the university is another important development in the process of transmitting knowledge. But most significantly the university institutionalized the function of discovering new knowledge.

In northern Italy during the mid-fifteenth century a number of factors converged, producing a series of fascinating developments. The success of the merchant economy had fostered a leisure class of young men. With the fall of Constantinople, scholars fled from the Byzantine empire into the universities of Europe to teach them. Both the universities and the guilds were well established within the social fabric. These factors comprise some of the ingredients for the beginning of the Renaissance.

Oddly, it was during this same period that the city of Venice, ruled by the guilds in their zenith, developed the first regular patent system (Boehm, 1967). Not only did the patent initiate the concept of rights of discovery, but it became a device by which the monarchs of the growing nation-states could reduce the powers of the guild. "As the new industries developed they acquired royal privileges to remain outside the guilds" (Hoselitz, 1948, p. 26). Unable then to control their membership and to protect the knowledge pertaining to their occupation, the influence of the guilds declined. Moreover, the commercial advantage to be gained by having the exclusive right to manufacture a new product enhanced the role of discovery as a social objective. Personal initiative began to gain in status over the more fraternal objectives of the guild system.

By the end of the fifteenth century the New World and the sea routes to the Far East had been discovered. At this time the level of specialization in Europe and the Far East were probably not much different. The slight advantage in technological development enjoyed by Europe, and the fact that the Europeans ventured to India and not the other way around, gave European society an impetus toward further development.

While Beniger (1986) focuses on the role of commerce in the Control Revolution, his detailed discussion of commercial trading practices reveals a strong link between commerce and information. The merchant sends an agent to a city to make purchases which can result in profit for both the agent, in the form of a commission, and for the merchant. Because communications in the sixteenth century were slow, the merchant must generally trust the agent to make the correct purchases. With a given purchase much information is created. The agent may require a receipt from the seller. He will record the transaction in his own books. He will put the goods on a ship and receive a bill of lading. When the goods arrive in Europe, the merchant will pay the shipping bill and obtain a receipt and a copy of the bill of lading. In his own books he will record the transactions of the agent, etc.

This simple example shows that information is created as a means of tracking the exchanges of money and goods. In modern society much the same information is recorded as was recorded them. Writing about the merchant in colonial America, Beniger states:

> ...the colonial merchant, a generalist who embraced all types of products and embodied all basic commercial functions, differed little from his counterpart in fifteenth-century Venice. Within two generations, however, these general merchants had been largely replaced by more specialized workers: shipowners, financiers, jobbers, transporters, insurers, brokers, auctioneers, retailers—a growing network of middlemen to process and move material goods. What merchants remained came increasingly to specialize in only one or two lines of goods, and to concentrate on a single commercial function: importing, wholesaling, retailing, or exporting. (Beniger, 1986, p. 185)

Here can be seen not only a close relationship between information and trade, but also that specialization reinforces this relationship. With the creation of each new middleman, at least two new transactions are created, each of which results in recorded information.

There are two distinct differences, then, between the East Indian farmer and the merchant in Venice. First, information is flowing toward the Venetian. Second, the merchant presumably has a number of agents and is, therefore, a locus of information.

Moving again to the colonial American period, Beniger's discussion of specialization among merchants points to a number of factors which encourage specialization. For example, there might have been a general merchant who decides to modify his business and specialize in importing liquor. First, he may be able to reduce the number of agents abroad. Certainly he can reduce the number of sellers abroad with which he has to deal. The amount of information about prices and availability of goods is reduced. The amount of information on his inventory will also be reduced. At the same time he creates for buyers an impression of expertise, if not actual expertise. Buyers may experience faster service or a more diverse or more readily available product line. Because the merchant is buying in larger quantities, he will probably be able to reduce his prices and undercut the competition, while retaining his profit margin.

Thus, there is a definite economic advantage for this merchant to specialize. Here again there is a strong connection between the commercial transaction and information. Forgetting for a moment the advantage he accrues in undercutting his competitors, the merchant would gain some advantage simply by reducing the amount and complexity of information.

Returning to Europe in the seventeenth century, another significant event in society's capacity to discover new knowledge was the development of scientific method and the social system of science. Going beyond the predominantly trial and error methods of prior ages, such notables as Galileo and Descartes contributed to the development of modern scientific methods of research. Not only has method been a valuable tool for discovering new knowledge, but it has also provided a common framework or language for the scientific community.

The social system of science which evolved at that time was an international one. According to Merton (1973, pp. 270-277) the norms of scientific behavior which developed were universalism, organized skepticism, communality, and disinterestedness.

Three of these norms are of particular interest in the discussion of science as an institution. Universalism intends that the scientific profession be open to everyone, regardless of their nationality or race. Communality implies that new knowledge is not the intellectual property of the discoverer, but belongs to the scientific community and society as a whole. Disinterestedness encourages the scientist to avoid being motivated by monetary rewards or fame and to pursue knowledge for the sake of knowledge.

It is universalism which makes this system international in character. In contrast to the secrecy of the alchemist or the trade secrets of the guild, it is a system which encourages the dissemination of new knowledge. The property rights of the scientist are generally limited to the claim of discovery.

This system developed among the men of several nations, most of whom belonged to an aristocratic class. In the norm of disinterestedness can be seen the stamp of this class and their notion of how a gentleman should behave. The concept of intellectual property has been integrated into the social system of science. But in fact, the norm of communality stand in direct contrast to the commercial concept of intellectual property that is embodied in the system of patents and copyrights. For generations after the birth of this social system, the men and women of science usually signed away their claims to any monetary benefits from their discoveries. These rights accrued to the universities, corporations, and governments that employed them.

It is only recently that scientists have begun to join financiers in establishing small research corporations, and more and more scientists are beginning to real large monetary rewards for their discoveries. Whether this kind of activity will undermine and substantially alter the social system of science remains to be seen. Veblen (1919/1969) indicates that there is something within the very character of the scientist and technician which makes him an unlikely candidate for a labor union or any other kind of organized activity aimed at economic protection. Looking back upon the long history of the guilds and the relationship between the knowledge of the specialist and the secrecy and other methods which were employed to protect the economic base of the specialist, the openness of the social system of science stands out as a grand anomaly.

In fifteenth and sixteenth century Europe numerous advances in technology enhanced the development of knowledge. While these inventions can be categorized in a variety of ways, there are two classes of technologies which are of particular interest. First are technologies which enhance the dissemination, storage, or retrieval of recorded knowledge. Second are technologies which enhance the discovery of new knowledge.

The invention of printing with movable type by Gutenberg about 1454 was an event of singular significance for the storage and dissemination of knowledge. It also contributed to the decline of the guilds, since technical information, written by experts, could be distributed broadly to anyone who could afford a book (Burke, ,1985, p. 116). This period also demonstrates one of the drawbacks of some technologies. Errors in the texts were standardized along with accurate information and were also distributed broadly.

In addition there was during this period another interesting connection between information and economics:

> A prime example of the proliferation of an already established text was the use of the press by the Church to reproduce thousands of printed indulgences. These were documents given to the faithful in return for prayer, penitence, pilgrimage or, most important of all, money (Burke 1985, p. 116).

During this period the indulgence became a sort of theocratic currency used by the popes to finance their grand building plans in Rome. The indulgence was itself sometimes used as money.

From this point can be traced the invention of numerous technologies which impact the dissemination, storage, or retrieval of information. These include photography, the phonograph, motion pictures, television, tape recording, video recording, and computers to name just a few.

The second class of technology, those which enhance the discovery of new knowledge, primarily include inventions which extend the perceptions or permit new types or degrees of measurement. These would include the telescope, microscope, Geiger counter, litmus paper, bubble chamber, particle accelerator, computers, etc. These are the special tools of the scientists which permit the observation of phenomena never before seen.

The invention of printing is often viewed as bringing to an end the oral tradition of transmission of knowledge. The oral tradition did undergo a change, in that it was no longer necessary to rely on such mnemonic devices as rhyme to pass information from one generation to another or from region to region. Nevertheless, the oral tradition did continue and is evident in modern society. Probably as much as fifty percent of education involves oral transmission of information from teachers to students. Walking into the reception area of a company, one can often see the current receptionist training the new one. In the grocery store one checker trains another. In a technical profession such as computer programming, it may require weeks if not months of orientation for a new programmer to become familiar with specific programs and systems. Films, videocassettes, and television can also be classified as means for the oral transmission of information.

Research on the workings of the invisible college has focused primarily on the exchange of information among scientists and other academic researchers. Researchers also comprise a group for whom the written word is of great importance. Yet it seems that no matter how much published information exists in books or journals, no matter how much is indexed in print or in electronic databases, the actual use of these to transmit information from one person to another is probably a small percentage compared to the vast invisible college that exists among the general populace.

From the seventeenth century onward knowledge grew rapidly, with new fields and disciplines branching off from the old much like a tree of knowledge. While the university had previously comprised a few specialties—primarily medicine, law, and theology—the process of specialization within the university took hold.

During this period there is evidence of synergy between disciplines. For example, electricity was "discovered" because astronomers asked if magnetism was what held the planets in orbit around the sun. In modern times this synergy is exemplified by the many new discoveries in biology which took place since the late 1940s, when unemployed physicists moved into research positions in molecular biology.

Such successes were probably influential in Campbell's (1969) proposal of the fish-scale model of interdisciplinary study. Reinforced by others, the importance of interdisciplinary approaches to discovering new knowledge has now been institutionalized within the university.

Nevertheless, various problems exist among the disciplines today. Bloom (1987) has described what is tantamount to a crisis in communication. Once again, economics enters the picture as social values influence the marketplace. The university must compete to some extent with the private sector and finds that it must spend much more for faculty in the sciences, engineering, and business fields than in the humanities or social sciences. Social values influence the curriculum, and the broad-based liberal arts education wanes in favor of the technical, occupation-specific education.

The accumulation of knowledge itself becomes a factor in the educational process. There is so much more for the high school student of today to learn than there was just two generations ago. Computers, DNA, and history since World War II are a few examples. It is possible that the more technical, occupation-specific education found in universities today is the result of the specialization process at work. If knowledge is growing exponentially, then one method of integrating knowledge into the social fabric would be to encourage specialized education at earlier ages. There is certainly evidence of strain on curriculum development in both high schools and universities.

Language also plays a role. Knowledge would not be advancing if there were not a parallel increase in terminology. New terms not only describe new phenomena but also become a short-hand jargon for communication among members of the discipline. This poses problems in indexing or subject analysis that are of special interest to the librarian. Often, however, members of the research community complain about this problem. In describing his interdisciplinary trek which resulted in the Gaia theory, James Lovelock wrote:

> Such journeys are lively, for the boundaries between the sciences are jealously guarded by their Professors and within each territory there is a different arcane language to be learnt. In the ordinary way a grand tour of this kind would be extravagantly expensive and unproductive in its yield of new knowledge; but just as trade often still goes on between nations at war, it is also possible for a chemist to travel through such distant disciplines as meteorology or physiology, if he has something to barter (Lovelock, 1979, pp. vii-viii).

Language serves much the same purpose as a secrecy for the guild. It protects the economic base of the discipline and to some extent controls the number of members in the discipline. It also seems understandable that a professor would be somewhat reluctant to divulge to an "uninitiated outsider" what had taken years of study and research to earn. Once again Lovelock's bartering provides an economic insight into the exchange of knowledge.

Since the invention of the computer, language has taken on new importance, as programming languages are invented to facilitate the use of computers. The significance of these languages is underscored by their acceptance by universities for fulfillment of foreign language requirements. Again, however, the knowledge of computer languages creates a boundary between the initiated and the uninitiated.

There seems also to be an interesting synergy between the development of new technology and war. The study of motion in physics frequently addressed problems related to sending cannonballs from one place to another. This developed into the field of ballistics, from which the field of rocketry derived much of its knowledge base. This further developed into sending missiles from one place to another, leading today to the concept of strategic defense, or the art of hitting one bullet with another bullet.

A skill that's quite different in character, such as computer programming, has also benefitted from ballistics. The programming algorithm for the binary search was derived from the artillery method for narrowing in on a target.

It appears that when societies expend great amounts of effort in the direction of either conquest or defense, they make significant investments in researching technologies that will provide an advantage over the opponent. The outcome of this investment is often new knowledge and new technologies that have application in the broader society after hostilities have ended.

Governments and corporations are major investors in research. Within the United States today there is a trend toward investing in research that will maintain or increase the economic status of the United States against other nations. There is also a concurrent trend toward keeping secret from other nations as much information as possible about this research. As an example President Reagan announced a plan to limit access by foreign nationals to research on superconductivity (McDonald, 1987). This trend runs counter to the norm of communality within the social system of science and poses yet another threat to that system (Shattuck, 1986).

Corporations have far less obligation to the public good than governments and are more secretive with the results of their research. The rise of the transnational corporation (TNC) poses a threat to the nation-state and quite probably to the open communication of scientific research as well. On the behavior of TNC's Toffler has stated:

> Sometimes cooperating with their "home" nation, sometimes exploiting it, sometimes executing its policies, sometimes using it to execute their own, the TNCs are neither all good nor all bad (Toffler, 1980, p. 338).

Some TNCs attempt to take advantage of the international division of labor by creating product specializations within nations:

> The transnational corporation (or TNC) may do research in one country, manufacture components in another, assemble them in a third, sell the manufactured goods in a fourth, deposit its surplus funds in fifth, and so on (Toffler, 1980, p. 336).

This diversification among nations may be motivated by more than cost savings in labor or material. There is evidence that it might also be motivated by a desire to keep secret the complete manufacturing process of a product or to distribute the risks associated with national political actions, such as nationalization of an industry (Mattelart, 1979).

There are two additional interesting aspects of the TNC that relate to information. First, is the ability of the TNC to utilize its information resources for economic gain:

> A new corporate officer has appeared in the executive suite—the "international cash manager," who remains plugged into the worldwide electronic casino twenty-four hours a day, searching for the lowest interest rates, the best currency bargains, the fastest turnaround (Toffler, 1980, p. 247).

Second is the growth of corporate intelligence centers and officers and what appears to be a trend to involve the special librarian in corporate intelligence gathering (Greene, 1988).

In examining the relationship between specialization and economics, factors effecting the distribution of knowledge cannot be overlooked. As an example, during the 1974 oil embargo filling-stations in the United States began to convert to self-service pumps. The gas station attendant has virtually disappeared as a specialization. The required knowledge for holding this position was not difficult to learn or crucial, but this position served in many instances as an informal apprentice position to the automobile mechanic. This forced a shift in training to vocational programs in high schools and technical schools. (The increasing complexity of automechanics has probably also reduced the amount of father to son training in this area.) Many companies are also cutting costs by eliminating the repairman and providing customers with toll free numbers to call (Toffler, 1980, pp. 286-288). More and more frequently the consumer is talked through the repair process. The numbers of repairmen are considerably reduced by this trend. Other occupations and professions requiring more education are also not immune from the marketplace distribution of specialization needs.

Adam Smith suggested that a specialization would distribute itself as far in the society as the marketplace would bear. This appears to be true, though it seems that the definition of "marketplace" may require further examination in this context. Besides being eliminated by the market, there is also the phenomenon of unusual positive feedback mechanisms arising among specializations, so that one specialization feeds on another in an every-increasing loop that is ultimately paid for by the consumer. A current example is the loop among doctors, lawyers, and insurance companies. Despite recriminations among them, these professions appear to be surviving quite well and are accounting for unprecedented percentages of gross national product. The question must be asked: What mechanisms, if any, do societies have for correcting the phenomenon of specializations going out of control?

A study of the distribution of knowledge must also take into account the programming of machines. Jacquard's loom invented in 1801 is often cited as the first example of the programmed control of production. ("The idea may have come from late eighteenth-century musical instruments programmed to perform automatically under the control of rolls of punched paper") (Beniger, 1986, p. 247). Since that time technological advances have increased the amount and complexity of instructions which can be transferred to machines. Microchips are employed today in products as diverse as the automobile and the doll.

Robots replace people on the assembly lines, performing operations from welding to optical inspections with higher levels of quality and quantity. This modifies the distribution of knowledge in society. Instead of the skill of welding being stored in the minds of a large number of welders, the skill is now stored in the minds of perhaps a handful of programmers. More likely, the skill is stored in the instructions, and the programmer will relearn the skill in an imaginary fashion only when a breakdown occurs or a modification is requested.

As society transfers more instructions and more knowledge to machines, specializations associated with that transfer such as electronic engineering and computer programming become critical. Here again secrecy plays a role. There are numerous instances of programmers encrypting their code or failing to document in order to maintain job security. There have also been cases of programmers forcing payment from customers by installing "bombs" that will erase the programs unless payment is received.

Surprenant (1983) has pointed out that this trend toward more and more sophisticated, artificially intelligent machines and computers is the real front in the technological war between Japan and the United States. The winner of this war will likely have an unprecedented economic advantage.

There are, however, disadvantages to transferring knowledge to machines. First, machines do not as yet have the capacity to knowingly transfer their knowledge from one machine to another. There is no living incentive to do so. Second, as happened with the introduction of printing, errors in the instructions are propagated with every copy. Such errors may not be readily apparent, and depending on the importance of the program to human decision-making, may cause disastrous consequences.

Finally, opportunity is lost. Besides the advantages of specialization outlined by Adam Smith, there are at least two others. One is the expression of talent, which is related somewhat to his concept of increased dexterity. But the second, and extremely important advantage, is the opportunity for discovery that accrues to the specialist. As he performs the same task over and over again, the opportunity to discover a new labor-saving method is much higher than for the non-specialist who may perform the task only occasionally. Accidental discovery is more likely, since the unexpected occurrence will be appreciated and understood. This form of opportunity is lost when work is transferred to machines. Serendipity is a human gift.

Computers and robots have the potential to alter the distribution of knowledge, as well as the growth of knowledge through lost opportunities. Even today decision-making programs are being used by executives to aid in determining courses of action. In a few years an executive may no longer be required to understand at a conceptual level all the factors that determine whether to initiate a new product. He will simply key in the data and wait for an answer.

Some advocates of artificial intelligence offer society an amazing future, producing a common misconception that computers think. People frequently forget that the computer is nothing more than a tool. Thought is intimately connected to life, and there will never be a machine, no matter how sophisticated the program, that truly thinks.

Finally, to understand the system of developing knowledge and specializations, the infrastructure of the system must be examined. The top of the specialization pyramid exhibits significant dependencies on prior achievements. Speculating on librarianship without electricity conjures an image of the profession at the turn of the century. Yet this unusual factor received critical examination by librarians at the Library of Congress as they considered the conversion of information to CD-ROM.

Returning to the ideas of Durkheim, the process of developing specializations includes the population factors mentioned by him—size and concentration of population. Returning to the ideas of Smith, economic advantages do occur in the division of labor. But obviously the system is even more complex than the concepts of Durkheim and Smith combined. Demographics and economics appear to interact in a complex fashion in which cause and effect cannot easily be assigned.

In the examples mentioned a technological innovation reduces the amount of human effort required to perform a task. Each innovation produces a quantity of "leisure," which is invested in other tasks to further enhance survival. When enough related innovations develop, these can coalesce into an occupation. For the specialization to appear in a society, the society must be disposed economically to accept it. The primary requirement would be the likely existence of a "market" for the products of the specialization. This suggests that the society as a whole must be surviving fairly well and that there must be a minimum size and concentration of population. As the specialization appears, this further influences the market and the population, allowing both to grow. The practice of the specialization and its interaction with other specializations can further increase the process of technological innovation. On the other hand, secrecy or other methods of transmission control are often associated with specializations to protect their economic viability.

At the institutional level, the invention of writing and the consequent specialization, librarianship, reduced reliance on generation to generation transmission of knowledge. The creation of enough leisure in pre-Renaissance Europe permitted the creation of the university. The transmission of knowledge not normally associated with a trade was institutionalized along with the professorial duty to discover new knowledge.

The examples given suggest that technological innovation and the production of leisure are important ingredients in the process. While innovation reduces human effort in the accomplishment of a task, it almost always requires an increase in overall energy consumption of the resulting human-machine aggregate. Although Adam Smith's delineation of advantages in specialization suggests that there is a saving in effort or per product effort, it is human effort only. The overall energy consumption per unit time increases, even in cases where the per product energy consumption might decrease. Of those factors which might correlate with the degree of specialization of a society, per capita energy consumption per unit time most likely has the strongest correlation.

In several examples there was a connection between information and energy in the form of money. Information was created to monitor the flow of money and tended to flow in the same direction as the money. The opportunity to understand the handling of information appears to be an integral part of the specialization process as well.

These descriptions and assumptions about specialization may provide some insights into the development of societies in the less developed countries (LDCs) and the Third World. While it is obvious that Western society has made extensive use of energy inputs from other countries and peoples to build a more advanced society, it is less obvious that the flows continue to favor the West. In the sphere of international development this may account for the failure of modernization theory, dependency theory, and adjustment theory (Dosa, 1985). Just as the export of agricultural products includes inherently the export of soil components for growing food, the international division of labor permits social growth only to those countries which are the locus of goods, services, money, and information.

> The family of a landless Indian peasant now spends about six hours a day merely finding the firewood it needs for cooking and heating. Another four to six hours are spent bringing water from the well, and a similar amount to graze cattle, goats, or sheep (Toffler, 1980, p. 355).

International development has provided energy in the form of money and knowledge in the form of specialists to the LDCs. Yet these have rarely succeeded, because they have not primed the pump of a self-sufficient specialization process. As Toffler has point out (1980, pp. 345-365), it is not necessary for LDCs to recapitulate the development of the West. Nevertheless, innovation in concert with a significant increase in per capita energy consumption would speed the development process.

The international division of labor, while it is a valuable economic theory, has overlooked the disadvantages of over-specialization. Some countries may specialize in information handling, as the United States appears to be doing at this stage in its development; those countries which specialize in unmechanized agriculture of non-food products have essentially eliminated their opportunity for further economic development.

In another organismic analogy, Toffler states:

> In short, we are moving toward a world system composed of units densely interrelated like the neurons in a brain rather than organized like the departments of a bureaucracy (Toffler, 1980, p. 344).

If the countries of the world are in a contest, a quest to be brain, then as Surprenant (1983) has pointed out, the United States must beware. As the contest moves from information handling to knowledge handling, the stakes are raised considerably. National secrecy will become increasingly important and threaten the existence of the social system of science in its present normative structure. An alternative solution would be to discard the theory of the international division of labor, cease justifying the West's advanced civilization on cultural barriers in other lands, and attempt to foster a self-sufficient specialization process in all countries.

A systems approach to specialization should produce some new understandings about social development. Rather than being the *result* of population factors, urban revolution factors, or economic factors, specialization can be viewed as a *process* that includes these factors. It can be viewed as a process that is intimately connected to life itself. Contrary to Toffler's belief that specialization and professionalism are under attack and that there is a growing movement to "restrain the power of the expert," (1980, p. 279), specialization as process will continue to be the means by which life organizes itself for enhanced survival.

Thus, social epistemology would be a perspective, a new way of looking at the development of knowledge. There exists already a treasure of information in history, sociology, economics, and librarianship on which this new discipline might draw. Besides investigating the social institutions and the new technologies related to discovering, storing, and transmitting knowledge, social epistemology would also recognize the importance of the human mind as the greatest portable storage device. The distribution of specializations in society and the oral transmission of information in the everyday world would receive particular attention. As emphasized by Shera, social epistemology would strive to know how societies know and how they put that knowledge to work.

REFERENCES

Beniger, James R. *The Control Revolution.* Cambridge, MA: Harvard University Press, 1986.

Bloom, Allan. *The Closing of the American Mind.* New York: Simon and Schuster, 1987.

Boehm, Klaus. *The British Patent System.* Cambridge: Cambridge University Press, 1967.

Bohm, David. *Wholeness and the Implicate Order.* London: Routledge & Kegan Paul, 1981.

Burke, James. *The Day the Universe Changed.* Boston: Little, Brown and Company, 1985.

Campbell, D. "Ethnocentrism of Disciplines and the Fish-scale Model of Omniscience." In M. Sherif and C. Sherif (Eds.), *Interdisciplinary Relationships in the Social Sciences* (1969) pp. 328-348. Chicago: Aldine.

Capra, Fritjof. *The Turning Point: Science, Society, and the Rising Culture.* New York: Simon and Schuster, 1982.

Childe, V. Gordon. *Man Makes Himself.* London: Watts & Co, 1936.

Dosa, Marta. "Information Transfer as Technical Assistance for Development." *Journal of the American Society for Information Science,* (1985) *36,* pp. 146-152.

Durkheim, Emile. *The Division of Labor in Society* (G. Simpson Trans.). New York: The Macmillan Company. (Original work published 1893), 1933.

Friedan, Betty. *The Feminine Mystique.* New York: W.W. Norton, 1963.

Gates, Jean Key. *Introduction to Librarianship* (2nd ed.). New York: McGraw-Hill Book Company, 1968.

Greene, H. Frances. "Competitive Intelligence and the Information Center." *Special Libraries, 79*(4) (1988) pp. 285-295.

Hoselitz, Bert F. "Guild." In Franklin J. Meine (Ed.), *American People's Encyclopedia: Vol. 10* (1948) pp. 26-27. Chicago: The Spencer Press, Inc.

Lacroix, Paul. *Manners, Customs and Dress during the Middle Ages and during the Renaissance Period.* London: Bickers and Son, 1874.

Lovelock, J.E. *Gaia: A New Look at Life on Earth.* Oxford: Oxford University Press, 1979.

Machlup, Fritz. *A History of Thought on Economic Integration.* New York: Columbia University Press, 1977.

Marsh, Robert. "University." In Franklin J. Meine (Ed.), *American People's Encyclopedia: Vol. 19* (1948) pp. 416-417. Chicago: The Spencer Press, Inc.

Mattelart, Armand. *Multinational Corporations and the Control of Culture: The Ideological Apparatuses of Imperialism.* Atlantic Highlands, NJ: Humanities Press, 1979.

McDonald, Kim. "Reagan's Plan to Limit Foreign Access to Data Opposed by Scientists." *Chronicle of Higher Education* (Sept. 9, 1987) pp. A1, A10.

Merton, Robert K. *The Sociology of Science.* Chicago: University of Chicago Press, 1973.

Ricardo, David. *On the Principles of Political Economy and Taxation.* London: G. Bell. (Original work published 1776), 1911.

Shattuck, John. "Federal Restrictions on the Free Flow of Academic Information and Ideas." *Minutes of the 107th Meeting of the Association of Research Libraries* (1986) pp. A1-A31. Washington, D.C.: Association of Research Libraries.

Sheldrake, Rupert. *New Science of Life.* Los Angeles: J.P. Tarcher, 1981.

Shera, Jesse. (1961). "Social Epistemology, General Semantics and Librarianship." *Wilson Library Bulletin, 35,* (161) pp. 767-770.

Smith, Adam. *Inquiry into the Nature and Causes of the Wealth of Nations.* New York: Random House, Inc. (Original work published 1776), 1937.

Surprenant, Thomas T. "Future Libraries: [Japanese Challenge to U.S. Supremacy in Computer Development]." *Wilson Library Bulletin, 58,* (1983) pp. 206-207.

Toffler, Alvin. *The Third Wave.* New York: William Morrow and Company, Inc, 1980.

Veblen, Thorstein. *Place of Science in Modern Civilization, and Other Essays.* New York: Capricorn Books. (Original work published 1919). 1969.

A BIBLIOGRAPHY OF LIBRARY MANAGEMENT IN SUB-SAHARAN AFRICA

Glenn L. Sitzman

The compiler of this bibliography has been guided by a very broad definition of "management." The intention has been not only to collect and record writings about the management of libraries in Sub-Saharan Africa but also to include works that may be of special interest or helpfulness to library administrators working in the Sub-Sahara, though the works may have no direct bearing on management in the terms that management is generally thought of.

Some critics may charge the bibliography with being eccentric, idiosyncratic, and inconsistent. It is, in fact, all of that. The eccentricities and idiosyncracies may be attributed to the compiler's recollection of suddenly finding himself the manager of a university library in the Sub-Sahara without managerial experience and with no compilation of writings such as this bibliography to turn to. The inconsistencies may be attributed to the compiler's decision not to list titles more than once, complicated by the human tendency to be inconsistent. Moreover, the attempt to present the material under various

Advances in Library Administration and Organization,
Volume 11, pages 267-293.
Copyright © 1993 by JAI Press Inc.
All rights of reproduction in any form reserved.
ISBN: 1-55938-596-0

headings in an effort to make the bibliography more manageable, in fact increased the possibility of scattering like material. Because of the multi-subjects of many articles, along with single entries for titles, users of the bibliography are advised not to rely entirely on the headings that break it into more manageable units.

The titles in the bibliography were taken from the compiler's various bibliographies on librarianship in Sub-Saharan Africa, compiled primarily from *Library Literature, Library and Information Science Abstracts* (*LISA*), and *Information Science Abstracts,* and published in the compiler's book *African Libraries* (Scarecrow Press, 1988) and in recent volumes of *Advances in Library Administration and Organization* (*ALAO*).

For those who will protest that this work is not scholarly, the compiler raises the question, Which of the scholars more qualified to produce such a bibliography has done so? Until some scholar does, the present bibliography may be of some use.

1. General Management

Abimbola, S. O. "Management by Objectives (MBO); Its Application to Libraries." *Nigerbiblios* 4(1979): 8-9, 11-13.

Abobunde, E. O. "Administration in a Professional Institution." *Nigerbiblios* 1(1976): 4-6, 8.

"African Network of Administrative Information (ANAI)." *Unesco Journal of Information Science* 4(1982): 143.

Ahiazu, Augustine I. "Towards Effective Management of Human Resources in Nigerian Libraries: An Evaluation of Cost Reduction Strategies." In *Management of Libraries in an Era of Scarce Resources. Proceedings of a Seminar, Benin University, Benin City, Nigeria, 18-20 June 1986,* edited by O. O. Oundipe, 30-57. Benin University, 1989.

Aiyepeku, W. A. "The Information Component in Decision-Making: A Framework for Analysis." *Nigerbiblios* 3(1978): 4-9.

Alemna, A. A. "Management of Libraries in Ghana: Concepts, Practices and Constraints." *Aslib Proceedings* 41(1989):: 217-223.

Benge, R. C. "Obstacles to Scientific Management in Nigerian Libraries." *Nigerian Libraries* 11(1975): 49-53.

El Hadi, Mohamed M. "The African Integrated Network of Administrative Information—AINAI: A Conceptual Project Proposal." *African Research & Documentation* 1(1976): 13-20.

————. "The Establishment of an African Administrative Training Materials Clearing-House at CAFRAD." In *Official Report of the African Seminar for Librarians and Documentalists of Administrative Information Services,* prepared by E. S. Asiedu, 169-183. 1975.

Hüttemann, Lutz, ed. *Establishment, Function and Management of a National Library and Document Service, Workshop Report: Harare* [*Zimbabwe*], *6-15 March 1985.* Bonn, German Foundation for International Development, 1985.

_____. *Management of a National Information and Documentation Network in Zambia: Workshop Papers; Lusaka, 15-24 February 1988.* Bonn, Lusaka, German Foundation for International Development and Zambia Library Association, 1988.

_____. *Management of National Documentation Centres, Malawi Workshop Papers, Blantyre, 6-14 March 1984.* Bonn, German Foundation for International Development, 1984.

Ifidon, Sam E. "Participatory Management in Libraries." *Bendel Library Journal* 2(1979): 4-10+.

_____. "Scientific Approach to Library Management." *African Journal of Academic Librarianship* 2(1984): 12-20.

Management of Libraries in an Era of Scarce Resources. Proceedings of a Seminar, Benin University, Benin City, Nigeria, 18-20 June 1986. Edited by O. O. Ogundipe. Benin University, 1989.

Nwafor, B. U. "Library Services and Management Studies." A Brief Address on the Occasion of JUMASA [Jos University Management Students Association] Week, 21-23 May 1981.

Nzotta, Briggs Chinkata. "Education for Library Management in African Library Schools." *Journal of Librarianship* 9(1977): 130-143, 157.

_____. "Management and the Core Curriculum in African Library Schools." *Nigerian Library and Information Science Review* 2(1984): 47-55.

_____. "Participative Management in Library Service." *Bendel Library Journal* 3(1980): 16-20.

Ogundipe, O. O. "The Response of Library Administration to Management Theories." *African Journal of Academic Librarianship* 4(1986): 26-30.

Ojiambo, Joseph B. "Transfer of Western Management Expertise to Developing Countries." In *Translating an International Education to a National Environment,* edited by Julie I. Tallman and Joseph B. Ojiambo, 65-81. Metuchen, N. J., Scarecrow Press, 1990.

Osundina, Oyeniyi. "Intuition or Research: Which Way to Better Governance of Libraries in Nigeria." *Bendel Library Journal* 4(1981): 36-40.

Rodrigues, A. J., W. Okelo-Ondongo, and R. J. P. Scott. "Management of Technological Change: Kenya Case Study." *Information Development* 4(1989): 399-471.

Thapisa, A. P. N. "Whither Human Being? Theories of Management as Applied to Library Management in Southern Africa." *International Forum on Information and Documentation* 12(1987): 14-20.

2. General Peripheral

Chimulu, Foster, et al. "Design of an Abstracting Service. Final Report [of] Working Group B." In *Implementation of Modern Documentation,* edited by Soud Timami, 129-160. Nairobi, Kenya, Coordinating Centre for Regional Information Training (CRIT), 1976.

Cornelius, David. "Ghana: A National Library Service." In *The Planning of Library and Documentation Services,* edited by C. V. Penna, 100-104. Paris, Unesco, 1970.

Dube, S. R. "The Zimbabwe National Library and Documentation Services: An Example for Eastern and Southern African Countries." In *Establishment of a National Information and Documentation Network* ... *Papers of the Seminar held in Dar-es-Salaam [Tanzania], February 16-24, 1989,* edited by O. C. Mascarenhas, 41-49. DSE [German Foundation for International Development], 1989.

Fayose, Philomena O. "Seminar Paper on New Directions in the Educational Functions of West African Libraries." *Ghana Library Journal* 3(1969): 16-23.

Ita, Nduntuei O. "Problems of Bibliographic Control in Nigeria." *Libri* 36(1986): 320-335.

Kaungamno, E. E. *Centralized Services for Libraries. The African Experience.* 1979. ERIC. ED 220 077.

_____. *Possibilities of an Integrated National Library Policy for African Countries.* 1978. ERIC. ED 220 078. First published by Tanzania Library service as a pamphlet, 1978.

Lazar, P. "Consideration on the Organization and Development of the National Information System in Developing Countries." *Library Herald* 11(1969): 32-43.

Lwanga, T. K. "A Proposal for the Basic Structural Organization of Documentation and Library Services in East Africa." In *Development of Documentation and Information Networks in East Africa,* 72-81. Bonn, German Foundation for International Development, 1974.

Mabomba, R. S. *Cataloguing Manual.* Zomba, University of Malawi Library, 1974.

_____. *A Manual for Small Libraries in Malawi.* Lilongwe, Malawi Library Association, 1981.

Nwafor, B. U. "The Ordeals of the Librarian in a War-Affected Library: The Nigerian Example." *Library Progress: an International Review in the Field of Libraries* 4(1971): 69-76.

Oketunji, Ibidapo. "The Book Crisis in Nigeria: Implications and Possible Solutions." *Library Scientist* 14(1987): 14-28.

Oluoch, A. R. "On Developing a National Bibliographic Agency." *Maktaba* 5(1979): 42-44. Also published in *The Development of Information: an African Approach,* edited by R. W. Thairu, 42-44. Nairobi, Kenya Library Association, 1979.

Ononogbo, Raphael U. "User Satisfaction in a Depressed Economy." *International Library Review* 21(1989): 209-221.

Sloane, Ruth C. "Patterns of Library Service in Africa." *Library Trends* 8(1959): 163-191.

Thairu, R. W., ed. *The Development of Information: An African Approach: Proceedings of the Third International Standing Conference of Eastern, Central and Southern African Librarians.* Nairobi, Kenya Library Association, 1979.

Tocatlian, Jacques. "Organizational Structure in East Africa in the Framework of the UNISIST Programme." In *Development of Documentation and Information Networks in East Africa,* 136-149. Bonn, German Foundation for International Development, 1974.

Udoh, D. J. E., and M. R. Aderibigbe. "The Problems of Development, Maintenance, and Automation of Authority Files in Nigeria." *Cataloging & Classification Quarterly* 8(1987): 93-103.

Wesley, Cecile. "National Information Policies and Networks in Morocco, Tunisia, Egypt and Sudan: A Comparative Study." *Alexandria* 2(1990): 23-38.

3. Acquisitions

Afre, S. A. "Stock Development and Management with the User in Mind." *African Journal of Academic Librarianship* 1(1983): 41-44.

Aguolu, I. F. "The Study of the Community Basis for Book Selection." *Bendel Library Journal* 4(1981): 18-21.

Akinfolarin, W. A. "The Acquisition of Books and Journals in Austere Times: The Ondo State University Library Experience [Nigeria]." *Library Review* 39(1990): 36-40.

Ali, S. Nazim. "Acquisition of Scientific Literature in Developing Countries." *Information Development* 5(1989): 73-115.

Ayeni, Emmanuel Olu. "The Benefits, Politics and Attendant Problems Associated with Gifts, Donations and Exchanges." *Library Scientist* 13(1986): 79-86.

Edem, U. S. "Serials Acquisition and Management in Nigerian Academic Libraries: Implications for Quality Library Services." *Information Services & Use* 9(1989): 161-170.

Ejiko, E. O. "The Organizational Structure and Functions of Collection Development Division: the Case of Ahmadu Bello University Library [Nigeria]." *Library Scientist* 9(1982): 26-35.

Ezennia, Steve E. "Problems and Achievements in Collection Building and Management in Anambra State, Nigeria." *Collection Management* 10(1988): 157-168.

Ifidon, Sam E. "Selection of Book Dealers: a Nigerian University Librarian's Dilemma." *Library Scientist* 9(1982): 14-25.

Jegede, O. "Problems of Acquisitions of Library Material in a Developing Country: University of Lagos [Nigeria] Library Experience." *International Library Review* 9(1977): 225-239.

Kwafo-Akoto, Kate O. "Acquiring Unpublished Population Documents in Africa: a Personal Experience." *Aslib Proceedings* 40(1988): 105-110.

Lauer, Joseph J. "A Methodology for Establishing the Size of Subject Collections, Using African Studies as an Example." *College and Research Libraries* 44(1983): 380-383.

N'jie, S. P. C. "Collecting Policies and Preservation: the Gambia." *IFLA Publications* No. 40. In *Preservation of Library Materials. Proceedings of the Conference Held at the National Libray of Austria, Vienna, April 1986,* volume 1, 24-30. New York, K G. Saur, 1987.

Njuguna, J. R. "Acquisition of Library Materials in Kenya: Problems and Prospects." A Paper presented at the IFLA Conference, Nairobi, Kenya, August 1984.

Nwafor, B. U. "Problems of Acquisition of Overseas and Local Materials." In *University Libraries in developing Countries,* edited by A.J. Loveday and G. Gatterman, 59-74. München, Saur, 1985.

Nzotta, Briggs C. "Acquisition Policy in a Developing Economy: A Case Study of Nigerian State (Public) Libraries." *Collection Building* 7, no. 4 (1985): 3-8.

————. "Written Acquisitions Policies in Public Libraries." *Nigerian Libraries* 9(1973): 83-89.

Oddoye, E. Oko. "Seminar on Problems of Book Provision in West Africa—Working Paper on the Ghanaian Case." *Ghana Library Journal* 5(1973): 40-47.

Olanlokun, S. Olajire, and H. S. Issah. "Collection Development in an African Academic Library During Economic Depression: The University of Lagos [Nigeria] Library Exerience." *Library Acquisitions* 11(1987): 103-111.

Onadiran, G. T., and R. W. Onadiran. "Acquisition Procedures in University Libraries in Nigeria." *Journal of Library and Information Science* 6(1981): 60-69.

Onuigbo, Wilson I. B. "Reprint Requests—A Tool for Documentation." *International Forum on Information and Documentation* 10(J1 1985): 7-9. Discussion: 11(Apr 1986) 40-41.

Rowse, Dorothea E. "The Creation of a Book Selection Policy, with Special Reference to African Materials." *Mousaion* 6(1988): 47-56.

Sanusi, K. A. "Processing in Acquisition Department of a University Library (Collection Development)." *Library Scientist* 13(1986): 87-98.

4. Academic Libraries

Adediran, B. O. "Centralization of University Library Services: Some Compelling Factors in Nigerian Universities." *College & Research Libraries* 35(1974): 360-363.

Aguolu, Christian C. "Centralization and Decentralization in African University Libraries: A Theoretical Critical Re-examination." *International Library Movement* 7(1985): 157-172. First published in *African Journal of Academic Librarianship* 2(1984): 27-33.

Alabi, G. A. "A Cost Comparison of Manual and Automated Circulation Systems in University Libraries: The Case of the Ibadan University Library." *Information Processing & Management* 21(1985): 525-533.

Asiagodo, G. D. "The Management of the Students' Reference and Reserve Collection at the Balme Library [University of Ghana]." *African Journal of Academic Librarianship* 4(1986): 49-55.

Dean, John. "Organization and Services of University Libraries in West Africa." In *Comparative and International Librarianship,* edited by Miles M. Jackson, 113-137. Westport, CT, Greenwood Press, 1970.

Diko, Inuwa. "Selective Dissemination of Information in Academic Libraries." *Library Scientist* 8(1981): 15-32.

Dipelou, J. O. "Administrative Problems in Academic Libraries with Particular Reference to Nigeria." *Unesco Bulletin for Libraries* 24(1970: 294-301).

————. "Objectives and Standards of Practice for University Libraries in West Africa." In *Standards of Practice for West African Libraries,* edited by John Dean, 31-44. Ibadan, 1969.

Edoka, Benson E. "Circulation Functions and Staffing Patterns in Nigerian University Libraries." Master's Thesis, Loughborough University of Technology, 1979.

Ekpenyong, G. D. "Faculty Status for Nigerian University Librarians." *Bendel Library Journal* 3(Dec 1980): 20-27.

Ifidon, S. E. *Essentials of Management for African University Libraries*. Lagos, Libriservice, 1985.

————. "Moving an Academic Library." *Journal of Academic Librarianship* 4(1979): 434-437.

————. "The Objectives of African University Libraries: The Nigerian Experience." *International Library Review* 10(1978): 43-50.

Jegede, Oluremi. "A Review of the Lagos University Library Manual Cataloguing Process." *International Journal of Law Libraries* 5(1977): 180-190.

Kadiri, J. A. "Problems with Non-book Materials in Nigerian Academic Libraries." *Audiovisual Librarian* 13(1987): 96-99.

Lawal, Olu O. "Austerity and Aspects of Bibliographic Services: The University of Calabar [Nigeria] Library." *Information and Library Manager* 8(1989): 13-16.

Mlotshwa, Peter Mggibelo. "General Management Principles in Zambian University Libraries." Master's Thesis, Loughborough University of Technology, 1982.

Morna, C. L. "Ghana's Universities Struggle to Cope with New Priorities." *Chronicle of Higher Education* 35(1988): 43-44.

Moys, Elizabeth M. "Problems Involved in the Creation of New University Libraries." *Unesco Bulletin for Libraries* 20(1966): 54-64.

Newa, John M. "Academic Status for University Librarians in Tanzania: Challenges and Prospects." *Library Review* 38(1989): 19-35.

Mwafor, B. U. "Management by Objectives in West African University Libraries: How Feasible?" *African Journal of Academic Librarianship* 4(1986): 3-8.

————. "The Problem of the Blank Cheque. (Description of the Organisation and Administration of the University of Jos [Nigeria] Library System. Being a Paper Presented at the University of Jos Library Senior Staff Seminar, 16 May 1980)." *Nigerbiblios* 5(1980): 9-15.

————. "What we do at Jos." A Paper presented before the Staff and Students of the Department of Library Science, Bayero University, Kano [Nigeria], 15 November 1982.

Nyirenda, J. E. "Organization of Distance Education at the University of Zambia: An Analysis of the Practice." *Distance Education* 10(1989): 148-156.

Ochai, Adakole. "Management Development Needs of Library Managers in University Libraries in Nigeria." *Library and Information Science Research* 7(1985): 357-368.

Ojiambo, Joseph B. "Participatory Management and its Relevance to Academic Libraries in Africa: With Specific Reference to English-speaking Africa." *Bookmark* 45(1986): 56-63.

Okomo, Elsie O. "Valuation of an Academic Library." *Australian Academic and Research Libraries* 22(1991): 19-23.

Osundina, Oyeniya. "Improved Accessibility and Undergraduate Use of the Academic Library." *International Library Review* 7(1975): 77-81.

Rathgeber, Eva M. "A Tenuous Relationship: The African University and Development Policymaking in the 1980s." *Higher Education* 17(1988): 397-410.

Salisu, Taofiq M. "Status of Academic Librarians: A Case Study from Nigeria." *College & Research Libraries* 411(1980): 333-338.

Sanni, Grace A. "Some Management Issues of Subject Specialisation with Reference to the University of Benin [Nigeria] Library." *Library Scientist* 14(1987): 44-56.

Sanusi, K. O. "Participation Management in Nigerian University Libraries: A Practical Application in the Case of Kashim Ibrahim Library [Ahmadu Bello University, Zaria, Nigeria]." *Library Scientist* 11(1984): 121-127.

Schlie, Theodore W., and Albert H. Rubenstein. *The Role of African Universities and Research Institutes in the Technology Transfer Process.* Evanston, IL, Dept. of Industrial Engineering and Management Sciences, Northwestern University, 1974.

Strategies for Survival by Nigerian Academic and Research Libraries during Austere Times: Proceedings of a National Seminar, edited by S. M. Lawani, et al. Nigerian Association of Agricultural Librarians and Documentalists and Academic and Research Libraries Section of the Nigerian Library Association, 1988.

Ugonna, J. A. "Developing Reference Services for University Faculties: A Study of Reference Usage Needs in a Nigerian University Library." *Libri* 27(1977): 305-324.

Unomah, J. I. "Student Utilization of Academic Libraries in Nigeria: an Assessment." *Journal of Library and Information Science* 10(1985): 170-182.

5. Archives

Afolabi, Michael. "Planning Factors Essential to the Establishment of University Archives." *African Journal of Academic Librrianship* 5(1987): 63-67.

"Archive Policy for French-speaking African Countries: Regional Seminar on Archives, Dakar, Senegal, 15 March to 9 April 1971." *Unesco Bulletin for Libraries* 26(1972): 84-87, 96.

Burke, Eric Edward. "Records Management in the Central African Archives." *Journal of the Society of Archivists* 1(1956): 62-66.

"Conference on the Problems of the Planning and Organization of Archives, Libraries and Documentation Centres in Africa, Abidjan [Ivory Coast], 11 to 17 September 1972." *Bibliography, Documentation, Terminology* 13(1973): 122-124.

Kamba, Angeline S., and Peter c. Mazikana. "Archive Repatriation in Southern Africa." *Information Development* 4(1988): 79-85.

Proceedings of the General Conference on the Planning of Archival Development in the Third World (Darkar [Senegal], 28-31 January 1975) / Actes de la Conférence Générale sur la Planicafication du Développement des Archives dans le Tier-monds. Edited by W. Lenz for International Council on Archives. München, Verlag Dokumentation, 1976.

6. Budget and Finance

Adedigba, Yakub A. "Budgeting in the Agricultural Libraries and Documentation Centres in Nigeria." *International Library Review* 20(1988): 215-226.

Angiating, Ashib Godwin. "An Evaluation of the Time and Cost of Copy and Original Cataloging in the University of Calabar [Nigeria] Library." *African Journal of Academic Librarianship* 4(1986): 18-25.

Boadi, B. Y., and P. Havard-Williams. "The Funding of Library and Information Services in West Africa." *International Library Review* 16(1984): 21-25.

Ehikhamenor, Fabian A. "Collection Development under Constraints." *Nigerian Library and Information Science Review* 1(1983): 42-56.

————. "Formula for Allocating Book Funds: the Search for Simplicity and Flexibility." *Libri* 33(1983): 148-161.

Gargett, Eric. "The Economics of Providing an African Library Service." *Rhodesian Librarian* 9(1977): 7, 24, 26, 28, 30.

Hüttemann, Lutz, ed. *Budgeting and Financial Planning: Papers and Proceedings of the Information Experts Meeting, 23-27 May 1983, Arusha, Tanzania.* Bonn, Deutsche Stiftung für Internationale Entwicklung, 1983.

Ifidon, Sam E. "Financial Support for West African University Libraries." *African Journal of Academic Librarianship* 5(1987): 21-25.

Kedem, Kosi A. "The Acquisition of Periodicals in a Foreign Exchange Starved Library: the Case of the Balme Library [University of Ghana]." *The Serials Librarian* 18(1990): 173-180.

Matanji, Peter. "The Problems of Journal Subscriptions and Possible Solution for the Academic and Research Libraries: Some Experiences from the University of Nairobi [Kenya]." *Maktaba* 11(1989): 5-9.

Nawe, Julita. "The Impact of a Dwindling Budget on Library Services in Tanzania." *Library Review* 37(1988): 27-32.

Nwafor, B. U. "Funding for University Libraries in the Third World." *Third World Libraries* 1(sum 1990): 23-27.

————. "Funding Third World University Libraries." Paper read in the Universities Library Section of IFLA, 1989.

Obiagwu, M. C. "Foreign Exchange and Library Collections in Nigeria." *Information Development* 3(1987): 154-160.

Ogundipe, O. O. "Sources of Funding: Problems and Issues." In *Management of Libraries in an Era of Scarce Resources: Proceedings of a Seminar, Benin University, Benin City, Nigeria, 18-20 June 1986,* edited by O. O. Gundipe, 15-29. Benin University, 1989.

Oluronsula, R., and E. O. Ajileye. "Periodical Retrenchment at the University of Ilorin Library [Nigeria]." *Library Review* 39(1990): 42-46.

Omoniwa, Moses A. "The 'Newer' Budgeting Techniques as Devices for Better Allocation of Resources in Nigerian Libraries." *Library Focus* 2(1984): 26-54.

Pankhurst, Rita. "Acquisitions Budget Strategy and its Implications in African University Libraries." *African Journal of Academic Librarianship* 1(1983): 21-29.

Phiri, Zilole M. K. "Book Budgets, Foreign Exchange Restrictions and their Impact on Collection Development in University, College, Technical and Research Libraries in Zambia: A Survey." *Zambia Library Association Journal* 15(1984): 30-50.

Samuel, Sarah. "The Relationship between the Organizational Placement and Budgeting in Some Selected Special Libraries in Zaria [Nigeria]." *Library Scientist* 12(1985): 124-131.

Umoh, P. N. "Financial Allocations, Budgeting Control and University Libraries." In *Management of Libraries in an Era of Scarce Resources: Proceedings of a Seminar, Benin University, Benin City, Nigeria, 18-20 June 1986,* edited by O. O. Agundipe, 83-94. Benin University, 1989.

7. Buildings and Furnishings

Aguolu, Christian Chukwunedu. "Problems of Physical Access to Nigerian University Libraries." *Bendel Library Journal* 3(1980): 9, 11-15.

Ahkidime, J. A. F. "The Librarian and Library Buildings in Nigeria." *NLA Newsletter* 63-64(Jl-Ag 1977): 3-6.

Amoikon, Michel K. *Structures, organisation et animation dans les bibliothèques en Côte d'Ivoire* (Buildings, Organization and Activities in Libraries in the Ivory Coast). Bordeaux, Agence de Cooperation culturelle et Technique, Ecole Internationale de Bordeaux, S. F. A. C., 1976.

Amosu, Margaret. "On the Planning of a New [Medical] Library." *Nigerian Libraries* 10(1974): 141-147.

Egbor, A. A. "Airconditioning and the Tropical University Library." Paper read at the Seminar on University Library Architecture, 30-31 May 1980, Ahmadu Bello University, Zaria, Nigeria.

Harvard-Williams, Peter, and J. E. Jengo. "Library Design and Planning in Development Countries." *Libri* 37(1987): 160-176.

Holdsworth, Harold. "Library Buildings in Newly Developing Countries." *Library Trends* 8(1959): 278-290.

Kwasitsu, Lishi. "The University of Calabar [Nigeria] Definitive Library Buildings: History and Future Development." *Libri* 35(1985): 218-226.

Loveday, Anthony J. "Zambia—an Experiment in Open Plan Librarianship." *Focus on International & Comparative Librarianship* 5(1974): 19-20.

Nwafor, B. U. "Adaptations of Buildings to University Library Use: a View from the Third World." In *Adaptations of Buildings to Library Use ...* edited by Michael Dewe, 190-198. Saur, 1987.

————. "Issues and Problems in the Preparation for the Planning and Design of University Library Buildings in the Developing Countries." In *Library Buildings: Preparations for Planning. Proceedings of the Seminar Held in Aberystwyth [Wales], 10-14 August 1987,* edited by M. Dewe, 208-214. München, Saur, 1989.

————. "The Spine or the Heart: the University of Jos in Search of a Library Building Model." *College & Research Libraries* 42(1981): 447-455.

Nwafor, B. U., and K. Mahmud, eds. *Tropical Library Architecture: the Proceedings of a Seminar Held 30-31 May 1980 at Ahmadu Bello University, Zaria, Nigeria.* Zaria, Kashim Ibrahim Library, Ahmadu Bello University for Committee of University Librarians of Nigerian Universities, 1985.

Nwali, L. O. "Librarians Participation in the Abubakar Tafawa Balewa University New Library Buildings [Bauchi, Nigeria]." *International Library Review* 22(1990): 283-298.

Nwamefor, Raphel Chianumba. "Nigerian Studies: Planning Library Buildings for Nigerian Universities." *International Library Review* 7(1975): 67-76.

Nwoye, S. C. "University of Nigeria, Nsukka, Building Brief for the Proposed New Library Building at Nsukka." *Nigerian Libraries* 17(1981): 36-47.

Oni-Orisan, B. A. "Library Accommodation: Standards and Realities." In *Management of Libraries in an Era of Scarce Resources: Proceedings of a Seminar, Benin University, Benin City, Nigeria, 18-20 June 1986,* edited by O. O. Ogundipe, 73-82. Benin University, 1989. First published in *African Journal of Academic Librarianship* 5(1987): 5-11.

Ozowa, V. N. "Planning University Library Buildings in Nigeria." *International Library Review* 20(1988): 375-386.

Packman, J. "Planning of New Library Buildings for University Ife, Designed Arieh Sharon: Notes on Ife University Library." *Nigerian Libraries* 3(1967): 96-98.

Plumbe, Wilfred J. "Ahmadu Bello University. Programme for Library Building, Zaria [Nigeria] Site, 4 October 1963." Brief to the architect.

————. "Climate as a Factor in the Planning of University Library Buildings In his *Tropical Librarianship,* [18]-28. Metuchen, N. J., Scarecrow Press, 1987. First published in *Unesco Bulletin for Libraries* 17, no. 6(1963).

————. "Federal University of Technology, Makurdi [Brief to the Architects for the University Library Building on the Permanent Site, June 1983]." In his *Tropical Librarianship,* [122]-141. Metuchen, N. J., Scarecrow Press, 1987.

————. "Furniture and Equipment in Tropical Libraries." In his *Tropoical Librarianship,* [29]-36. Metuchen, N. J., Scarecrow Press, 1987. First published in *Unesco Bulletin for Libraries* 15, no. 5(Sep/Oct 1961).

————. "University of Malawi." Brief to the architect, discussed at a meeting on March 4, 1966.

Roda, Jean-Claude. "Le nouveau bâtiment de la bibliothèque du Centre universitaire de la Réunion" (The New Building of the University Center Library, Réunion). *Bulletin des bibliothèques de France* 21(1976): 329-335. "Erratum": 538-539.

Rousset de Pena, Jean. "Construction of Libraries in Tropoical Countries." *Unesco Bulletin for Libraries* 15(1961): 263-270.

————. "La nouvelle bibliothèque centrale de l'Université de Dakar [Senegal]" (The New Central Library of the University of Dakar). *Bulletin de bibliothèques de France* 11(1966): 293-304.

Zeine, Ramsey. "The Need to Reconsider Basic Factors Affecting the Design of University Libraries." Paper read at the Seminar on University Library Architecture, Ahmadu Bello University, Zaria, Nigeria, 30-31 May 1980.

8. Communications Internally

Adedeji, C. Folasade. "Communication among Staff in a Library." *Nigerian Libraries* 10(1974): 57-62.

Dramé, Cheick Oumar. "La société moderne africaine au sud du Sahara: quelques problèmes et perspectives de développement de la communication documentaire dan les services de bibliothèque" (Modern African Society South of the Sahara: Some Problems and Perspectives of Developing Documentary Communications within Library Services." *Libri* 33(1985): 348-362.

Igwe, Paul O. E. "Overcoming Communication Barriers in a Multi-campus Teaching Hospital through the Use of Two-way Radio: a Nigerian Example." *Bendel Library Journal* 7(1984): 8-19.

Wamulwange, Margaret s. "Informal Communication—a Feasible Alternative in Zambia?" *Zambia Library Association Journal* 17(1985): 19-30.

9. Computers and Information Service

Borchardt, Peter, ed. *Gestion des Services d'Information, Rapport d'un stage realisé a Kigali [Rwanda] 20-31 octobre, 1986* (Management of Information Services, Report of a Training Program Carried out at Kigali...). Bonn, Kigali, German Foundation for International Development and Organisation for the Management and Development of the Kagera River Basin, 1987.

Cooney, Sean. "Criteria for a User-oriented Cost-effective Information Service: an Analysis of the East African Literature Service." *Special Libraries* 65(1974): 517-526.

Eyitazo, Adekunle O. "Status Report on the Attitude of Automated Library System Vendors to Investing in Nigeria." *Program* 23(1989): 247-256.

Fajemirokun, F. A. "Establishing an African Data Bank." In *Proceedings of the International Symposium on Management of Geodetic Data, Copenhagen, Denmark, 24-26 Aug 1981*, 50-57. Copenhagen, Geodetic Institute, 1981.

Fenn, Tom, et al. "Guidelines for Establishing Automated Libraries in Developing Countries." *Computers in Libraries* 10(1990): 21-28.

Hüttemann, Lutz, ed. *Establishment and Management of a National Information Service in Botswana, Workshop Papers, Gaberone, 23-27 February 1987*. Bonn, Gaberone, German Foundation for International Development and Botswana National Library Service, 1987.

Igwe, Paul O. E. "The Electronic Age and Libraries: Present Problems and Future Prospects." *International Library Rekview* 18(1986): 75-84.

Mg'andu, Bathesheba. "The 1984 DSE/ESAMI Workshop on Management of Information Services: an Appraisal." *Zambia Library Association Journal* 16(1984): 13-29.

Musana, A., J. N. Kiyimba, and L. Hüttemann, eds. *Management of Information Services: Workshop Papers, Arusha [Tanzania], 11-22 April 1988*. Bonn, Arusha, Kigali [Rwanda], German Foundation for International Development, Eastern and Southern African Management Institute, and Organisation for the Management and Development of the Kagera River Basin, 1988.

N'Jie, B. K. "Management of Technological Change with Focus on Automation." *Information Development* 4(1989): 259-282.

Olorunsola, R. "A Case for the Application of Computers in Nigerian Libraries." *Library Scientist* 13(1986): 46-54.

Olukolade, Olushola Anthony. "Difference between a Data Base Management System and an Information System." Master's thesis, University of Pittsburgh, 1980.

Pakkiri, Devi. "Plans to Computerize UZ [University of Zimbabwe] Library Services: Prospects and Problems." *Zimbabwe Librarian* 20(1988): 61-63.

Shayne, Mette. "Computerised Data Searching for the African Scholar." *African Research & Documentation* 43(1987): 8-15.
Timami, Soud, ed. *Establishment of Information Services.* Nairobi, Kenya, 1977. (CRIT series 5/77)
Were, Jacinta. "Problems of Automating Libraries in a Developing Country: Kenya." In *Training Workshop on Use of Computers in Information Handling: a Report,* edited by Lutz Hütteman, 97-103. DSE [German Foundation for International Development], 1986.

10. Cooperation

Aboyade, 'Bimpe. "Building Collection through Exchange—the Ibadan University Experience." *Nigerian Libraries* 5(1969): 69-73.
Adedigba, Yakub A. "The Design of a Local Network for the Agricultural Research Libraries in Ibadan, Nigeria." *Nigerian Library and Information Science Review* 2(1984): 13-27.
Adekunle, W. A. O. "Library Cooperation in Nigeria: the Role of National Library." *Nigerbiblios* 3(1978): 10-11, 14-15, 22.
Adeyemi, Nat M. "Cooperation among Libraries in Nigeria: a Pilot Study." Ph. D. thesis, University of Pittsburgh, 1975.
Aje, S. B. "Cooperative Acquisition in Nigeria. In *Resource Sharing of Libraries in Developing Countries: Proceedings of the 1977 IFLA/ Unesco Presession Seminar for Librarians from Developing Countries, Antwerp University, August 30- September 4, 1977,* edited by H. D. L. Vervliet, 24-32. Munich, K. G. Saur, 1979.
Alemna, A. A., and I. K. Antwi. "Library Cooperation Practices of Univerities in Ghana." *International Library Review* 22(1990): 273-282.
Antwi, I. K. "Co-operation and Resource Sharing among Nigerian Libraries." *International Library Movement* 6(1984): 124-136.
Banjo, A. O. "Library Resource Sharing: Shared Approach to Using Information." In *Management of Libraries in an Era of Scarce Resources: Proceedings of a Seminar, Benin University, Benin City, Nigeria, 18-20 June 1986,* edited by O. O. Agundipe, 58-72. Benin University, 1989.
Batubo, F. B. "Library Co-operation." *International Library Review* 20(1988): 517-532.
Boadi, Benzies Y. "Regional Library Cooperation for Development in Africa." *IFLA Journal* 10(1984): 370-376.
Bujra, Abdalla S. "Meeting on Setting up Networks of African Research Institutes on Research Information, Dakar [Senegal], 1-3 December, 1978." In *Report: Consultative Meeting on Information Needs ...* prepared by Francis K. Inganji and T. Moeller, 46-51. Nairobi [Kenya], Coordinating Centre for Regional Information Training (CRIT), 1979.
Dikko, I. "Cooperative Acquisitions: A Model for Nigeria." Paper submitted to the National Library of Nigeria's Advisory Committee on Library Cooperation, 1976.
Dipeolu, J. O. "Sharing Resources among African University Libraries—Some Problems and Solutions." *African Journal of Academic Lilbrarianship* 2(1984): 44-47.

El Hadi, M. "Feasibility of Establishing Network and Clearinghouse Activities." In *Official Report of the African Seminar for Librarians and Documentalists of Administrative Information Services,* prepared by E. S. Asiedu, 60-101. 1975.

Esezobor, J. E. "Regional or Institutional Cooperation: Which is Better?" *Nigerian Libraries* 12(1976): 61-63.

Harrison, Albert. "Cooperative Acquisition and the National Bookstock." *Rhodesian Librarian* 4(1972): 37-38, 40.

Inoti, Virginia I., and Peter Matanji. "Interlending and Document Supply in Kenya." *Information Development* 6(1990): 158-162.

Jegede, Oluremi. "The Possibility of Cooperative Acquisition of Legal Materials among Some Libraries in the City of Lagos [Nigeria]." *International Journal of Law Libraries* 3(1975): 197-207.

Johnson, Norman. "Library Co-operation [in Central Africa]." *Library Association of Central Africa Newsletter* 5,2(Apr 1965): 24-30; 5,3(Je 1965): 36-43.

————. The Relevance of New Techniques to Interlibrary Cooperation, with Special Reference to Computerized Joint Catalogues and Tulex Communication." *Rhodesian Librarian* 42(1972): 40-46.

Kibirige, Harry M. *Local Area Networks in Information Management.* Greenwood Press, 1989.

Kufa, J. C. "Problems of Resource Sharing in Developing Countries." *Zimbabwe Librarian* 21(1989): 40-41.

Kwalo, Mrs. S. A. "Planning Interlending Systems for Developing Countries: a View from Zambia." *Interlending Review* 9(1981): 4-6.

Lor, Peter J. "The Southern African Interlending Scheme: Some Results of a Comprehensive Survey." *Interlending & Document Supply* 15(1987): 101-107.

Lwanga, T. K. "Inter-library Cooperation in East Africa: Initial Stages to Formal Cooperation." *EALA Bulletin* 13(Jy 1972): 5-16. First published in *Focus on International & Comparative Librarianship* 2(1971): 5-11.

Made, S. H. *Project on Resource Sharing in Southern and Central Africa: Feasibility Study (Part 1 and 2).* Unesco, 1988.

Mvula, H. S. T. "Interlibrary Loans in Malawi: The Case of University of Malawi Libraries—Situation and Proposals." *MALA Bulletin* 4(1986): 30-36.

Ngwenya, A. M. L. "Cooperation in Book Acquisition." *Zimbabwe Librarian* 20(1988): 8, 10-14.

Nwafor, B. U. "The Costs of Interlending and Document Supply." Paper read at the IFLA Pre-session Seminar, 1989.

Nwoye, S. C. "Library Co-operation: Some Proposals for Organization in Nigeria." *Nigerian Libraries* 1(1964): 119-124..

————. "Planning Interlibrary Systems for Developing Countries: A View from Nigeria." *Interlending Review* 8(1980): 116-118.

Obokoh, N. P. "Other Libraries' Books in our Campuses—The Forgotten Aspect of Library Cooperation: The University of Port Harcourt [Nigeria] Pioneering Effort." *Bendel Library Journal* 6(1983): 82-90.

Odeinde, T. Olabisi. "Towards Effective Library Cooperation in Nigeria: Cooperative Acquisitions." *Nigerian Libraries* 12(1976): 55-60.

Ofori, A. G. T. "Library Cooperation in Ghana: The Public Libraries Point of View." *Ghana Library Journal* 1(1964): 60.

Oguara, E. T. A. "Cooperative Cataloguing." *Nigerian Libraries* 12(1976): 83-88.

Omolayole, O. O. "Co-operative Acquisition Scheme in Nigeria—A Progress Report." *Lagos Librarian* 9(1982): 48-58.

Otike, J. N. "The Concept of Co-operation and Its Implications to Research Libraries in Kenya." *Maktaba* 11(1989): 28-37.

――――――. "Resource Sharing in Special Libraries: the Kenyan Experience." *Collection Management* 12(1990): 153-166.

Qobose, Edwin N. "Interlibrary Lending in Botswana: Practices, Problems and Prospects." *Interlending & Document Supply* 18(1990): 12-17.

"Recommendations Made for Library Cooperation in Ghana." *Law Library Journal* 54(1961): 237-238.

Seriki, T. A. B. "Problems of Interlibrary Cooperation among Nigerian Medical Libraries." *Special Libraries* 64(1973): 566-570.

Sheriff, G. M. *Resource Sharing in West Africa: Some Implications for the Development of National Information Policies.* 1977. ERIC. ED 176 764.

Sorieul, Françoise. "La coopération interbibliothèques en Afrique: Resultats d'une enquête de prospective" (Interlibrary Cooperation in Africa: Results of a Survey). *Argus* 12(1983): 119-123.

Tawete, Felix K. *The Need for Resource Sharing in Tanzania.* 1977. ERIC. ED 176 760.

Uba, D. E. "Library Cooperation in Nigeria." *Nigerian Libraries* 11(1975): 213-220.

――――――. "Library Cooperation in Technical Services in Nigeria." *Nigerian Libraries* 8(1972): 163-175.

Varley, Douglas Harold. "University Library Co-operation in Tropical Africa: the Leverhulme Library Conference, Salisbury, 1964." *Libri* 15(1965): 64-71.

Wise, M. C. "Library Cooperation in East Africa." *East African Library Association Bulletin* 10(1968): 16-21.

Young, Mrs. R. D. E. "University Library Co-operation." *Ghana Library Journal* 1(1964): 56.

11. Legislation

Abidi, S. A. H. *Public Library Laws in East Africa: Comparative Analysis.* Kampala [Uganda], 1982. mimeograph.

Bagrova, I. Y. "Natsional'nye biblioteki razvivayushchikhsya stran: voprosy zakonodatel'nogo obespecheniya" (National Libraries of Developing Countries: Questions of Legislation). *Bibliotekevodenie i Bibliografia za Rubezhom* 111(1987): 3-17.

Bello, Nassir. "The Importance of Library Legislation: a Case of National Library of Nigeria." *Pakistan Library Bulletin* 22(1991): 1-4.

Boadi, B. Y., and Peter, Havard-Williams. "Legislation for Library and Information Services in Anglophone West Africa." *Libri* 33(1983): 9-21.

Knox-Hooke, S. A. "The Law Relating to Public Libraries in West Africa. a Comparative Study with the United Kingdom Public Library Laws." Thesis, Library Association, 1966.

Lajeunesse, Marcel, and Henri Sene. "Les problemes de législation en matiere de services de bibliotheque et d'information dans les pays africains d'expression francaise" (Legislative Problems in the Field of Library and Information Services in French-speaking Africa). *Libri* 34(1984): 271-288.

Umo, Margaret G. "A Survey of Legal Deposit Laws in Nigeria." *Library Focus* 4(1986): 1-21.

12. Middle Management

Ochai, Adakole. "Management Development Needs of Lower and Middle Managers in University Libraries in Nigeria." *Dissertation Abstracts International* 46(1985): 827-A.

13. Personnel

Abodunde, E. O. "The Annual Performance Evaluation Report." *Nigerbiblios* 4(1979): 13-16.

Adelabu, Adedeji. "Personnel Problems in Nigerian University Libraries: In Search of a Realistic Solution." *International Library Review* 3(1971): 355-363.

Adeniyi, Chris Ishola. "Personnel Problems in Nigerian University Libraries." Master's thesis, Loughborough University of Technology, 1983.

Agada, John. "The Search for an Appropriate Level of Training for Practising Libraries in Developing Countries: The Nigerian Experience." *Journal of Librarianship* 17(1985): 31-48.

Aguolu, Christian Chukwunedu. "Staffing in Nigerian University Libraries." *Herald of Library Science* 29(1990): 24-37.

Akinyotu, Adetunji. "Scientific Job Allocation and Staff Deployment in Libraries: A Necessary Step towards Professional Recognition." *Nigerian Libraries* 10(1974): 131-140.

Aladejana, Adebisi. "Scientific Management: Staff Performance Appraisal Techniques." *Nigerian Libraries* 11(1975): 55-63.

Ampitan, Edwards J. "A Survey of Professional Opinion on Academic Status of Librarians in Nigerian Universities." *Library Focus* 5(1987): 99-109.

Antwi, I. K., and L. O. Nwali. "Staff Development of Librarians: The Case of the Abubakar Tafawa Balewa University Library, [Bauchi] Nigeria." *Library Management* 11(1990): 30-34.

Asiagodo, G. D. "Staff Development for the Professional Staff of a University Library: The Case of the Balme Library, University of Ghana." *Ghana Library Journal* 7(Nov 1989): 15-21.

Bozimo, Doris Oritsewenyimi. "Paraprofessional to Professional Status: One Assessment of the 'Ladder Principle'." *Education for Information* 1(1983): 335-344. Also published in *Library Scientist* 10(1983): 120-139.

Bozimo, Doris O., and Abudullohi Mohammed. "BLS [Bachelor of Library Science] Product and the Job Market in Nigeria: an Analysis of the Job Advertisements." *African Journal of Academic Librarianship* 5(1987): 45-49.

Darch, Colin. "The Status of Professional Librarians in African Universities." *International Library Review* 7(1975): 497-502.

Dean, John. "Training and Management for Library Personnel: Professional Education in Nigeria." *Nigerian Libraries* 2(1966): 67-74.

Edoka, B. E. "Staff Recruitment in Libraries: The Nigerian Situation." *International Library Review* 11(1979): 93-104.

Ene, Ngozi. "Status and Role of the Public Librarian." *Nigerian Libraries* 15(1979): 64-74.

Farid, M. *The Development of Information Manpower Resource.* 1982, ERIC. ED 235 833.

Harrison, Kalu U., and Peter Havard-Williams. "Motivation in a Third World Library System." *International Library Review* 19(1987): 249-260.

Hunter, Lucilda. "The Recruitment and Training of Middle-level Manpower in the Public Library Service." *Sierra Leone Library Journal* 3(1977): 3, 5-6.

Hüttemann, Lutz, ed. *Manpower Training Needs: Proceedings and Papers of the Information Experts Meeting, Harare [Zimbabwe], 18-21 March 1985.* Bonn, German Foundation for International Development, 1985.

Kelly, M. J. F. "Computer Utilisation and Staffing in Zambia: A Survey Conducted in Late 1986." *Information Development* 2(1987): 283-292.

Mabomba, Rodrick S. "Manpower Training Requirements for Library and Information Service in Malawi: A Survey Report." *MALA Bulletin* 3(1982): 13-18.

Newa, John M. "Academic Status for University Librarians in Tanzania: Challenges and Prospects." *Library Review* 38(1989): 19-35.

Nkereuwen, Edet E. "Issues in the Correlation between Job Performance, Job Attitudes and Work Behaviour among the Staff in Academic Libraries." *African Journal of Academic Librarianship* 4(1986): 10-17.

————. "Issues on the Relationship between Job Satisfaction, Job Attitudes and Work Behaviour among the Staff in Academic Libraries." *Information Services & Use* 10(1990): 281-291.

Nwafor, B. U. "A Comparative Analysis of Selected Advertisements for Senior Staff Positions in Nigerian Academic Libraries." *Nigerian Libraries* 9(1973): 67-73.

————. "Staff Development in Nigerian Libraries." In *Aspects of African Librarianship: A Collection of Writings,* compiled and edited by Michael Wise, 166-181. Mansell, 1985.

Nwagha, Georgiana K. N. "Deployment of Professional Librarians: A Barrier to the Availability of Publications in a Developing Country." *College & Research Libraries* 44(1983): 168-172.

Nzotta, Briggs C. "A Comparative Study of the Job Satisfaction of Nigerian Librarians." *International Library Review* 19(1987): 161-173.

————. "Factors Associated with the Job Satisfaction of Male and Female Librarians in Nigeria." *Library & Information Science Review* 7(1985): 75-84.

Ochai, Adakole. "The Generalist versus the Subject Specialist Librarian: A Critical Choice for Academic Library Directors in Nigeria." *International Library Review* 23(1991): 111-120.

Ogunrombi, Sam A. "Faculty Status for Professional Librarians: A Survey of Nigerian University Libraries." *International Librasry Review* 23(1991): 135-140.

Ogunsheye, F. A. "New Proposals for Structure of Library Personnel and Curricula for the Various Levels or Categories." Paper presented at the Colloquium on Education and Training for Librarianship in Nigeria, University of Ibadan, Nigeria, 15-19 March 1974. mimeographed.

Okoro, Okechukwu M. "Prejudice and Change in Librarianship: A Critique of Library Recruitment Policies in Nigeria." *International Library Review* 23(1991): 1-9.

Oloko, Beatrice Adenike. "Some Correlates of Client Evaluation of Public Library Employees in Nigeria." *Libri* 31(1981): 95-107.

Oluwakuyide, Akinola. "Status: the Problem of Nigerian Librarians." *Special Libraries* 62(1971): 283-286.

Onyechi, Nnamdi I. "Full Academic Status for Nigerian University Librarians through the Divisional Library/Subject Specialist Plan." *Libri* 25(1975): 183-198.

Onyeonwu, Winifred. "Personnel Problems of Library Boards." *Bendel Library Journal* 1(1978): 11-14.

Osundina, Oyeniyi. "Academmic Status for University Librarians in Nigeria: What it Takes." *Nigerian Libraries* 8(1972): 117-122.

Osundwa, J. N. "Designing a Curriculum for In-service Training of Library Administration Course for Library Assistants in Special Libraries in Kenya." In *Designing a Curriculum for the Training through Refresher Courses of Qualified Library Assistants ... Kenya Library Association, 23-31.* Nairobi, Coordinating Centre for Regional Information Training (CRIT), 1978.

Plumbe, Wilfred J. "Staff Education and Training in African University Libraries." In his *Tropoical Librarianship, 55-72.* Metuchen, NJ, Scarecrow Press, 1987. First published in *Northern Nigeria Library Notes* 2/3(1964-65): 131-148.

_____. "Salary Scales and Recruitment for Librarianship in Nigeria." *WALA News* 2(1958): 157-163.

Rosenberg, Diana, and Brigid O'Connor. "Training at the Grassroots: An Integrated Approach to Training Library Assistants in Southern Sudan." *Information Development* 4(1988): 14-20.

Urquidi, J. "Status of Librarians [Report of a Conference Held at Dakar, Senegal]." *IFLA Journal* 3(1977): 384-386.

Wina, Danson K. "Academic Status for Academic Librarians: The Zambian Experience." *Zambia Library Association Journal* 17(1985): 49-63.

14. Planning

Adediran, 'Fola. "Design and Operation of Reference Systems in Libraries and Information Centres." *Nigerian Libraries* 9(1973): 51-55.

Aderinto, Mosebolatan Adeoye. "Centralised Technical Services Procedures in Oyo State [Nigeria] State Polytechnic Libraries: Ibadan Polytechnic Experience." Master's thesis, Loughborough University of Technology, 1983.

Affia, George B. "Library Development Planning: The Case of Nigeria." In *Aspects of Library Development Planning,* edited by J. S. Parker,s 225-235. Mansell, 1983.

_____. "The University of Port Harcourt [Nigeria] Library: An Idea for its Growth and Development." *African Journal of Academic Librarianship* 1(1983): 73-76.

Alegbeleye, Bunmi. "Disaster Control Planning in Nigeria." *Journal of Librarianship* 22(1990): 91-106.

Amoa, Kwame. "Some Aspects of the Problem of Information Requirements for Development Planning in Africa." In *Report: Consultative Meeting on Information Needs,* prepared by Francis K. Inganji and T. Moeller, 54-59. Nairobi [Kenya], Coordinating Centre for Regional Information Training (CRIT), 1979.

Benge, Ronald Charles, and E, A, Olden. "Planning Factors in the Development of LIbrary Education in English-speaking Black Africa.' *Journal of Librarianship* 13(1981): 203-222.

Bourne, Charles. *Planning for a National Research Information Center. United Republic of Tanzania.* Paris, Unesco, 1975.

Broome, E. Max. "The Organization and Planning of Library Development in AFrica." *Unesco Bulletin for Libraries* 25(1971): 246-251.

Camara, Alioune Badara. "Implementing an Information Strategy for Sub-Saharan Africa: The First Stages." *Information Development* 6(1990): 55-61.

Communication Planning. Washington, DC, Academy for Educational Development, Clearinghouse on Development Communication, 1978. ERIC. ED 163 1976. Focus on West Africa.

Conférence sur les Problèmes de la Planification et de l'Organisation des Archives, Bibliothèques et Centres de Documentation en Afrique (Conference on the Problems of Planning and Organization of Archives, Libraries and Documentation Centers in Africa). Dakar [Senegal], Association Internationale pour le Développement de la Documentation des Bibliothèques, et des Archives en Afrique, 1972.

De Heer, A. N. "Rural Library Service Project: Draft Proposal." *Zambia Library Association Journal* 9(1977): 1-6.

Development of Public Libraries in Africa: the Ibadan [Nigeria] Seminar. Paris, Unesco, 1954.

Dim, Peter Tarzomon. "National Development Plans and the Integration of Library Planning in a Developing Country: Nigeria as a Case Study." Ph. D. thesis, Loughborough University of Technology, Dept. of Library and Information Studies, 1983.

Elmaki, Laila Ibrahim A. "Planning Library and Information Services in Developing Countries, with Special Reference to the Sudan Public and School Libraries." Master's thesis, Loughborough University of Technology, Dept. of Library and Information Studies, 1983.

Gehrke, Ulrich. "Information for Development: Some Problems of National Co-ordination, Regional Co-operation and International Assistance." *INSPEL* 19(1985): 166-198.

_____. *Kenya: Planning for a National Information and Documentation System.* Paris, Unesco, 1975.

Haeringer, Danielle. *Documentation et planification au Gabon* (Documentation and Planning in Gabon). Gabon, Ministère de la Planification du Développement et des Pakrticipations, Commissariat Général au Plan, Direction des Projets, 1981.

Igwe, Ukoha O. "Planning Library Extension Service in Nigeria." *Library Scientist* 13(1986): 19-34.

Ilomo, Charles S. "Practice, Experience and Lessons of Library Development Planning in Tanzania." In *Aspects of Library Development Planning*, edited by J. S. Parker, 236-255. Mansell, 1983.

Istasi, Cecile Wesley. "Planning Guidelines for a National Scientific and Technical Information System in the Sudan." Ph. D. thesis, University of Pittsburgh, 1976.

Kaungamno, Ezekiel. "A National Plan for the Development of Library Services." *EALA Bulletin* 14(Sep 1974): 7-24.

Lundu, Maurice Chimfwembie. "Information Services and Activities in the Eastern, Central and Southern African Region: The Next Five (5) Years." In *1984: Challenges to an Information Society: Proceedings of the 47th ASIS Annual Meeting, Philadelphia, Pennsylvania, October 21-25, 1984*, compiled by Barbara Flood and others, 90-91. Published for the American Society for Information Science. Knowledge Industry Publishers, 1984.

Lwanga, T. K. "A Brief Note on the Development of Library Services in Uganda: The Need for Coordination." *Ugandan Libraries* (special issue) March 1975: 75-79.

Mohrhardt, F. E., and C. V. Penna. "National Planning for Library and Information Services." *Advances in Librarianship* 5(1975): 61-106. Includes Nigeria.

Msuya, Jangawe. "Planning and Automation of Libraries in Development Countries: A Systems Analysis Approach." *Library Review* 39(1990): 29-32.

Mwasha, A. Z. *Some Considerations for the Planning of Village Libraries in Tanzania.* 1979. ERIC ED 220 084.

Odini, Cephas. "Library Planning with Special Reference to Developing Countries." *Library Review* 38(1989): 42-52.

————. "Planning for Public Library Development in Development Countries with Special Reference to African Countries." *Libri* 40(1990): 33-48.

Ononogbo, Raphael U. "Implementing a National Scientific and Technological Information System in Nigeria: Actions and Inputs Needed." *Nigerian Library and Information Science Review* 2(1984): 89-108.

Pala, Francis Otieno. *The Seychelles: Reorganization and Development of Libraries, Museums and Archives.* Paris, Unesco, 1977.

Penna, C. V. *Planning of Library and Documentation Services.* 2d ed. Rev. and enl. by P. H. Sewell and Herman Liebaers. Paris, Unesco, 1970.

Phiri, Zilole M. K. "Groundwork for Implementing AACR2 in the University of Zambia (UNZA) Library." *Zambia Library Association Journal* 17(1985): 31-38, 64-71.

"Planning Documentation and Library Networks in Africa." *Unesco Bulletin for Libraries* 30(1976): 306-307.

Report on Use of Information and Documentation for Planning and Decision Making. A Seminar Held by NIR [National Institut of Development and Cultural Research] and the German Foundation for International Development (DSE), Gabarone [Botswana], 1-5 Sep 1980. Editor: Francis Inganji. Gabarone, University College of Botswana, 1981.

Shio, Martin J. "The use of Information for Planning and Decision Making." In *Report on Use of Information ... Gabarone, 1-5 Sep 1980,* edited by Francis Inganji, 8-16. Gaberone, University College of Botswana, 1981.

Symposium on Documentation Planning in Developing Countries at Bad Godesberg, 28-30 November 1967. Bonn, German Foundation for Development Countries, Central Documentation, 1967.

"Unesco Organized a Meeting of Experts on Planning Documentation and Library Networks in Africa (NATIS) at Brazzaville (People's Republic of the Congo), from 5 to 10 July 1973 [i.e. 1976]." *Bibliography, Documentation, Terminology* 16(1976): 229.

Womboh, Simmons H. "A Plan for the Development of Selected Technological University Libraries in Nigeria." *Collection Management* 8(1986): 79-99.

15. Preservation and Maintenace

Badu, Edwin Ellis. "The Preservation of Library Materials: A Case Study of University of Science and Technology in Ghana." *Aslib Proceedings* 42(1990): 119-125.

Ezennia, Steve E. "The Harmattan [dry dusty wind from the Sahara] and Library Resources Management in Nigeria: An Appraisal of the Effects, Problems and Prospects." *Library & Archival Security* 9(1989): 43-48.

Ogundipe, O. O. *Conservation of Library Material in Tropical Conditions. The Example of Nigeria.* 1980. ERIC. ED 211 037.

Plumbe, Wilfred J. *The Preservation of Books in Tropical & Subtropical Countries.* Kuala Lumpur, Oxford University Press, 1964.

_____. "Preservation of Library Materials in Tropical Countries." *Library Trends* 8(1959): 291-306.

_____. "Storage and Preservation of Books, Periodicals and Newspapers in Tropical Climates: A Select Bibliography." *Unesco Bulletin for Libraries* 12(1958): 156-162. Also issued as a separate by Unesco.

Talabi, J. K. "Maintenance Needs of Educational Equipment in Nigeria." *Journal of Education Television* 12(1986): 49-53.

16. Public Libraries

Antwi, I. K. "The National Library of Nigeria: A Case Study of the Bauchi State Branch." *Aslib Proceedings* 42(1990): 127-135.

Dikko, I. "The Library Board and Public Library Services." Paper delivered at NLA [Nigerian Library Association] Borno State Annual Conference, Maiduguri, 1982.

_____. "The Potential Users of the Public Library in Nigeria." A Conference paper delivered at the Plateau State Division of the Nigerian Library Association, Jos, 1979.

Egor, F. O. "A Preliminary Study of the Clientele Structure of Public Libraries: Bendel State Library, Benin City [Nigeria]." *Bendel Library Journal* 7(Je 1984): 46-57.

Ene, Ngozi. "The Operations of the Mobile Library Service, Bendel State Library [Nigeria]." *Bendel Library Journal* 1(1978): 14-17.

Giorgis, Kebreab W. "Planning and Organizing Public Libraries in Ethiopia for the Period 1975-2000." *Unesco Bulletin for Libraries* 30(1976): 78-82, 100.

Gwabin, John Nuhu. "User Satisfaction Survey of Kaduna State Library Services [Nigeria]." *Library Scientist* 13(1986): 71-78.

Igwe, P. O. E. "Institutional Libraries as Surrogates for Public Libraries: An Alternative Option for Developing Countries with Poor Public Library Systems." *Education Libraries Journal* 32(1989): 44-52.

Nzotta, Briggs C. "The Administration of Branch Libraries in a Developing Country: A Case Study [Nigeria]." *Public Library Quarterly* 9(1989): 47-60.

Ogunsheye, F. Adetowun. "Objectives and Standards of Practice for Public Libraries in West Africa, part 2 [with discussion]." In *Standards of Practice for West African Libraries,* edited by John Dean, 53-65. Ibadan, 1969.

Okorie, Kalu. "Objectives and Standards of Practice for Public Libraries in West Africa, part 1." In *Standards of Practice for West African Libraries,* edited by John Dean, 47-50. Ibadan, 1969.

Onyeonwu, Winifred O. "Organising Children's Book Club." *Bendel Library Journal* 2(1979): 49-54.

Otinkorang, Robert Adjei. "The Problem of Mobile Library Planning, Design, Construction and Development in Anglo-phone Countries with Particular Reference to Ghana." Master's thesis, Loughborough University of Technology, 1980.

17. Public Relations

Afolabi, Michael. "The Role of Exhibitions in Publicising University Libraries: A Nigerian Case Study [of Ahmadu Bello University]." *African Journal of Academic Librarianship* 4(1986): 57-64.

Ajibero, Matthew Idowu. "Public Relations and and Publicity in Nigerian Public Libraries." *Library Focus* 5(1987): 38-48.

Akinpelu, G. O. "Public Relations in University Libraries." *Bendel Library Journal* 3(1980): 24-28.

Kane, Kenneth. "Library Promotion." *MALA Bulletin* 5(1988): 38-49.

Onadiran, G. T., and R. W. Onadiran. "Nigerian University Library Services: Students Opinion." *Journal of Library and Information Science* 11(1986): 45-60.

Opubor, Alfred E. "Effective Public Relations and Presidential Democracy." *Bendel Library Journal* 3(1980): 33-39.

Osundina, Oyeniyi. "The University Library in Nigeria and the Need for Public Relations." *Nigerian Libraries* 5(1969): 55-61.

Qobose, Edwin Nkareng. "Library Promotion: Programmes in a Public Library." *Botswana Library Association Journal* 6(1984): 25-33.

18. Records Management

Muhenda, MKary Basaasa. "My Invaluable Experience in Current Records Management." *Records Management Journal* 2(1990): 15-20.

Nthunya, Emma. "Report on Records Management Seminar, Held at the Eastern and Southern African Management Institute (ESAMI), Arusha, Tanzania, from 18-30 Jan 1981." *Lesotho Books and Libraries* 2(1981): 13-17.

19. Rural Libraries

Adimorah, E. N. O. "Training for Rural Library and Community Information Centre Management." *Education for Information* 9(1991): 55-59.

Deboeck, G., and B. Kinsey. *Managing Information for Rural Development. Lessons from Eastern Africa.* 1980. (NTIS. PG83-247122)

International Workshop on Development and Dissemination of Appropriate Technologies in Rural Areas, Kumasi, Ghana, 1972. *Workshop Report.* Berlin, German Foundation for Developing Countries, Seminar Centre for Economic and Social Development, 1972.

Musana, A., and Lutz Hüttemann, eds. *Management of Agricultural Information Services, Course Material; Arusha 19-30 October 1987.* Bonn, Arusha, German Foundation for International Development and Eastern and Southern African Management Institute, 1988.

Naber, Gerrit. "Rehabilitating an Agricultural Library in Mozambique." *Information Development* 6(1990): 100-104.

Oruma, Oviss. "The Problem of Information Management in AGriculture." *Quarterly Bulletin of the International Association of Agricultural Librarians and Documentalists* 29(1984): 91-94.

Philip, Abraham. "Organization and Management of Rural Libraries." *Maktaba* 7 no. 2(1980): 45-50.

Sharr, F. A. "Functions and Organization of a Rural Library System." *Unesco Bulletin for Libraries* 26(1972): 2-7.

20. School Libraries

"The Administration of School Libraries." *Anambra State [Nigeria] School Libraries Association Bulletin* 10 no. 2(Dec 1981): 6-16.

Agunwa, C. O. "The Organsiation of Library Services for Primary Schools in Anambra State [Nigeria]." *Anambra/Imo States School Libraries Association Bulletin* 8(1979): 58-64.

Allen, Joan. *Organization of Small Libraries: A Manual for Educational Institutions in Tropical Countries.* London, Oxford University Press, 1961.

Dean, John. "Objectives of the College and School Library." *Nigerian Libraries* 5(1969): 78-82.

Elaturoti, D. F. "Management of Media Centres in Nigeria: The Abadina Media Resource Centre Experience." *Lagos Librarian* 9(1982): 77-80.

Fadero, Joseph Olantunji. "Objectives and Standards of Practice for School Libraries in West Africa." In *Standards of Practice for West African Libraries,* 69-81. Ibadan, 1969.

Jalloh, Mohammed Habid. "A School Library Service for Sierra Leone: A Proposal and Development Plan for the Establishment of School Library Resource Centres in Sierra Leone." Master's thesis, Loughborough University of Technology, 1980.

Mwacalimba, Hudwell. "Manpower Training and Provision for School Libraries." *Zambia Library Association Journal* 16(1984): 27-34.

Nwakoby, F. U. *Organizing Resource Centre Materials for Use.* Anambra/Imo States [Nigeria] School Libraries Association, 1977? (Occasional paper no. 111)

Nzotta, Briggs C. "Power and Authority in the Administration of College and Education Libraries in Nigeria." *African Journal of Academic Librarianship* 4(1986): 32-39.

Obokoh, N. P. "Alternative Revenue and Material Sources for Secondary School Libraries in Nigeria." *Library Focus* 3(1985): 50-61.

Ogunleye, Gabriel Olubunmi. "Manpower Aspects of Secondary School Libraries in the 6-3-3-4 Education System in Nigeria: The Case of Ondo State." *Library Review* 37 no. 4(1988): 28-34.

Otike, J. N. "Staffing Secondary School Libraries in Kenya." *Information Development* 4(1988): 98-102.

Sinnette, Elinor D. "Administration of the School Library in Nigeria." *Nigerian Libraries* 5(1969): 83-87.

Touchard, W. *Developing African Secondary School Libraries.* ERIC. ED 297 781.

21. Security and Vandalism

Antwi, I. K. "The Problem of Library Security: The Bauchi [Nigeria] Experience." *International Library Review* 21(1989): 363-372.

Nwamefor, Raphael Cianumba. "Security Problems of University Libraries in Nigeria." *Library Association Record* 76(1974): 2244-2245.

Okoye-Ikonta, Gabby I. "Book Thefts and Mutilation in Nigerian University Libraries." *Library Scientist* 8(1981): 89-100.

Olorunsola, Richard. "Crimes in Academic Libraries: University of Ilorin [Nigeria] Library Experience." *Library Scientist* 14(1987): 29-43.

Oluwakuyide, Akinola. "Noise in Libraries: Causes and Control." *Special Libraries* 65(1974): 28-31.

Onadiran, G. T. "Book Theft in University Libraries in Nigeria." *Archival Security* 8(1988): 37-48.

————. "Library Users as Security Problems in Africa." *International Library Movement* 8(1986): 37-43.

Thapisa, A. P. N. "Book Security Systems Administration at the University of Botswana Library." *Botswana Library Association Journal* 4(1982): 11-17.

22. Special Libraries or Materials

Agar, Janet. "The Department of Agriculture Library, Zambia." *Quarterly Bulletin of the International Association of Agricultural Librarians and Documentalists* 21(1976): 122-125.

Agyei-Gyane, L. "The Development and Aministration of the Africana Collection in the Balme Library, University of Ghana, Legon." *Libri* 37(1987): 222-238.

Ajewole, G. A. "Controlling the Objectives of the National Library [of Nigeria]." *Nigerbiblios* (1976): 20-21, 24.

Ali, S. Nazim. "Science and Technology Information Transfer in Developing Countries: Some Problems and Suggestions." *Journal of Information Science* 15(1989): 81-93.

————. "Serials Management in Developing Countries." *The Serials Librarian* 18(1990): 147-154.

Banjo, A. Olugboyega. "Problems in the Storage and Dissemination of Newspaper Information: a Nigerian Example." *INSPEL* 19(1985): 65-80.

Chantal, Jean de. "The Institute of Public Administration Library, Achimota, Ghana." *Canadian Library* 20(1963): 121-122.

Fatuyi, E. O. A. "The Plan, Design and Set-up of the Leather Research Institute of Nigeria (LERIN) Library." *Library Focus* 5(1987): 80-98.

Ifebuzor, Christopher C. "Centralization versus Decentralization of Law Libraries and Law Library Services in Nigerian Universities." *Law Library Journal* 80(1988): 605-617.

Kwong, Rosemary Ng Kee. "Communication Channels in the Access to and Transfer of Information from Research to Practice [in the Mauritius Sugar Industry Research Institute]." *Quarterly Bulletin of the International Association of Agricultural Librarians and Documentalists* 35(1990): 19-24.

Long, Nina P. "Twinning of Hospital Libraries—International Resource Sharing." *Bulletin of the Medical Library Association* 74(1986): 374-375.

McIlwane, I. C. "The Subject Organisation of Materials on Africa: An Overview of Recent Work." *African Research & Documentation* 46(1988): 17-30.

Mazikana, Peter C. "A Strategy for the Preservation of Audiovisual Materials." *Audiovisual Librarian* 14(1988): 24-28.

Mothae, B. D. "Basic Outline of the Administration and Management of Special Libraries in Lesotho—(Research in Progress)." *Lesotho Books and Libraries* 3(1982/1983): 14-15.

MpHepo, Swema. "Organising a Small Library: Telecommunications Library (Maselema) [Malawi]." *MALA Bulletin* 5(Dec 1989): 2-3.

Musisi, Jafred S. "Developing, Organization and the Working Process in Parliamentary Libraries in Eastern, Central and Southern Africa." In *Parlament und Bibliothek* 238-249. New York, Saur, 1986.

Nweke, Ken M. C. "Managing Information Resources in Nigerian Special Libraries." In *Information, Knowledge, Evolution: Proceedings of the 44th FID Congress, Helsinki, 28 August-1 September 1988,* edited by Sinikka Koshiala and Ritva Launo, 421-430. Amsterdam, Elsevier Science Publishers, 1989.

Ojo-Igbinoba, M. E. "The Role and Management of Newspapers in Nigerian University Libraries." *International Library Review* 23(1991): 83-90.

Okocha, Kingsley Ferewisky. "Effective Science and Technology Information Resources Management and the Role of Nigerian Agricultural Libraries in Food Production." *Quarterly Bulletin of the International Association of Agricultural Librarians and Documentalists* 35(1990): 25-30.

Okorafor, E. E. "Maintaining Local Newspaper Collections in Nigerian Libraries." *Information Development* 3(1987): 161-166.

Omondi, Washington A. "Problems in Collection and Preservation of Music Data in Kenya and Suggested Solutions to the Problems." *Fontes Artis Musicae* 33(1986): 108-117.

Osiobe, Stephen A. "A Study of the Use of Information Sources by Medical Faculty Staff in Nigerian Universities." *Journal of Information Science* 12(1986): 177-183.

Parker, J. Stephen. "Developing Information Systems in the Water and Sanitation Sector." *Information Development* 6(1990): 215-222. [Includes Uganda, Ethiopia, Tanzania]

Rooke, Andrew, and A. Msiska. *Problems with the Acquisition and Bibliographic Control of Official Documents and their Accessibility to Citizens and Researchers: the University of Zambia Library Experience.* 1980. ERIC. ED 208 803.

Schüller, Dietrich. "Handling, Storage and Preservation of Sound Recordings under Tropical and Subtropical Climatic Conditions." *Fontes Artis Musicae* 33(1986): 100-104.

Shio, Martin J. "Management of Information in Government." In *Report on Use of Information ... Gabarone, 1-5 Sep 1980,* edited by Francis Inganji, 26-35. Gaberone, University College of Botswana, 1981.

Stout, Dorothy L. "Preparing a Kenyan Field Guide." In *Frontiers in Geoscience Information: Proceedings of the Twenty-fourth Meeting of the Geoscience Information Society, November 6-9, 1989, St. Louis, Missouri,* edited by Mary B. Ansari, 209-212. Geoscience Information Society, 1990.

Thomsen, P. "The Establishment of a Library Service to Visually Handicapped People in African Developing Countries." *IFLA Journal* 11(1985): 36-42.

Utor, J. K. "The Use of Research Libraries in Zaria [Nigeria]: Two Case Studies." *Library Scientist* 13(19868): 56-70.

Walsh, Gretchen. "African Language Materials: Challenges and Responsibilities in Collection Management." In *Africana Resources and Collections,* edited by Julian W. Witherell, 77-107. Metuchen, NJ, Scarecrow Press, 1989.

Winjobi, Samuel Ayodele. "Management Problems of Government Special Libraries in Development Countries with Particular Reference to Agricultural Libraries in Nigeria." Master's thesis, Loughborough University of Technology, 1979.

Woakes, Harriet. "Recent Developments in the Use of Audiovisual Materials in Nigeria: Implications for Librarians." *Audiovisual Librarian* 12(1986): 26-31.

Woakes, Harriet, and Grace Toni Gandu. "The Development of an Index to Pictorial Materials in the Kashim Ibrahim Library, Ahmadu Bello University [Nigeria]." *Audiovisual Librarian* 13(1987): 209-214.

23. Standards

Barnshaw, Anne. "Establishing and Maintaining Professional Standards in Zimbabwe's Libraries." *Zimbabwe Librarian* 16(1984): 8-9.

Ifebuzor, Christopher C. "Wanted: Standards for Academic Law Libraries in Nigeria." *Law Librarian* 18(1987): 81-86.

Ifidon, Sam E. "Establishment of Standards for Bookstock in West African University Libraries.l" *Libri* 33(1983): 92-106.

Kulleen, P. C. "Standards for Public Libraries in Zambia." *Zambia Library Association Journal* 11(1979): 86-93.

Nwafor, B. U. "Standards for Nigerian Academic Library Buildings (a Paper Read at the Nigerian Library Association Conference, Kano, Nigeria, 1-6 December 1980)." *Nigerian Libraries* 16(1980): 71-81.

Oboro, Daniel O. "Public Libraries Standards in Nigeria." *Bendel Library Journal* 1(1978): 6-8, 10-11.

Odumosu, Olu. "Standards for Nigerian Special Libraries in Post-military Era." *Nigerian Libraries* 15(1979): 75-82.

Ogundipe, O. O. "Personnel Standards for University Libraries." *Library Scientist* 9(1982): 1-13.

Podmore, Ann. "Establishing Educational Standards and Training for Librarianship." *Zimbabwe Librarian* 16(1984): 10-13.

Rappaport, Philip. "Objectives and Standards of Practice for Special Libraries in West Africa." In *Standards of Practice for West African Libraries,* edited by John Dean, 85-91. Ibadan, 1969.

Schick, Frank L. "Performance Standards, Guidelines and Criteria for Administrative Services." In *Offocial Report of the African Seminar for Librarians and Documentalists of Administrative Information Services,* prepared by E. S. Asiedu, 102-115. 1975.

24. Statistics

Aje, Simeon B. "Library Statistics in Africa." In *Bowker Annual,* 1975: 360-364.

Allen, Geoffrey G. "The Management Use of Library Statistics." *IFLA Journal* 11(1985): 211-222.

Dieolu, J. O. "Library Statistics, Library Standards, and Library Development." *Nigerian Libraries* 9(1973): 57-65.

Nwoye, S. C. "Essence of Library Statistics. *Nigerbiblios* 1(1976): 17-18.

Rooke, Andrew. "Zambian Library Statistics—Time to Start Now!" *Zambia Library Association Newsletter* 4(1982): 17-19.

25. Studies and Surveys

Adeyemi, Nat M. "Library Operations Research—Purpose, Tools, Utility, and Implications for Developing Libraries." *Libri* 27(1977): 22-30.

Ahiakwo, D. N. "Forecasting Techniques and Library Circulation Operations: Implications for Management." *Library and Information Science Research* 10(1988): 195-210.

Edoka, Benson E. "Assessment Techniques in Library Studies." *Nigerian Libraries* 15(1979): 48-58.

Kimble, Helen. "A Reading Survey in Accra [Ghana]." *Universitas* 3(1958): 77-81.

Mchombu, K. *User Studies: How to Identify Potential and Actual User Needs.* 1987. ERIC. ED 299 978.

Tiamiyu, Mutawakilu A., and Isola Y. Ajiferuke. "A Total Relevance and Document Interaction Effects Model for the Evaluation of Information Retrieval Processes." *Information Processing and Management* 24(1988): 391-404.

BIBLIOGRAPHY OF SUB-SAHARA AFRICAN LIBRARIANSHIP, 1990

Compiled by Glenn L. Sitzman

PREFACE

This bibliography is the fourth (and probably last) annual supplement to "Bibliography of African Librarianship," published in the compiler's *African Libraries* (Scarecrow Press, 1988). It is the compiler's intention to cumulate the titles thus far compiled, plus titles compiled in 1991. Any complications after the cumulation will have to made by another bibliographer. Although this undertaking has not proved to be a thankless task, it is, nevertheless, an anomalous work when one considers that the compiler has had to work without access to primary works and that one of the abstracting services on which the bibliography is based is at least three hours away. Distances and library facilities inadequate to the task make verification and correction difficult when slipups occur in the compiler's notes. It is therefore this compiler's hope that the work can be carried on by a bibliographer with training in African studies and ready access to a large and growing Africana library.

The compilation presented here brings the titles in the combined bibliographies to almost 4,300. The 274 titles added here are fairly evenly

Advances in Library Administration and Organization,
Volume 11, pages 295-318.
Copyright © 1993 by JAI Press Inc.
All rights of reproduction in any form reserved.
ISBN: 1-55938-596-0

divided among works of a rather general reference (88); works referring to individual countries, except Nigeria (95), and works focused on Nigeria (91). These proportions follow the pattern observed in the earlier compilations. This is not, however, a necessarily accurate representation of current publications, because fifty-four titles (almost 20 percent) are retrospective. The term "retrospective" is used in this compilation to include any works from 1989 or before that have been provided from sources other than the three standard indexes and abstracting services on which the bibliographies are primarily based.

Several items published in the early 1990s were trieved from the *Bibliography of Library Economy* by H.G.T. Cannons, published in 1927 and reprinted in 1970. They came to light when a chance reference to Cannons came to the compiler's attention in his searches. Special thanks are extended to B. U. Nwafor (Nigeria) and Japhet N. Otike (Kenya), who kindly provided approximately 50 titles, unpublished as well as published, that have not appeared in the indexes. In this respect, an observation made by Mr. Nwafor in a letter of November 5, 1990, is apt for whoever attempts to compile future bibiographies of African librarianship. With reference to a list of his own works which he had sent to the compiler, Mr. Nwafor wrote, "I did not realise I've up to 29 articles not previously featured in your bibliographies. Which raises some issue as to the comprehensiveness of bibliographies relating to our part of the world—that only through personal contacts can they approximate exhaustiveness."

It is because of the need to contact individuals personally regarding their works, both published and unpublished, and because of historical material, both ephemeral and substantial, that have not been recorded in compilations of ready access that a comprehensive and exhaustive bibliography of librarianship in the Sub-Sahara probably can never be accomplished by one bibliographer working alone, if, indeed, it can be achieved at all. It seems imperative that the project devolve to an interested organization with personnel and financial resources to pursue the kind of undertaking necessary to search archives, examine old historical publications, and solicit information concerning speeches, addresses, papers read at conferences, and such like material that was written down and filed someplace but never published, not to speak of the quantity of material currently produced.

Once more it is the compiler's pleasure to acknowledge with thanks permission to use the libraries of the University of Puerto Rico, both at Mayagüez and Río Piedres, as well as the helpfulness of library personnel on both campuses.

Finally, it should be pointed out that some citations are not as bibliographically complete as the compiler would have them. They have been included, as received or found, in the thought that if a researcher knows that they exist the full citation may be tracked down. Abbreviations sometimes appear without explanation because the compiler could not decipher them locally. Three that are used several times in the compilation without being explained in all cases are, DSE for Deutsche Stiftung für Internationale Entwicklung (German Foundation for International Development); IAMSLIC, for International Association of Marine Science Libraries and Information Centers; and SADCC, for Southern African Development Coordination Conference.

GUIDE TO ORGANIZATION OF BIBLIOGRAPHY

Africa in General

General and Peripheral
French-speaking Africa
Academic Libraries
Bibliographies and Bibliography
Book Trade, Printing, and Publishing
Cataloging and Classification
Documentation and Information Science
Library Education and Training
School and Children's Library Services and Literature
Special Libraries, Services, and Subjects

Africana

Inter-Regional and Regional

Inter-Regional
Eastern Africa
  General
  Library Education
  Public Libraries
Southern Africa
West Africa

International Meetings

1989. Dar es Salaam, Tanzania, Establishment of a National Information and Documentation Network

Individual Countries

Botswana
Djibouti
Ethiopia

Gambia
Ghana
  General
  Academic Libraries
    University of Ghana
    University of Science and Technology
  Library Education
  School and Children's Library Services
Ivory Coast
Kenya
  Bibliography
  Library Education
  Academic Libraries
  Special Libraries
Lesotho
Malawi
Mauritius
Mozambique
Namibia
Nigeria
  Academic Libraries
    Ondo State University
    University of Calabar
    University of Ilorin
    University of Jos
    University of Nigeria
  Children's Library Service
  National Library of Nigeria
  Public Libraries
    Bauchi State
  School Libraries
  Secondary School and College Libraries
  Special Libraries, Materials, and Services
    Agriculture
    Law
    Medicine and Health Science
    Science and Technology
Somalia
Sudan
Swaziland
Tanzania
Uganda
Zambia
Zimbabwe
  Library Education
  Professional Associations

Academic Libraries
School and Children's Library Services
Special Libraries

Africa—General and Peripheral

Adeyemi, Nathaniel M. "Information Needs of Local Governments." In *An Information Strategy for IDRC for Africa: Proceedings,* 37-44. IDRC, 1988.

Broadbent, Kieran P. "The Importance of Information Sharing in Developing Countries: Marine Science as an Example." In *Marine Science Information throughout the World: Sharing the Resources,* edited by Carolyn P. Winn, et al., 3-6. International Association of Marine Science Libraries and Information Centers, 1989.

————. "Information Needs for Rural Development." *Information Development* 6(1990): 49-54.

Camara, Alioune Badara. "Implementing an Information Strategy for Sub-Saharan Africa: the First Stages." *Information Development* 6(1990): 55-61.

Economic Commission for Africa. "A PADIS Perspective on Elements of a Strategy for the Development of Information Infrastructure and Services in Sub-Saharan Africa." In *An Information Strategy for IDRC for Africa: Proceedings,* 169-180. IDRC, 1988.

Hüttemann, Lutz, ed. *Coordination and Improvement of National Information Services: a Report.* DSE, 1986. DOK 1347 A/a.

An Information Strategy for IDRC for Africa: Proceedings. IDRC, 1988.

Kemp, Ivor. "Books and Library Development for Developing Countries." *COMLA Newsletter* 65(Sept 1989): 4-5.

Lendvay, Olga. "Disponibilidad y Apoyo de la Formación en el Campo de Información para Países en Desarrollo" (Availability of Support for Training in the Field of Information for Developing Countries). *Revista AIBDA* 9(1988): 43-54.

Lloyd, Peter. "The International African Institute and the Book Famine in Africa." *African Research & Documentation* 51(1989): 23-26.

Lumande, Edward. "The Skeleton of a Net Work of Scientific and Technical Information." In *An Information Strategy for IDRC for Africa: Proceedings,* 45-47. IDRC, 1988.

Lundu, Maurice Chimfwembe. "The Information Gap: Reflections on its Origins and Implications." *Information Development* 5(1989): 223-227.

Mabomba, Rodrick S. "The Development of Librarianship in the Third World: a View from Africa." Paper presented at the IFLA Conference, Brighton, UK, August 1987.

Maps of Africa. Cape Town, South Africa Library, 1989.

Mchombu, Kingo. "Transformation of Rural Communities: the Role of Information." In *An Information Strategy for IDRC for Africa: Proceedings,* 2-16. IDRC, 1988.

Morin-Labatut, Gisèle. "Is there a User in House? Connecting with the User of Information Services." *Information Development* 6(1990): 43-48.

Newa, John M. "Libraries in National Literacy Education Programmes in Africa South of the Sahara: the State-of-the-Art." *International Library Review* 22(1990): 73-94.

Newton, Sarah. "'Have You Anything to Declare?' Working Abroad." *Library Association Record* 92(1990): 215.

Nwafor, B. U. "Copyright and the Developing Countries." Paper read at the IFLA Conference, Stockholm, August 1990.

————. "IFLA's Core Programme on the Advancement of Librarianship in the Third World. 1: An African Viewpoint—A Script in the Sky?" *Focus on International and Comparative Librarianship* 17(1986): 27-28.

Ojiambo, J. B. "Transfer of Western Management Expertise to Developing Countries." In *Translating an International Education to a National Environment,* 65-82. Metuchen, NJ, Scarecrow Press, 1990.

Olden, Edward Anthony. "Opinion Paper: Sub-Saharan Africa and the Paperless Society." *Journal of the American Society for Information Science* 38(1987): 298-304.

Philip, Abraham. "Organization and Management of Rural Libraries." *Maktaba* 7(1980): 45-50.

Poulsen, Ulla. "Afrika tur-retur" (Africa Round Trip). *Bogens Verden* 69(1987): 470-472.

Suzuki, Yukihisa. "On the Franklin Book Programs: 1952-1978." *Toshokan-Kai* (The Library World) 41(1989): 27-30. In Japanese.

Tabachnick, B. Robert. "Libraries Can Play a Part in Overseas Development Projects." *College & Research Libraries* 50(1989): 819, 821-825.

Tiamiyu, Mutawakilu A. "Sub-Saharan Africa and the Paperless Society: a Comment and a Counterpoint." *Journal of the American Society for Information Science* 40(1989): 325-328. A reply to E. A. Olden; see above.

Zwagobani, Elliot. "Modern Information Tools and Technologies: Constraints in an African Context." In *An Information Strategy for IDRC for Africa,* 88-99. IDRC, 1988.

Africa—French-speaking Africa—Academic Libraries

"Library in the Sahara." *Scientific American* 102, no. 9(Feb 26, 1910): 182. Cites as its source a report "published in the latest number of the *Revue du Monde Musulman.*".

Nwafor, B. U. "Issues and Problems in the Preparation for the Planning and Design of University Library Buildings in the Developing Countries." In *Library Buildings: Preparations for Planning. Proceedings of the Seminar Held in Aberystwyth, 10-14 August 1987,* edited by M. Dewe, 208-214. München, K. G. Saur, 1989.

Otike, Japhet. "SCAUL and its role in the Development of University Libraries in Africa." *Outlook on Research Libraries* (August 1990): 9-11.

Africa—Bibliographies and Bibliography

Cannons, H. G. T. *Bibliography of Library Economy: A Classified Index to the Professional Periodical Literature in the English Language Relating to Library*

Economy, Printing, Methods of Publishing, Copyright, Bibliography, etc., from 1876 to 1920. New York, Burt Franklin, 1927 (reprinted 1970).

Gladden, Earle M. "African Portuguese Books." *Booklist* 86(Apr 15, 1990): 1612-1613.

Gorman, G. E. "African National Bibliographies as Selection Resources." *International Library Review* 21(1989): 495-508.

Gupta, Davendra K. "Lotka's Law and its Application to Author Productivity Distribution of Psychological Literature of Africa for the Period 1966-1975." *Herald of Library Science* 28(1989): 11-21, 318-326.

Hütteman, Lutz, ed. *Librarianship and Documentation Studies: a Handbook of Teaching and Learning Materials.* DSE, 1985. DOK 1310 C/o.

Iwuji, H. O. M. "Librarianship and Oral Tradition in Africa." *International Library Review* 22(1990): 53-59.

Jones, Eldred. "The Noma Award for Publishing in Africa—Ten Years On" [a Bibliographical Essay]. *Scholarly Publishing* 21(1990): 108-116.

Africa—Book Trade, Printing and Publishing

MacLam, Helen. "A New Iniative in Third-World Publishing: African Books Collective." *Choice* 27(Oct 1989): 265.

Africa—Cataloging and Classification

Aderibigbe, M. R., and D. J. E. Udoh. "LC Subclass PL8000-8844: a Case for Revision." *Cataloging & Classification Quarterly,* 10, no. 3(1990): 77-90.

Africa—Documentation and Information Science

Abate, D. "Essential Features of a National Information and Documentation Network: a PADIS Perspective." In *Establishment of a National Information and Documentation Network ... Papers of the Seminar held in Dar-es-Salaam, February 16-24, 1989,* edited by O. C. Mascarenhas, 76-84. DSE, 1989.

————. "Improvement of National and Regional Information Services: an Assessment of Problems and Solutions Prescribed under the PADIS Programme." In *Coordination and Improvement of National Information Services: a Report,* edited by Lutz Hüttemann, 78-92. DSE, 1986. DOK 1347 A/a.

Akinlade, T. O. "Software Engineering in a Developing Country." *Information Technology for Development* 5(1990): 69-72.

Ali, S. Nazim. "Databases on Optical Discs and their Potential in Developing Countries." *Journal of the American Society of Information Science* 41(1990): 238-244.

Boyle, Peter. "Sectoral Information Services, Systems and Needs in SADCC: Collaborative Programmes and Project." In *An Information Strategy for IDRC for Africa,* 181-195. IDRC, 1988.

Doust, Robin W. "Computerisation in the Third World Library." *Wits Journal of Librarianship and Information Science* 5(July 1988): 69-85.

Fenn, Tom, Norman L. Weatherby, and Susan Kingsley Pasquariella. "Guidelines for Establishing Automated Libraries in Developing Countries." *Computers in Libraries* 10(1990): 21-28.

Africa—Library Education and Training

Aina, L. O. "Continuing Education Programmes and the Role of Library Schools in English Speaking Africa." *Training and Education* 6(1989): 43-52.
Hüttemann, Lutz. "Information and Training for Africa: the Role of the German Foundation for International Development (DSE)." *Information Development* 6(1990): 84-88.

Africa—Public Libraries

Odini, Cephas. "Planning for Public Library Development in Developing Countries with Special Reference to African Countries." *Libri* 40(1990): 33-48.

Africa—School and Children's Library Services and Literature

Osa, Osayimwense. "African Children's Literature from the 1976 Legon Seminar to the 1987 Zimbabwe International Book Fair." *International Review of Children's Literature and Librarianship* 4(1989): 34-41.
Segun, Omowunmi. "Children's Magazines in Africa." *Bookbird* 28(1990): 4-5.
Take, Kiyoshi. "Controversy over *Little Black Sambo*." *Toshokan Zasshi* 83(1989): 374-377. In Japanese.

Africa—Special Libraries, Services, and Subjects

"Activities of Farmers' Organizations: Pools of Information." *Quarterly Bulletin of the International Association of Agricultural Librarians and Documentalists* 34(1989): 148-149. First published in *Farming for Development* no. 3, 1988.
Alafiatayo, Benjamin O. "The ARIPO [African Regional Industrial Property Organization] Approach to Patent Search and Examination." *World Patent Information* 11(1989): 71-75.
Freeman, Robert R., and Deborah T. Hanfman. "REGIS: a Prototype Regional Information System for African Agriculture." In *IAMSLIC at a Crossroads: Proceedings of the 15th Annual Conference*, edited by Robert W. Burkhart and Joyce C. Burkhart, 55-64. International Association of Marine Science Libraries and Information Centers, 1990.
Menou, Michel J., and Thiendou Niang. "General Programme for Training in Agricultural Information [Meeting in Rome, 1988]." *Education for Information* 8(1990): 41-43.
Mills, D. M. "The Patent System and Development: African Viewpoint." *World Patent Information* 11(1989): 147-151.
"REGIS [Regional Information System for African Aquaculture]: Intelligent Documents on African Aquaculture." *Quarterly Bulletin of the International Association of Agricultural Librarians and Documentalists* 34(1989): 153.

Africana

"Access to Sources for African History." *African Research & Documentation* 49(1989): 31-34.

D'Ooge, Craig. "Window on Africa: a Visit to the Nairobi Field Office." *Library of Congress Information Bulletin* 49(1990): 164-165.

Eyers, John. "The London School of Hygiene and Tropical Medicine and the African Health Literature." *African Research & Documentation* 49(1989): 2-9.

Henn, Barbara J. "Securing Asian and African Materials for Library Collections: Practical Advice and Considerations." *Technical Services Quarterly* 5(1988): 41-48.

Kalisa, Beryl Graham. "Africa in Picture Books: Portrait or Preconception." *School Library Journal* 36(Feb 1990): 36-37.

Loh, Eudora. "Africa, Asia, Europe, and Latin America [Publications Received between May 1988 and May 1989]." *Government Publications Review* 16(1989): 619-625.

Maack, Mary Niles. "Scholarly Resources for the Study of the Third World: The Case of Africa." In *Libraries and Scholarly Communication in the United States: the Historical Dimension,* edited by Phyllis Dain and John Y. Cole, 111-133. Greenwood Press, 1990.

Rowse, Dorothea E. "The Creation of a Book Selection Policy, with Special Reference to African Materials." *Mousaion* 6(1988): 47-56.

Tanno, Yasuko. "African Studies in Japan." *African Research & Documentation* 49(1989): 28-31.

Inter-Regional and Regional

"Improving Library Services in Eastern and Central Africa." *Quarterly Bulletin of the International Association of Agricultural Librarians and Documentalists* 34(1989): 179. First published in *Spore* no. 22(Aug 1989).

Jenkins, J. "Some Trends in Distance Education in Africa: an Examination of the Past and Future Role of Distance Education as a Tool for National Development Case Studies of Kenya, Zambia, Zimbabwe]." *Distance Education* 10(1989): 41-53.

Made, S. H. *Project on Resource Sharing in Southern and Central Africa: Feasibility Study (Part 1 and 2).* Unesco, 1988.

Neill, J. R. "Collection Development and Dependence within the SADCC Configuration of Eastern, Central and Southern African States." In *Librarianship and Documentation Studies: A Handbook of Teaching and Learning Materials,* edited by Lutz Hüttemann, 121-128. DSE [German Foundation for International Development], 1985. (DOK 1310 C/o)

Inter-Regional and Regional—Eastern Africa

Ng'ang'a, James M. "Inter Library Lending in East Africa." In *Librarianship and Documentation Studies: A Handbook of Teaching and Learning Materials,* edited by Lutz Hüttemann, 7-22. DSE [German Foundation for International

Development], 1985. (DOK 1310 C/a)

Otike, Japhet. "Bibliographic Control in East Africa in the 1980s." *Information and Library Manager* 8, no. 4(1989): 18-25.

————. "Document Reproduction and Supply in East Africa." *Library Review* 39(1990): 21-27.

Were, Jacinta. "Computerized Union List of Periodicals in Eastern Africa." *Maktaba* 7, no. 2(1980).

Inter-Regional and Regional—Eastern Africa—Library Education

Otike, Japhet. "The Education and Training of Information Personnel in East Africa." *Libri* 39(1989): 110-126. LISA gives the title: "The Training of Information Personnel in East Africa."

Inter-Regional and Regional—Eastern Africa—Public Libraries

Abidi, S. A. H. "Public Library Laws in East Africa: Comparative Analysis." Kampala, 1982. unpublished mimeographed paper.

Inter-Regional and Regional—Southern Africa

Carleton, Patricia. "Library Development and International Assistance in Six Southern African Countries." Master's thesis, University of North Carolina at Chapel Hill, 1989.

Haag, Dietrich E. "Compilation of the Register of Investigations into Librarianship in Southern Africa." *South African Journal of Library and Information Science* 57(1989): 328-338.

Inganji, Francis. "The Southern African Development Information System (SADIS) and Resource Sharing among the SADCC Countries." Gabarone, 1982. Unpublished mimeographed paper.

Kotei, S. I. A. "Southern African Development Coordination Conference: SADCC— A Subsystem for PADIS." *Maktaba* 7, no. 2(1980): 21-33.

Maclean, Jay L., and N. I. Jhocson. "ICLARM's Information Activities in Africa." In *IAMSLIC at a Crossroads: Proceedings of the 15th Annual Conference,* edited by Robert W. Burkhart and Joyce C. Burkhart, 49-54. International Association of Marine Science Libraries and Information Centers, 1990.

Nyirenda, C. I. D. "The Provision of Appropriate Reading Material for School Children in the Southern African Region." In *Librarianship and Documentation Studies: A Handbook of Teaching and Learning Materials,* edited by Lutz Hütteman, 33-48. DSE, 1985. (DOK 1310 C/a)

Inter-Regional and Regional—West Africa

Maack, Mary Niles. "The Role of External Aid in West African Library Development." A paper presented at the IFLA conference, Nairobi, Kenya, August 1984.

International Meetings

1989, Dar es Salaam, Tanzania, Establishment of a National Information and Documentation Network.
Mascarenhas, O. C., ed. *Establishment of a National Information and Documentation Network ... Papers of the Seminar Held in Dar-es-Salaam, February 16-24, 1989.* DSE, 1989.

Individual Countries

Botswana

Kgosidintsi, T. F. "Information Needs of Small Scale Business Enterprises: A Case Study of Botswana." In *Librarianship and Documentation Studies: a Handbook of Teaching and Learning Materials,* edited by Lutz Hüttemann, 49-68. DSE, 1985.
Qobose, Edwin N. "Interlibrary Lending in Botswana: Practice, Problems and Prospects." *Interlending & Document Supply* 18(1990): 12-17.

Djibouti

Dawe, M. P. St. J. "Création d'une bibliothèque à l'Assemblée nationale de Djibouti" (Creation of a Library at the National Assembly of Djibouti). *Bulletin d'Informations de l'Association des Bibliothécaires Français* 142(1989): 15-20.

Ethiopia

Gabre-Tsadik, Degife, and Sushman Gupta. "Postgraduate Research Trends in Ethiopia." *Information Development* 6(1990): 72-76.
Pankhurst, Rita. "Librarianship Education in Ethiopia." *Information and Library Manager* 8(1989): 5-9.

Gambia

N'Jie, B. K. "Management of Technological Change with Focus on Automation." *Information Development* 4(1989): 259-282.

Ghana

Alemna, Anaba A. "Cataloguing and Classification Practices in Ghanaian Libraries." *Ghana Library Journal* 7(Nov 1989): 48-55.
_____. "Information and Economic Recovery in Ghana." *Information Development* 5(1989): 206-209.
_____. "Opportunities in Librarianship: Alternatives for the Ghanaian Graduate." *Ghana Library Journal* 7(Nov 1989): 36-41.

————. Publishing and the Book Trade in Ghana." *Scholarly Publishing* 21(1990): 99-107.

————. "The State of Education and Library Services in Ghana." *Annals of Library Science and Documentation* 35(1988): 111-115.

Ayiku, M. N. B. "A Case Study in Process Automation in Ghana." *Information Development* 4(1989): 117-156.

Badu, Edwin Ellis. "The Use of Computers in Ghana Libraries: Justification and Constraints." *Ghana Library Journal* 7(Nov 1989): 30-35.

Cabutey-Adodoadji, E. "Collection Development: A Hypothetical Perspective." *Ghana Library Journal* 6(1988): 20-30.

Kwei, C. "Bibliographic Control: the Interntional Concept and the National Effort." *Ghana Library Journal* 6(1988): 31-39.

Nyarko, Kwame. "The Book Industry in Ghana." *Ghana Library Journal* 6(1988): 9-19.

Oddoye, David E. M. "The Ghana Library Association: The First 25 Years." *Ghana Library Journal* 7(1989): 1-14.

Opare-Sem, D. K. "Need for Scientific and Technological Information (STI) in Development." *Ghana Library Journal* 6(1988): 40-51.

Quakyi, Kofi Totobi." "Opening Address [at the Second Biennial Congress of the Ghana Library Association, Accra, 11-12 Sept 1986]". *Ghana Library Journal* 6(1988): 4-8.

"The State of the Nation's Information Provision and Service: 2nd Biennial Congress of the Ghana Library Association, Accra, 11-12 Sept 86." *Ghana Library Journal* 6(1988): 1-62.

Ghana—Academic Libraries

Alemna, A. A. "Collection Development in University Libraries in Ghana: Some Observations." *Collection Building* 10(1989): 47-51.

————. "User Education in University Libraries in Ghana." *Education Libraries Journal* 33(1990): 40-47.

Badu, Edwin Ellis. "Technology in University Libraries in Ghana." *Aslib Proceedings* 42(1990): 111-117.

Ghana—Academic Libraries—University of Ghana

Asiagodo, G. D. "Staff Development for the Professional Staff of a University Library: The Case of the Balme Library, University of Ghana." *Ghana Library Journal* 7(Nov 1989): 15-21.

Kedem, K. A. "The Acquisition of Periodicals in a Foreign Exchange Starved Library: The Case of the Balme Library." *Serials Librarian* 18(1990): 173-180.

Robertson, Kathleen. "Information Technology: A Report from West Africa." *Canadian Library Journal* 46(1989): 367-369.

Ghana—Academic Libraries—University of Science and Technology

Badu, Edwin Elllis. "The Preservation of Library Materials: A Case Study of University of Science and Technology Library in Ghana." *Aslib Proceedings* 42(1990): 119-125.

Ghana—Library Education

Alemna, A.A. "Acquisitions and Collection Development Education in Ghana." *Library Acquisitions: Practice and theory* 14(1990): 53-59.

Ghana—School and Children's Library Services

"International Children's Book Day 1989." *Bookbird* 27(Sept 1989): 19.
Sackey, Juliana. "IBBY/Unesco Workshop in Ghana." *Bookbird* 27(Nov 1989): 18.

Ivory Coast

Couture, Carol, and Marcel Lajeunesse. "L'archivistique, instrument de développement: le cas de la Cote d'Ivoire" (Archival Science, Instrument of Development: the Case of the Ivory Coast). *Archivaria* 29(winter 1989-90): 18-32.
Gra, Patricia. "Perspectives of Information Development on Marine Science in West Africa: The Case of Cote d'Ivoire [Ivory Coast]." In *Marine Science Information throughout the World: Sharing the Resources,* edited by Carolyn P. Winn, et al., 27-31. International Association of Marine Science Libraries and Information Centers, 1989.

Kenya

Burke, Enid, ed. *In Search of a System for the Dissemination of Research Findings and Technology in Kenya.* University of Nairobi, 1973. (IDS Occasional Paper no. 7)
Ng'ang'a, J. M. *Development of Libraries in Kenya, 1900-1967.* Nairobi, 1981. mimeographed.
Njuguna, J. R. "Acquisition of Library Materials in Kenya: Problems and Prospects." Paper presented at the IFLA Conference, Nairobi, Kenya, August 1984.
Otike, Japhet. "The Concept of Cooperation and its Implication to Research Libraries in Kenya." *Maktaba* 12(1989):
Rodrigues, A. J., W. Okelo-Odongo, and R. J. P. Scott. "Management of Technological Change: Kenya Case Study." *Information Development* 4(1989): 399-471.
Were, Jacinta. "Problems of Automating Libraries in a Developing Country: Kenya." In *Training Workshop on Use of Computers in Information Handling: A Report,* edited by Lutz Hüttemann, 97-103. DSE, 1986. (DOK 1346 A/a)

Kenya—Bibliography

Ochola, Francis W. "The Kenya National Bibliography and Universal Bibliographic Control." *Maktaba* 7, no. 2(1980): 8-18.

Kenya—Library Education

Otike, Japhet. "Education of Information Personnel in Kenya." *Outlook on Research Libraries* 11(1989): 9-12.

————. "The Training and Education of Information Professionals in Kenya."
   Information and Library Manager 8(1989): 11-16.

Kenya—Academic Libraries

Ng'ang'a, James M. "Development of Kenyatta University College Library 1972-84." In
   *Librarianship and Documentation Studies: A Handbook of Teaching and Learning
   Materials,* edited by Lutz Hüttemann, 69-88. DSE, 1985. (DOK 1310 C/a)
Tanui, Tirong arap. "Moi University Library: A New Library in a New University."
   Information Development 5(1989): 235-239.
————. "Psychology and Culture in Information Retrieval: With Special Reference
   to Moi University Library." *Libri* 39(1989): 185-191.

Kenya—Special Libraries

"Core Agricultural Literature Project: Progress Report, 1st Quarter 1990." *Quarterly
   Bulletin of the International Association of Agricultural Librarians and
   Documentalists* 35(1990): 102-103.
Lilech, John F. "Kenya Institute of Administration Library as a National Liaison Centre
   and Focal Point for Information and Administration for Development."
   Maktaba 7, no. 2(1980): 1-8.
Otike, Japhet. "The Development of Special Libraries in Kenya with Particular
   Emphasis on Problems and their Possible Solutions." Master's thesis,
   Loughborough University, 1985.
————. "Resource Sharing in Special Libraries: the Kenyan Experience." *Collection
   Management* 12(1990): 153-166.
————. "The Role of a Special Librarian in the Dissemination of Information with
   Particular Reference to Kenya." Paper presented at the Kenya Library
   Association (KLA) Annual Seminar held in February 1987.
————. "The Work of a Special Library: The Experience of the Kenya National
   Museum." *International Library Review* 21(1990):
Stout, Dorothy L. "Preparing a Kenyan Field Guide." In *Frontiers in Geoscience
   Information: Proceedings of the Twenty-fourth Meeting of the Geoscience
   Information Society, November 6-9, 1989, St. Louis, Missouri,* edited by Mary
   B. Ansari, 209-212. Geoscience Information Society, 1990.

Lesotho

Moshoeshoe, Matselio Mamahlape. "Content Analysis and Description of Documents:
   Evolution Challenge to Lesotho." In *Information, Knowledge, Evolution:
   Proceedings of the 44th FID Congress, Helsinki, 28 August-1 September 1988,*
   edited by Sinikka Koshiala and Ritva Launo, 133-143. Amsterdam, Elsevier
   Science Publishers, 1989.

Malawi

Howse, Foster G. "Bibliographic Control, Standardization and Malawiana." *MALA
   Bulletin* 5(Dec 1988): 14-26.

Kane, Kenneth. "Library Promotion." *MALA Bulletin* 5(Dec 1988): 38-49.

Kinney, Jane. "National Networking: The Case of Malawi." *Quarterly Bulletin of the International Association of Agricultural Librarians and Documentalists* 34(1989): 180-183.

Kulemeka, Anne B. "Library Provision for Children in Malawi." *MALA Bulletin* 5(Dec 1988): 50-57.

Phiri, Vuwa. "The Bibliographic Control of Reports, Seminar Papers, Teaching Manuals and Other Categories of Grey Material in Malawi." *MALA Bulletin* 5(Dec 1988): 27-29.

Zembe, Nestore L. "A Step Ahead in the Use of Computers in Malawi Libraries." *MALA Bulletin* 5(Dec 1988): 58-60.

Mauritius

Kwong, Rosemary Ng Kee. "Communication Channels in the Access to and Transfer of Information from Research to Practice [in the Mauritius Sugar Industry Research Institute]." *Quarterly Bulletin of the International Association of Agricultural Librarians and Documentalists* 35(1990): 19-24.

"Libraries of Mauritius." *Literary Year-Book,* 1907:677; 198:771. Cited by Cannons, p. 72.

Mozambique

Naber, Gerrit. "Rehabilitating an Agricultural Library in Mozambique." *Information Development* 6(1990): 100-104.

Namibia

Pieterse, Pat. "The Public Library Service of South West Africa/Namibia." *Cape Librarian* 33(1989): 2-6.

Nigeria

Ahiauzu, Augustine I. "Towards Effective Management of Human Resources in Nigerian Libraries: An Evaluation of Cost Reduction Strategies." In *Management of Libraries in an Era of Scarce Resources: Proceedings of a Seminar, Benin University, Benin City, Nigeria, 18-20 June 1986,* edited by O. O. Ogundipe, 30-57. Benin University, 1989.

Ezennia, Steve E. "The Harmattan and Library Resources Management in Nigeria: An Appraisal of the Effects, Problems and Prospects." *Library & Archival Security* 9(1989): 43-48.

Nwafor, B. U. "The Five M's or the 1972 ALA Conference as seen by a Nigerian Participant." *Northern States Library Notes* 7(1973): 54-59.

――――. "A Librarian Father and Children in Conversation." *Education Libraries Bulletin* 30, no. 3(autumn 1987): 36-40.

_____. "Librarians and the Quest for Truth." *Bendel Library Journal* 7(1984): 58-64.

_____. "Library Services and Management Studies." A Brief address on the occasion of JUMASA Week [Jos University Management Students Association], 21-23 May, 1981.

_____. "Nigerians and Reading: A Preliminary Observation." Paper presented at the Annual Conference of the Plateau State Division of the Nigerian Library Association, Jos, 28 June 1985.

Nwafor, B. U., and K. Mahmud, eds. *Tropical Library Architecture: The Proceedings of a Seminar Held 30-31 May 1980 at Ahmadu Bello University, Zaria, Nigeria.* Zaria, Kashim Ibrahim Library, Ahmadu Bello University for Committee of University Librarians of Nigerian Universities, 1985.

Nwafor, B. U., and A. B. Ojoade. "Library Statistics in Nigeria: An Assessment." Paper presented at the Workshop on Information Statistics Organised by the Nigerian National Commission for Unesco, Lagos, 12-16 Nov. 1985.

Ogundipe, O. O., ed. *Management of Libraries in an Era of Scarce Resources: Proceedings of a Seminar, Benin University, Benin City, Nigeria, 18-20 June 1986.* Benin University, 1989.

_____. "Sources of Funding: Problems and Issues." In *Management of Libraries in an Era of Scarce Resources ...* edited by O. O. Agundipe, 15-29. Benin University, 1989.

Osiobe, Stephan A. "Free Access: Providers and Users of Information—Reactions in a Developing Economy." *Library Review* 38, no. 4(1989): 7-14.

Nigeria—Bibliographies and Bibliography ·

Gupta, D. K. "Scientometric Study of Biochemical Literature of Nigeria, 1970-1984: Application of of Lotka's Law and the 80/20-Rule." *Scientometrics* 15(1989): 171-179.

Nigerian Periodicals Index. B. U. Nwafor, ed. vol. 1-   1986-

Nwafor, B. U. "The Organisation and procedures for the Production of the *Nigerian Periodicals Index.*" Paper presented at the Indexing Workshop Organised by the Committee of University Librarians of Nigerian Universities, Jos, 10-12 Nov. 1985.

Okorafor, E. E. "Indexing of Nigerian Newspapers for Effective Research." *Information Development* 5(1989): 228-234.

_____. "Newspaper Indexing in Nigerian Libraries." *The Indexer* 17(1990): 35-38.

Nigeria—Documentation and Information Science

Akinlade, T. O. "Information Technology in Nigeria: Problems and Prospects." *Information Technology for Development* 4(1989): 667-676.

Alegbeleye, G. O. "Patterns of Information Systems in Nigeria." *Records Management Journal* 1(1989): 29-35.

Anyanwu, L. O., and P. D. McElroy. "Improving the Performance for Majors in Computer Science in the Nigerian Universities." *Computers and Education* 14(1990): 403-408.

Azubuike, Abraham A. "Document Subject Matrix as a Factor of Precision in Computerized Information Retrieval Systems." *Quarterly Bulletin of the International Association of Agricultural Librarians and Documentalists* 35(1990): 81-85.

_____. "System Analysis Imperatives for Computer Catalogue Design." *Libri* 39(1989): 237-250.

Eyitayo, Adekunle O. "Status Report on the Attitude of Automated Library System Vendors to Investing in Nigeria." *Program* 23(1989): 247-256.

Okoye, G. "A Nigerian Experience in Office Automation Project." *Information Development* 4(1989): 283-314.

Ubogu, Felix N. "Library Application Software Packages in Nigeria: a Survey." *Program* 24(1990): 291-296.

Nigeria—Libraries and Education

Nwafor, B. U. "The Library and the Educational Process." *Nigerian Journal of Education: a Journal of Educational Studies and Research* 1(1977): 181-186.

Nigeria—Library Education

Agumanu, Joan N. "Education and Training for Nonprofessional Library Staff in Nigeria." *Journal of Education for Library and Information Science* 30(1989): 68-69, 141-143.

Iroka, Luke A. "Library Orientation and Instruction for Medical Students." *International Library Review* 21(1989): 481-485.

Nwafor, B. U. "Education for Librarianship in Nigeria." *Northern Nigerian Library Notes* nos. 2&3(Oct 1964-Jan 1965): 122-130.

_____. "Education for University Librarianship in Nigeria." In *Proceedings of the First Annual National Conference on Education for Librarianship in Nigeria, Kano, Department of Library Science, Bayero University, 14-17 April 1984*, edited by M. I. Ajibero, 67-77. 1988.

_____. "Nigerian Libraries' Library and Information Science Collections: A Preliminary Study." *Nigerian Library and Information Science Review* 3(1985): 71-74.

_____. "The Training of Nigerian Librarians." *Far Flung Flong Afar: Journal of the Old Students' Associatin, Ealing School of Librarianship* 1(Oct 1964): 11-14.

Nwakoby, Martina A. "Physical Facilities and Resources for Education in Librarianship in Nigeria." *Journal of Education for Library and Information Science* 31(1990): 76-87.

Ochogwu, Michael G. "Alternatives in Librarianship: Prospects and Problems for the Nigerian Graduate." *Journal of Education for Library and Information Science* 30(1989): 275-284.

Nigeria—Library Education—University of Maiduguri

Nweke, Ken M. C. "Information Technology Used for Education for Information in the Maiduguri Library School, Nigeria." *Education for Information* 7(1989): 43-49.

Nigeria—Library Education—University of Nigeria

Amucheazi, O. N. "Teaching of Library Science in Nigeria: With Special Reference to the Department of Library Science, University of Nigeria, Nsukka." *COMLA Newsletter* 65(Sept 1989): 6-7.

Nigeria—Library Education—University of Port Harcourt

Obokoh, N. P. "Alternating Work and Education: A Sandwich Programme for an Undergraduate Diploma in Library Science." *Library Review* 38, no. 5(1989): 22-28.

Nigeria—Academic Libraries

Alegbeleye, Bunmi. "Disaster Control Planning in Nigeria." *Journal of Librarianship* 22(1990): 91-106.

Edem, U. S. "Serials Acquisition and Management in Nigerian Academic Libraries: Implications for Quality Library Services." *Information Services & Use* 9(1989): 161-170.

Nkereuwen, E. E. "Computers and the Nigerian Academic Library Service in the 21st Century." *Information Services & Use* 8(1988): 229-237.

Nwafor, B. U. "The Bibliographic and Information Climate for Research in Nigeria." A University of Jos Postgraduate Open Lecture Delivered on 11 March 1985. Jos, 1987.

————. "Problems of Acquisition of Overseas and Local Materials." In *University Libraries in Developing Countries,* edited by A. J. Loveday and G. Gatterman, 59-74. München, K. G. Saur, 1985.

————. "Standards for Nigerian Academic Library Buildings: a Paper Read at the Nigerian Library Association Conference, Kano, Nigeria, 1-6 December 1980." *Nigerian Libraries* 16(1980): 71-81.

————. "Welcome Address." In *Proceedings of the National Seminar on Strategies for Survival by Nigerian Academic and Research Libraries during Austere Times,* edited by S. M. Lawani, 1-2. NAALD and Academic and Research Libraries Section, Nigerian Library Association, 1988.

Oke, Olufunso. "Library Service without Book Loans: a Future Strategy for Nigerian University Libraries?" *Library Review* 38, no. 4(1989): 37-41.

Oni-Orisan, B. A. "Library Accommodation: Standards and Realities." In *Management of Libraries in an Era of Scarce Resources: Proceedings of a Seminar, Benin University* ... edited by O. O. Gundipe, 73-82. Benin University, 1989.

Umoh, P. N. "Financial Allocations, Budgetary Control and University Libraries." In *Management of Libraries in an Era of Scarce Resources* ... edited by O. O. Ogundipe, 83-94. Benin University, 1989.

Nigeria—Academic Libraries—Ondo State University

Akinfolarin, W. A. "The Acquisition of Books and Journals in Austere Times: The Ondo State University Library Experience." *Library Review* 39(1990): 36-40.

Nigeria—Academic Libraries—University of Calabar

Lawal, Olu O. "Austerity and Aspects of Bibliographic Services: The University of Calabar Library." *Information and Library Manager* 8(1989): 13-16.

Nigeria—Academic Libraries—University of Ilorin

Olorunsola, R., and E. O. Ajileye. "Periodical Retrenchment at the University of Ilorin Library." *Library Review* 39(1990): 42-46.

Nigeria—Academic Libraries—University of Jos

Nwafor, B. U. "The Library Director as Student and Library Assistant." Paper presented at the University of Jos Senior Library Staff Seminar on 19 Nov. 1982.
_____. "The Problem of the Blank Cheque. (Description of the Organisation and Administration of the University of Jos Library System. Being a Paper Presented at the Univerisity of Jos Library Senior Staff Seminar, 16 May, 1989)." *Nigerbiblios* 5(1980): 9-15.
_____. "What we do at Jos." Paper presented before the staff and Students of the Department of Library Science, Bayero University, Kano, 15 Nov. 1982.

Nigeria—Academic Libraries—University of Nigeria

Iwueke, Damian C. "Archives Collection at Nnamdi Asikiwe Library, University of Nigeria, Nsukka." *COMLA Newsletter* 66(Dec 1989): 2-3.

Nigeria—Children's Library Services

Nwafor, B. U. "The Characteristics of the Post-primary School Magazines of the Former Eastern Nigeria." *East Central State School Libraries Bulletin* 2(1973): 7-18.

Nigeria—National Library

Antwi, I. K. "The National Library of Nigeria: A Case Study of the Bauchi State Branch." *Aslib Proceedings* 42(1990): 127-135.

Nigeria—Public Libraries

Chijioke, Mary Ellen. "Public Library Services as Information Networks: Nigeria in the Twenty-first Century." *Journal of Librarianship* 21(1989): 174-185.
Igwe, P. O. E. "Institutional Libraries as Surrogates for Public Libraries: An Alternative Option for Developing Countries with Poor Public Library Systems." *Education Libraries Journal* 32(1989): 44-52.
Nzotta, Briggs C. "The Administration of Branch Libraries in a Developing Country: A Case Study." *Public Library Quarterly* 19(1989): 47-60.

Nigeria—Public Libraries—Bauchi State

Antwi, I. K. "The Development of Public Libraries in Nigeria: The Case of Bauchi State Library Service." *Aslib Proceedings* 41(1989): 285-293.

Nigeria—Secondary School and College Libraries

Nwafor, B. U. "The Library in the Teacher Training College." Paper read at the Annual Conference of the Benue and Plateau States Division of the Nigerian Library Association, Jos, 26 February 1977.

Nwali, L. O. "Students Use of Library Resources in a Polytechnical Institution in Nigeria: A Case Study of Ibadan Polytechnic Library System." *Aslib Proceedings* 42(1990): 137-146.

Nzotta, Briggs Chinkata. "An Evaluative Study of Collections, Personnel and Services of College of Education Libraries in Nigeria." *Herald of Library Science* 28(1989): 305-317.

Nigeria—School Libraries

Apeji, E. Adeche. "The Development of School Library Services." *International Library Review* 22(1990): 41-51.

Elaturoti, David F. "Use of Resource People in the Generation of Learning Materials for Nigerian Schools." In *Voices from Around the World: Selections from the Annual Proceedings of the International Association of School Librarianship,* edited by Philomena Hauck, 119-123. Metuchen, NJ, Scarecrow Press, 1989.

Shaibu, Samaila. "School Media Resource Services in Nigeria: The Past, Present and Future Prospects." *Education Libraries Journal* 32(1989): 32-43.

Nigeria—Special Libraries, Materials, and Services

Adaramola, E. S. "Non-print Media Services in Nigerian Libraries at the Cross-roads." *Audiovisual Librarian* 15(1989): 151-154.

Nweke, Ken M. C. "Managing Information Resources in Nigerian Special Libraries." In *Information, Knowledge, Evolution: Proceedings of the 44th FID Congress, Helsinki, 28 August-1 September 1988,* edited by Sinikka Koshiala and Ritva Launo, 421-430. Amsterdam, Elsevier Science Publications, 1989.

Obokoh, N. P. "Bibliometric Study of Research Fields of Nigerian Geographers, 1957-1978." *Bulletin (Special Libraries Association, Geography and Map Division)* 158 (Dec 1989): 18-29. *Erratum,* no. 159(Mar 1990): 76-77.

Nigeria—Special Libraries, Materials, and Services—Agriculture

Adedigba, Yakub A. "User Education in Research Institutes' Libraries in Nigeria." *Quarterly Bulletin of the International Association of Agricultural Librarians and Documentalists* 35(1990): 73-76.

Okocha, Kingsley Ferewisky. "Effective Science and Technology Information Resources Management and the Role of Nigerian Agricultural Libraries in Food Production." *Quarterly Bulletin of the International Association of Agricultural Librarians and Documentalists* 35(1990): 25-30.

Pouris, A. "A Scientometric Assessment of Agricultural Research in South AFrica." *Scientometrics* 17(1989): 401-414, Article contains comparisons with Nigeria.

Nigeria—Special Libraries, Materials, and Services—Law

Dada, T. O. "Short Course in Law Library Services for Nigerian Law Libraries: a Palliative for a Raging National Problem?" *International Journal of Legal Information* 17(1989): 32-42.

Nigeria—Special Libraries, Materials, and Services—Medicine and Health Services

Afolabi, Michael. "The Literature of Onchocerciasis, 1960-1981: Compiled by the Medical Library of the Ahmadu Bello University." *International Library Review* 21(1989): 487-493.

Nigeria—Special Libraries, Materials, and Services—Science and Technology

Aderibigbe, M. R. "The Nigerian Patent System and the New Industrial Poicy." *World Patent Information* 12(1990): 95-99.

Aina, L. O. "The Use of Patent Literature by Nigerian Scientists." *INSPEL* 23(1989): 164-169.

Akinboro, E. O. "Analysis of the Publications of Research Scientists of the National Cereals Research Institute, Nigeria." *Quarterly Bulletin of the International Association of Agricultural Librarians and Documentalists* 35(1990): 77-80.

Alabi, G. A. "The Citation Pattern of Nigerian Scientists." *International Library Review* 21(1989): 13.

Apeji, E. Adeche. "Satisfying Readers' Information Needs in a Nigerian Research Institute." *Annals of Library Science and Documentation* 35(1988): 149-155. Article focuses on the Library of the Rubber Research Institute of Nigeria.

Ehikhamenor, F. A. "Aspects of the Publication Cycle of Physical Scientists in Some Nigerian Universities." *Journal of Information Science* 16(1990): 257-264.

————. "Productivity of Physical Scientists in Nigerian Universities in Relation to Communication Variables." *Scientometrics* 18(1990): 437-444.

Nweke, Ken M. C. "The Language and Format of the Literature Used by Research Scholars in Zoology at the Ibadan University, Nigeria." *Annuals of Library Science and Documentation* 35(1988): 128-133.

Spencer, S. M. "The Relative Effectiveness of Programmed Instruction in the Teaching of Chemical Concepts: A Case Study of Schools in Ibadan." *Education and Training Technology International* 26(1989): 241-247.

Somalia

Ismael, S. Yusuf. "Establishment of a National Information and Documentation Network in Somalia." In *Establishment of a National Information and Documentation Network ... Papers of the Seminar Held in Dar-es-Salaam, February 16-24, 1989,* edited by O. C. Mascarenhas, 25-32. DSE, 1989.

Sudan

Wesley, C. "Information Services for Current Research in the Sudan." In *Librarianship and Documentation Studies: A Handbook of Teaching and Learning Materials,* edited by Lutz Hüttemann, 97-112. DSE, 1985. (DOK 1310 C/a)

Weyers, Richard W. "Sudan's National Documentation Centre." *African Reserarch & Documentation* 49(1989): 10-15.

Swaziland

Nhlapo, M. M. "The Place of a Documentation Centre in the Supply of Information in Swaziland: Problems and Prospects." In *Coordination and Improvement of National Information Services: A Report,* edited by Lutz Hüttemann, 21-35. DSE, 1986. (DOK 1347 A/a)

Stewart, Shelagh, and Richard Pathak. "Ndzevane Education Resource Centre." *Journal of Multicultural Librarianship* 3(1989): 83-84.

Wamala, E. "An Overview of the Study of Information in Swaziland." In *Coordination and Improvement of National Information Services: A Report,* edited by Lutz Hüttemann, 11-20. DSE, 1986. (DOK 1347 A/a)

Tanzania

Karugila, J. M. "German Records in Tanzania." *African Research & Documentation* 50(1989): 12-18.

Mascarenhas, O. C., ed. *Establishment of a National Information and Documentation Network in Tanzania: Papers of the Seminar Held in Dar-es-Salaam, February 16-24, 1989.* DSE, 1989.

Naas, Ragnhild. "Barnebokmese for første gang i Tanzania" (First Time for Children's Book Fair in Tanzania). *Bok og Bibliotek* 55(1988); 34.

Newa, John M. "Academic Status for University Librarians in Tanzania: Challenges and Prospects." *Library Review* 38(1989): 19-35.

Uganda

Birungi, P. K. "Establishment of a National Information and Documentation Network in Uganda: The Status Quo." In *Establishment of a National Information and Documentation Network: Papers of the Seminar Held in Dar-es-Salaam, February 16-24, 1989,* edited by O. C. Mascarenhas, 17-24. DSE, 1989.

Zambia

Msadabwe, E. M. "Ranfurly Library Service Helps the Branch Library at Kalabo, Zambia." *Library Association Record* 90(1988): 661.

Nyirenda, J. E. "Organization of Distance Education at the University of Zambia: An Analysis of the Practice." *Distance Education* 10(1989): 148-156.

Zimbabwe

Dube, S. R. "The Zimbabwe National Library and Documentation Services: An Example for Eastern and Southern African Countries." In *Establishment of a National Information and Documentation Network* ...: *Papers of the Seminar Held in Dar-es-Salaam, February 16-24, 1989*, edited by O.C. Mascarenhas, 41-49. DSE, 1989.

Gurira, J. "An Alternative Approach to the Realization of Rural Library Service for Zimbabwe." *Zimbabwe Librarian* 21(1989): 30-31.

Hopkinson, Alan. "Libraries and Library Automation in Zimbabwe: A Brief Overview." *African Research & Documentation* 51(1989): 19-22.

"Libraries of Rhodesia." *Literary Year-Book,* 1907: 676; 1908: 771. Cited by Cannons, p. 72.

Made, S. M. "Library Situation in Zimbabwe: An Historical Background to the Establishment of the National Library and Documentation Service (NLDS)." *Wits Journal of Librarianship and Information Science* 5(1988): 171-197.

Ngwenya, A. M. L. "Cooperation in Book Acquisition." *Zimbabwe Librarian* 20(1988): 8, 10-14.

Zimbabwe—Library Education

Thorpe, D. M. "Library Education in Zimbabwe." *Zimbabwe Librarian* 21(1989): 26-29.

Zimbabwe—Professional Associations

Hikwa, L., and T. Takawira. "Conference 1987 and A. G. M.: Library Needs, Initiatives and Problems in the Next Decade." *Zimbabwe Librarian* 20(1988): 3-4.

Pakkiri, Devi. "The Zimbabwe Library Association from CABSALA to ZLA." *COMLA Newsletter* 65(Sept 1989): 11.

Sibanda, I. "Keynote Address [at the opoening of the 1989 Annual General Meeting and Conference of the Zimbabwe Library Association]." *Zimbabwe Librarian* 21(1989): 4-7.

Zimbabwe—Academic Libraries

Kufa, Jacob C. "The University of Zimbabwe Library in a Growing Academic Community." *African Research & Documentation* 51(1989): 1-7.

Pakkiri, Devi. "Plans to Computerize UZ Library Services: Prospects and Problems." *Zimbabwe Librarian* 20(1988): 61-63.

Zimbabwe—School and Children's Library Services

Matsika, K., and E. R. T. Chuirare. "Trends in the Development of Libraries in Zimbabwe with Special Reference to School Libraries." *Zimbabwe Librarian* 21(1989): 20-24.

Vardell, Sylvia M. "Books in the Classroom." *Horn Book* 65(1989): 669-670.

Waungana, Ellen. "The Home Library Movement of Zimbabwe." *Bookbird* 28(May 1990): 18-19.

————. "IBBY-Asahi Reading Promotion Award 1990." *Bookbird* 27(Nov 1989): 19.

Zimbabwe—Special Libraries

Hadebe, B. "The National Library and Documentation Service and the Future Development of Government Libraries." *Zimbabwe Librarian* 21-(1989): 14-18.

"An Information Digest for Health Works in Zimbabwe." *Zimbabwe Librarian* 20(1988): 74-75.

Maya, R. S. "Process Automation in the Pharmaceutical Industry: A Case study of Process Automation at the CAPS Holdings Drug Factory." *Information Development* 4(1989): 253-258.

Nengomasha, Catharina. "The National Archives and Automation: Records Centre Experience." *Zimbabwe Librarian* 20(1988): 55-59.

BIOGRAPHICAL SKETCHES
OF THE CONTRIBUTORS

Jane Rogers Butterworth is a graduate research assistant at Clarion University of Pennsylvania. She holds a Bachelor of Arts in English and a Master of Arts in History.

Jane A. Dodd is Business Reference Librarian at the Sterling C. Evans Library, Texas A&M University, College Station.

Miriam A. Drake is Dean and Director of Libraries at the Georgia Institute of Technology, Atlanta.

Dr. Ahmad Fouad M. Gamaluddin is Director of the Graduate Library Science program at Clarion University of Pennsylvania. His areas of specialization in library education include technical services and international librarianship.

Suzanne D. Gyeszly is Coordinator for Social Sciences at the Sterling C. Evans Library, Texas A&M University, College Station.

Ray Hall is Head Reference Librarian at the University of Tennessee, Chatanooga.

Steven M. Hutton is a graduate student of the School of Information and Library Science, The University of North Carolina, Chapel Hill.

Rashelle S. Karp is Associate Professor in the Department of Library Science, Clarion University of Pennsylvania.

Marjorie E. Murfin is a reference librarian in the Information Services Department, Ohio State University Libraries, Columbus. She holds the rank of Associate Professor and her research interests are in analysis of the reference process, including measurement, evaluation, and patron responses and behavior. Active in the American Library Association, she was the 1987 recipient of the Isadore Gilbert Mudge citation for distinguished contributions to reference librarianship.

Dr. Kenneth Oberembt is University Librarian at the American University, Cairo, Egypt. Active in the American Library Association, he has served on committees in the Library Administration and Management Association.

Dr. J. Fred Olive III is Head, Educational Technology Services, Mervyn H. Sterne Library, The University of Alabama, Birmingham.

Virginia Tiefel was voted 1984 Ohio Academic Librarian of the Year by the Academic Library Association of Ohio. Active in the American Library Association, she was awarded the Miriam Dudley Award in 1986 by the Association of College and Research Libraries.

Glenn L. Sitzman retired from the Carlson Library, Clarion University of Pennsylvania. He has worked as a librarian and traveled in Africa.

INDEX

Abdel-Motey, Yaser, 233
Accreditation, 230
Adams, C.H., 105
Adult student [definition], 115
Adult student, (*see* non-traditional student)
African Libraries, 295
"Aggravation Quotient," 27
Aguilar, William, 126, 127
Albano, C., 100
Altman, J.H., 103
American Library Association, 101, 134, 135, 138, 140, 229
American University in Cairo, 76
Anderson, Charles, 9
Anderson, A.J., 98, 99
Anxiety, and non-traditional students, 119
"Aproachability," [of reference librarians], 4
Arizona State University, 157, 172
Armstrong, Scott, 132, 133, 135
Arrigona, Daniel, 10
Artificial Intelligence (full text), 147
Asbury, Herbert, 31
Asanian, Carole B., 117
"Ask Fred," 161

Association of Research Libraries Information Access, 140
Atkinson, Joan L., 230
Atomism as cultural constraint, 84
Audience (for special automated programs), 165
Auld, L.W.S., 226, 229
Authoritarianism as cultural constraint, 83
Ayubi, Nazih N.M., 83

Balenger, V.J., 103
Barker, R.L., 98
Barron, Daniel, 237
Barrow, J.C., 54
Bass, B.M., 52, 54, 57, 61
Bates, Doug, 227
Baumol, William, 22
Beder, Hal, 117
Behrman, S., 100, 102
Bell, Chip R., 46
Benefit measures, reference service, 26
Benefits: [definitions], 26; inferred, 27; (of reference service) outcomes, 27-30; research, 28; external, 31

Benham, Frances, 238
Beniger, James R., 249, 253-4, 260
Bennett, L.L., 102
Bennett, Yvonne S., 125
Bibliographic instruction, 124
Bibliographic instruction, American
    University-Cairo, Library, 90
Billings, Harold, 236
Birney, Ann, 238
Bitnet, 42
Blackwelder, J., 115
Blair, I.L., 100
Blanchard, K.W., 56
Bloom, Allan, 257
Boehm, Kraus, 253
Bogdanich, Walt, 15
Bohm, David, 251
Bolger, E., 99
Borden, J., 107
Borgardus, E.S., 55
Boyles, A., 107
Brawner, L.B., 100
Brickell, Henry, 117
Broomall, J.K., 115
Brown, C., 100
Brown, Karen, 124
Brownlee, E.U., 106
Bryant, D.C., 100
Bunge, Charles, 2, 15, 23, 29
Bureacracy of permission, 84
Burich, Nancy, 128
Burke, James, 256
Burson, L.E., 105
Byrne, R., 99

Calder, B.J., 52, 57, 58
Campbell, D., 257
Cannons, H.G.T., 296
Capra, Fritjof, 250
Career change, 117
Carlson, G., 15
Carl systems, 147, 168
Carnegie Mellon University, 145, 170

Cartwright, D., 55
Carvalho, J., 99
Carver, D.A., 51
Casey, D.W., 101
Cashman, J., 58
Caskey, R., 99
Censorship, of information, 138
Challenges, for leaders, 50
Childe, V. Gordon, 247, 252
Children, 38
Childress, C.P., 104
Christensen, Paul, 237
Chugh, R.L., 101
Clancy, tom, 131
Clark, C.K., 100
Clark, E., 100
Clayton Library, 100
Client as library user, 45-46
Cline, Gloria, 8, 9
Cluff, E. Dale, 227, 236
Cochran, Judith, 80
Cochran, Lynn S., 13, 14, 33
Coffman, Steve, 237
Comes, J.F., 52, 59, 60
Communality, in science, 255
"Computer culprits," 218
Computer science (full text), 146
Concepts, technology transfer, 77
Conflict, regarding volunteers, 98
Connant, R.W., 234, 235
Consultants (local systems), 179
Cooper, G., 98, 100
Cooper, M.D., 26, 29, 31
Corbett, E.V., 98
Cost allocation [reference service], 7
Cost benefit analysis, reference
    service, 26
Cost effectiveness, measures, 14
Cost effectiveness, paraprofessional,
    professional staff, 21
Cost effectiveness and self
    improvement, 23

Cost measure, reference question
success, 16
Courrier, Y., 237
Courtney, Nancy, 123, 124, 128
Cowser, R.L., Jr., 123
Cribben, M.M., 98
Crittenden, S., 103
Cronin, Blaise, 22
Cultural constraints, 78; atomism,
84; authoritarianism, 83;
elitism, 78; groupism, 88
Cunningham, L.L., 55, 56, 57
Curriculum development, 231

Dalrymple, H., 100
Dansereau, F., 51, 58
Davidow, William H., 44
DeCandido, Graceanne A., 138
Deckoff, M.J., 100
Dervin, Brenda, 26, 28, 29, 31
Detweiler, M.J., 101
Dewey, Melvil, 218
Dipboye, R.L., 61
Disbenefits [definition], 26
Disinterestedness, in science, 255
Division of Labor in Society, 247
Dodson, K., 102
Dolnick, S., 98, 99
Dosa, Marta, 263
Dowell, Arlene T., 234
Dragon, A.C., 52, 53, 60, 61
Dumont, Paul, 232
Durkheim, Emile, 247, 252
Dyadic linkage model, 58

Economics and support (locally
developed databases), 175
Effectiveness measures, 14; cautions,
15; input, output, process, 14-15
Egypt, children's libraries, 78
Eisenhut, L., 100
Elitism as cultural constraint, 78
El-Koussy, Abdel Aziz, 85

Ellison, J.W., 4
Elster, J., 106
Engleberg, Stephen, 136
Evaluation (local systems), 179

Faculty status, American University-
Cairo, 79
Fairfax Couty, VA, Public Library,
28
Farnsworth, Clyde H., 137
Farrington, A., 98, 99
Fees for service, 27
The Feminine Mystique, 249
Fiedler, F.E., 55
Fitch, R.T., 103
Flanagan, A., 98, 99
Fleishman, E.A., 56
Flood, Barbara, 27
Foerstel, Herbert N., 139
Ford, Robert B., Jr., 125
Frankie, S., 52, 53, 59
Fredenburg, A.M., 107
Freedom of Information Act, efforts
to weaken, 132-133
Freireich, S., 107
Friedan, Betty, 249
Futas, Elizabeth, 227
Future (of local systems), 188

Gabehart, Alan, 231
Gale, S.R., 99, 101
Gallo, P., 105
Galloway, R. Dean, 123
Galvin, Thomas J., 234
Garvey, William D., 30
Gates, Jean Key, 251
Gaughan, T.M., 100
Gensen, T.S., 100
Gephart, W.J., 55, 56, 57
Gerhard, G.W., 107
Getz, Malcolm, 28, 31
Gibb, C.A., 54, 55
Goals, 163

Goals, 163; setting and community
    involvement, 164
Goldhor, Herbert, 30
Gorman, G.E., 231, 232
Graen, G., 51, 58
Gray, Lucy, 36
Gray, S.T., 101, 102, 107
Green, S.K., 103
Greene, H. Frances, 260
Greer, E., 98
Griffiths, Jose Marie, 27
Groupism as cultural constraint, 88

Haeuser, M., 100
Haga, W.J., 51, 58
Hagedorn, Ann, 139
Hall, Edward T., 78
Hall, Linda M., 117, 118
Halpin, A.W., 56
Hamady, Sania, 79, 85, 89
Hameister, D.R., 120
Hannaford, C., 105
Hartridge, Digby, 231
Hass, F.W., 55
Havener, Michael W., 21
Hayden, Colo, 100
Haynes, R. Brian, 30, 31
Henderson, J.A., 103
Hernon, Peter, 29
Hersey, P., 56
Hiatt, Fred, 132
"High Performance Computing Act
    of 1991," 41
Hill, J., 100
Hine, Betsy N., 119
Hirschorn, Michael W., 116
Hoagland, Sister M.A., 105
Hofmann, C.M., 100
Holden, S., 100
Hopwood, Derek, 80
Horn, Zoia, 123
Hoselitz, Bert F., 252, 253
Howard, Sheila, 125

Howarth, E., 101
The Hunt for Red October, 131

Identity, library school within the
    institution, 230
Ihrig, A.B., 101
Impact (of local systems), 186
Information, censorship, 138
Information, finding, 42
The Information Machine, 156
Information types (for locally
    created databases), 165
Information, U.S. Government
    classification, 132
Inglewood, C.A. Public Library, 100
In magic, 158
Inopac, 155
Inspec (Carnegie Mellon University),
    145
Integrated Academic Information
    Management System, 154
Intelligent Reference Information
    System, 156
Internet, 39, 41
Iovacchini, Eric V., 117, 118

James, T.O., 57
Jarlsberg, J., 100
Jenkins, H., 106
Jenner, J.R., 101, 102, 103
Jensen, Rebecca, 31
Johnson, Ian M., 233
Johnson, Jean S., 127
Jones, I., 105
Josephine, Helen, 237

Kaminer, W., 99
Kantor, Paul, 3, 5, 9, 10, 24, 28, 31
Kaplan, Fred, 134, 136
Kappner, Augusta, 118, 122, 123
Karp, R.S., 97, 99
Kascus, Marie, 126, 127
Keenan, Lori M., 120-121, 126

Keltner, C., 100
Kendall, K.S., 106
Kenkel, M.B., 106
Kies, C., 98
King, Judith D., 5
King, Radford, 31
Klauber, Julie, 232
Knowbots [information finders], 42
Knowles, Malcolm S., 125
Kochoff, S.T., 100
Korman, A.K., 55
Kramer, Joseph, 31
Kratcoski, P.C., 103

Lacroix, Paul, 252
Lane, Edward, 88
Langrish, J., 30
Lardner, George, Jr., 132
Lawson, Lonnie, V., 21
Leaders, characteristics, 54
Leadership behavior description
        questionnaire, 52, 59; behavior
        observation, 55; contingency
        theories, 55; definitions, 54;
        development, 92-93; Dyadic
        Linkage Model, 58; Hersey
        and Blanchhard Model, 56;
        Ohio State Model, 56;
        Research studies, 53, 58; styles,
        54; traits, 54; transformational,
        50, 51
Leclair-Marzolf, M., 100
Leila, Ali, 83, 89
Lenox, David, 228
Lessin, Barton M., 127
Lester, June, 230
Levine, E., 98, 101
Levinson, R.W., 100
Lewin, M., 97, 98
Libraries, existing online, 40
"Library anxiety," 119
Library association, 99
"Library Awareness Program," 139

*Library Education and Employer
        Expectations*, 236
Library Education Survey, 218-222
Library of the future, 40
Library and Information Science
        Schools, 46
Library management role, 46-47
Library service, undervalued by
        society, 46
Library users, customers, clients, 46
LIS II (Carnegie Mellon University),
        145
Loewenthal, N., 115
Logan, G.K., 100
Longeway, B., 98
Lopez, Manuel, 3, 4, 8
Lovelock, J.E., 258
Lucas, L., 101, 106
Luloff, A.E., 103
Lutzker, Marilyn, 122, 123, 124

Mac NOTIS, 168
Machlup, Fritz, 248
Mahfouz, Naguib, 85
Management Development, 93
Management, meaning for
        Egyptians, 80
Mann, R.D., 55
Marsh, Robert, 253
Martin, M.S., 58
Martin, Rosemary, 231
Masek, D.B., 99
Mason, Robert M., 27
Mathews, Eleanor, 10
Mattelart, Armand, 259
McClam, T., 105
McClure, Charles, 16, 23
McDonald, Kim, 134, 259
McFadden, Robert D., 139
McMurdo, George, 4
Mech, Terrence, 8, 9-10
Medical Information Quick, 154,
        172

Meek, Janet, 119
Mellon, Constance A., 119
Merton, Robert K., 255
Mick, Colin, 1
Miles, A., 51, 52, 57, 58
Miller, J.M., 107
Miller, Ruth H., 119
Miller, William, 5
Mitchel, Steven E., 132, 133
Moe, Ronald C., 137
Molenda, Claudia, 4
Moody, Marilyn, 138
Moore, K.L., 6, 24
Morrow-Howell, N., 102, 103
Morton, Sandy I., 138
Mubarak, Suzanne, Mrs., 78
Mui, A., 102, 103
Munson-Benson, T., 100
Murfin, Marjorie, 15, 23, 29
Murk, P.J., 102, 103
Murphy, A.K., 55
Murphy, Marcy, 3, 4, 5, 6, 7, 8

Naimer, Janet Naul, 232
National Academy of Sciences, 136
National Agriculture Library, Tech-
    nology Transfer Program, 193
National Commission on Libraries
    and Information Science, 138
National Research and Education
    Network, 39, 41
National Technical Information
    Service, privatization, 138
Nature of Library Services, 45
Netting, F.E., 99
Ney, N.J., 106
Nightingale, D.S., 97, 107
"No News," 140
Non-traditional student [definition],
    115; anxiety, 119; career
    change, 117; comparison to
    others, 120; return to school,
    116; stress, 118

Nordstrom, Brian H., 116, 117
Norman, Colin, 137
North, David M., 136
Northwestern University, 161, 174
NSFNET, 42
NUINFO, 161, 174
Nwafor, B.U., 296
Nyren, K., 99

Obrokta, C., 105
Obstacles, to library progress, 43
OCLC/Amigros Collection analysis
    CD, 204, 207
OCLC/Epic Service, 211
Off-campus services, 125-126
Ohio State University Leadership
    Model, 50, 56, 60
O'Neill, P.C., 101
Ordover, Janusz, 22
Organizational development, 93
Orgren, C.F., 228
Otike, J.N., 296
Outcome measures, reference
    service, 15
Overmyer, E., 100
Ozawa, M.N., 103

Palmer, Monte, 83, 89
Palmour, Vernon, 3, 6
Park, C.S., 99
Park, Robert L., 140
Parker, M.A., 103
Parsons, M.P., 100
Pastine, Maureen, 29
Patai, Raphael, 80, 83, 89
Patron major (subject), 17
Patron status, 17
Payment for service, (see fees for
    service)
Pear, Robert, 131, 133
Pearce, J.L., 99, 102
Pemberton, Michael, 232
Pennsylvania State University, 159

Penzias, Arno, 39
Personnel (for local systems), 177
Petgen, E.A., 100
Pfeifer, D.B., 100
Pike's Peak District Library, 149, 173
Pincus, Walter, 132
Pitlak, Robert, 30
Planning, 102
Poa, M.L., 238
Postman, Neil, 38
Prentice, Ann, 232
Problems (local systems), 181
Professional education, 226
Professional ranks, American
    University-Cairo, Library,
    79-80
Program budgeting, for reference
    service, 7, 8-9
Project Jefferson, 151, 153, 164
Project Mercury (Carnegie Mellon
    University), 145

Quality, of library service, 44
Queeny, D.S., 117

Raffel, Jeffrey, 3, 5, 7, 9
Random alarm mechanism, in
    reference service, 8
Ray, G.W., 107
Rees, Alan M., 237
Reference and Adult Services
    Division, 21
Reference desk time, 4; tasks, 4-5, 6;
    use of, 4-5
"Reference is an expensive service,"
    [a false impression], 3
Reference expert, 156
Reference question subject, 19;
    complexity, 16; success cost
    measure formula, 16
Reference questions, costing
    methods, 2; hourly costs, 3;
    unit cost, 9;

Reference service; benefit measures,
    14; cost allocation, 7; cost
    benefit analysis, 26; cost
    comparisons, 16, 25; cost
    measurement (in hours, in
    minutes), 3, 5, 6; disadvantage
    in hourly measurements, 6;
    effectiveness comparisons, 24;
    effectiveness and student
    status, 17-18; formula
    approximation, 10-11;
    program budgeting, 7, 8-9; self
    testing, 24; visibility and cost,
    3-4
Reichlin, S., 102, 103
Remote access interface design, 158
Research Center for Group
    Dynamics, 55
Return to school, by adults, 116
Ricardo, David, 248
Risk taking, 47
Robbins, J.B., 230
Robbins, S.P., 56, 58
Roberts, Kenneth W., 217
RoboRef, 158
Role episode process, 58
Rothstein, Samuel, 7, 9
Rubin, A., 103, 105
Rubin, Nancy, 115
Rutledge, J., 100

San Diego State University, 155, 172
Sannwald, W.W., 100
Saracevic, Tefko, 28, 31
Sardar, Ziauddin, 80, 92
Sassone, Peter G., 27
Satisfaction, of people using
    libraries, 47
Savage, N., 98
Schlessinger, B.S., 238
Schmidt, W.H., 54
Schrage, Michael, 136
Schuckett, S., 100

Schumacher, M., 98, 99
Scott-Stevens, Susan, 77
Secrecy planned for shuttle mission,
    132
Sedlacek, W.E., 102, 103
Seguin, M.M., 100
Selaiha, Nehad, 88
Self inprovement [of reference
    services], 23-24
Self testing, reference service, 24
Seligman, L.G., 51, 52
Sergent, M.T., 102
Shattuck, John, 133, 134, 259
Sheldrake, Rupert, 251
Shelflist count, 203-207
Shera, Jesse, 245
Sheridan, Jean, 117, 118, 125
Sherif, Khalid, 3, 5, 7, 9
Silling, M.A., 116, 117
Simmons, Randall, 232
"Situational Frame," 78
Skory, V., 102
Slavin, R.E., 62
Smith, Adam, 247, 248
Smith, A.L., 101
Smith, Alice G., 37, 48
Smith, Edward Reid, 231
Smith, Josephine Metcalfe, 218
Smoke, Helen Lloyd, 231
Smolowe, Jill, 140
Snider, A., 102
Souza, M.B., 101
Sparks, R., 52, 58
Special Library Association,
    testimony on access to
    information, 138
Specialization, definition, 246;
    process, 247
Spencer, Carol, 6, 7, 8
Spillers, Lisa, 227
Staff advancement, American
    University-Cairo, Library, 86-87
Staff development, 230

Standera, Oldrich, 27
Stanton, E., 102
Starr-Schneidkraut, N., 26, 29, 31
Statistical Package for the Social
    Sciences, 62
Steffen, Susan, S., 119
Steiner, P., 51, 52, 57, 58
Stephan, J.F., 99, 101, 102, 103
Stoffle, Carla J., 122
Stogdill, R.M., 54, 55, 56, 60
Stress, and non-traditional student,
    118
Strickland, C., 100
Stringer, Herbert, 38
Stuart, M., 22, 27
Student major subject, 17, 19;
    reference service cost
    effectiveness, 17-18
Student status, reference service cost
    effectiveness, 17-18
Subject of reference question, 19
Sullivan, Harold J., 139
Surprenant, Thomas T., 261, 264

Tabor, F.T., 98
Tannenbaum, R., 54
Taylor, B., 100
Taylor, K., 104
Technology, 195
Technology (of locally created
    databases), 168
Tedrick, T., 102, 103
Texas A&M University, 158
Thomson, James, 218
Thorelli, I.M., 103, 105
Thornton, Mary, 132
Tiller, Kathleen, 123, 124, 128
Time (to develop local systems) 185
Toffler, Alvin, 248, 259, 260, 263,
    264
Tomaiuolo, Nicholas G., 122, 125
Totten, Herman L., 227
Trainer, L., 98, 99, 101

Training, 230
Trait studies, 53, 58
Traits, of leaderrship, 54
Transformational leadership, 50-51
Tucker, M.P., 99
Tuckett, Harold W., 122

Uncover, 148
Unit cost, reference questions, 9
Unit costs, reference service, 9
U.S. Department of Commerce, 137
Universalism in science, 255
University of California, San Diego, 158, 177
University of Cincinnati, 172, 254
University of Houston, 156, 173
University of Southern California, 151, 174
USC info, 151
Users, clients, 46; customers, 47
Uttal, Bro, 44

Vafa, A., 105
Vander Linde, G., 238
Van House, Nancy, 23, 31, 32
Varlejs, Jana, 236
Veblen, Thorstein, 255
"Vertical Dyad Theory," 51
Vittitow, D., 106
Volunteer service value, 97
Volunteers, 97; advertising, 104; budgeting, 103; conflicts, 98; evaluation, 105-6; interviewing, 104; law, 103; orienting, 105; planning, 102; preplanning, 102; recruiting, 104; recognition, 106; solutions, 101; training and supervision, 105
Vondvan, F., 238

Wagner, Collette A., 118, 122, 123
Walch, David B., 238
Walsh, John, 136
Warmann, Carolyn, 12, 14, 33
Warner, A.S., 101
Warner, R.M., 238
Watson, Margaret, 233
Watson, T., 100
Webster's NInth New Collegiate Dictionary, 75
Weech, Terry, 3, 5
Weinberg, B.M., 103
Weinschenk, D., 105
Wells, L.B., 101
Wessel, C.J., 6, 24
Whaley, C., 103
Whipple, M., 104
Whitlatch, Jo Bell, 15
Williams, Dorothy, 233
Williams, R.F., 103
Wilson, M., 107
Wilson, S.R., 26, 29, 31
Wisconsin-Ohio Reference Evaluation Program, 4, 11, 15, 25
Witucke, Virginia, 126
Wolfe, D, 103
Wyman, Andrea, 120, 128

Yassin, El Sayed, 83, 89

Zander, A., 55
Zemke, Ron, 46
Zipkowitz, Fay, 227
Zischka, P.C., 105

Advances in Library Administration and Organization

Edited by **Gerard B. McCabe,** *Director of Libraries, Clarion University of Pennsylvania*
and **Bernard Kreissman,** *University Librarian Emeritus, University of California, Davis*

REVIEWS: "Special librarians and library managers in academic institutions should be aware of this volume and the series it initiates. Library schools and University libraries should purchase it."
— *Special Libraries*

"... library schools and large academic libraries should include this volume in their collection because the articles draw upon practical situations to illustrate administrative principles."
— *Journal of Academic Librarianship*

Volume 1, l982, 148 pp. $73.25
ISBN 0-89232-2l3-6

CONTENTS: Introduction, *W. Carl Jackson.* **Continuity or Discontinuity-A Persistant Personnel Issue in Academic Librarianship,** *Allan B. Veaner.* **Archibald Cary Collidge and "Civilization's Dairy: Building the Harvard University Library",** *Robert T. Byrnes.* **Library Automation: Building and Equipment Considerations in Implementing Computer Technology,** *Edwin B. Brownrigg.* **Microforms Facility at the Golda Meir Library of the University of Wisconsin, Milwaukee,** *William C. Roselle.* **RLIN and OCLC - Side by Side: Two Comparison Studies,** *Kazuko M. Dailey, Jaroff Grazia and Diana Gray.* **Faculty Status and Participative Governance in Academic Libraries,** *Donald D. Hendricks.*

Volume 2, 1983, 373 pp. $73.25
ISBN 0-89232-214-4

CONTENTS: Introduction, *Bernard Kreissman.* **Management Training for Research Librarianship,** *Deanna B. Marcum.* **Subject Divisionalism: A Diagnostic Analysis,** *J.P. Wilkinson.* **Videotext Development for the United States,** *Michael B. Binder.* **The Organizational and Budgetary Effects of Automation on Libraries,** *Murray S. Martin.* **The Librarian as Change Agent,** *Tom G. Watson.* **Satellite Cable Library Survey,** *Mary Diebler.* **Deterioration of Book Paper,** *Richard G. King, Jr.* **Evaluation and the Process of Change in Academic Libraries,** *Delmus E. Williams.* **Towards a Reconceptualization of Collection Development,** *Charles B. Osburn.*

Strategies and Long Range Planning in Libraries and Information Centers, *Michael E.D. Koenig and Leonard Kerson.* Project Management: An Effective Problem Solving Approach, *Robert L. White.* A Preliminary and Selective Survey of Two Collections of Juvenilia, *Michele M. Reid.* Biographical Sketch of the Contributors.

Volume 3, 1984, 320 pp. $73.25
ISBN 0-89232-386-8

CONTENTS: Introduction, *Gerard B. McCabe.* International Exchange and Chinese Library Development, *Priscilla C. Yu.* Measuring Professional Performance: A Critical Examination, *Andrea C. Dragon.* The Turnover Process and the Academic Library, *James G. Neal.* Subject Bibliographers in Academic Libraries: An Historical and Descriptive Review, *John D. Haskell, Jr.* University of California Users Look at Melvyl: Results of a Survey of Users of the University at California Prototye Online Union Catalog, *Gary S. Lawrence, Vicki Graham and Heather Presley.* Job Analysis: Process and Benefits, *Virginia R. Hill and Tom G. Watson.* College Library and Nonusers, *Nurieh Musavi and John F. Harvey.* David Milford Hume, M. D., 1917-1973, *Mary Ellen Thomas.* The Association of Research Libraries 1932-1982 50th Anniversary. The Impact of Changes in Scholarship in the Humanities Upon Research Libraries, *Ralph Cohen.* The ARL at Fifty, *Stephen A. McCarthy.* ARL/LC: 1932-1982, *William J. Welsh.* The Influence of ARL on Academic Librarianship, Legislation, and Library Education, *Edward G. Holley.* Biographical Sketch of the Contributors.

Volume 4, 1985, 233 pp. $73.25
ISBN 0-89232-566-6

CONTENTS: Introduction, *Bernard Kreissman.*The Third Culture: Managerial Socialization in the Library Setting, *Ruth J. Person.* Public Library Unions: Bane or Boon?, *Rashelle Schlessinger.* Satisfaction with Library Systems, *Larry N. Osborne.* Budgeting and Financial Planning for Libraries, *Michael E.D. Koening and Deidre C. Stam.* Library Support of Faculty Research: An Investigation at a Multi-Campus University, *Barbara J. Smith.* Staff Development on a Shoestring, *Helen Carol Jones and Ralph E. Russell.* The Impact of Technology on Library Buildings, *Rolf Funlrott.* Whither the Book? Considerations for Library Planning in the Age of Electronics, *Roscoe Rouse, Jr.* Attempting to Automate: Lessons Learned Over Five Years, Pittsburgh Regional Library Center, *Scott Bruntjen and Sylvia D. Hall.* Annotated Bibliographer of Materials on Academic Library Service to Disabled Students, *Rashelle Schlessinger.* Biographical Sketch of the Contributors.

JAI PRESS

Volume 5, 1986, 307 pp. $73.25
ISBN 0-89232-674-3

CONTENTS: Introduction, *Gerard B. McCabe.* **A Longitudinal Study of the Outcomes of a Management Development Program for Women in Librarianship,** *Ruth J. Person and Eleanore R. Ficke.* **Volunteers in Libraries,** *Rashelle Schlessinger Karp.* **The History of Publishing as a Field of Research for Librarians and Others,** *Joe W. Kraus.* **The Response of the Cataloger and the Catalog to Automation in the Academic Library Setting,** *Joan M. Repp.* **Accredited Master's Degree Programs in Librarianship in the 1980s,** *John A. McCrossan.* **Collection Evaluation - Practices and Methods in Libraries of ALA Accredited Graduate Library Education Programs,** *Renee Tjoumas and Esther E. Horne.* **Integarted Library System and Public Services,** *Marcia L. Sprules.* **Bibliographic Instruction (BI): Examination of Change,** *Fred Batt.* **The University Library Director in Budgetary Decision Making,** *Susan E. McCargar.* **Getting From Here to There: Keeping an Academic Library in Operation During Construction/Rennovation,** *T. John Metz.* **Three Studies of the Economics of Academic Libraries,** *Paul B. Kantor.* Bibliographical Sketches of the Contributors. Author Index. Subject Index.

Volume 6, 1987, 323 pp. $73.25
ISBN 0-89232-724-3

CONTENTS: Introduction, *Bernard Kreissman.* **Proactive Management in Public Libraries - In California and in the Nation,** *Brian A. Reynolds.* **Library Resource Sharing in Massachusetts, Traditional and Technological Efforts,** *Robert Dugan and MaryAnn Tricarico.* **On the Nature of Information Systems,** *Charles B. Osborn.* **Fiscal Planning in Academic Libraries: The Role of the Automated Acquisitions System,** *Carol E. Chamberlain.* **Taking the Library to Freshmen Students via The Freshmen Seminar Concept,** *John N. Gardner, Debra Decker and Francine G. McNairy.* **Conceptualizing Library Office Functions as Preparation for Automated Environment,** *Edward D. Garten.* **A Survey of the Sixth-Year Program in Library Schools Offering the ALA Accredited Master's Degree,** *Alice Gulen Smith.* **The Evolution of an Endangered Species: Centralized Processing Centers and the Case of the University of South Carolina,** *University of South Carolina.* **Libraries and the Disabled Persons: A Review of Selected Research,** *Marilyn H. Karrenbrock and Linda Lucas.* Biographical Sketches of the Contributors. Author Index. Subject Index.

Volume 7, 1988, 287 pp. $73.25
ISBN 0-89232-817-7

CONTENTS: Introduction, *Gerard B. McCabe.* **A Comparative Study of the Management Styles and Career Progression Patterns of Recently Appointed Male and Female Public Library Administrators (1983-1987),** *Joy M. Greiner.* **Library Services for Adult Higher Education in the United Kingdom,** *Raymond K. Fisher.* **Chinese Theories on Collection Development,** *Priscilla C. Yu.* **An Overview of the State of Research in the School Library Media Field, with a Selected Annotated Bibliography,** *P. Diane Snyder.* **A Comparison of Content, Promptness, and Coverage of New Fiction Titles in Library Journal and Booklist, 1964-1984,** *Judith L. Palmer.* **Librarians as Teachers: A Study of Compensation and Status Issues,** *Barbara I. Dewey and J. Louise Malcomb.* **Academic Library Buildings: Their Evolution and Prospects,** *David Kaser.* **Accreditation and the Process of Change in Academic Libraries,** *Delmus E. Williams.* **College and University Libraries: Traditions, Trends, and Technology,** *Eugene R. Hanson.* **A Reference Core Collection for a Petroleum Library,** *Nancy Mitchell-Tapping, Valerie Lepus, Rashelle S. Karp, and Bernard S. Schlessinger.* **Private Institutions and Computer Utilization in Community Service and Education: The Case of the Abdul-Hamid Shoman Foundation,** *As'ad Abdul Rahman. Abdul-Hameed Shoman Public Library, Nahla Natour.* Bibliographical Sketches of the Contributors. Index.

Volume 8, 1989, 302 pp. $73.25
ISBN 0-89232-967-X

CONTENTS: Introduction, *Bernard Kreissman.* **Quality in Bibliographic Databases: An Analysis of Member-Contributed Cataloging in OCLC and RLIN,** *Sheila S. Intner.* **The Library Leadership Project: A Test of Leadership Effectiveness in Academic Libraries,** *Eugene S. Mitchell.* **Applying Strategic Planning to the Library: A Model for Public Services,** *Larry J. Ostler.* **Management Issues in Selection, Development, and Implementation of Integrated or Linked Systems for Academic Libraries,** *Elaine Lois Day.* **Acquisitions Management: The Infringing Roles of Acquisitions Librarians and Subject Specialists-An Historial Perspective,** *Barbara J. Henn,.* **Development and Use of Theatre Databases,** *Helen K. Bolton.* **The Academic Library and the Liberal Arts Education of Young Adults: Reviewing the Relevance of the Library-College in the 1980s,** *Peter V. Deekle.* **College Libraries: The Colonial Period to the Twentieth Century,** *Eugene R. Hanson.* **Library Administrators' Attitudes Toward Continuing Professional Education Activities,** *John A. McCrossan.* **A Core Reference Theatre Arts Collection for Research,** *Sharon Lynn Schofield, Helen K. Bolton, Rashelle S. Karp, and Bernard S. Schlessinger.* **The**

Library Buildings Award Program of the American Institute of Architects and the American Library Association, *Roscoe Rouse, Jr.* **Bibliography of Sub-Sahara African Librarianship, 1986-1987,** *Glenn L. Sitzman.* Bibliographical Sketches of the Contributors. Index.

Volume 9, 1991, 262 pp. $73.25
ISBN 1-55938-066-7

CONTENTS: Introduction, *Gerard B. McCabe.* **Administrative Theories, Business Paradigms and Work in the Academic Library,** *Allen B. Veaner.* **Whatever Happened to Library Education for Bibliotherapy: A State of the Art,** *Alice Gullen Smith.* **Three Libraries: Use of the Public Library Planning Process, an Analysis Accompanied by Recommendations for Future Users,** *Annabel K. Stephens.* **Book Piracy and International Copyright Law,** *Serena Esther McGuire.* **Investigation of the Motivational Needs of Corporate Librarians: A Framework,** *Sohair Wastawy-Elbaz.* **Libraries, Technology, and Access: the Statewide Automation Planing Process in New York,** *Frederick E. Smith and George E.J. Messmer.* **The National Szechenyi Library Budapest - Hungary,** *Elizabeth Molnar Rajec.* **The Royal Scientific Society Library of Jordan,** *Nahla Natour.* **A Collection for a Brokerage Firm Library,** *Kris Sandefur, Lori Rader, Bernard Schlessinger, and Rashelle Karp.* **Bibliography of Sub-Sahara African Librarianship, 1988,** *Glenn L. Sitzman.* **The I.T. Littleton Seminar - Introduction,** *Cynthia R. Levine and D.F. Bateman.* **Perspectives on the Information Needs of the Agricultural Researcher of the 21st Century,** *J. Edmond Riviere.* **Computing Technology and Libraries,** *Henry E. Schaffer.* Biographical Sketches of the Authors. Index.

Volume 10, 1992, 298 pp. $73.25
ISBN 1-55938-460-3

CONTENTS: Introduction, *Bernard Kreissman.* **Long-Range Strategic Planning for Libraries and Information Resources in the Research University,** *Robert M. Hayes.* **Computerized Matchmaking; The Researcher and the Collector,** *Patricia A. Etter.* **Bibliographic Instruction: Examining the Personal Context,** *James R. Coffey and Theodora T. Haynes.* **The Role of Citation Analysis in Evaluating Chenmistry Journals: A Pilot Study,** *Sandra E. Goldstein.* **The Process of Cost Justification,** *Thomas J. Waldhart.* **The Development of Library Lighting: The Evolution of the Lighting Problems We are Facing Today,** *Ellworth Mason.* **What do Liberal Arts College Deans Think About the Library?,** *Larry Hardesty.* **General Education in Colleges and Universities: An Annotated Bibliography of Journal Articles 1985 - March, 1990,** *Rashelle Karp, Sandra Yaegle, Faith Jack, and Polly Mumma.* **Bibliography of Sub-Sahra African Librarianship, 1989,** *Glenn L. Sitzman.* About the Authors. Index.

Advances in Serials Management

Edited by **Marcia Tuttle** *Head, Serials Department
University of North Carolina—Chapel Hill* and
Jean G. Cook, *Serials Librarian, Iowa State University*

REVIEWS: "This should be considered an essential addition to general library science collections as well as those serving the needs of library science students."

— *Library Resources and Technical Services*

" This is a welcome addition to the canon of serials literature."

— *Journal of Academic Librarianship*

" .... a solid body of practical information of substantial value to administrators and practitioners in large libraries."

— *Wilson Library Bulletin*

"...this series is a welcome addition to the professional literature."

— *Library Journal*

Volume 4, 1991, 275 pp. $73.25
ISBN 1-55938-189-2

CONTENTS: Reflections on the Origins of European Journals, *Gordon Graham.* **Management of Serial Records in the Integrated Catalog,** *Judith Niles, Pam Burton, Tyler Goldberg, Melissa Laning.* **The** *Newsletter on Serials Pricing Issues:* Teetering on the Cutting Edge, *Marcia Tuttle.* **ISDS: The Unfinished Revolution,** *Jim E. Cole.* **Coffee at the Carolina Inn: The Discussion to End all Discussions,** *Cynthia D. Cowan and Michael Markwith.* **Users of the Brave New Catalog: Electronic Access to Periodical Articles,** *Wilma Reid Cipolla.* **The Claim Function in Serials Management,** *J. Travis Leach and Karen Dalziel Tallman.* **But Serials are Different!,** *Christian M. Boissonnas.*

Also Available:
Volumes 1-3 (1986-1989) $73.25 each

JAI PRESS INC.

55 Old Post Road - No. 2   P.O. Box 1678
Greenwich, Connecticut 06836-1678
Tel: (203) 661-7602   Fax: (203)661-0792